Burma

ROBERT I. ROTBERG
Editor

BURMA

Prospects for a Democratic Future

THE WORLD PEACE FOUNDATION
and
HARVARD INSTITUTE FOR INTERNATIONAL DEVELOPMENT
Cambridge, Massachusetts

BROOKINGS INSTITUTION PRESS / *Washington, D.C.*

Library of Congress Cataloging in Publication Data:

Burma : prospects for a democratic future / Robert I. Rotberg.
editor.
p. cm.
        Includes bibliographical references and index.
    ISBN 0-8157-7582-2 (cloth)
    ISBN 0-8157-7581-4 (pbk.)
    1. Burma-Politics and government-1998- 2. Political culture-Burma. 3. Burma-
Economic policy. 4. Burma-Social policy.
I. Rotberg, Robert I. II. World Peace Foundation.
    JQ751.A91 B87 1998
    320.9591'045-ddc21

                                                                98-8987
                                                                CIP

9 8 7 6 5 4 3 2 1

Typeset in Times Roman

Composition by Oakland Street Publishing
Arlington, Virginia

Printed by R.R. Donnelley and Sons Co.
Harrisonburg, Virginia

Acknowledgments

THIS BOOK grew out of a collaborative research project and conference (held in December 1996, at Harvard University) sponsored by the Trustees of the World Peace Foundation and the Director and Fellows of the Harvard Institute for International Development. Most but not all of the chapters in this book were originally delivered at that conference, and then revised. The conference itself is summarized in David I. Steinberg, *Burma: Prospects for Political and Economic Reconstruction,* WPF Reports, 15 (Cambridge, MA, 1997). Steinberg also contributed in significant and formative ways to the design of the original conference; without his initial enthusiasm and support the project might never have become a reality. The authors and editor of the book are also permanently indebted to Dana Francis, of the WPF staff, for her assiduous editing of the book and for seeing the book through many stages to publication. She was ably assisted by Emily Edson, Maeve McNally, and Sarah Lischer of the WPF. The book was proofread by Carlotta Ribar, and the index was prepared by Mary Mortenson.

—R.I.R.

Myanmar or Burma?

BURMA WAS long the name of the country between India and Thailand. In the nineteenth century there were Upper and Lower Burmas, and the hill territories. Eventually, under colonial rule, and at independence, there was one Burma. It took its name from the Burmans, the majority people of Burma and a people unrelated ethnically to most of the other peoples who came to be incorporated into modern Burma. Only when the State Law and Order Restoration Council (SLORC) installed itself in power after the 1988 student pro-democratic protests and their brutal repression by the army (which formed the SLORC) did the SLORC decide to re-name the country Myanmar. The democratic forces of the National League for Democracy (NLD), which overwhelmingly won the 1990 national election, refuse to accept Myanmar as the name of their country. The editor of this book abides by the NLD decision to resist a name change that was invented by a regime that has no national legitimacy. Hence Burma is used in the title and throughout the chapters, despite the resistance of the some of the chapter authors themselves. It should be clear that any criticism of the use of Burma rather than Myanmar should be directed at the editor, and not at individual authors. Using Burma and not Myanmar also accords with the policy of the World Peace Foundation, the Harvard Institute for International Development, and the U. S. Department of State.

In December 1997, Burma's leaders dissolved the SLORC and created a new ruling group called the State Peace and Development Council (SPDC), composed of many of the same people. This book uses the name SLORC since that was the ruling council in place at the time the chapters were written.

Contents

Part Two: The Military

Part Three: Economic Considerations

Part Four: Health and Education

Part Five: Looking Forward

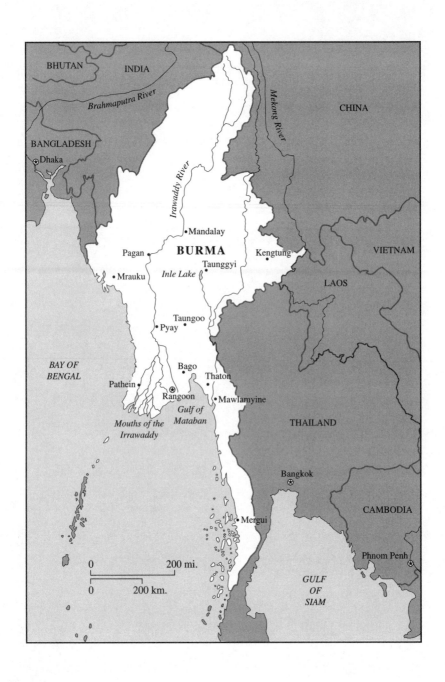

Prospects for a Democratic Burma

Robert I. Rotberg

BURMA IS an evil anachronism. Amid a post–Cold War era that has largely embraced democracy and its liberating consequences, Burma is a throwback to an earlier, more nakedly brutal period of dictatorial excess. Since being defeated overwhelmingly in the 1990 elections, the State Law and Order Restoration Council (SLORC), a steely military junta, has repressed dissent, detained Nobel laureate Aung San Suu Kyi, and violated the human rights and civil liberties of countless Burmese.

Aung San Suu Kyi's National League for Democracy (NLD) received 82 percent of the vote in 1990, two years after soldiers had gunned down about 3,000 protesting students and Buddhist monks in Rangoon, Mandalay, Sagaing, and other cities and towns.

The SLORC placed Suu Kyi under house arrest from 1989 to mid-1995. Throughout the rest of that year and during the last months of 1996, the SLORC also intermittently prevented Aung San Suu Kyi from addressing her followers or meeting openly with the NLD leadership. Her telephone line was cut from time to time. On one occasion a mob recruited by the SLORC attacked her car. Her free movement outside her home was also limited in December 1996, when students at the University of Rangoon and the nearby technical institute protested peacefully in the streets. In January 1997, the SLORC arrested a number of students, including supposed members of Suu Kyi's party. The avenue outside Suu Kyi's house was blocked by the SLORC from November 1996 through early February 1997.

Conditions for Aung San Suu Kyi and her democratic followers improved lit-tle throughout much of the rest of 1997. Her difficulties made no discernible impression on the Association of Southeast Asian Nations (ASEAN), which admitted Burma to membership in July. Aung San Suu Kyi, as well as the United States and the countries of the European Union, had implored ASEAN not thus to legitimize the SLORC's hegemony in Burma. But ASEAN, led decisively in this case by Mahathir Mohamed, prime minister of Malaysia, turned a collective deaf ear. As the chapters that follow by Andrew Selth, Mohan Malik, and Marvin Ott make abundantly clear, ASEAN had three overriding goals: to engage the rulers of Burma "constructively" to moderate the SLORC's repressive policies; to bring Burma into ASEAN to counter China's increasingly tight embrace of the SLORC and its paramount influence inside Burma—a potential threat to ASEAN; and to refuse to be dictated to by the West.

President Clinton officially declared Burma, as ruled by the SLORC, a pariah state. In April 1997 he prohibited all future American investments there. Several U.S. states and cities had previously legislated against purchasing goods from any corporations doing business in Burma, and a number of apparel makers, soft drink purveyors, and others had closed down their activities in Burma. After President Clinton's ban, only Unocal and Texaco, of prominent U.S.-based firms, remained active in Burma. Mark Mason's chapter on foreign trade and investment provides the full picture of Burma's minor place in Southeast Asian economic activity.

President Clinton in April, and Secretary of State Madeleine Albright at the ASEAN meeting in July, called the SLORC a collection of drug trafficking thugs. Sixty percent of the heroin that enters the United States comes from Burma, most-ly via China, or via India and Thailand, and Secretary Albright echoed the chap-ters in this book by Robert Gelbard and Bertil Lintner in criticizing the SLORC for sponsoring as well as profiting from the drug trade out of Burma.

Neither the U.S. attempts to intervene diplomatically on behalf of Burma's fledgling democratic movement nor the European Union's decision to bar Burma from trade preferences altered the SLORC's approach to Aung San Suu Kyi or made it any more receptive to democracy in Burma. Indeed, the SLORC blamed Aung San Suu Kyi for obstructing the process of maturing change in Burma and for her failure to acquiesce in the SLORC's control of Burma. Robert Taylor's chapter presents some of the reasons of political culture why military rulers of Burma distrust and disdain democracy. Mary Callahan's chapter like-wise demonstrates how little democracy Burma ever knew and how alien democracy is to Burma, despite the so-called democratic era of the 1950s. Josef Silverstein's chapter, however, emphasizes the democratic tendencies within traditional Burmese culture and shows how those democratic tendencies have long been manifest.

There is more to Burma than the Burmans, and there are plural political cultures, not just a single, dominant political culture. But, as much as the SLORC might disagree, Aung San Suu Kyi's overwhelming victory in 1990 was no fluke. She and her party are still overwhelmingly favored by all the peoples of Burma.

Burma's 45 million residents include about 28 million ethnic Burmans from southern and central Burma, and about 17 million members of the Shan, Karen, Kyaw, Mon, Kachin, and dozens of other ethnic groups. The failed 1990 elections and all subsequent informal methods of gathering opinion show that nearly all of these Burmese support Aung San Suu Kyi's opposition to the SLORC and her determined quest for democracy. Some may question her quietly gentle, civil, tactics. Some of the ethnic groups are unsure about her attitudes toward their lingering preferences for autonomy within the Burmese state. But, in opposition to the repressive might of the SLORC, now only Aung San Suu Kyi has legitimacy, charisma, and staying power.

The SLORC is a collective decisionmaking body with about twenty members and three acknowledged leaders, Army commander-in-chief Gen. Than Shwe, Army deputy commander-in-chief Gen. Maung Aye, and Director of Defense Services Intelligence Lt. Gen. Khin Nyunt. Too little is known, however, about the precise way in which decisions are arrived at within the SLORC, or even the extent to which the top three have absolute vetoes or qualified vetoes. However, there is a general understanding that most decisions are made by consensus, which could account for the inconsistent manner in which the SLORC treated Suu Kyi and protesters in 1996.

Army Gen. Ne Win took power in a coup in 1962, ruled despotically, and plunged Burma into isolation from the world until 1986. Now nearly ninety, he still wields occasional authority from the background. Local army district commanders seem to have remarkable autonomy in their rural areas, and conceivably even in the cities.

The army (as Selth's chapter authoritatively discusses) is among the largest in Asia, with approximately 300,000 men. But students of the Burmese military report that the army is poorly equipped, mostly with second-hand Chinese equipment, and is under-trained. It is an army primarily organized to repress its own people and keep internal order. The army has been used to impress civilians in a version of the corvee. Compulsory work on roads and forced child labor have been widely documented. The military also collects tribute in the form of rice or other commodities.

The army has long battled ethnic armies on the country's borders, but most of those conflicts resulted in standoffs. Using diplomatic means, and in some cases promising de facto autonomy, nearly all of the outstanding civil wars were concluded in 1995 and 1996. A series of wary truces took the place of steady hostilities, as Lintner and Ananda Rajah relate at length in their chapters.

Despite its large military budget, Burma is one of the poorest countries in Asia. The precise depth of Burma's poverty remains uncertain, with estimates ranging from $200 to $700 annual per capita GDP, but it is clear that much of Burma's economy is not recorded on official books or is otherwise hidden from direct scrutiny. David Dapice is one of the few Western economists who have examined the Burmese economy from afar as well as from inside. His chapter is appropriately pessimistic about the possibility of sustained economic growth.

More than 60 percent of the world's heroin comes from the poppy fields and refineries of Burma. It finds its way north and east through China and Thailand and then on to the United States, with some also smuggled into northeastern India. It is estimated that fully half of the Burmese economy (and its foreign trade) is drug derivative. Teak and jade are important exports, most of which are not openly declared. Like narcotics, most of the jade and the teak are exported initially through Thailand and China.

Burma once was the world's largest rice exporter, but its exports are now limited (although rice remains the largest official earner of foreign exchange). Natural gas deposits have been discovered in the Andaman Sea; a controversial pipeline is being constructed across Burma into Thailand to generate electricity near Bangkok.

Burma's relations with its neighbors are now more significant politically and economically than ties with Britain, the former colonial power; with Japan, Burma's wartime ruler; or with the United States as a world power. Indeed, now that the SLORC has obtained acceptance from ASEAN, joining Laos as a new member, it may intensify its currently limited relations with ASEAN beyond Thailand (although investment from Singapore and Malaysia has long been significant). Importantly, none of the leaders of ASEAN has yet met Aung San Suu Kyi. The influence on Burmese policy of the United States, Japan, Australia, and the countries of the European Community is limited, especially after their failure to stay ASEAN's hand in July.

China could but probably will not significantly influence Burma's political trajectory. China wants a compliant Burma on Yunnan's southern border. It may harbor geopolitical ambitions in that direction as well, but for the moment it is content to support the SLORC and the SLORC's repression of popular protest and other "dangerous" behavior. China has armed the Burmese military (for a price). Frank Jannuzi outlines Burma's heavy reliance on Chinese arms, but says that their importance to the SLORC can be overstated. The SLORC's success against ethnic insurgents resulted more from improved logistics than from Chinese arms, Jannuzi contends.

China's merchants and officials in Yunnan have greatly profited from the trade in drugs and other commodities that crosses from Burma. Some of these same traders, and others, have made heavy investments in Mandalay and Rangoon. It is evident that, without China, Burma could be more easily isolated. Some form of sanctions conceivably could also be implemented, but not without Chinese agreement and cooperation. It is unlikely, moreover, that China has any direct official acquaintance with, or much interest in, Aung San Suu Kyi and her democratic movement.

Except for the period from 1948 to 1962 (excluding the military caretaker government from 1958 to 1960), when Burma began experimenting with participatory governance and embryonic forms of democracy (which Callahan examines), the country has known only harsh, sometimes capricious, military rule since the Japanese invasion and the end of British colonialism. There is little tradition of democracy or the rule of law, although students of Burma hark back to the 1920s, when the British were in control, to establish the roots of a Burmese democratic spirit, as Silverstein makes clear. Economically, Burma is as badly off as it is because of Ne Win's compulsive autarky, which kept Burma out of most non-narcotics international trade and contact throughout the 1960s and 1970s.

Aung San Suu Kyi, apolitical and self-exiled before then, emerged as the heroine of the 1988 protests. She quickly became the spokesperson of the oppressed and the nation's leading strategist of democratic reform. Since her release from house arrest, she has called for dialogue with the SLORC and promised to meet civility with civility. But there have been no talks and no obvious overtures.

In order to encourage some form of dialogue with the SLORC, Aung San Suu Kyi favored pressure against rather than acceptance of Burma by ASEAN, opposed constructive engagement—the policy of using incentives to nudge the SLORC toward an accommodation with democratic tendencies, and believed that generalized sanctions might help stimulate meaningful discussions. She accepted no responsibility for the student protests of early 1997 and does not wish to be the excuse for further SLORC-initiated repression.

Her problem, the SLORC's problem, and Burma's tragic conundrum is how, short of an unlikely (and bloody) people's uprising, to facilitate or initiate an acceptable transition from military to popular rule. Suu Kyi believes, like all charismatic opponents of seemingly impregnable but illegal regimes, that time is on her side. She also assumes that a reluctance on the part of ASEAN to embrace the current government of Burma—plus the enforced (or voluntary) disinvestment from Burma of multinational energy, manufacturing, textile, and other concerns—could influence the behavior of the greedy stalwarts of the junta.

Opportunities for increased rent-seeking may indeed motivate some of the members of the SLORC. With increased economic activity, only possible during a transition to democracy, could come multiple new sources of licit and illicit wealth.

The SLORC is also motivated, individually and severally, by power and security or the fear of losing both. Whether or not Aung San Suu Kyi would accept a Chilean (Pinochet) model of democracy is unknown. Whether it could work in a country with such a weak democratic tradition is also unclear. But some version of the Chilean model—some method of maintaining military privileges and rent-seeking, and preventing retribution—may be favored now or soon by the more forward-looking members of the SLORC.

That the SLORC contains different tendencies and styles of leadership is well known. Whether any of the key figures are ready in 1997 to respond to internal and external pressures, and to begin to normalize their relations with the democratic movement, is not clear. But the SLORC in 1996 appeared to stay its hand in some troubling instances, seemed to be responding to ASEAN and world scrutiny and criticism, and seemed to exhibit an ambivalence in responding to Aung San Suu Kyi and the student demonstrators.

The prognosis for Burma is not particularly optimistic. But the SLORC's recent behavior patterns, the fundamental weakness of the economy, the potentially critical role of ASEAN, the democratic aura that permeates world thinking in the wake of the collapse of Soviet Communism and the freeing of South Africa, and the obvious fact that Suu Kyi's moral and political credibility is undiminished provide modest hope that Burma, too, can soon begin to move toward a democratic future.

When it does, the economy, presumably freed from SLORC-imposed artificial constraints, can begin to grow rapidly. There are many opportunities in almost all sectors of the economy for foreign direct investment. But even in the best of all possible futures, with the acceptance by the SLORC of the results of the 1990 elections and the ushering in of a democratic central government, Aung San Suu Kyi would face formidable obstacles. The ethnic groups would be suspicious of her Burman background, and would continue to distrust rule by even her central government. The enormous national educational and medical deficits, which the chapters by John Brandon and David Chandler describe, as well as serious and numerous infrastructural impediments, could overwhelm her budgetary resources. The military now swallows half of the official budget and probably more. So a freed Burma would need large-scale and sustained international friendship and assistance, as well as committed new corporate investment. If a government led by Aung San Suu Kyi were to try to tackle the drugs trade, it would have many additional problems, not least with several of the strong ethnic leaderships. As David Steinberg notes, political liberalization must be driven both internally and externally, with foreigners playing important roles in bringing transparency and information to a closed and isolated country.

A transition to democratic rule in Burma is thus not an end in and of itself, but a means to the achievement of a better future (what this book is primarily about) for all those who live within the contemporary borders of Burma.

Part One

POLITICAL
CONSIDERATIONS

CHAPTER I

The Evolution and Salience of Burma's National Political Culture

Josef Silverstein

IT HAS BECOME an article of faith of the present leaders of Burma to claim that "national and regional peculiarities as well as historical, cultural, and religious backgrounds together with the stage of economic development," excuse Burma from adhering to its treaty obligations and granting its people the rights their leaders acknowledged when they voted favorably for the adoption of the Universal Declaration of Human Rights at the United Nations in 1948.[1] In putting forward their oft-repeated arguments that Burma is different from other nations, especially those in the West, Burma's spokesmen declare that the government is guided by the values and institutions of its national and political culture, and rejects the efforts of outsiders to use human rights "as a tool to interfere in the domestic affairs of states."[2]

In its broadest sense, culture is defined by Spiro as "a system of traditional ideas, beliefs, and values which, expressed in public symbols, are shared by, acquired from, and guide the action of the members of a social group."[3] Political culture is a subset of culture and reflects the values and attitudes of a society toward political power. It both explains and justifies the way power is organized and used by those in authority and the responses of the people. Because political culture is part of national culture, the two must be considered together.[4] It is assumed that when the political system is synchronized with the political culture, it will be honored and accepted by the people, and internal peace and harmony will prevail.

Has there always been an unchanging national and political culture in Burma, and does it still form the basis of the values and ideas of the leaders and the people?

Are the military leaders in Burma ruling in accordance with the precolonial political culture or are they propounding new ideas and values and shrouding them in
myths about and interpretations of old ideas as justification for their form of rule?

Those who seek to explain and justify the present totalitarian system imposed
initially by the military in 1962, and made even more severe in 1988, argue that
the present soldier-rulers are acting consistently with the traditional values and
attitudes that the people know and accept. Despite modern education, exposure
to the world beyond Burma, and changes in thought and behavior, the political
culture of the past is more acceptable than alternative values, beliefs, institutions,
and processes that originated abroad and either were imposed by foreign rulers
or advocated by indigenous elites who internalized them during the period of
colonial rule or later, while living, studying, or working abroad.[5]

This chapter advances three theses:

1. Burma's political culture in the precolonial period was plural and localized,
not singular and universal. The political culture of the dominant Burmans dif-
fered fundamentally from that of the non-Burmans living in the hills surrounding the Irrawaddy heartland and the delta.

2. The political culture of Burma is not immutable. It began changing following contact with the outside world and particularly after the advent of colonial rule. It is an amalgam of ideas and values drawn from Buddhist and non-
Buddhist sources that reflect changes resulting from colonialism, war, and exposure to the outside world. The gap between the Burmans and the non-Burmans
began closing in 1945, but neither was able to adjust and adapt its responses to
the other; as a result, Burma's political culture remained plural and, in some
cases, antagonistic as some leaders looked for ways to transcend differences and
others to institutionalize them.

3. The ideas and values expressed by today's political opposition—Burman
and non-Burman—flow from the mainstream of Burma's contemporary political culture and are a major reason why an overwhelming majority of people support the parties and leaders who oppose the authoritarian dictatorship of the military and its efforts to impose its values on the nation.

To put the present state of political culture into perspective, it is necessary to
consider the salient elements of traditional Burmese political culture.

Religion as the Basis of Burmese Culture

The culture of the Burmans, Mons, and Arakanese, living in the Burmese
heartland, was based on Buddhism. It developed at the outset of the Pagan

Dynasty (eleventh century C.E.), following King Anawratha's adoption of Theravada Buddhism, and was propagated throughout his kingdom. It continues to form the values, attitudes, and ideas of the believers to the present. Animism, in various forms, including *nat*, or spirit, worship, was the basis of religious beliefs before Buddhism and persists to the present despite early efforts by Anawratha to stamp it out. Today, the spirit shrines in front of the houses of Burman Buddhists attest to animism's survival as part of the national faith.[6] Early Roman Catholic priests and, later, Protestant missionaries had relatively little success in converting Buddhists.

Among the non-Buddhist ethnic minorities, animism, including spirit worship, was the basis of their belief and value systems. Protestant missionaries, especially American Baptists, who came to Burma in the nineteenth century, had wide success in converting ethnic minorities. Christianity, together with other non-Buddhist religions, continues to be the basis of the beliefs and values of non-Burmans, who represent approximately 35 percent of the total population.

Several beliefs drawn from Buddhism are reflected in Burma's political culture. Man, Buddhism teaches, is chained to the wheel of rebirth (*samsara*); existence is impermanent (*anicca*), substanceless (*anatta*), and filled with suffering (*dukkha*). The Buddha taught that the believer can escape the wheel of rebirth by following the Eight-Fold Path. "If you follow this path, you will put an end to suffering. But each has to struggle for himself."[7] Thus, the faithful tended to be inward-looking, concentrating on self, and doing good works in order to earn merit toward their next rebirth. Spirit worship, astrology, and numerology also influenced the people, and they looked to these sources as well to guide and influence their behavior.

Buddhism "prescribed the rules of relationship between parents and children, teacher and pupil, wife and husband, friend and comrades, masters and servants . . . each [person] had to discharge his duties faithfully."[8] Age and status defined the personal hierarchy of authority that the believer automatically accepted. During the period of Burman rule, from the eleventh to nineteenth centuries, the faithful were unconcerned about the state and society in which they lived and did not speculate about whether or not it could be changed or improved. The ordinary Burman took no interest in palace politics and avoided contact with the government and its agents. The political system was accepted as found, and the king's right to rule and his power over life and death was not questioned. There was no speculation about such questions as the rule of law and what constituted good government. From birth, being taught that government was one of the five evils all must face and endure, people believed that it was important to avoid standing out and to have as little to do with the king's representatives as possible.

Unity of Monarchy and Religion as the Basis of Traditional Burman Buddhist Political Culture

At the heart of Burman political culture was the "Burmese monarchy [which was] distinguished by three features: the sacrosanctity and central position of kingship, absolutism and the undifferentiated functions of kingship."[9] The king was the absolute ruler of all the people and patron of the faith. His right to rule came from the merit he accumulated in previous existences. The palace was believed to be located at the center of the universe. By holding the palace, controlling the regalia of office, and defending the faith, the king's right to rule was unquestioned. He devoted much of his resources to pagoda-building and other religious activities in order to continue to make merit.

In theory, the king was expected to uphold the ten moral precepts and observe the four kingly laws and seven kingly rules. In reality, there was no power or authority to which he was accountable. Challenges to his rule came from those, usually with some connection to the royal family or the court, who sought to replace him as the god-king—not to alter the existing system. So long as he upheld and protected the faith and maintained the loyalty of his family and members of the court, his rule was unquestioned. The king was so intimately connected with Buddhism, that until the last monarch was exiled, and foreign non-Buddhist rulers took over, it was inconceivable for anyone to consider the survival of the faith and the kingdom without a king to protect both.

The Absence of Independent or Semiautonomous Bureaucracies

The political system did not admit the existence of independent or semiautonomous bureaucracies outside the control of the king. Consistent with the Buddha's declaration that there was no superiority in rank, but only superiority in piety and length of observance of the vows, the religious orders in Burma were locally supported and controlled. However, they were drawn together under a religious hierarchy centered in the palace. The king appointed and maintained the office of the *thathanabaing*, head of the faith, who, in most cases, was his religious teacher before the king ascended to the throne. The primate had power to discipline *pongyis* (monks), and *sanghas* (religious orders), and to rule on religious disputes through a hierarchy of religious leaders, whom he appointed or dismissed. Through the thathanabaing, he exercised his authority over the behavior and beliefs of the religious orders, the monks, and the people.

The king named the royal councilors at the palace and the hierarchy of administrators who implemented his rule throughout the realm. There was no class of independent, trained administrators who filled the offices on the basis of merit and expertise. All served at the king's pleasure. When he was strong and his rule was stable, his administrative appointees outside the palace formed a network covering the Burman heartland, collecting taxes and performing other duties as charged. They were not concerned with the mundane problems of the village.

The king commanded the army and appointed its leaders, usually from the royal family. Because of their royal connection and control of armed forces, they posed a threat to the king; they were in a position to topple and replace him.

Both the religious and secular bureaucracies were unstable. So long as the appointees held the king's favor they continued in office. When they lost his support, they were removed; when the king died or was replaced on the throne, all office-holders had to return to the palace and receive new appointments from his successor. Usually reappointments or replacements took time.

The villages functioned as self-contained political units supporting the local monks and monasteries, providing for village defense, maintaining order, and deciding local issues. In theory, the king was absolute and his rule applied everywhere and to everything; in fact, the villages enjoyed a large degree of local autonomy.

The Class Structure of Society

In the pre-British period, Burman society was divided between royalty and the people. The latter were organized in two broad classes: the *ahmudan* and the *athi*. The ahmudan owed personal service to the king in lieu of paying taxes, and were organized into military companies or service units. There was a heavy concentration of ahmudan villages around the palace areas where they could be called quickly into service when needed. Otherwise, they farmed royal lands or their own property, which they gained either through prior service or inheritance.

The athi were ordinary farmers, artisans, and others who paid taxes in lieu of service. They, like the ahmudan, were subject to corvee labor and conscription as auxiliary foot soldiers in times of war. In areas beyond the palace, there were villages where ahmudan and athi lived together, intermingling and intermarrying as the class structure was not rigid.

In both classes, men owed direct allegiance to their patron—among the ahmudan, their captain, and among the athi, the *myothugyi*. The captains and patrons stood between their clients and the king's representative. Even the village headman had only limited direct authority over the villagers and he, too, had to make his complaints and requests to the patron rather than directly to a particular resident. If a patron of athi became too severe or demanding, his clients could, and often did, slip away and accept the patronage of another in a distant area. Members of the ahmudan were less likely to leave their villages because they were tattooed with the symbols of their military formations and could easily be identified and returned.[10]

The Political Culture of the Non-Burmans

Among the non-Burmans living in the hills surrounding the Burman heartland, the Buddhist-centered political culture applied differently. In theory, the Burman king claimed authority over all people and their lands. In fact, a kind of feudal arrangement existed whereby, in exchange for acknowledging the suzerainty of the Burman king, providing soldiers, and giving tribute, minorities lived under their own rulers, according to their own laws and traditions, practiced their own religions and cultures, and used their own languages. The Burmans made no effort to assimilate minorities, although a degree of noncoercive assimilation occurred at the points where Burmans and minorities lived in close proximity.

Because the minorities lived apart from one another and had different religions, languages, and cultures, they continued to remain separate and distinct, never forming an alliance and rival center of power to the Burman kings. With animistic beliefs as the basis of their cultures and traditions, they were organized in different ways, and their political systems varied from authoritarian and centralized to quasi-democratic and decentralized. The introduction of Christianity among many of the minorities changed their value systems and political cultures and separated them further from the Burmans.

Following the fall of Pagan in the thirteenth century, the Shan, a large ethnic minority whose homeland was in the eastern part of Burma, rose to power as the successors of the Burmans. Those who held power adopted the political culture of their predecessors in exercising their rule, but they were unsuccessful in holding the kingdom together, mainly because of internal conflicts. When a new Burman dynasty rose in the fifteenth century, the Shan retreated to their historic lands where they ruled their own people according to their own traditions and values.

Throughout the pre-British period, when strong Burman kings held the throne and the system remained intact, the relationship between the Burman rulers and the minorities was generally harmonious. When weak Burman kings ruled or during periods when there were disputes over the throne, the minorities, especially those living at great distances from the capital, often threw off Burman rule and either gave allegiance to a foreign state or sought to remain free. Throughout this long period of history, the minorities retained their separate identities, values, and beliefs.

Real change in the political culture of Burma occurred as the British secular, rational-legal system was introduced and applied by the new rulers of Burma in the wake of the British conquest. The 122 years of British rule (1826–1948) introduced changes that had a major impact on the new elite and the people. Under strong and determined secular rulers, Burma's traditional values and beliefs about authority, power, and place either synthesized with, coexisted with, or were replaced by new values.

Some of the more significant ideas that affected Burma's political culture were:

1. *The Separation of Religion from the State*

The exile of the last king and the separation of the state and church undermined the basis of traditional political culture. The new rulers rejected both the form of rule and the Buddhist-based laws, rules, and decrees. They replaced them with an administrative system that functioned under permanent lines of authority, radiating from the center to the borders of the colony. Its rule was based on reason and law; it drew its inspiration from Judeo-Christian ideas and values, as well as British customary law. The administrative system was modeled on the pattern developed in India.

The British were unwilling to be patrons and protectors of the Buddhist faith, and refused to take over the practice of the Burman king in appointing the thathanabaing and supporting his rulings on religious questions. The religious administrative structure continued without formal government sanction and slowly died out. The colonial rulers drew a distinction between upholding many of the rulings of the ecclesiastical courts, which continued to operate after the end of Burman rule, and backing the orders and rulings of the thathanabaing. In 1895, when the last thathanabaing appointed by a Burman king died, the British rulers refused to participate in selecting a successor. Local religious orders and individual monks found themselves free to pursue their own religious practices and ideas as central control and discipline broke down.[11]

Along with separating the church and state in governing Burma, the British also altered the educational system. Under the Burman kings, the local monasteries served as the nation's schools and the children were given instruction in religion, reading, and writing. That system made the Burmans one of the most literate people in the region.

Initially, the British saw a utility in maintaining and even improving the traditional education at the elementary level. In lower Burma, as early as 1866—after its annexation following the Second Burmese War in 1852—the British sought to expand the curriculum by adding secular subjects, such as arithmetic and geography, which were taught by lay teachers. The British were prepared to pay for the change, provide books, and repair buildings. After the complete annexation of Burma in 1886, the experiment ended when the thathanabaing ruled against continuing the practice and implementing it in upper Burma.[12]

Throughout British rule, traditional education continued in the rural areas at the *pongyi kyaungs*, which intellectually separated rural students from their urban counterparts. It also left them unprepared to move into the emerging modern sector of society and take jobs in the modern economy.

The parents of children in the cities and large towns turned to Christian missionary and government schools as replacements for the monastery schools. In the missionary schools, Buddhist religious education was supplanted by moral training based on Christian teachings. It was offered to students whose parents allowed them to participate. The major educational emphasis was placed on the study and use of English, mathematics, science, and history, all of which were intended better to prepare students for the changing economy and administration of Burma. At the state-run schools, both English and Burmese were used as the languages of instruction of modern subjects. In most cases, the level of education was worse than that offered in the missionary schools. Many students continued their religious studies at the pongyi kyaung while attending the new Western schools. With their loss of place in the political culture as a major support for the political system and as the primary educators of Burma's youth, some of the clergy turned to political activity and were in the forefront of the nationalist movement. Most, however, retreated into their monasteries and accepted lesser roles in society.

2. *"Replacement of the God-King with a Secular Government"*

The British bureaucratic government of Burma was organized on a rational-legal basis with new codes of law, courts, lawyers, and judges in place of the despotic and arbitrary Burman rulers. When the king and his court were swept aside, the God-king was replaced by a foreign governor under the colonial authority in India. There was a permanent hierarchy of Western administrators reaching from the capital in Rangoon to the smallest village in the countryside. Its members, who were well-educated and trained in administrative skills, developed language skills and knowledge of the people and country after coming to Burma. Administrators, with the backing of the law, police, and military, were able to make the colonial system felt throughout the land. The military and police were led by Britons, and the ranks were recruited from Indians and Burma's ethnic minorities. In this and other ways, the balance of power shifted from the Burmans to the minorities and foreigners, upsetting the political culture of Burma; only after World War I did the recruitment policy for middle and upper rank administrators open to Burmans. At the local level, authority was made territorial instead of personal. The village headman replaced the patron as the officer between the people and the state who was responsible for law and order and the collection of taxes. The new system proved better than its predecessor in giving the government in Rangoon direct access to and control of the population, but it depersonalized local authority, broke up the pattern of patron and client, and made the headman a salaried employee of the state.

In place of personal patron-client relations there emerged the man of power in the village who could get things done. Such a person was believed to have *pon* (power), *gon* (influence), and *awza* (authority) as reflected in his personal wealth and ability to perform a variety of services. He, rather than the headman, emerged as the real leader in the village.[13] Later, after independence, he usually was the governing party representative or had some other connection with government.

In a relatively short time, a new secular administration under foreign rulers swept away the traditional government of Burma and created a system that provided safety for the people and order in the colony. It was a new form of authoritarian rule that was more efficient and effective than its predecessor and was accepted by the people.

3. *The Introduction of New Patterns of Thought including Western Liberal Ideas about Political Authority, Limited Government, Popular Participation, and Civil and Political Rights*

The colonial system created a new indigenous elite, which, by the twentieth century, became concerned with the here and now as well as with the hereafter; its ideas and values challenged the fatalism of the traditional Buddhist view that nothing could be done about this existence. The new thought patterns of the Burman elite were based on the Western political ideas and practices learned at school, through foreign literature and local newspapers. Burmans began to organize politically to protect pagodas and pongyi kyaungs from desecration and disrespect by non-Buddhist visitors. Within a few years, the movement became political with young Burmans exercising their freedoms under law through party formation, voting, participation in parliament, and a variety of other direct actions, including a university student strike against colonial policy on higher education.

In the years following World War I, the new Burman elite moved along two opposite paths: while those in the cities and large towns mobilized the popula-

tion for constitutionalism, liberal democracy, and independence, the rural population moved toward a return to the values and institutions of the precolonial
period.[14] The Hsaya San Revolt of 1930-1932, which erupted in rural areas of
lower Burma, sought to force the British out of the country and to restore the
monarchy. It failed because it drew only modest support from the rural population and hardly any from those in the urban areas.[15]

In displacing religion and political absolutism, colonialism made it possible
for the new elite to undergo a revolution in thought that challenged everything
from the traditional values of the past to the British right to rule Burma. The people learned to separate religion from politics and came to believe that conditions
as they found them were not immutable; rather conditions, like everything else,
were subject to change. They also came to believe that they could change society and even gain Burma's freedom if they made the effort. Newspapers, books,
radio, and films were important conduits for the transmission of Western ideas
and values, which were embraced by some members of the elite and rejected by
others. Some took the lead in reviving the use of Burmese as the language of literature and popular communication, others studied the political ideas popular in
Europe, China, India, and the United States to guide their thinking, and some
borrowed whole systems as the basis for reorganizing Burma's society and polity. University students challenged older leaders through movements and parties
to mobilize the people and worked to change Burma from a colony to an independent state. Western-educated Burmans separated religion from their political
beliefs as they looked for ways to shift the source of authority from religious to
secular and worked to modernize government by establishing it on a popular
basis and making it responsive to the will of the people. Out of this ferment, a
new political culture emerged.

World War II saw Japan replace Great Britain as the ruler of Burma. Burma's
leader Ba Maw sought to revive the monarchical tradition in modern dress and
rhetoric, but few, if any, gave real support to his pretensions and efforts. When
the war ended, he and his ideas were swept aside as a new political elite came
forward with ideas about the polity and economy that reflected the changes in
political thought and values that the western-educated Burmans had undergone
since the arrival of the British. The contesting leaders were intent on building a
strong, modern, independent state, modeled on those in the West, but they were
divided over which model was more appropriate. In the brief period between the
war's end and Burma's independence, there was widespread political ferment
with no one advocating a restoration of the traditional political culture of
Burma's pre-British past. With Aung San in the lead, the constitution of 1947
reflected the new ideas the Burmans had accepted and internalized during the

century of British rule as well as their determination to create a state on the basis of secular and popular rule.[16]

4. *The Continued Separation of Ministerial Burma from the Hill Areas*

The British continued the traditional separation of the Burmans and the minorities in the surrounding hill areas. In doing so, they deepened and widened the divide, not only physically, but culturally as well. By establishing indirect rule in the hill areas the British ensured the survival of local cultures, traditions, and leaders. The separation between the peoples of the two areas made it possible for the minorities to remain politically static while changes among the Burmans moved ahead. The British recruited members of the minorities for the police and military, which aligned them with British power and, along with the spread of Christianity in the hill areas, strengthened the divide between Burmans and non-Burmans.

In 1922, the British created a federation of the Shan states that drew them together and further widened the gap between the largest ethnic minority and the Burmans. It reinforced traditional rule in the Shan states and isolated that area from the political ferment in Ministerial Burma.

If colonial rule helped to strengthen and perpetuate the diverse cultures of the minorities, it also deprived their youth of modern education and the ability to interact with their Burman contemporaries. The minorities did not participate in the nationalist and other political movements of the interwar years (1918–1939) and did not develop independent responses to the world beyond Burma and the challenges that it posed. They knew little of the West, other than what they learned from the Christian missionaries in their midst, and they were unprepared in 1945 for a weakened Britain unable to remain their protector and guide.

Although a few minority leaders, especially among the Shan, participated in discussions between British and Burman leaders about the future of the country, they were the exception and not the rule. Minorities were divided among themselves and neither created strong common political movements nor developed strategies and goals for dealing with changing conditions in and outside of Burma.

In 1947, minorities were faced with decisions about their future that most were unprepared to make. Some of the leaders were willing to trust their Burman counterparts, while most were not. Some sought the benefits of being part of a unified state while others were fearful of losing their identities, cultures, and sense of independence. Most were prisoners of their pasts and carried their fears of Burman domination into the present and future. When called on to help write a constitution for the new state of Burma, they were not clear about what they wanted from the new political arrangement and how to achieve it. They feared central authority under Burman domination and sought ways to preserve their autonomy and identities, and remained uncertain about the benefits of being part of a larger political unit where their numbers were too small, in most cases, to make a real difference. Without experience in voting, forming parties, and developing coalitions with other minorities for common ends, most had no clear ideas about what the new political system, without British protection, would mean for them. Most minorities entered the Union of Burma reluctantly, knowing that the gap between the Burmans and themselves was filled with bad memories and there was no time available for making adjustments to meet the challenge of transition and the future.

When Burma became free, the divisions between the peoples were still there; the structure of the state preceded the emergence of a new political culture. Although the state was based on the liberal democratic ideas of the leaders who achieved independence, there was no general agreement in the nation about the result of their handiwork. The political culture was plural and the people were still divided over what it included and left out. Even before the new state came into existence, there were threats of rebellion and secession, which hardened as the date of independence drew near. In an environment of growing hostility and unwillingness to compromise, the politics of fear replaced the politics of compromise and consensus; the people were unable to make the new political system work.

If the new political system of independent Burma was intended to inculcate the ideas of individual freedom through liberal democratic institutions and the acceptance of diversity through a quasi-federal system, it never really got started.

Although all seemed to agree on the idea of popular rule, they were divided between those who advocated the adopted system and those who wanted to substitute the models offered by authoritarian socialist and communist states in Eastern Europe and China. Those who wanted a strong central state sought to undermine the quasi-federal state, even before it took root. Those who defended the religious pluralism embedded in the new constitution were challenged by others who wanted a religious-based state, or at least the elevation of Buddhism to the state religion.

Widespread impatience and dissatisfaction with the constitution and the ideas that it supported were reflected in the rebellions and insurrections, which, in some cases, continue to the present. The Communists sought to overthrow the liberal democratic state while several minorities fought to gain independent status outside of the union. The internal wars were complicated by invasion from the north and fears among the nation's leaders that China's civil war threatened the integrity and independence of Burma.

Despite the near anarchy and dismemberment in the first years of independence, the Union of Burma held firm. The people generally remained loyal to their new state, and the minorities, with the exception of the Karen, stood firmly in support of the Union against those who would dismember it and in defense of liberal democracy against authoritarianism.

During the constitutional period, a growing number of citizens participated in the three national elections held between 1950 and 1960 and supported the governments elected. They enjoyed their political and civil rights as protected by the constitution, a free press, and a national secular educational system. The military, under civilian control, played a key role in pushing the rebellious forces away from the nation's heartland, making it possible for the agricultural and extractive economy to thrive and grow. Under the leadership of U Nu, prime minister for most of the period, the nation had a man who was committed to educate citizens about the ideas and values of the emerging political culture of inclusion of all through blending liberal democratic and socialist values and ideas drawn from the West and traditional Theravada Buddhism. In his frequent speeches to the nation and his writings, U Nu drew on Buddhist teachings and religious parables to convey this message, while never failing to take note of the religious pluralism of the nation. He never hesitated to explain and expound on liberal democratic ideals and values as basic to a free and diverse society, and he never hesitated to defend the ethnic and cultural diversity of Burma as a strength of the nation.[17] But, with too little time for the new ideas and system to be established, and with divided messages and voices both in and out of his party, U Nu and the nation were unprepared in 1962 for a new challenge by the military to the emerging political culture and institutions.

The military, under Gen. Ne Win, held an alternative set of ideas and beliefs as the basis for a different political system. Ne Win feared a breakup of the Union of Burma because the constitution permitted the Shan and Karenni states the right of secession. He also argued that, following the death of Aung San, the governing Anti-Fascist People's Freedom League (AFPFL), under Nu, had departed from the socialist goals of the pre-war nationalist movement and was taking Burma down a capitalist road. The military seized power, set the democratic constitution aside in favor of a military dictatorship and overlaid the federal system with an administrative network that created a unitary state. Ne Win and supporters of the change declared its actions consistent with the traditional political culture of precolonial Burma as well as with nationalist pre–World War II goals; therefore they were more understandable and acceptable to a majority of the people than the Western ideas and values of the 1947 constitution.

In line with the isolation of Burma before the nineteenth century, Ne Win initially closed the country to the outside world in order to give the nation time to solve its internal problems: ending disunity, restructuring the state, and making it strong and able to resist alien ideas and values from abroad, which, it was argued, were destroying the unique culture and identity of the people and the land.

The new authoritarian culture of Burma, which Ne Win sought to impose, cloaked change in traditional dress. Although despotism was the legacy of pre-colonial Burma, the authoritarian values and institutions adopted by Ne Win and the military were not drawn from the traditions of Burma under its kings but from the East European socialist state models. The centralized administrative system erected by the military was also patterned after the British colonial system, where authority reached into the village and touched every resident, not on the semifeudal system employed in the times of the kings. It was backed by a permanently mobilized military whose primary mission was internal control. Under the old system, the palace was considered the center of the universe, and anyone who occupied it was recognized as the legitimate ruler. The rule of Ne Win—with all power in the hands of one person supported by a small council of handpicked supporters—may have had the appearance of a kingship of old but without a moral sanction. It was a poor imitation of the past. In 1974, the military wrote a constitution that perpetuated its rule through a one-party system. This blend of the old authoritarian rule with the new constitutionally legalized dictatorship, distorted both the precolonial and liberal democratic ideas and values as the basis for the new political culture that it authored.

Socialism, not Buddhism, was the basis of the military's ideology of the state. The rulers thought of themselves as modern men in tune with the ideology embraced by Europeans, Asians, Africans, and Latin Americans who were in the process of throwing off the intellectual and neocolonial shackles of Western capitalism and building new states on the basis of socialist ideas and values. By 1987, socialism failed, and in order to lighten external debt, the military rulers were forced to ask the United Nations to declare Burma a least-developed country, even though it failed to meet the criteria for such a designation. The government's inability to manage the economy and provide the necessary goods and services to the people was a major reason for the popular peaceful revolution of 1988.

The political culture of the military rulers included the objective of a united and strong Burma. The rulers saw the survival of separatism between the Burmans and minorities as a result of the colonial policy of "divide and rule," which led to a weak state, subject to foreign interference and possible invasion. Federalism and the preservation and propagation of minority cultures were post-independence means of perpetuating separatism and keeping Burma divided and weak. The basis for a strong united nation, the military argued, was the creation of a unitary state, the use of a single language and the development of a national culture based on Burman values and ideals. In order to achieve this goal, the military had to end rebellion and internal war. The military offered two alternatives, the carrot of inviting the opposition to end its rebellion and return to society—or the stick of facing continuous warfare and defeat, to unite and Burmanize the society.[18] It refined its policy in 1974 by shifting to a political solution—the inclusion of a nominal federal system in a new constitution while leaving real power in the hands of the central government. The military hoped that this combination would win the approval of the ethnic minorities who were not in revolt, and end their support for insurgent armies.

The new political culture of the military offered no rights to the citizens without duties. Citizens could take up any occupation "permitted by the state within the bounds of the socialist economy," they could use their own language and follow their own customs so long as "unity and solidarity of the national group, security of the state and the social order" was not undermined. Individuals had the right of free speech and publication "unless such freedom [was] contrary to the interest of socialism."[19]

The political culture that the military sought to impose struck shallow and weak roots in the society; when the people could no longer accept military rule and the ideas and values that it sought to impose on the nation, they took to the streets in the summer of 1988 and peacefully called for the revival of the political culture and spirit of 1947. Only the military's violent suppression of their demands halted the march for change.

After more than nine years of brutal military dictatorship, there is strong evidence that the political culture of the people remains plural, with alternative sets of ideas, values, and leadership contesting and shaping the thoughts and actions of the people.

On Sept. 18, 1988, when the military violently suppressed the peaceful revolution and displaced the 1974 constitution and the party leaders to whom it had transferred power, it restored outright despotism. The military justified its actions by declaring that the nation was faced with political disunity, threats to national sovereignty, and the dismemberment of the state. It ruled by decree and martial law, enacting new rules and laws as well as restoring old ones from the colonial and constitutional periods.

Faced with an angry and resistant population and worldwide criticism of its violent seizure of power, the military rulers decreed a national election for members to a reconstituted national assembly. This was believed to be the first step in the restoration of democracy. Although 233 parties were registered, two stood out: the National Unity Party (NUP), the new name for the Burma Socialist Program Party the military created in 1962 and to whom it transferred power in 1974; the National League for Democracy (NLD), the party of Daw Aung San Suu Kyi, the daughter of the martyred father of Burma's independence, and several former Burma military officers who had broken with Ne Win in the preceding two decades. The NLD stood for the restoration of democracy, civilian rule under law, and the re-establishment of human and civil rights. The military allowed the election to be free and fair, and the NLD won overwhelmingly, gaining 392 seats to 10 for the NUP.

Faced with a rival claimant, the NLD, the military rulers announced that the ruling body, the State Law and Order Restoration Council (SLORC) was "not bound by any constitution . . . is ruling the country with martial law...[that it is] a military government and . . . is . . . recognized by countries of the world and the United Nations. During the interim period before the emergence of a government formed under a firm constitution, the SLORC [will rule]."[20]

Having suppressed the Burman population in Burma's heartland, the SLORC sought to bring unity to the nation through an offer of cease-fires to all ethnic groups in revolt. Returning nominally to the political culture of precolonial times, it offered its ethnic rivals temporary autonomy within their own areas—possession of their weapons, control of the areas they held, freedom to live according to their own traditions and cultures, and the right to pursue their economic activity—in exchange for halting their fighting against the state and breaking off contact with other minorities in revolt. The SLORC specifically refused to discuss and settle outstanding political issues, saying they belonged to the future constitutional government of Burma.

Although fourteen cease-fire agreements were signed, three minority groups were still at war in early 1997. Meanwhile, in minority areas the military seizes property, demands free labor, and abuses the population without restraint.

Without popular support and ruling by fear and intimidation, the SLORC has slowly sought to impose new political values and processes on the people. Its long-term goal is nothing less than changing the political culture of Burma. In 1992, it organized a national convention with handpicked members under tight control that continued to deliberate (in 1997) and write the principles for a new constitution. The convention's immediate objective was to write a basic law that would give the military permanent political control at all levels of government. The Convention says and does nothing without the prior approval of the SLORC.[21] By discussing the work and results of the Convention in the press, on radio and television, the military propagates its ideas and values and prepares the nation to accept them.

Despite the efforts of the military to monopolize all means of communication and push relentlessly for the acceptance of the values and ideals that it advances, there are alternative ideas and values in the marketplace that have found wide support and approval by the people, both Burman and non-Burman. Articulated best by Aung San Suu Kyi, they draw on the ideas embedded in the political culture that gave rise to the independence movement and the 1947 constitution, and were reaffirmed by the peaceful marchers in the summer of 1988. At the time, Aung San Suu Kyi noted that, "In the quest for democracy the people of Burma explore not only the theories and practices of the world outside their country but also the spiritual and intellectual values that have given shape to their own environment."[22]

Aung San Suu Kyi also recalled the themes of her father, Aung San, in his campaign for independence by asking the people for disciplined support and unity, not violence and division. Finally, she called for the restoration of a multiparty democratic system of government. By returning to the idea of freedom located at the heart of Buddhism and to the liberal democratic ideas imported from the West, she wrote that, "The people of Burma want not just a change in government but a change in political values."[23]

To achieve a free and democratic society through peaceful means, Aung San Suu Kyi called for dialogue between equals—the military rulers and the leaders of the people. "Dialogue," she said, "is not debate. There will be disagreements and arguments. Dialogue does not involve winners and losers. It is not a question of losing face. It involves finding the best solutions for the country."[24]

Dialogue between equals implies freedom and limited government. "Human beings the world over need freedom and security that they may be able to realize their full potential." The longing for a form of governance that provides security without destroying freedom goes back a long way. Aung San Suu Kyi noted that it was Mencius, the Chinese scholar, long before the Greek and other Western philosophers, who said that "in a nation the people are the most important, the state is next and the rulers the least important."[25]

The people of Burma responded to the NLD and Aung San Suu Kyi's call for a return to democracy, freedom, and government under law. These were not new ideas; they were part of the political culture that the nationalist leaders in the post–World War II period inscribed in the constitution and used as their guide in erecting the institutions of government. When these democratic ideas were recalled in the summer of 1988, the people responded and called for their return as the basis of Burma's polity.

Even after the military brutally suppressed the peaceful marches, created the SLORC, and used violence and intimidation to impose its will, the ideas did not disappear. Through the speeches and writings of Aung San Suu Kyi and other NLD leaders, they were repeated. They resonated with the people. During military rule before 1988, the people learned to use more subtle and indirect means to keep their demands and struggle alive. They made their strongest statement in the 1990 election when they overwhelmingly voted for the NLD. They continued, even though many of their leaders were arrested, imprisoned, abused, and killed.

When Aung San Suu Kyi was released from six years of house arrest in 1995, pro-democracy activists defied the SLORC's decrees about assembling in large groups, and courted arrest and imprisonment by attending the weekly meetings outside her house in Rangoon to hear and talk with her. They continue to defy authority by listening to foreign shortwave broadcasts, secretly viewing videos smuggled from abroad, and viewing the movie *Beyond Rangoon*. They eagerly follow the satire of the comics at the *pwes*, the traditional entertainment of the countryside, where punning, double entendres, and sarcasm are the staple weapons for challenging the pomposity and authority of the rulers. For people who believe in magic, numerology, and astrology, as well as Buddhism, they read and understand symbols. The NLD's adoption of the ordinary peasant's straw hat as its symbol in the 1990 election sent a message that, like the hat that protects the head of the wearer from the sun and rain, the NLD would cover and protect the people, if chosen to lead. Like many Burmese, Ne Win believed in numerology, and he scheduled important events on dates that added up to the number nine, which was thought to be lucky. The public knew, however, that there was no magic in number nine when Ne Win's party lost the May 27 national election in 1990. No matter how good the government's intelligence and how cruel the punishment for breaking the SLORC's rules, in 1997 the people's defiance continued, even in the face of an unrelenting dictatorship.

On the question of unity between the Burmans and non-Burmans, Aung San Suu Kyi set forth some of her party's ideas in a message that she delivered on the 1996 anniversary of the 1947 Panglong Conference where her father and the leaders of some of the minorities had agreed voluntarily to form a union. She recalled that the NLD said, in February 1989, that no single ethnic group would have special privileges. Nor would rightful privileges be curbed. The party, she said, would work "toward the right of all indigenous races to set out their policies in political, economic, and administrative fields."[26]

Aung San Suu Kyi reminded her listeners that on Aug. 29, 1990, following a meeting between the NLD and the United Nationalities League for Democracy (a loose confederation of the NLD parties), delegates called for racial and political equality among all peoples, the right to autonomy under the constitution, and the assurance of democracy and human rights. They agreed that there would be no right to secede. They agreed to go back to the ideas of Aung San, as stated at the AFPFL preconstitutional convention, on the basic characteristics of a state within the union; they agreed that states shall have autonomy and democratic political institutions in order to govern in their areas; finally, they agreed that state legislation would be subject to review by the national legislature when conflicts arose.[27]

Aung San Suu Kyi reminded her listeners that it was the intention of the elected government in 1990 to convene a National Coordination Convention for all indigenous races to develop ideas and principles regarding democracy, stability, peace, unity, and solidarity of the indigenous peoples for the future constitution.

These ideas and declarations go beyond 1947 by proposing that within each state, legislative and administrative bodies must be formed for minorities that were too small to have states of their own. They would be allowed certain language and cultural rights. The NLD has not adopted any additional principles; instead, it looks forward to the convening of a meeting between leaders of the two groups where they can take up lingering as well as new questions, formulate other principles, and work out details.

Since 1988, the minorities and Burmans have learned a great deal about one another. The minorities offered protection and aid to the Burman students, monks, and others who took refuge among them. In addition to hosting Burmans, they have aided in training them militarily and have fought together against the Burmese army. In 1988, the ethnic minority and Burman groups living in the border areas formed the Democratic Alliance of Burma (DAB), a broad front coalition; in 1990, the Karen gave refuge to seven Burman elected members to parliament and supported their formation of the National Coalition Government of the Union of Burma, the rival government to the military in Rangoon. With nearly a decade of close contact, the minorities and Burmans have come to know a great deal about each other and have found common ground in the struggle against military rule.

As early as 1984, the minorities, organized as the National Democratic Front, publicly agreed to end their efforts to secede from the Union of Burma and, together with the Burmans, to build a viable federal union wherein they would have equality and some right of self-determination. Also, in 1990, the leaders of the DAB created a study group to examine the past in Burma to learn why the 1947 constitution failed to achieve national unity and peace and to study the constitutions of foreign nations to learn how other countries have dealt with similar problems. The study group has drafted several proposed constitutions that it has circulated both inside of Burma and abroad to international scholars for comments, criticism, and alternative ideas. In all of the drafts, the principles of federalism, democracy, self-determination, human rights, and civilian rule are developed and incorporated into constitutional language. The authors are determined to try to anticipate and solve as many problems as possible before agreeing to a new national constitution. The DAB, like the NLD, looks forward to one or more preconstituent assembly meetings so that through dialogue they can develop a common vision and goals for the future political system in Burma.[28]

The issue of national unity is still a central question for Burma. The past decade has provided a means whereby the Burmans and the minorities have come to know one another, and both are looking for ways to build a peaceful permanent union. This reflects a major change in the political culture of Burma from the ideas and values expressed just before and during the 1947 constituent assembly. Today, the leaders of both groups are working for unity; the question remains how to achieve it. Both agree that the military approach to the problem is unacceptable and inconsistent with the values and goals of the people.

There never was a single political culture shared by Burmans and non-Burmans. Instead, the culture has been plural, drawing on different sources and seeking different ends. Colonial rule affected the political cultures of the Burmans and the non-Burmans in strikingly different ways: while introducing new values and beliefs among the Burmans that were assimilated in different ways, the traditional values and ideas of the minorities were reinforced and perpetuated into World War II. But the time between the war's end and independence was too short to allow for the amalgamation of the different beliefs and values; as a result, the constitution was flawed, and civil war and disunity resulted.

Today there is an emerging national culture that is secular and democratic, not religious and authoritarian. It reflects the diversity in values and beliefs among the people. It calls for a political system with a significant degree of decentralization under civilian control. Real changes toward a broader national political culture are evolving from an increase in communication between Burmans and non-Burmans, a result of the 1988 migration of young educated Burmans to the minority areas and their common abuse by an illegal, self-chosen military junta and the army it commands. Aung San Suu Kyi is the only leader today who enjoys the overwhelming trust of a majority of Burmans, minority leaders, and their followers. Together, they are on record in favor of a democratic political system that honors and respects human rights. They reject the declarations of the SLORC's spokesmen that world criticism of its despotism "is a tool to interfere in the domestic affairs of states." Rather, they see the United Nations, through its Burma resolutions and criticism of the SLORC by democratic governments as fulfilling the international purposes of the UN Charter to "achieve international cooperation in solving international problems of an economic, social, cultural, or humanitarian character, and in promoting and encouraging respect for human rights and for fundamental freedoms for all without distinction as to race, sex, language, or religion."[29]

With the people in support of the leaders of the opposition, who are advancing the emerging national political culture, the people of Burma, and not the SLORC, may yet find solutions that all can accept and live with peacefully.

Notes

1. Statement by His Excellency, U Ohn Gyaw, Minister of Foreign Affairs and Chairman of the Delegation of the Union of Myanmar, in the General Debate of the Fifty-first Session of the United Nations General Assembly. New York, 27 September 1966, 4, mimeo.

2. Ibid.

3. Melford Spiro, *Kinship and Marriage in Burma* (Berkeley, 1977), xi.

4. Maung Maung Gyi, *Burmese Political Values: The Socio-political Roots of Authoritarianism* (New York, 1983), 9.

5. Michael Aung Thwin, "1948 and the Myth of Independence," in Silverstein (ed.), *Independent Burma at Forty Years: Six Assessments* (Ithaca, 1989), 19–34.

6. Donald Eugene Smith, *Religion and Politics in Burma* (Princeton, 1965), 14.

7. Ibid., 5.

8. Maung Maung Gyi, *Burmese Political Values*, 36.

9. Ibid., 14.

10. John S. Furnivall, *An Introduction to the Political Economy of Burma* (Rangoon, 1938, 2nd rev. ed.), 37-41; Victor B. Liberman, *Burmese Administrative Cycles: Anarchy and Conquest, c. 1580-1760* (Princeton, 1984), 101–107.

11. Smith, *Religion*, 48–51.

12. Ibid., 58–61.

13. Manning Nash, *The Golden Road to Modernity* (New York, 1968), 76–79.

14. Ba Maw, *Breakthrough in Burma: Memoirs of a Revolution 1939–1946* (New Haven, 1968), 7-15; Maung Htin Aung, *A History of Burma* (New York, 1967), 282–298.

15. Patricia Herbert, *The Hsaya San Rebellion (1930-1932) Reappraised* (Melbourne, 1982).

16. Josef Silverstein, *The Political Legacy of Aung San* (Ithaca, 1993; rev. ed).

17. Silverstein, *Burmese Politics: The Dilemma of National Unity* (New Brunswick, 1980), 134-161; U Nu, *Toward Peace and Democracy* (Rangoon, 1949); U Nu, *From Peace to Stability* (Rangoon, 1951); U Nu, *Burma Looks Ahead* (Rangoon, 1953); U Nu, *Forward With the People* (Rangoon, 1955).

18. Government of Burma, *Internal Peace Parley (Historical Document No. 1)* (Rangoon, 1963) (mimeo); Silverstein, "First Steps on the Burmese Way to Socialism," *Asian Survey*, IV (1964), 720–721.

19. Silverstein, *Burma: Military Rule and the Politics of Stagnation* (Ithaca, 1977), 130–131; Government of Burma, *The Constitution of the Socialist Republic of the Union of Burma* (Rangoon, 1974).

20. SLORC, *Announcement No. 1/90*, 27 July 1990, para. 6, 21.

21. Janelle M. Diller, *The National Convention in (Burma) Myanmar: An Impediment to the Restoration of Democracy* (New York, 1996).

22. "Speech to the Mass Rally at the Shwedagon Pagoda," in Aung San Suu Kyi and Michael Aris (ed.), *Freedom from Fear* (Hammondsworth, 1991), 198–204.

23. "In Quest of Democracy," in *Freedom from Fear*, 178.

24. Aung San Suu Kyi, "Transcript of Aung San Suu Kyi Interview," BurmaNet, 13 May 1994.

25. Aung San Suu Kyi, *Empowerment for a Culture of Peace and Development*, Manila, Nov. 21, 1994, 6, mimeo.

26. National League for Democracy, "Daw Aung San Suu Kyi's Message at the 1996 Union Day Anniversary Held at Her House," Feb. 12, 1996, mimeo. All succeeding information taken from this document.

27. "Bogyoke Aung San's Address at the Convention Held at Jubilee Hall, Rangoon, on 23 May 1947," in Silverstein, *Political Legacy of Aung San*, 151–158.

28. National Council of the Union of Burma, "Federal Union of the Burma Constitution" (draft), 1995.

29. *The Charter of the United Nations*, Art. 1, paras. 3, 4.

CHAPTER 2

Political Values and Political Conflict in Burma

R. H. Taylor

THE DIMENSIONS of political conflict in Burma are symbolized by the inability of the most visible antagonists to agree on the name of the state when speaking and writing in languages other than that of most of the population of the country itself. Because the substitution of the transliterated Myanmar for the familiar Burma was imposed by a military regime with dubious claims to legitimacy in the eyes of its opponents, it has found little use in the United States. The fact that we all have become accustomed to Thailand for Siam and Sri Lanka for Ceylon is beside the point in the current circumstances.

More important, this symbolic divide is representative of a deep division in political values that has evolved in different communities and interest groups within Burma during the past century. What appears to be essentially a contemporary political clash between the forces of militarism and the forces of democracy can equally be interpreted as a clash between the values of an allegedly "traditional" indigenous communalism versus the values of modern and "Western" individualism. Which set of values runs deeper in the society at the present time will determine the eventual outcome whatever the possible effects of external political and economic pressures. But values change over time at different rates in different social strata even if more slowly than their defenders and protagonists usually believe. Change is occurring, but slowly.

There is a temptation, because of the new-found currency and emotion that Burmese politics now evoke, to see the political issues of the country as sui generis. In fact, of course, the clashes of values and forces now seen there have been present, to different degrees and at various levels of conflict, in all of the countries of Southeast Asia and most of the remainder of Asia and Africa for the past century or so. By putting the issues of Burma into comparative historical perspective, the debate over plausible and effective policy options will become more realistic than when merely superimposing the values of the societies of North America and northwestern Europe on a set of historical and sociological forces different from those now found in wealthy industrialized, urban societies.[1]

The Legitimacy of the State

The most fundamental clash of values currently perceived in Burma is over the basis of the legitimacy of the state and its ability to structure social and political relations. The State Law and Order Restoration Council (SLORC) rests its claims to legitimacy on its ability to maintain and protect a number of values held dear by itself, and, it believes, by the majority of the population. These include nationalism, national defense, economic development, and the preservation of indigenous religious, cultural, and social institutions. Opponents advance the argument, more familiar to those in the West, that legitimacy comes from the consent of the people as expressed through the ballot box.

Although much has been written about the radical transformations of Burmese society during the past 150 years, relatively little has been written on the comparative basis of legitimacy and consent in the country. There are several reasons for this paucity, one of which is that the issue itself is relatively recent in historical terms. Legitimacy is itself a modern concept.

There exists in Burma, as in Southeast Asia generally, no fully developed indigenous theory of the state. Rather, the historical principles of state "legitimacy" found in practice have been derived from theories developed in the classical literatures of India, China, or Europe and then adapted to Southeast Asian conditions as the modern state evolved.[2] In consequence, the study of state legitimacy requires the "reconstruction" of theories from historical practice together with the analysis of contemporary attempts to develop lasting formulations in the face of rapidly changing political, economic, and social conditions.

Another reason is that the foundations of the state seem fragile in comparison with those of the major states of East and South Asia, as well as Europe. The absence of indigenous theories of the state, combined with the consequences of colonial rule and its effects on different social strata, has allowed the foundations of the state to remain contested. Politics in the region often centers on the nature of the basis of the state. Regime crises therefore tend to raise more fundamental questions than just who governs; they tend to reopen debates about the way the polity should be governed. The absence of an indigenous historical consensus on and a consistent theory of the foundations of the state before the nineteenth century has allowed imported European ideas of ethnicity and justice to compete with older indigenous ideas about the "cosmological" basis of power, thus encouraging a search for acceptable formulations for state foundations in the late twentieth century that attempt to combine these essentially antagonistic concepts.[3]

Evolution of the State

As I have argued elsewhere, the nature of the state in Burma has changed significantly during the past two hundred years, as has the context of its existence and the nature of its leading personnel.[4] These changes have been largely the consequence of altered external and internal factors that established new conditions for state construction and maintenance, and have had very different effects during various epochs on the nature of the society and its economic and other institutions. What is striking, however, is the similarity in effect of indigenous popular ideas about the foundations of the state in both pre-colonial and post-colonial times, despite the addition of European-derived secular, republican, and socialist images. Shortened and simplified, my thesis is as follows.

The pre-colonial or monarchical state in Burma, which arose with the establishment of the Restored Toun-goo dynasty in 1597, and continued under the Kon-baung dynasty (1752–1885), had its foundations primarily in the moral and political authority that a system of semireligious symbolism and ritual provided the monarchy and its agents in an essentially subsistence economy that had few bases of authority other than patron-client relationships. The Theravada Buddhist *sangha*, or monkhood, and the sanctioning of monarchical authority that Buddhist thought provided, plus the sumptuary laws of the state, coupled with a low level of demand by a small population in a largely self-sufficient economy, meant that politics centered around the distribution of status rewards and authority within the monarchical state's increasingly bureaucratized structures. These remained largely unquestioned despite progressive structural alterations. Although the bureaucratic and administrative structures of the state changed in the face of new domestic and external challenges and opportunities between 1752 and 1885, the foundations remained little altered and the monarchical state's authority largely unquestioned.[5]

In classical Burmese politico-religious theory, the monarchy existed in the face of humanity's natural and egotistical greed in order to promote righteousness and thereby regulate man's moral condition.[6] According to Buddhist thought, the state and the monarchy had developed originally because of the inherent greed of each individual. Personal acquisitiveness led to the growth of jealousy, envy, and covetousness, which in turn led inevitably to conflicts over ownership and usufruct. The resulting disorder led humanity to realize that it required some authority over itself to keep acquisitiveness in check. The people then elected a king (*thamatta*, the contemporary Burmese word for president), a person of superior moral qualities, from among themselves to control their greed and establish order. Thus, humanity came to recognize the need to have a temporal authority so that the individual could pursue a moral life to his or her short-term material disadvantage but long-term spiritual benefit.[7]

This traditional conception of the foundations of the state, explained in what might be seen as a variant of the "social contract" theory, did not include the idea of the state in relation to society, as such. Rather there was assumed to be an individual contract between each person and the monarch that in turn sanctioned hierarchical patron-client relations from the top to the bottom of the social order. Indeed, classical Burmese thought did not have a term for society as such and only subsequently did Burmese writers develop concepts and words to take account of this essentially modern notion, the twin of legitimacy.

The imposition of British colonial rule between 1824 and 1886 resulted not only in the displacement of the monarchical state and the power it provided the wielders of authority, but also imposed the bureaucratic and legal institutions and structures of the British Indian empire on "ministerial Burma proper," but not "Frontier Areas" Burma. The social and political consequences of that geographical and administrative system divide continue to shape political perceptions in and out of the country today.

During the process of colonial state creation and for the subsequent sixty-two years of British rule, the state was dependent upon the military power of the British Indian army and a high level of legal coercion supported by the power of a relatively efficient, externally oriented bureaucratic machine unhindered by effective local political demands to maintain its authority.[8] In terms of the history of the locus of state authority in Burma, the colonial state possessed little basis for popular acceptance other than its claim to modernity, economic efficiency, and necessity, and this fragile self-justification was rapidly undermined with the rise of modern nationalist sentiments and increasing social instability during the first decades of the twentieth century. Nonetheless, the colonial state managed to restructure economic and social relations of the majority of the lowland population in significant ways, giving rise to an export-oriented agrarian society with complex class and ethnic structures. These changes led to the growth of the new political forms and ideas that provided the basis for Burmese nationalism.

Nationalism

But informing and giving power to these new nationalist ideals were conceptions of political legitimacy similar in their assumptions to the basis of moral and political authority in the pre-colonial world. Thus, the first articulators of modern Burmese nationalism in the 1910s and 1920s harkened back to the symbolism of monarchical Burma, including identifying nationalism with the defense of Buddhism and the resurrection of a state that governed like that of the Burmese kings. Modern thought was thus mediated by ideas of social relations derived from the institutions of the monarchical state.[9]

The generation of nationalist leaders who emerged in the 1930s and took state power from the British in 1948, turned—despite their knowledge of European socialism—to the same indigenous pool of ideas about the foundations of the state, even though when independence was regained in 1948, the state initially took the constitutional form of the republican and secular state. But soon, in the face of widespread revolt led by communist and ethnic separatist movements, government leaders sought legitimacy for the state through ideas founded in the Buddhist traditions of the past. Prime Minister U Nu turned to religious symbols and moral appeals in order to gain support for the state and the perpetuation of its authority. The Buddhist "revival" of the 1950s, with its centerpiece, the four-year-long *Sangayana* (Sixth Buddhist Council or synod), reenacting the shoring up of the state's foundations conducted by Burma's penultimate king, Mindon Min, in the 1860s, is a clear indication of the significance attached to these foundations.[10] Nu's constitutional amendment in 1961 making Buddhism the state religion was the culmination of this process but set off in its wake protests from other religious groups opposed to the implied preferential recognition given to the religion of the majority.

Socialism

Following the coup of 1962, the army took direct control of the state, and began, at first haltingly and then with greater intent, to reconstruct the foundations of the state on an avowedly nonsectarian, but implicitly and explicitly indigenous, cultural basis. The foundations of the state that the army chose to emphasize also harkened back to the moral ideals of the Buddhist kings, but recognizing the religiously plural society of twentieth-century Burma, the army attempted to establish a secularist moral order based upon Buddhist-derived ethical beliefs that are widely shared throughout Burmese society.[11] Building from the language of Burmese Marxism, itself translated into Burmese idiom through Buddhist terminology, and recognizing that force alone is insufficient for the creation of state legitimacy, the army assumed an ideological hegemony that combined the moral notions of the state found in the pre-colonial order with those found in twentieth-century Marxist thought.[12] The basis of these ideas was stated in the basic ideological text of the Burma Socialist Program Party (BSPP), *The System of Correlation of Man and His Environment.*[13]

Like the thought of monarchical Burmese Buddhism, the ideology of the Party emphasized the egotistical nature of humanity and the fact that people only enter society for selfish purposes; they cannot live alone and fulfill either their spiritual or material needs. These social constraints naturally work against humanity's nature and people constantly need to keep "within bounds" their "self-aggrandizement and desire for freedom." Society is capable of doing so to a certain extent through institutions such as marriage and the family, but the rise of individualism poses new challenges for those in authority. It is at this point that the ideology reveals implicitly the role of socialism as a state-controlled economic system designed not to establish social and economic equality but to control humanity's egotism, the basis of its greed.

The document states that: "Our socialist economy shall be based on the dialectical unity of the individual and social interests of the citizens of the Union of Burma. Our socialist economy is a system which will achieve a harmony between the individual and the social interests of the people."[14] Socialism was seen as the means to keep in bounds humanity's natural acquisitiveness which, if allowed full rein, would not be to either the individual's or society's long term advantage. The case for the justification and legitimization of the modern authoritarian state begins to emerge at this point.

Given the egotistical nature of humanity, it must be guided away from greed by a higher authority. Under modern conditions, the ruling party replaced the monarch as the guiding institution of the state and therefore the maintainer of order. The implicit authoritarianism of the ideology becomes explicit because the function of the party, through the system of democratic socialism, is to give guidance to others in order to limit their greed. The party was to reorient the views of the people in order to eradicate "fraudulent practices, profit motive, easy living, parasitism, shirking and selfishness."[15] The result was to deny the legitimacy of any source of power outside the state, whether economic, social, or moral, and to attempt to concentrate attention upon the state itself as the center of human identity. Thus the state assumed the cloak of the nation and sought to be the only legitimate sanction of authority. The Buddhist sangha was brought back under its control in 1980, and while religious freedom was allowed, the legitimacy of ethnic and other identities with any political, as opposed to cultural content giving rise to anti-state movements, was forbidden.[16]

Urban crowds rejected the socialist/military government in 1988 because of economic mismanagement and the government's isolation from public opinion. Despite that rejection and the apparent peculiarity of the socialist state's foundations in Burma, in comparative historical perspective there are important similarities in the experience of the Burmese state and others in Southeast Asia. Ironically, it has been socialism that has, to a large extent, created the structures that have preserved so much of traditional Burma. While laissez faire capitalism did a great deal to destabilize and reorder social and political relations in colonial Burma, it has been socialism that has ensured that there was so little change until the collapse of the BSPP regime in 1988.[17] Thailand, which was characterized in the late 1940s as a more traditional and less modern society than British Burma, has become one of the most diversified and politically complex societies in Asia as a consequence of its deep and intense involvement since the 1950s with the world capitalist order. By contrast, Burma has been, relatively speaking, frozen in aspic.[18]

Clash of Values

The political, economic, and social isolation of Burmese society during the three decades since the early 1960s took place in a period in which value changes and challenges were the order of the day in many neighboring societies. The turbulence of Thailand's politics, the rise of an articulate, business-oriented middle class, the politicization of universities, and the expansion of an independent press—forcing the army to concede power at various times during the past two decades and more—stands in marked contrast to the value stasis in Burma.[19] The value conflicts found in Burma today represent the result of the depth of the challenge that modernity poses for the traditional values of Burmese society. The intensity of that conflict is enhanced by the intellectual and experiential backgrounds of the major public antagonists, Daw Aung San Suu Kyi, who for many represents the National League for Democracy (NLD) and its call for a new basis of legitimacy, and the SLORC and its military leaders. While the political understanding of Aung San Suu Kyi was shaped by years of living under first Indian and then British democracy, which she assumes to be the norms of life, the military has been conditioned by education and career experiences to reject such values as not only foreign, but actually subversive of the nation it is pledged to defend.

As with periods of political crisis in other countries in Southeast Asia during the past half century, the current impasse, symbolically represented by the opposition of Aung San Suu Kyi to the SLORC, is about fundamental issues of how the state is to be legitimized.[20] While the SLORC appeals implicitly to Burmese cultural traditions and contends that the NLD and those who support it at home and abroad are set on undermining Burmese political and cultural independence, it bases its immediate and explicit public foundation for continued rule on the historical role of the armed forces as the founder and savior of national independence.

In arguments that appear self-serving and disingenuous to its critics and opponents, the army advances views that I believe are genuinely held by the officer corps and those who work most closely with it. Like individuals who work in any institution, the army officers are aware of its deficiencies and mistakes, and the foibles of its personnel. Personal rivalries exist and ambitions and hopes are nurtured, but underlying these natural human motives there remains a strong sense of corporate solidarity that is based on shared training, shared experiences, and a sense of beleagueredness that is reinforced by the hostility shown the regime by the Western world as well as its internal opponents.

As an organization that dates its origins to the formation of the Burma Independence Army (BIA) in 1941, but which traces its inspirational roots back to the great days of the Burmese monarchs, the army sees itself as the primary defender of the country's independent spirit. The new Military Museum in Rangoon is revealing of the modern army's view of itself. From fighting forces of the kings, through to the army's struggle against the Japanese, the British, Karen, and Communist insurgents at the time of independence, and the CIA-backed Kuomintang in the early 1950s, to subsequent conflicts with other insurgent-cum-separatist groups in more recent years, the army portrays itself as continually fighting to maintain the unity and integrity of the country.

As the official version of the army's role in the making of contemporary Burma makes explicit, the military's ability to regain independence and maintain national sovereignty has been achieved in the face of the unwitting opposition of civilian politicians who looked to interests other than those of the Burmese people for their support. In this view, independence was lost by the decadence and self-indulgence of the last Kon-baung kings who failed to maintain sufficient and sufficiently modern military forces to ward off the encroaching Europeans. Rather than acknowledging the failure of the final monarchs to come to terms with modernity, they only see the national disgrace of military defeats in 1824, 1856, and 1885.

During the colonial period, while some politicians were content to work in Rangoon with the colonially inspired parliamentary structures and the legal sys-

tem that allowed the Burmese to lose much of their patrimony to foreign land-
lords and capitalists, the "real" soul of the country rested with the workers and
farmers who rose up in the strikes and peasant revolts of the 1930s against colonial rule only to be put down, largely undefended by the Burmese politicians, by
the superior force of the British Indian army.[21] The alleged duplicity of civilian
politicians continued in the post-independence period when winning elections or
maintaining office, no matter with whom one had to compromise, was seen as
more important than the army's conception of the "national interest."[22]

Having created a political image of the past that sees non-military enemies
of the state throughout the past 150 years, the army also claims that not only
has it sacrificed to regain and maintain national independence, it has also filled
the policy void that the civilian politicians failed to acknowledge. The new
army museum, like official military accounts of the past, points to the role of
the 1958-60 Caretaker Government in reaching border agreements with China
and ending the "feudal" rule of the *sawbwas*. That these were policies anticipated before the army assumed sole control is not noted in these accounts.
While the economic failures of the thirty years of BSPP/army rule are acknowledged, and attributed to the BSPP, rather than the army as the main prop of that
party, the government emphasizes the current role of the army in furthering
infrastructure development and general economic development in the face of
external and internal political opposition.

Critics of the regime, as well as historians of modern Burma, will find much
to dispute in the government's one-sided account of how the country arrived at
its present position. The distribution of praise and blame is rarely, if ever, as one-
sided as the official version of history asserts. But a self-serving vision of history is not a uniquely Burmese military problem. The regime's opponents also
advance self-serving, distorted and overly simplistic reconstructions of the past.
The lack of recognition of the variable foci of power during the 1950s, and the
insecurity of life during that period, is the most glaring. One of the great political strengths of the army's arguments is that they do resonate with many older
people's views of the major crises in modern Burmese history—from the loss of
independence to the conflicts with various separatist groups, and the insecurity
of the 1940s and 1950s. Moreover, they are arguments that can be advanced in
the mantle of nationalism and Burmese cultural traditions.

In opposition to these historically justified and deep-seated values, and the
more ephemeral ones of recent historical interpretations, about the legitimacy of
the SLORC-dominated state in Burmese political history, Aung San Suu Kyi and
the NLD stand for the simple and now largely universally unquestioned republican notion that the state, regardless of its origins and contested history, must

reflect the views of the electorate as expressed at the ballot box. The denial by the SLORC of the political consequences of the 1990 elections, which saw the NLD win 60 percent of the vote and 80 percent of the seats in the never-formed legislature, is thus seen as the capping proof of the insincerity of the SLORC's protestations that it wishes to see the establishment of democracy in Burma just as much as anyone else.

Burmese Elections

The history of elections in Burma is not without interest.[23] Though the first elections, for municipal councils with extremely restricted franchises, were held in British Burma as early as the 1880s, what we might think of as "national" elections (though restricted to the core seven divisions of diarchical rule in "Burma proper") first were introduced in 1922. Elections during the 1920s were often seen as tools of British domination as much as the expression of the public will, and were widely boycotted by nationalist politicians. Only in the election of 1936, in which previously boycotting groups joined in, did participation rates exceed 50 percent. Under the electoral systems of the 1920s, 1930s, and 1940s, the electoral rolls were structured around concepts of ethnicity and social and economic rank; it would be difficult to argue that these were structures designed to create a cohesive nation.

Not until the 1947 election, which formed the basis of the first post-independence parliament, could it be said that a "national" election took place. Even then in fifty-six of the non communal constituencies the ruling Anti-Fascist People's Freedom League (AFPFL) candidates were unopposed. In those areas where real contests took place, the participation rate was less than 50 percent. The official reason advanced for the low turnout was the political instability that pervaded the country in the turbulent years after the Japanese occupation and the struggle for independence. The fact that the electoral process itself, and the nature of the independence agreement that provided its justification, were strongly criticized by politicians of the left and right who attacked the AFPFL for the terms of independence that it had accepted, may have also played a role. The call for a boycott was apparently as strong then as in the 1920s.

The participation rate in the post-independence elections remained low until 1960. The phased elections of 1951, occurring as the military could gain control over an area in order to establish sufficiently peaceful conditions for a ballot to occur, saw a turnout of about 20 percent, 1.5 million voters out of an electorate of 8 million. The 1956 election saw a doubling of the turnout rate with an increasingly high level of competition at the ballot box. Participation in the last multiparty election, in 1960, which resulted in the return of former Prime Minister U Nu to power after the eighteen-month military Caretaker Government, apparently achieved the highest level of participation (approximately 56 percent according to sources available to me) of any Burmese election until that of 1990.

During the BSPP period, the military organized the country's only national referendum to approve the 1972 socialist constitution. The result was a 95 percent turnout with more than 90 percent approving the constitution. Given the one-party military dominance of the period, this is hardly surprising; nor was it a true indication of public opinion. But perhaps with the exception of the 1960 election, what election in Burma was a "true" expression of public opinion? The elections of the colonial period were widely seen as unfairly structured and designed to achieve the ends of the foreign rulers. The elections of 1947 and the 1950s were held in circumstances of great controversy, internal unrest, and contested legitimacy. The election of 1960, while formally a contest between U Nu and his associates against his former AFPFL colleagues U Kyaw Nyein and U Ba Swe, was more widely seen as a referendum against the nature of the policies and programs the military had conducted from 1958 to 1960.[24]

Given the absence of other forms of evidence, one can only speculate on the grounds of popular support for Aung San Suu Kyi and the NLD in the 1990 elections. Clearly, the economic and political failure of the old socialist order with which the military was intimately involved and the repressive tactics of the army before and after the 1988 coup against Maung Maung's one-month government, provided a basis for widespread hostility to any political groups that represented the past. Although many other parties not descended from the BSPP emerged, none of significance other than the NLD had such a clear lack of affiliation with failed movements and individuals from the 1950s and 1960s thanks to its identification with Aung San Suu Kyi.[25]

The individual basis of continuing support for the NLD, to the extent that it still exists in different sectors of society, may stem from different and less generalized motives. One might argue that for many in the poorer and less politically involved sections of the society, where literacy is at a premium but discomfort is a daily reality, the coming of Aung San Suu Kyi, with her charismatic link through her martyred father with the failed promises of independence in 1947, may have heralded a new millennium. But for veterans of Burmese politics from the 1950s and 1960s, her arrival on the scene may have had a more instrumental appeal. Through her and the NLD many of the failed leftists' thwarted ambitions—as the result of having lost out in previous political and internal military conflicts—could be realized. This is not to say that they do not hold their beliefs about the good of the country as firmly and honestly as their onetime military associates. For some of the old leftists who, with former military men, form part of the core of the party, the NLD provides an opportunity, however mistaken, to achieve the influence they lost to the army in the late 1960s.[26]

Many of the NLD's most avid and brave supporters have been students and other youth. For the generation of students born since 1962, which has never lived under any regime not dominated by the military, the expression of change, opportunity, and modernity offered by the ideas of democracy, individualism, and life as lived outside Burma is extremely attractive. Knowledge about what life is like in advanced capitalist countries is well known to alert and energetic emerging middle class youth, despite the relative isolation of the country from the outside world until recent years. The economic and cultural consequences of embracing the developmental consequences of the consumer society that is implicit in modern capitalist democratic societies is less well appreciated.

Conclusion

In this chapter I have attempted to delineate, in an oversimplified form, two contrasting sets of values and political concepts of authority in contemporary Burmese political life. One centers on the maintenance of tradition and the symbols of national independence that are seen as incompatible with the swift introduction of civilian rule through the free and unfettered contest of political parties. The other poses a concept of individual electoral rights and obligations that implies a wholesale jettisoning of existing political forms for the invocation of democratic institutions and democratic norms de novo. Both the premises of these positions and their logical consequences are, however, misleading because politics and values do not interact in the simplistic manner implied.

Consider, for example, the trajectory of Thai politics during the past thirty or forty years. One might have expected such a simplistic clash of the values of a constructed tradition and an idealized modern future to have existed and persisted there. But opportunities and experiences led civilian and military political groups to recast their values to fit changing circumstances. Although the Thai generals of the 1950s stood for tradition and preservation of an existing, idealized, social order, they set in motion forces of economic and social change which created the social groups, including business persons, lawyers, journalists, and academics, who accused the military of undermining tradition in the name of economic aggrandizement and self-interest. But that followed a period in which non-governmental, non-military, social groups accumulated the capital and institutional independence that allowed them to contest on more equal terms for power with those who felt that they had a right to rule. There emerged a political struggle between much more equal social forces than now exist in Burma. The turbulent politics of contemporary Thailand did not emerge overnight and no one would say they are perfect. But they are more open and democratic than those of Burma.

There is no certainty that Burma will follow the same path. Some would not see that path as desirable. Others would argue that an outcome more similar to that in Indonesia may emerge. But even in Jakarta in the 1990s there is more political movement and uncertainty than was the norm in Rangoon for many years before 1988. A debate about the basis of the state is possible, even if attempts to establish independent political institutions are still stymied. Ironically, Thailand, the Southeast Asian polity in which the debate over the basis of the legitimacy of the state has led to the most radical political change, has been able to maintain the outward trappings and inner morality of more traditional political authority.

Notes

1. This is not, however, to accept the claims of some political leaders about some unique form of "Asian values." Values reflect the interests, experiences, and sociological structures of societies and groups within societies, not their geographical or ethnic origins.

2. This point is made for Indonesia in particular, and by implication for the remainder of the region, by Benedict R. O'G. Anderson, "The Idea of Power in Javanese Culture," in Claire Holt (ed.), *Culture and Power in Indonesia* (Ithaca, 1972), 1.

3. The classic statement is Robert Heine-Geldern, *Conceptions of State and Kingship in Southeast Asia* (Ithaca, 1956).

4. R.H. Taylor, *The State in Burma* (London, 1987). The most important changes were consequences of the rise, transformation, and fall of the British-Indian Empire to which Burma was largely, if not always formally, attached from 1824 to 1948.

5. Much as many modern European states can trace a lineage back to the Roman empire, so the state in Burma can trace itself back to the much earlier Pagan dynasty (c. 849–1287), but it is too much to argue that the foundations of the pre-colonial state are found at Pagan. For details of the nature of the early modern state in Burma, see Victor B. Lieberman, *Burmese Administrative Cycles: Anarchy and Conquest c. 1580–1760* (Princeton, 1984); William J. Koenig, "The Early Kon-baung Policy, 1752–1819: A Study of Politics, Administration and Social Organization in Burma" (unpublished Ph.D. dissertation, School of Oriental and African Studies, University of London, 1978); Myo Myint, "The Politics of Survival in Burma: Diplomacy and Statecraft in the Reign of King Mindon, 1853-1878" (unpublished Ph.D. dissertation, Cornell University, 1987).

6. Lieberman, *Burmese Administrative Cycles,* 65.

7. The Theravada Buddhist view is summarized in Stanley J. Tambiah, *World Conqueror and World Renouncer: A Study of Buddhism and Polity in Thailand against a Historical Background* (Cambridge, 1976), 13–14. For a Burmese version, see Aung San, "Naingnganyei Amyomyo," *Dagun Maggazin* ["Kinds of Politics," *Dagon Magazine*], CCXXXIV (1940), 61–71.

8. See the excellent discussion of the role of violence and coercion in Burmese politics in Mary Patricia Callahan, "The Origins of Military Rule in Burma" (unpublished Ph.D. dissertation, Cornell University, 1996), especially Ch. 3: "Coercion and the Colonial State," 79–130.

9. See Donald Eugene Smith, *Religion and Politics in Burma* (Princeton, 1965), 81–139; E. Michael Mendelson, *Sangha and State in Burma: A Study of Monastic Sectarianism and Leadership,* John P. Ferguson (ed.), (Ithaca, 1975), 173–235; Patricia Herbert, *The Hsaya San Rebellion (1930–32) Reappraised* (Melbourne, 1982), 8–9.

10. Mendelson, *Sangha and State in Burma*, 236-357, especially 270–276.

11. Some Muslim and Christian leaders of separatist movements would deny the possibility of such a formulation.

12. For a discussion of the use of socialist imagery in contrasting versions of modern Burmese political thought, see Robert H. Taylor, "Burmese Concepts of Revolution," in Mark Hobart and Robert H. Taylor (eds.), *Context, Meaning and Power in Southeast Asia* (Ithaca, 1986), 79–92.

13. *The System of the Correlation of Man and His Environment: The Philosophy of the Burma Socialist Programme Party* (Rangoon, 17 January 1963).

14. *The System of Correlation*, 25.

15. Ibid., 8–19. The 1988 urban uprising against the government seriously questioned the state's foundations in a way they were not 200 years ago. But the underlying theory of the state does not appear to have been seriously questioned. It should be noted that these beliefs are expressed, in altered but parallel form, by "democratic" leaders such as the late U Nu, the last civilian Prime Minister and one of the leaders of the 1988 opposition. In one of his early writings he expressed similar views on the individual's relationship with authority and the need to have a state to control man's natural unruliness and greed. The title of this work, *Man, the Wolf of Man*, expresses this view for it is from the Burmese translation of the line in Hobbes's *Leviathan*, "Man is to man a wolf." See Richard Butwell, *U Nu of Burma* (Stanford, 1969), 34.

This essay is not the place to explore Burmese economic thought but such a study would be revealing of a number of attitudes toward the market and value that also contradict the assumptions of the liberal world. For example, John S. Furnivall noted in 1957 that economic policy under the former civilian Socialist government ". . . was complicated by the mistaken notion, generally current among Burmans, that everything has its 'proper' price, dependent on the cost of production." This led to significant market distortions and an assumption that the state had a right, indeed an obligation, to absorb the difference between the market price and the import price. "Preface to the Third Edition," *An Introduction to the Political Economy of Burma* (Rangoon, 1957, 3rd edition). For a more positive account of the consequences of Burmese economic thought than that provided by the trenchant Furnivall, see Ernst F. Schumacher, "Buddhist Economics," in Robert H. Taylor, *Handbooks of the Modern World: Asia and the Pacific* (New York, 1991), II, 1503–1509. These ideas inspired Schumacher's subsequent *Small Is Beautiful: A Study of Economics as if People Mattered* (London, 1973).

16. Tin Maung Maung Than, "The Sangha and Sasana in Socialist Burma," *SOJOURN: Social Issues in Southeast Asia*, III (1988), 26–61.

17. As Furnivall made clear in his seminal *Colonial Policy and Practice: A Comparative Study of Burma and the Netherlands Indies* (Cambridge, 1948).

18. I have attempted to explore some of the causes and consequences of this situation in the 1992 Kingsley Martin Memorial Lecture at Cambridge University, published as R. H. Taylor, "Disaster or Release: J. S. Furnivall and the Bankruptcy of Burma," *Modern Asian Studies*, XXIX (1995), 45–63.

19. See the stimulating accounts in Suchit Bunbongkarn, "Elections and Democratization in

Thailand," and Anek Laothamatas, "A Tale of Two Democracies: Conflicting Perceptions of Elections and Democracy in Thailand," in Taylor (ed.), *The Politics of Elections in Southeast Asia* (Cambridge, 1996), 184–200, 201–223.

20. Or previously portrayed as Aung San Suu Kyi versus Gen. Ne Win, a form of conflict that the Western media find most appealing as in the recent political opposition of Megawatti Sukarnoputra versus President Suharto in Indonesia.

21. The fact that the acting Governor of Burma was the only Burmese head of the colony at the time of the Saya San revolt is illustrative of the kind of duplicity that the official army view of history attaches to civilian politicians.

22. See especially Callahan, Ch. 9, "Coups, Counter-Coups, Elections and Purges: The Tatmadaw Comes of Age," in *Origins of Military Rule in Burma*, 444–511, where this point is documented more solidly than I have seen elsewhere.

23. I have given one version in "Elections in Burma/Myanmar: For Whom and Why?" in Taylor (ed.), *Politics of Elections in Southeast Asia,* 164–183.

24. These policies were widely applauded at the time by Western observers and governments for their economic efficiency, openness to the market, and avowed anti-communism.

25. The return to political prominence, even if briefly, of former Prime Minister U Nu and former Brigadier Aung Gyi distracted attention from a welter of other lesser-rank politicians from four decades earlier who attempted one last hurrah.

26. It is interesting to note similar thinking between some senior members of the NLD and the army. When I visited NLD headquarters in July 1989, the day after the party admitted that two of its members, unbeknown to the leadership, had planted a bomb in Rangoon city hall killing a sweeper, several former army officers advanced the view that the party needed its own internal intelligence organization to keep track of members' behavior and intentions. In regard to economic policy, it is important to note that the party apparently not only opposes foreign direct investment now because of its alleged support for continued SLORC rule, but will do so if it takes power on the grounds, according to Aung San Suu Kyi, in an interview with a British business representative in September 1996, that the NLD does not intend to allow Burma to "become" a low wage manufacturing economy like other East Asian countries.

CHAPTER THREE

On Time Warps and Warped Time
Lessons from Burma's
"Democratic Era"

Mary P. Callahan

AGAINST OPPOSITION leader Aung San Suu Kyi's criticisms that the State Law and Order Restoration Council (SLORC) is suppressing peaceful democratic forces, Burma's generals respond with such quaint rallying cries as, "Oppose ax handles who rely on external elements, act as stooges and hold negative views." Against western charges of constructing a "Fascist Disneyland," the junta's public relations team exhorts the citizenry to "Crush all internal and external destructive elements as the common enemy."[1]

To the outside observer, the sloganeering of the military (in Burmese, tatmadaw) regime suggests a time warp. The exhortations and rallying cries proffered in newspaper editorials, on omnipresent red billboards, and on television announcements have their origins in the Fort Bragg psychological warfare training provided in the 1950s to a handful of young Burmese army officers (e.g., U Kyaw Sunn) who now hold positions on the SLORC's Information Committee and other prominent government bodies. To the junta, however, that very period—when the American training was sought as a way out of the country's geostrategic predicament on the frontlines of the Cold War—continues to inform much of the regime's attitudes toward politics, economics, and the world community.

Burma's period of constitutionalism, civilian rule, and contested elections after independence, is often labeled by contemporary pro-democracy activists as Burma's "democratic era." From 1948 until 1958, and from 1960–1962, Burma's political system looked like one of the more promising young democracies in the postcolonial world. Why did a decade of constitutionalism and electoralism lead to the first military takeover in 1958 and then to the more authoritative, enduring military intervention in 1962? Was democracy doomed in Burma? Is there something inherently authoritarian about Burmese culture, as some have argued? Or were Ne Win and his military simply a predatory political force, dating back to the army leadership's formative experiences in anti-colonial student union politics in the 1930s? Do the 1950s hold the answers for the 1990s and beyond?

Those who call the country Burma have somewhat warped readings of a troubled historical time, while those who call it Myanmar seem trapped in a time warp. In particular, I argue that the 1950s do not hold the solutions for Burma in the 1990s and beyond. Instead, I suggest that a careful reading of the 1950s generates sobering warnings about the complex and deep historical roots of Burma's contemporary troubles.

The "Democratic Era"

From 1948 until 1962, the Burmese political system was structured by the 1947 constitution, which included many of the basic provisions associated with democratic rule: Sovereignty was held to "reside in the people"; equality of rights and opportunity were guaranteed for all citizens; subject to the demands of public order and law, citizens were guaranteed liberties of expression, assembly, and association; and an independent judiciary was established, including a Supreme Court which would "issue directions in the nature of habeas corpus. . . ."[2]

To provide for minority rights in this majority-rule parliamentary system, the 1947 constitution also established a federal framework (although the word, "federal," never appears in the document, as Silverstein has pointed out).[3] A bicameral legislature was established, guaranteeing representation to minority ethnic groups in the Chamber of Nationalities. In ethnic minority-dominated regions, a variety of solutions were enshrined in the constitution. All the Shan states were amalgamated into one, which was guaranteed constitutionally a right of secession after ten years. The supreme legislative body in the Shan State was the elected fifty-member State Council, while in local areas, the hereditary Shan princes—the sawbwas—were allowed to retain their traditional powers and authority. Likewise, the Karenni (or Kayah) states were reconstituted as a single state with a similar secession guarantee. In Kachin State, which was provided no secession rights, a nineteen-member state council was constituted to run state-level affairs, with local duwas (Kachin princes) and traditional headmen reinstated to run local administration. The Chin people were granted fewer rights and privileges, and their territory was called a "Special Division." The status of the territorial authority over three other major ethnic groups—the Mons, Karens, and Arakanese—was left open in the constitution, to be decided after independence.

In the implementation of these constitutional arrangements, the early years of independence witnessed national-level parliamentary elections in 1947, 1951, 1956, and 1960. The Anti-Fascist People's Freedom League (AFPFL), the former wartime resistance organization turned political party, was victorious in the first three elections. In the 1960 election, U Nu's Pyidaungsu (Union) Party won a decisive victory over the military-supported Stable Faction of the collapsed AFPFL. Turnouts in these elections were often higher than 70 percent, and in accordance with Western expectations of electoral systems, electoral losers vacated their offices and winners took over.

Furthermore, as the 1950s wore on, the very real possibility of a loyal opposition began to emerge in the form first of the National United Front (NUF) and later in two successor parties formed after the breakup of the AFPFL. Growing out of a faction that broke off from the AFPFL in 1950 under the title of "Red Socialists," the NUF developed into a viable opposition party, gaining forty-seven seats in the 1956 Chamber of Deputies election, including numerous seats previously considered "safe" by the AFPFL. In that election, the NUF vote represented more than 30 percent of the popular vote, as compared to only 48 percent for the AFPFL.[4] Beyond its polling strength, the NUF also commanded extensive media attention and succeeded in organizing trade union and peasant organizations outside of the AFPFL's umbrella structure. In many ways, the success of the NUF in the 1956 election and the election of U Nu over the military-backed candidate in 1960 represented clear steps toward institutionalizing a competitive parliamentary system.

Problems of the "Democratic Era"

While on paper, these developments seemed indicative of progress toward sustainable liberal democratic institutions and processes, the legacies of the colonial and wartime period gave a very different meaning to these Western-style processes. For Burma's young leaders, the overriding priority in the drafting of the first constitution was not to establish a democracy but to get the British out of Burma once and for all. In fact, democratizers of the 1990s may be surprised that the word "democracy" does not appear in the 1947 constitution. This was not an oversight by the batch of first-time constitution writers who came together in 1947. Although the constitution—which was written by U Chan

Htoon and other lawyers trained in the British system—looks like it was based on the liberal principles enshrined in the British Government of Burma Act of 1935, the resulting document also reflects Aung San's oversight in its more socialist and anti-liberal provisions for the construction of a strong state. In actuality, the leaders of Burma at independence had no interest in the promotion of liberal democracy.

The leaders of Burma in the 1950s came of age in student union politics associated with the nationalist movement in the 1930s. Their nationalist program embraced the anti-imperialist, utopian socialist project, which they came to understand through their translation and study of the writings of Karl Marx, Vladimir Ilyich Lenin, Josef Stalin, George Bernard Shaw, and Sidney and Beatrice Webb. For the nationalists, democracy was the system of the colonizer, and as such represented that which Burma's young leaders had fought to expel. The identification of democracy with imperialism grew particularly thorny as the AFPFL united front began to splinter in the postwar period; Aung San and AFPFL leaders came under heavy pressure for giving too many concessions to the British imperialists in arranging the transfer of power agreement.

Hence the 1947 constitution embodied this distrust of democracy, placing emphasis not on individual rights and limitations of state intrusions in individual lives but instead on the empowerment of the state so that the great economic disparities wrought by imperialism could be leveled. To the degree that there was any concern for democratic institutions such as elections, it was to develop those procedures and practices that would ensure more equitable distribution of social resources. In Aung San's writings, for example, there is a clear ambivalence regarding the focus on democracy that emerged during World War II. In one of his last public speeches, Aung San laid out his "Basis of Burmese Democracy," which included eight elements ranging from the nationalization of the means of production, the provision of workers' rights and social insurance, and the establishment of the judicial system based "on popular conception." For Aung San and many of his colleagues, regaining control over Burma's wealth on behalf of the people of Burma was of paramount importance, not the array of legal provisions that protect individuals in a Western-style democracy. "Only by building our economic system in such a way as to enable our country to get over capitalism in the quickest possible time can we attain a true democracy."[5]

This anti-imperialist, anti-capitalist focus can be seen in Prime Minister U Nu's introduction of the motion to adopt the 1947 constitution, when he began his speech to the Constituent Assembly by explaining "what Burma . . . will be":

> I might say, at once, that it will be Leftist. And a Leftist country is one in which the people working together to the best of their power and ability

strive to convert the natural resources and the produce of the land . . . into consumer commodities to which everybody will be entitled according to his need. . . . [I]n such a country the aim of production is not profit for the few but comfort and the happiness of a full life for the many.[6]

Even earlier, the emphasis on the need to build a strong state and the disregard for the establishment of liberal democratic institutions was made particularly clear by Aung San, never a "liberal democrat." He wrote in 1941, "What we want is a strong state administration as exemplified in Germany and Italy. There shall be only one nation, one state, one party, one leader. There shall be no parliamentary opposition, no nonsense of individualism."[7]

The Emphasis on Unity and Uniformity

Throughout the early years of independence, the concerns that individualism would undermine the nationalist project resulted in an emphasis not on the liberal democratic pursuit of difference and competition but instead on unity and uniformity, an emphasis which would lead first to the near collapse of the AFPFL and its government and later to widespread government and party repression of the free expression of dissenting opinions. At first, Aung San and the leadership of the AFPFL—which in 1945 was a united front of rather incompatible political parties, including socialists, communists, and conservative elements—were able to enforce uniformity and to command unity immediately after World War II in the struggle to gain independence from the returned British regime. But as soon as the British agreed in January 1947 to grant Burma independence a year later, each of the constituent parties in the united front began to press for its own vision of the future, and the united front and the government it had organized in 1948 unraveled. Having grown out of a highly decentralized resistance organization, where no dialogue and consensual processes were possible under wartime conditions, the AFPFL never developed any mechanisms to accommodate and resolve conflicting political views, visions, and objectives.

As the AFPFL leadership drifted rightward, the more left-leaning spokesmen of the majority of the rank-and-file of the League led their followers into rebellion against the government.[8] At least one-third of the army followed the Communist Party underground in 1948, as did the majority of the nationwide People's Volunteer Organization, ostensibly a veterans' affairs group but in reality the paramilitary wing of the AFPFL. In 1949, the Karen National Defense Organization revolted, prompting the defection of the Karen Rifles and Karen-dominated artillery units from the government's army. By this time, important cities such as Mandalay, Maymyo, Prome, and even Insein (a suburb of Rangoon) fell to insurgent control. By the time Ne Win assumed his position as Supreme Commander in 1949, he commanded only two thousand remaining troops. At the time, most observers referred to the Government of the Union of Burma as "the Rangoon Government," reflecting the actual extent of territory U Nu controlled.[9]

The Elimination of Dissent

While what remained of the AFPFL leadership was able by 1952 to regain the upper hand in this civil war against their former colleagues, this experience institutionalized certain mechanisms that excluded many expressions of dissent. From the days leading up to independence, the leadership of the national front pressed the unconditional emphasis on unity and uniformity. For example, in his address to the AFPFL Convention in May 1947, Aung San ranked as top priority the purge of the national front: "[The] AFPFL and affiliated people's organizations should carry out a thorough cleansing process right through in order to be purged of rottenness in the blood."[10]

As the civil war escalated, tolerance for dissenting points of view evaporated. Throughout the first decade of independence, the U Nu government and the military invoked emergency provisions and other legal devices to eliminate criticism of the shaky government by imprisoning critics (at times for years before they were even brought to trial), suspending habeas corpus, shutting down newspapers and arresting their editors and publishers, banning novels that "were deemed likely to cause disaffection against the Government," and closing down student unions.[11]

One of the more repressive tools, Section 5 of the Public Order (Preservation) Act (PO(P)A) of 1947, was strengthened soon after the outbreak of the civil war at independence in order to allow local police to arrest possible rebels and detain them indefinitely, even without any significant evidence of criminal or treasonous acts. Over the next decade, PO(P)A was used by both national-level and local politicians and their followers to detain many opposition politicians; in fact, nearly every major opposition politician—including U Ba Pe, Thakin Ba Sein, Thakin Lwin and his brother—was detained under Section 5 PO(P)A during the 1950s, some for more than two years without ever coming to trial. It is not surprising that many of the thousands of PO(P)A arrests occurred in the months leading up to the national elections of 1951, 1956, and 1960. As one newspaper editorial noted: "[P]olitical rivals, or just any cantankerous person who exercised his freedom to speak out against the AFPFL, have been arrested and held without trial."[12]

This is not to argue that the era of parliamentary rule in Burma was a total facade. Rather, the particular unity-conscious focus of Burma's young leaders coupled with the exigencies of a collapsing state led to harsh methods of ensuring that unity. It also impeded the development of party and government institutions that could tolerate and process competition and difference in political ideas.

The Problem of Authority throughout Independent Burma

To pacify the countryside at the outbreak of the insurrection, the Nu government revived the village and town militia units that had fought in the anti-Japanese resistance during World War II. Organized under local politicians loosely connected to the Socialist Party in the AFPFL, these units were armed with either homemade weapons or weapons abandoned by retreating British and Japanese soldiers during the war.[13] Called by various names (People's Peace Guerrillas, Sitwundan, Pyusawhti), these units were not tied in to a centrally-based chain of command; they were formed in their home villages and rarely moved or saw action beyond village and town limits. Discipline was weak among many of these militia groups, and throughout the 1950s there were frequent reports of robbery, banditry, bribery, and murder committed by their members. Moreover, once formed to fight against the insurgents, these militia also became electoral tools of local political bosses, who deployed them during election campaigns to ensure victories for themselves or their followers.[14] Consequently, throughout the 1950s, elections often were characterized by thuggery and violence, with political murders not uncommon.[15] Although the government tried several times to disarm and demobilize these militia groups as well as to bring the local political bosses under more central party control, its efforts were never successful.

Already crippled by the 1947–48 flight of most of the top grade and senior civil servants, the independent Union government unwittingly destroyed any possibility of building the strong central state of Aung San's dreams by launching this highly decentralized campaign to salvage the AFPFL government in the first few years after independence.[16] By relying on the decentralized forces of local politicians to fight off the very real threat to the government during 1948-1952, the Nu government revived and strengthened local power bases. Those bases continued throughout the 1950s to block central government efforts to obtain the economic resources and the cooperation from outside of Rangoon that were needed to finance the League's ambitious socialist economic program.

Moreover, the areas near the British-drawn borders of Burma were even further beyond the "reach of the state."[17] Under British rule, for the first time ever, these regions officially were delineated as parts of a territory called Burma. Initially, the British called these regions "frontier areas," then later, "excluded" areas, and they were left largely untouched by the British rulers. Authority rested in the hands of selected indigenous leaders of the Shans, Chins, Arakanese, and Kachins.[18] In the postwar era, a complicated set of agreements was reached at the second Panglong Conference, in February 1947, which gave substantial local autonomy to the Shans and Kachins, while providing some constitutional measure of autonomy to the Chins. At the time, Aung San and AFPFL leaders were confident that the peoples of the minority regions would develop loyalty to the Union of Burma as the socialist economic development programs brought wealth, progress, and comfort. However, as the civil war derailed the AFPFL's economic and social programs, the weakened government was too busy fighting off threats to Rangoon to worry about these regions, some of which launched separatist insurgencies.

State-Building throughout Burma

What is significant about relations between the government of central Burma and the leaders of the minority groups in the border areas is that throughout modern history, there has never been a time when the territory that comprises Burma has been integrated in any meaningful way. During the colonial period, residents of central Burma, including Burmans and Karens, had no reason or opportunity to visit the frontier areas. Those Burmans and Karens in government service or the military police were posted only in Burma proper; only British or Indian civil servants were deployed to the frontier, and even they were sent only on the rarest occasions. Residents of the frontier areas likewise made few journeys into central Burma. Unlike in central Burma, the British established no government schools in the Excluded Areas, and graduates of indigenous schools from these regions were not admitted to college or university in Burma proper (although the sons of some Shan princes were educated in England). As Smith argues, throughout most of the colonial period, "the Frontier Areas remained largely forgotten" by the British and largely unknown for the Burmans.[19]

Although the 1947 constitution did establish institutions such as the Chamber of Nationalities in Rangoon that brought minority leaders into the capital on a regular basis, the only significant reverse traffic came under the auspices of the army. In the early years of independence, the military ordered its ethnic Burman troops out to distant minority-dominated regions to fight against communist insurgents. In 1952, U Nu also sent the army to the Shan State to displace some of the princes and set up an army administration when the U.S.-backed Kuomintang (KMT)—fleeing from the communists in China and also gearing up to retake China in the future—began moving deeper into Burma.[20] Some Shan leaders resisted this attack on local power and later led armed, anti-Rangoon, separatist movements that fought the government until the mid-1990s.

This move of army field and staff commanders into the administration of the frontier of Burma represented the first real—albeit unconscious—attempt at building state institutions that stretched across more of the territory than just the central region. No state institution in either pre-colonial or colonial Burmese history had ever established centralized control throughout the territory enclosed by the borders drawn by the British in the nineteenth century. The construction of the loosely integrated federal system in the 1947 constitution was at best a fantasy, based on a dream that participation of national minorities in legislative politics in Rangoon would forge an overarching national identity. In fact, minority participation in the 1950s legislature probably did more to reinforce ethnic identification than it did to create a sense of shared purpose, identity, and future.

The significance of the tatmadaw's being at the helm of this first-ever state-building enterprise cannot be overstated. When the AFPFL assumed power in 1948, there was little in the way of state machinery or resources left from the collapsed colonial regime to take over. After the insurrections in 1948–1949, there was even less. However, as the 1950s wore on, the army emerged among the three major national institutions as the only one capable of building nation-wide structures of authority. In the early 1950s, the army became significantly more centralized and more institutionally capable of exerting influence over territories beyond the greater Rangoon area than either of the other two major institutions that comprised the state—the ruling AFPFL and the bureaucracy. This point can be illustrated at one very basic level: By around 1954, the army was able to order locally-recruited members of its field units to move to other parts of Burma, and the War Office orders were followed with some degree of consistency. Neither the AFPFL nor the bureaucracy were able to do the same thing at any point in the 1948-1962 period.

Assessing the 1950s

An assessment of the 1950s is relevant to understanding politics in Burma today. In fact, interpretations of the 1950s are often the stone on which different political views of contemporary politics are engraved. Those who oppose the

SLORC's rule harken back to the days of elections, civilian rule, and the parliamentary processes of the 1950s. Those who are sympathetic to or supportive of authoritarian rule conjure up the images of the political instability that undermined economic and social development in that period; according to this view, politicians were too corrupt or weak to bring Burma out of anarchy.

This chapter suggests that neither of these judgments is based on informed readings of the years between independence and the coup in 1962. The 1950s may have been a period of "civilian" rule in Rangoon, but how "civil" or "civilian" was political life upcountry under the strong arms of local political bosses and their pocket armies? And one would be hard pressed to label the 1951, 1956, or 1960 elections as entirely free and fair given the thuggery and violence that surrounded them and the use of Section 5 PO(P)A by the governing party to weaken the opposition. Furthermore, such key democratic values as the freedom of expression were greatly circumscribed by the AFPFL government's extensive use of emergency measures and Section 5 PO(P)A to stifle the political opposition.

By the same token, the 1950s were not without significant democratic advances. In spite of AFPFL repression of dissent, a viable loyal opposition was emerging by the end of this period; few would denigrate the significance of this development for the institutionalization of democratic processes.[21] Additionally, the economic and social chaos that engulfed Burma in the postwar era was not caused directly by political mismanagement, corruption, or infighting. Instead, Burma was a newly independent nation-state struggling to assert authority within boundaries drawn by a colonizer and inhabited by peoples who historically had never looked to Rangoon for direction. The historical lack of integration throughout the territory was far more influential in laying conditions for the civil war between the government and separatist movements than was the political ineptitude of the Burman civilian rulers in Rangoon. Furthermore, the shortcomings of economic policies probably had more to do with the collapse of the international commodities market after the Korean war than with corruption. The politicians may have been responsible for the violent, unfair nature of elections during this period, but it must not be forgotten that units of the army also threatened voters and stuffed ballot boxes in the 1956 and 1960 elections.

Was the collapse of the parliamentary system inescapable? I would suggest that although the parliamentary collapse was never preordained, it was, however, inevitable that this parliamentary system should look very different by the end of its first decade of existence. From the beginning there were incompatible tensions that could be glossed over in the somewhat rushed production of constitutional arrangements in 1947, but these problems could not be resolved in an enduring way without innovation, accommodation, and change. Most importantly, the patched-together constitutional "solutions" for the minority-dominat-ed areas simply aggravated existing tensions by putting off any serious dialogue about how to harmonize never-before integrated portions of this territory into a functional nation-state. This was not a new problem; in fact, the relatively more powerful colonial regime had never tried to do so, recognizing that Burma was not governable in the reaches of territory that stretched beyond the limited sys-tems of roads, telegraph wires, and railroads. I would suggest that Burma was even less governable in the early post-independence years, characterized as they were by civil war, economic decay, and political instability.

In assessing the 1950s, it is clear that democratic, parliamentary politics was not the problem that crashed the system. The problem was governability, and this problem was found not only in border areas but also in the regions where rail-roads and telegraphs could transport policies. Tax records indicate that the AFPFL regime never attained the level of collections of land, customs, and income taxes that the British had obtained in its heyday of laissez-faire, minimalist rule. What little in the way of state institutional capacity was bequeathed by the British to the AFPFL disintegrated in the chaotic early years of independence. Between the mass resignations of most senior civil servants in 1947–1948 and the AFPFL's desperate devolution of power to local political bosses at the outbreak of the civil war, there were very few skilled administrators, tools, or resources left for the Nu government to deploy to implement policy, collect taxes, or even just maintain the status quo. Beyond Rangoon—and even within Rangoon—the state was decrepit and inept. Set against the centuries-old centrifugal aspirations of the frontier area peoples, the Nu regime was in no position to start the state-building that would have been necessary to win the loyalty of the national minorities by distributing social resources fairly and justly to minorities and Burmans alike. In the throes of these turbulent conditions, Aung San's oft-quoted promise to the frontier people at the Panglong Conference, "If Burma [proper] receives one kyat, you will also get one kyat," was soon forgotten.

The Arrival of Military Rule

Was strong, authoritarian rule under military leadership inevitable in postwar Burma? It was never inevitable that this tatmadaw would emerge from the chaos of mutinies, defections, and materiel losses in 1948-1949 as the powerful force that would dominate state and society for more than thirty years. In the throes of that chaos, there were few signs that the military leadership (or anyone else) could even envision such a future. The tatmadaw was but one of numerous armies that emerged at independence in 1948; many were illegal, anti-state armies but there were also quasi-legal paramilitary squads maintained by cabinet members and other politicians in the Socialist party and the AFPFL. The "democratic era" was replete with challenges both to and within the tatmadaw and the state, challenges often backed by arms and violence.

In part, the tatmadaw's development of the governing capabilities that made military rule possible came at the order of its civilian rulers when the army was deputed to many parts of Burma to fight communists and KMTs, to enforce martial law or to establish military administration during internal crises. The military was alone among the state's three major institutions—the others being the bureaucracy and the AFPFL—in consolidating some kind of authority that stretched to the borders. But the development of the Cold War also privileged the tatmadaw among the institutions in Burmese society. Responding to the insecurity of Burma's geographical and ideological position in the Cold War, the War Office, Gen. Ne Win, and some field commanders bought arms on the world market and negotiated programs of military assistance with virtually no oversight by civilian politicians.[22] In fact, the tatmadaw took a leading role in managing the impact of the world economy and of the international states' system in the 1950s; by the end of the decade, the army fully managed the impact of the world economy on the national economy through its import-export operations under the Defense Services Institute.[23] Its effectiveness and autonomy in doing so contrasted with the position of the ruling AFPFL, and suggests yet another early source of the army's growing strength vis-à-vis other institutions within the postcolonial state. As weak civilian institutions came apart under the domestic and global pressures of the 1950s, the tatmadaw was busy with what can only be seen in hindsight as state-building activities. At the time, however, there was no evidence of any grand scheme to build an army capable of running the Burmese polity over the next several decades.

Implications for the Future

A careful analysis of postwar history demonstrates that the 1950s do not hold the solutions for Burma in the 1990s and beyond. In fact, if anything, the 1950s provide some sobering warnings for both those who call the country Burma and those who call it Myanmar. In many ways, the most serious political problems of the country today are the same ones faced by the AFPFL government in the 1950s (and arguably by the colonial regime prior to World War II). The most serious dilemmas today are the unworkable nature of federalism in this multi-ethnic society, the continued crisis of state capacity, and the institutional intolerance for any forms of dissent.

On the first dilemma, there is a degree to which the assumptions which underlie the concepts of both Burma and Myanmar—that is, the delineation of a nation-state stretching across the territory bounded by the British-drawn borders—are impossible propositions. Given the financial and topographical barriers to integration, no state in the modern era has ever even come close to the Weberian ideal of exerting authority throughout the territory. But beyond simply the non-integration of this territory, there are clear and recent historical barriers to the realization of this "Burma" (or "Myanmar"). In the colonial period, frontier areas were deliberately kept separate from central administrative operations. Additionally, during the Japanese occupation, British and U.S. special forces operating in border areas encouraged minority peoples to hate and kill ethnic Burmans, and promised the minorities political independence from the Burmans in the postwar period.[24] These two discrete historical projects contributed directly to the start of separatist movements in these regions in the 1950s and 1960s and reinforced the difficulties of developing any basis for establishing an integrated polity. As Smith has observed: "Over the years, there have been few moments of lasting reconciliation or compromise."[25]

Some might argue that the recent cease-fire movement in ethnic war zones represents a step toward enduring reconciliation and compromise.[26] However, these arrangements are nothing more than temporary, ad hoc answers to complex, centuries-old structural problems. As many observers have noted, the cease-fires have broken down in a number of regions. Additionally, the agreements have provided ethnic groups with the authority to hold on to their arms, to police their territory, and to use their former rebel armies as private security forces to protect both legal and illegal business operations. This authority, however, is due to run out when the SLORC's hand-picked National Convention completes its new constitution. At that point, it is difficult to imagine that the SLORC will be able to convince ethnic warlords to turn in their weapons peacefully. In some respects, this ad hoc attempt at a kind of federal system which provides extensive local autonomy for minority groups along the border areas represents the most extreme concession of central control over Burmese territory in modern history, even more extreme than U Nu's plans in 1962 to grant statehood to the Mons and Arakanese and to consider seriously Shan and Kayah efforts to exercise their secession rights.[27]

This problem would not go away if a democratically-elected government were to take over the regime. In such a scenario, how would a democratic government be able to collect taxes or implement social or economic policy in—for example—the Kokang region, where local elites are profiting greatly from being left alone? Without access to the economic resources such as gems and teak in the border areas, how would a democratic regime alleviate the suffering of local populations throughout the frontier regions who are trying to claw their way out of two generations of war? Some ethnic group leaders currently question whether democratic leaders from central Burma would really commit national resources to development programs for the border areas. As one ethnic Pao leader told Smith: "The issue of democracy is often put before ethnic nationality questions, but in our view it [the ethnic question] needs to come first." With the world focusing on Aung San Suu Kyi and her party, some ethnic leaders worry that the needs of their people are not being considered, either by the National League for Democracy or by the well-meaning democratizers around the world.[28]

A Comparative Perspective on the Dilemmas of Ethnicity

From a comparative perspective, there are very few instances in which a post-colonial, multi-ethnic state has been able to democratize its political system at the same time that it builds administrative, economic, and cultural linkages between geographically dispersed ethnic communities. Prime Minister Jawaharlal Nehru may have engineered the most successful case of this combined project in leading India to significant progress in assuaging multi-ethnic tensions. However, that process also led to the Pakistan solution, which may still prove to have been the wrong answer for India. In fact, if Hindu nationalists seeking to convert India into a Hindu nation-state win power in the near future, India's 110 million Muslims will no doubt react badly with grave consequences for the democracy.

Furthermore, as recent history in the former Soviet Union, eastern Europe and some African nations (such as Somalia) has shown, federal systems in which the state components are constitutionally defined largely by ethnicity (as tied to territory), and in which the institutional, economic, and cultural linkages between ethnicities are minimal, frequently have not proven to be viable solutions to the problems of multi-ethnicity in a modern society. A federal constitution—such as the one envisioned by the NLD that would revisit the 1947 constitutional provisions or the one envisioned by the SLORC that would maintain the current range of ethnic states while establishing new "self-administered areas" for smaller minorities (such as the Pao, Palaung, and Kokang in the Shan State)—is not likely to produce a sustainable, integrated Burma.

For this kind of integration to take place, a future regime might need to try some of the tactics of consociationalism, such as providing for mutual veto in decision-making, education and mass media in other languages, and army, university, and/or bureaucracy recruitment and promotion practices that favor previously excluded minorities.[29] However, these kinds of policies face a major obstacle in Burma. Elsewhere, they have generally been successful in countries where there is either a ruling ethnic group (of either majority or minority status) that for some reason has been pressured to give up its privileged position and to commit itself to proportionally fewer demands on national resources in the future (e.g., contemporary South Africa) or in a society where there is no clear single majority group (e.g., Lebanon from 1943-1975). Although it is difficult to measure, in the current environment it seems unlikely that ethnic Burmans—most of whom have never had access to reliable information about the plight of Karen, Kokang, Shan, or other minority groups and have developed little in the way of cross-ethnic empathy—will be content to give up university places, officer commissions, or other opportunities to recruits from other nationality groups.

Other Dilemmas for the Future

In terms of the second dilemma—state capacity—the SLORC regime has developed to perhaps their highest form the tools of coercion and repression to maintain its hold over the government. However, the apparently unthreatened monopoly over guns and prisons necessary to hold on to power does not translate into any kind of significant capacity or capability in what is perhaps the regime's most pressing task: transforming Burma into a more modern, market-oriented, and productive society. In fact, many overseas investors have pulled their capital out of Burma because the regime's nine-year track record has shown little progress toward restructuring the agrarian economy into one that could support export-driven production. Will a democratically-elected regime have any greater success in this arena? From the experiences of other transitional societies that have attempted to liberalize their markets and democratize concurrently, it seems clear that this, too, is a very difficult process which generates economic losers who become constituents for anti-democratic politicians.[30] Not every member of society will be better off under a democratic or market system. Hence, the dislocations created in society can lead to a backlash that may be serious in a democratic regime at the helm of a weak state such as Burma.[31]

Finally, regarding the third dilemma, the four decades since the 1950s have not given Burma any real experience with political institutions that allow,

accommodate, and incorporate dissent, dialogue, and difference. Although it
seems clear that the current regime is unwilling to risk reforms in this regard, the
opposition also exhibits characteristics that seem rather intolerant of and inimical to the development of democratic processes. For example, in January 1997,
the opposition National League for Democracy (NLD) expelled Than Tun and
Thein Kyi, two elected members of the never-convened parliament, for insubor-
dination when they refused to sign a mandate giving the NLD's Central
Executive Committee full power to act on behalf of the party. Than Tun and
Thein Kyi claimed after the expulsion that their differences with party leaders
were over whether to compromise in the process of bringing the SLORC to the
negotiating table. According to Than Tun: "We are trying to put up these different ideas and ways for the NLD to survive through these difficult times. . . . We
must get dialogue first. . . . the SLORC is ignoring us all the time. They [the
NLD] want to stick to principles. To get compromise you must not always stick
to principles."[32] Given the nature of political repression, it is difficult to know
whether such actions are justified (i.e., if the NLD had strong evidence that the
two members were SLORC plants, as some diplomats have suggested) or representative or taken out of context. However, anti-government student groups and
political parties over the last nine years have shown a distinct tendency either to
expel purveyors of minority views (who then form their own party or group) or
to fragment around leaders of uncompromising positions.

Some might argue that intolerance for dissent suggests a cultural flaw in the
Burmese personality. However, I remind the reader that the 1950s were not a
completely lost cause for democratic practices and institutions. While in practice, the elections, constitutionalism, and civilian rule had their flaws and proved
untenable in the crises of the 1950s, Burmese culture did not impede the emergence of such promising developments as loyal opposition (even under great
repression), an independent judiciary, and a mobilized electorate. Instead, I
would argue that there may be a more historically discrete factor that accounts
for institutionalized intolerance across the generations of "democratic,"
"Socialist," and the SLORC's Burma. Under colonial, parliamentary, socialist,
and post-1988 military rule, conflicts over views, visions, and policies have
always been winner-take-all battles. As most national-level leaders (including
the NLD executive committee in early 1997) have conceived of themselves as
fighters against an old regime or imperialism or authoritarianism, they have
behaved as though the only answer to conflict was to eliminate it; moreover, the
only way to eliminate conflict was to enforce unity and solidarity. The future of
Burma will continue to look bleak until its leaders develop organizational frame-
works that manage and moderate conflict.

The leaders of contemporary Burma—both within and outside the government—appear to be trapped in their own kind of time warp as far as this last dilemma is concerned. Common to both the SLORC and the NLD is an overarching emphasis on unity and solidarity that is simply inimical to the development of institutional mechanisms that can accommodate the needs and demands of the broad range of social forces that exist throughout the country. This political debate could come right out of the debates of 1946–47, during which Aung San was attempting to rally disunited forces to stand up to the British one more time for the cause of independence: "We must take care that 'United we stand' not 'United we fall.' [sic] . . . Unity is the foundation. Let this fact be engraved in your memory, ye who hearken to me, and go ye to your appointed tasks with diligence."[33] As a means to independence, this unified show of force was probably critical in moving the British to grant independence. However, unity became an end in itself, and in many ways by virtue of historical habit, politics has never grown out of this phase.

Notes

1. See the SLORC's essay on "Information and Public Relations," in *Kye-Mon* (The Mirror), (30 January 1997).

2. From "The Constitution of the Union of Burma," Maung Maung, *Burma's Constitution* (The Hague, 1961, 2nd ed), 258–301.

3. Josef Silverstein, *Burma: Military Rule and the Politics of Stagnation* (Ithaca, 1977), 185–205.

4. Hugh Tinker, *The Union of Burma: A Study of the First Years of Independence* (London, 1967, 4th ed), 90.

5. "Bogyoke Aung San's Address at the Convention Held at the Jubilee Hall, Rangoon, on the 23rd May, 1947," in Silverstein (ed), *The Political Legacy of Aung San* (Ithaca, 1993), 151–161. Aung San actually wrote very little in his lifetime, and this particular volume brings together most of the extant speeches and publications. See Silverstein's excellent introduction to the volume, in which he interprets and contextualizes the maturing albeit nebulous political thought of Aung San.

6. From the translation of U Nu's speech to the Constituent Assembly, 24 September 1947, in Union of Burma Government, *Burma's Fight for Freedom* (Rangoon, 1948).

7. "Blue Print for Burma," in *The Political Legacy of Aung San*, 19–22.

8. For a discussion of the rightward drift of the AFPFL leadership during these years, see Robert H. Taylor, *The State in Burma* (London, 1987), 217–290.

9. U San Nyein and Myint Kyi, *Myanmar Politics from 1958 to 1962* [in Burmese], I (Rangoon, 1991), 95.

10. "Bogyoke Aung San's Address at the Convention Held at the Jubilee Hall, Rangoon, on the 23rd May, 1947," in *The Political Legacy of Aung San*, 151–161.

11. Quotation is from a news story about the police seizure of copies of a novel by Bhamo Tin Aung, *The Nation* (20 November 1953). He served several years in jail for having published two novels that were critical of the government. Regarding newspaper harassment, Ludu U Hla—the leftist editor of the Mandalay daily the *Ludu*—was arrested a number of times during the 1950s for publishing articles that contained not only criticism of the government but also bona fide typographical errors.

It is interesting to note that many of these repressive tools were revitalized versions of the same ones the British regime used to suppress the nationalist movement leaders during the 1920s and 1930s.

12. *The Nation* (20 June 1958). Compare the concerns raised in the editorial with the concerns raised by Aung San regarding British colonial practices in 1946:

Quite a considerable number of politicians and law-abiding citizens have been arrested or prosecuted under the Defence Act for various alleged charges, both political and criminal.
. . . I must also point out the scandalous way in which the Defence Act is abused. Several of those charged with criminal offences were at first arrested and detained under the Defence Act for six months, at the end of which instead of being released, they were detained further by bringing cases in dug up or framed up against them.

From his "Critique of British Imperialism," Address Delivered to the Second Session of the Supreme Council of AFPFL, 16 May 1946, in *The Political Legacy of Aung San*, 119–120.

This characterization of the use of Section 5 PO(P)A should not be taken to imply that the law was not used for its original purpose of containing the rebellion. However, even in that regard it was greatly abused. For example, a number of Karens were detained under Section 5 in January 1949 when the Karen insurrection broke out; all were held without trial and without the furnishing of any evidence to a court that linked them to the insurrection until June 1951, when the Supreme Court approved their habeas corpus application. [The *Nation*, 10 July 1951.] Additionally, newspapers also reported incidents in which police officers made arrests under Section 5 PO(P)A of individuals suspected of certain non–PO(P)A crimes when there was not enough evidence to arrest them for the crimes of which they were suspected. See, for example, the case of the Rangoon trishaw union leaders who were suspected of murdering the vice-president of the Chinese Chamber of Commerce; there was not much evidence to link the trishaw union leaders to the murder, so the Rangoon police arrested them under Section 5. [The *Nation*, 2 October 1951.]

13. In return for fighting against insurgents, the Socialist and AFPFL leadership guaranteed militia leaders such as Saya Hti (in Meiktila) or Thakin Kyi Shein (in Lewe)—who were also political bosses upcountry—ferry and fishery licenses, control over the distribution of government loan programs for cultivators, trading licenses for merchants, licenses to operate public transit and alcohol shops, and unofficial promises to ignore the smuggling of rice, teak, gold, and other commodities in the regions controlled by their followers [author's interview with Thakin Kyi Shein, 10 February 1993].

14. See the reports of the enquiry commission that looked into the cases of election fraud and intimidation by local politicians and their militia in the 1956 parliamentary elections in Government of the Union of Burma, *Reports of the Parliamentary Election Petition Enquiry Commission (Extracts)* (Rangoon, 1959).

15. For a description of political violence in one region (Mergui) during the 1950s, see my article, "The Sinking Schooner: Murder and the State in Independent Burma: 1948–1958," in a forthcoming volume edited by Carl Trocki on democracy in Southeast Asia (to be published by Cornell University Southeast Asia Program in late 1997).

16. James Guyot, "Bureaucratic Transformation in Burma," in Ralph Braibanti (ed), *Asian Bureaucratic Systems Emergent from the British Imperial Tradition* (Durham, N.C., 1966), 354–443.

17. Term drawn from Vivienne Shue, *The Reach of the State: Sketches of the Chinese Body Politic* (Stanford, 1988).

18. Under the Japanese Occupation, part of the Shan states were ceded to Thailand, Japan's ally, while the Chin and Kachin hill regions and Arakan were simply written off by the weakened regime in Rangoon. Not surprisingly, these were the areas in which U.S. and British expeditionary forces organized indigenous resistance during the war and from which they launched the campaign to "liberate" Burma in 1944.

19. Martin Smith, *Ethnic Groups in Burma: Development, Democracy and Human Rights* (London, 1994), 23.

20. U Nu initially attempted to bring the region under some kind of centralized control so that the borders could be defended from further Kuomintang incursions; his great concern was that the presence of the US.-backed anti–People's Republic of China force in Burmese territory might serve as a pretext for a Chinese invasion or annexation of that territory. However, the sawbwas balked at Nu's proposals for a kind of power sharing that would lesson the sawbwas' authorities while strengthening the Rangoon government's powers in the region. This ultimately led to Nu sending in the tatmadaw.

21. See Robert Dahl, *Polyarchy: Participation and Opposition* (New Haven, 1972).

22. In 1949, Gen. Ne Win negotiated arms deals with the Indian government and on the black market in Italy in the early period of the civil war when Great Britain and the United States refused to sell arms or provide assistance to the tatmadaw. Purchasing missions which included War Office, field command, and navy and air force staff, traveled around the world and brought back fighter-bombers from the Israelis, Italian advisors to establish the first ammunition factory, and U.S. counterintelligence trainers from the CIA.

23. In September 1950, Maj. Aung Gyi established the Defense Services Institute (DSI) as a commissary-style supply system to provide soldiers with consumer items at low prices. By 1960, DSI operated international shipping lines, banks, and the largest import-export operation in the country. See Maj. Kyaw Soe, "The Defence Services Institute" (n.d., probably 1958–1960); at the Defence Services Historical Research Institute, Document DR 8117.

24. Andrew Selth, "Race and Resistance in Burma, 1942–1945," *Modern Asian Studies,* XX (1986), 483–507.

25. Martin Smith, "Burma at the Crossroads," *Burma Debate* (Nov/Dec. 1996), 4–13.

26. Lt. Gen. Khin Nyunt initiated the cease-fire negotiations with ethnic rebel groups in 1989 soon after the Communist Party of Burma collapsed. Since 1989, seventeen of the twenty-one major anti-government forces (with as many as 50,000 troops) have concluded cease-fire agreements with the SLORC. Ibid., 7.

27. Chapter X of the 1947 constitution guaranteed to the Shan and Kayah (or Karenni) states the right to secede from the Union no earlier than ten years after independence. In order to invoke this clause, the state had to pass a secession resolution by two-thirds of the members of the State Council, after which the Union President would order a plebiscite to be held to poll the people of the state.

28. Khun Okker, foreign affairs spokesperson for the National Democratic Front, quoted in Smith, "Burma at the Crossroads," 8.

29. Arend Lijphart, *Democracy in Plural Societies* (New Haven, 1977), 25–52.

30. Philippe C. Schmitter, "Dangers and Dilemmas of Democracy," *Journal of Democracy,* V (1994), 57–73.

31. See also the rather cynical assessment of the potential for this kind of backlash in transitional societies in central Europe in Richard C Morais, "Beware of Billionaires Bearing Gifts," *Forbes* (7 April 1997), 82–87. For a systematic analysis linking the mode of transition to the type of backlash, see Gerardo L. Munck and Carol Skalnik Leff, "Modes of Transition and Democratization: South America and Eastern Europe in Comparative Perspective," *Comparative Politics,* XXIX (1997), 343–362.

32. Reuters, 4 February 1997.

33. From "Bogyoke Aung San's Address at the Convention Held at the Jubilee Hall, Rangoon, on the 23rd May, 1947," in *The Political Legacy of Aung San*, 151–161. The last sentence apparently is a translation of a Pali proverb.

CHAPTER 4

From Isolation to Relevance
Policy Considerations

Marvin C. Ott

IT HAS BEEN three and a half decades since the army seized power in Burma. For nearly all of that period Burma has been of little strategic or foreign policy interest to the United States. While momentous events were occurring elsewhere in Southeast Asia, the authorities in Rangoon adopted a policy of autarkic isolation that effectively marginalized their country internationally. The brutal suppression of political opposition in 1988 and the emergence of Aung San Suu Kyi as a democratic icon gave Burma international prominence—but as a human rights rather than a strategic or foreign policy concern. However, China's rapid emergence as an economic and military power in Asia and its growing influence in Burma plus the effort of the ASEAN countries to draw Burma into the Southeast Asian mainstream, have created a new foreign policy equation that the United States has been slow to recognize.[1]

The Burmese Road to Isolation

Of all the newly independent nations of postcolonial Africa and Asia, none had brighter prospects than Burma. In addition to a rich endowment of natural resources and an agricultural sector that regularly produced a large exportable surplus of rice, Burma possessed a well-educated, English-speaking elite, a literate work force, and a tradition of British jurisprudence. Burma's promise was reflected in the international stature of U Nu, the new nation's first president. In the 1950s the only two Southeast Asian leaders of comparable standing were Ho Chi Minh of Vietnam and Sukarno of Indonesia.

Burma, along with India and Yugoslavia, became a prime mover in the Nonaligned Movement, the most prominent Third World political initiative of the day. U Nu was one of a relatively few Third World leaders who enjoyed respect and support throughout the developing world and the West. It did not take long for Moscow and Beijing to decide that their initial denigration of leaders like U Nu as colonial puppets was a major tactical blunder.

By the time of the Bandung Conference in 1955, the Comintern's peaceful coexistence line was in full flower. Bandung was a seminal event, the first time that the leaders of virtually all the newly independent states of Africa and Asia had met together. The conference gave birth to the nonaligned movement. It also provided China with an opportunity to gain the trust of leaders who often viewed international communism with distrust and fear. That task fell to China's suave diplomatic genius, Chou En-lai. U Nu was a prominent target of the Chinese foreign minister's blandishments.[2]

Against this background, the self-imposed isolation of Burma following the military coup of 1962 is all the more striking. Perhaps only North Korea has remained more tightly sealed off for the last four decades. Burma's isolation, which cut off the country from its neighbors as well as the international community, has only begun to ease in the last two years or so. In a region where senior officials meet with their counterparts almost weekly through organizations like the Association of Southeast Asian Nations (ASEAN), ASEAN Regional Forum (ARF), and Asia-Pacific Economic Cooperation (APEC), much of the senior leadership of Burma is now venturing out for the first time to visit capitals that are only an hour's plane flight away.

The reasons for Burma's mutation into a modern-day hermit kingdom include a preoccupation with endemic ethnic separatism, the peculiar mentality of former ruler Gen. Ne Win, the paradoxical inheritance of nonalignment which became redefined as noninteraction, and the response to growing international criticism of the military regime's crude authoritarianism. The generals who controlled Burma responded to their foreign critics by withdrawing deeper into their national shell. Xenophobia became a leitmotif of state policy.

For most countries, a policy such as theirs would have quickly proved nonviable because of an economic dependence on external trading partners or security concerns that made foreign linkages imperative. But for Burma, the constellation of forces and the course of events in Southeast Asia permitted a policy of national invisibility. For most of the 1960s and 1970s, the region was preoccupied with warfare in Indochina (plus a briefer conflict between Indonesia and

Malaysia and within Indonesia) and Marxist insurgencies. Beyond that, national and regional energies were consumed by an economic transformation that resulted in national incomes more than quadrupling in a generation across much of Southeast Asia.

The great rivalries of the Cold War played out elsewhere in the region with the U.S. military presence centered largely on Indochina and the Philippines. Although communist-inspired guerrilla movements attracted American attention elsewhere in Southeast Asia, Burma seemed to settle into a pattern of low-grade perpetual skirmishes resolving nothing and going nowhere. Finally, Burma's geographical location at the periphery of South and Southeast Asia helped it stand aside from major developments in both regions.

For the Southeast Asian countries, Burma rapidly faded out of sight and out of mind. ASEAN emerged in the 1970s and 1980s as a close knit club of like-minded states focused on high economic growth. Burma was outside the club, out of step, and increasingly irrelevant. Only Thailand, with a shared 1,100-mile border, had any sustained interests at stake. Those were largely confined to semi-licit commercial deals between logging companies affiliated with the Thai army and either Burmese army or ethnic military commanders. As Burma's once buoyant economy sank under the weight of the Burmese Road to Socialism, other countries, including Japan and the United States, that might have been attracted by economic opportunity, looked elsewhere.

Processes of Change

In the last few years all this has begun to change. The end of the Cold War terminated the strategic competition that gave focus to great power interests in the region. Four decades of nearly continuous warfare in Indochina came to an end. With the removal of the Cold War overlay, economic growth and modernization moved more clearly to the top of Southeast Asia's agenda. Security concerns quietly shifted to a preoccupation with China's emergence as Asia's indigenous great power.

Southeast Asian uneasiness concerning Beijing's capabilities and intentions has been reinforced by China's growing presence in Burma. For the first three decades of Burma's post-colonial independence, China's influence in Rangoon was sharply limited by its substantial, provocative, and futile support for a Burmese Communist Party (BCP) insurgency against the government. But with Beijing's renunciation of its BCP policy and Rangoon's international isolation after the bloody repression of democracy activists in 1988, the picture changed dramatically. On Aug. 6, 1988, even as prodemocracy demonstrators clashed with police in Rangoon, China and Burma signed a border-trade agreement. Two months later, a high level Burmese delegation went to China and the first shipment of Chinese arms arrived the following August. Thus began an increasingly intense relationship that has drawn Burma deeply into China's embrace. The public record is striking. In four years Burma has purchased an estimated $1.4 billion in Chinese arms including F-6 and F-7 fighter aircraft, tanks, armored personnel carriers, radars, three frigates with missile capability, patrol boats, rocket launchers, and small arms.[3] Bertil Lintner, a veteran Southeast Asia correspondent, recounts a conversation on the Burmese border with a Chinese resident who described one nighttime convoy of more than 500 military trucks crossing the border from China headed south.[4] This is a profoundly important military relationship, with Burma receiving hardware, expertise, training, and technology from China. In return, China gains a market for its huge military industry and probably access to intelligence on movements through the busy shipping lanes from the Indian Ocean into the Malacca Straits. Most significant is the fashioning of a relationship in which the State Law and Order Restoration Council (SLORC) is effectively dependent on Beijing for its survival and Burma becomes a Chinese client state.

Economically, China's presence, particularly in northern Burma, has exploded. In ten years, crossborder trade went from $15 million to more than $800 million. A flood of inexpensive Chinese goods now dominates the Burmese consumer market. Large numbers of Chinese traders and undocumented immigrants have changed the demographic profile of northern Burma. Today, Mandalay is described by visitors as a predominantly Chinese city dominated by Chinese money, much of it invested in hotels, restaurants, and bars. Chinese construction crews are building and upgrading highways, bridges, and railroads through northern Burma to the sea, while Chinese officials describe Burma as a potentially lucrative outlet to the Indian Ocean for Chinese trade. For China, the Burma market is a key to the economic development of its southwest—a region that is lagging in China's headlong race to fulfill the late Chinese Premier Deng Xiaoping's dictum: "To get rich is glorious." Burma is also an important source of raw materials. Of course, a growing Chinese economic presence reinforces Burma's military/security dependence.

There has been occasional speculation, and some official concern, in Southeast Asia that China seeks more than trade along Burma's coast. Lintner reports:

> Most alarming, from the perspective of ASEAN [the six nations comprising the Association of Southeast Asian Nations], was the fact that some

of the equipment for the Burmese navy had to be installed and at least partially maintained by Chinese technicians. To ASEAN strategists, this meant that the Chinese had gained a toehold in the maritime region between India and Southeast Asia for the first time.[5]

Reporters have speculated about listening posts and possible Chinese naval bases on Burmese islands near the mouth of the Malacca Straits, though little supporting evidence has surfaced publicly. But in 1994 the Indian navy reportedly detained a Chinese survey ship with electronic monitoring equipment in Indian waters. At the same time, three boats, variously described as fishing or cargo vessels, flying the Burmese flag but crewed by Chinese, were detained by Indian patrol craft. No fish or cargo were on board.[6]

China and Burma have further tightened their bonds through an impressive number of bilateral VIP visits. The highlights include a week-long visit to China by Burmese Gen. Khin Nyunt (the military intelligence chief generally regarded as the most powerful single member of the junta), accompanied by four ministers, the commander of the Northern Military Region, four deputy ministers, and a large number of senior officials. That visit was Khin Nyunt's fourth official trip to China. Sixteen months later he was back, accompanying Gen. Than Shwe, chairman of the SLORC, for another weeklong visit. It was Than Shwe's third trip to China. A month earlier Than Shwe had hosted a senior Chinese leader and had described China as "the Myanmar people's most trusted friend."[7]

From a geopolitical perspective, Burma's approach to its huge northern neighbor is anomalous in that Rangoon has accepted a deepening dependence on the only country in a position to threaten its vital security interests. It is unclear whether Burma's leaders have fully thought through the implications of their actions. When this question was posed to the military intelligence officers who work with Khin Nyunt, it was evident that it was of great interest and no little controversy among them.[8]

For Southeast Asia, all these factors—economic, security, and political—have cast Burma in a new light. As the rest of the region's forests are systematically exploited and despoiled, Burma's still large (but rapidly diminishing) stands of tropical hardwoods have become a magnet. As regional wage rates rise with living standards, Burma's substantial pool of low-wage labor (much of it with some proficiency in English) is increasingly attractive to investors. Nothing drives government policy in contemporary Southeast Asia like the smell of money. ASEAN's push for greater international influence and regional effectiveness underscored the fact that the association could not encompass all of Southeast Asia without Burma. At the same time, Burma's increasingly close security relationship with China has generated a growing disquiet in other regional capitals. These developments have altered Burma's regional status from irrelevant embarrassment to an important source of opportunity and potential danger. Paradoxically, this perception has probably been enhanced by the emergence of Burma as a cause célèbre among human rights activists in Europe and North America. Systematic abuses that went largely unnoticed before 1988 now have become the focus of major media and government attention in the West. The days of ignoring Burma, for good or for bad, are long over.

Meanwhile, to a lesser degree, developments within Burma have compelled Rangoon to look outward. The huge disparity between the performance of the Burmese economy and its immediate neighbors has become impossible for the authorities in Rangoon to ignore. To be a poverty pocket in a rich neighborhood is to invite contempt. And contempt is one thing a proud, even arrogant, regime cannot abide. It also has become increasingly difficult for the SLORC to dismiss the growing crescendo of Western political criticism, and with it the ascension of democracy leader Aung San Suu Kyi to the status of international icon. This is true if only because outraged Western governments have their collective foot across the windpipe of badly needed international financial assistance.

Regional Response

Over the past two years ASEAN has more clearly defined its policy toward Burma as "constructive engagement," meaning an effort to build economic and political ties to Rangoon. As such, it is diametrically opposed to U.S. policy, which is to pressure Rangoon into political reform with economic sanctions and political ostracism. The result has been a growing debate between ASEAN and Washington. In 1996 the Administration sent two special envoys to ASEAN capitals to press Washington's case—to little apparent effect. The essential ASEAN view is that a policy of isolation and pressure toward Burma only heightens the regime's insecurity, causing it to resort to greater repression at home and to turn to its only perceived friend abroad—China.

The main rationale behind constructive engagement is to counteract China's use of Burma to extend its military and political reach into Southeast Asia. ASEAN's response has been to try and draw Burma into the ASEAN fold in order to offer an alternative to Beijing. The second reason for constructive engagement stems from regional nationalism. The success of ASEAN and its member states has nurtured a growing pride, confidence, and sense of regional cohesion. ASEAN has become, in the minds of many, a bulwark against overweening foreign influence in Southeast Asia. ASEAN members now want to "complete" the organization's membership by encompassing all ten countries, including Burma, that are geographically part of Southeast Asia. With the admission of Burma and Laos in July 1997, only Cambodia remains outside the ASEAN fold.

Senior ministers from Singapore, Thailand, the Philippines, and Vietnam have led delegations to Burma. Both Khin Nyunt and Than Swe have visited ASEAN capitals. In 1994, Burma attended its first ASEAN ministerial meeting as an invited guest of Thailand, the host government. In December 1995, Burmese representatives also attended the ASEAN summit of heads of government as guests. In 1996, Burma acceded to the ASEAN Treaty of Amity and Cooperation and acquired formal observer status with an expectation of full membership to follow. Meanwhile, Burma joined the region's multilateral organization for security dialogue, the ASEAN Regional Forum. The forum provides a vehicle for sustained military and intelligence dialogue between Rangoon and its prospective ASEAN partners. All of this represents ASEAN's reach toward Burma, but it also demonstrates Rangoon's receptivity.

Certainly, some in ASEAN realize that Burma's membership brings risk to the association in at least three respects. First, ASEAN's remarkable cohesion will surely suffer as less like-minded states join the fold. It is far from certain that the "ASEAN way" of decision-making will work when it must accommodate regimes as diverse as Vietnam, Singapore, the Philippines, and Burma. Second, if Burma tries to use ASEAN as a shield against Western criticism, the association may find itself tarred with the brush of Burmese atrocities. Third, Rangoon's dependence on China raises the disturbing prospect that Burma will become a proxy for Chinese interests and policies within ASEAN.

The matter of setting a firm date for Burmese membership in ASEAN became the source of some apparent controversy within the association. Malaysia was the most outspoken in urging early membership, i.e. in 1997. However, Indonesian Foreign Minister Ali Alatas, speaking after an informal ASEAN foreign ministers' meeting in late 1996, said that ASEAN "would not rush into" admitting Burma. The Philippines publicly advocated a go-slow approach. Alatas cited doubts about whether the Burmese economy met all the technical standards of membership. But the more important concern was probably embarrassment over very public incidents of crude repression directed by the SLORC against the National League for Democracy (NLD), the democratic opposition in Burma.[9] The ASEAN governments did not want to be seen as responding to Western human rights pressures both as a matter of regional pride and because each government is vulnerable to some criticism on this score. But neither did they want to be seen as apologists for the sort of thuggish practices that the SLORC resorts to so regularly.

In the end, it was Malaysia as the host to the 1997 ASEAN ministerial meetings that prevailed. In late July, the ASEAN foreign ministers meeting in Kuala Lumpur formally admitted Burma and Laos into the grouping. Cambodia was left in limbo given the conflict and uncertainties in the wake of a de facto coup. U.S. Secretary of State Madeleine Albright sharply criticized the admission of Burma. The Malaysian foreign minister responded dryly, "I can't help it if she is uncomfortable."[10]

Each of the ASEAN governments has its own bilateral agenda vis-à-vis Burma, driven in varying degrees by economic, political, and security considerations.

Thailand

As immediate neighbors, Thailand and Burma share a long border, a difficult, often conflicted, history, and a perspective of mutual suspicion tempered by opportunities for shared economic benefit. The Thai-Burmese relationship is an extraordinarily complex one and as much of it as possible is kept hidden from outsiders.

But it is no secret that a large proportion of the heroin produced in the Golden Triangle finds its way to the West via trafficking routes through Thailand. Logging companies affiliated with the Royal Thai Army (RTA) have long been active inside Burma with the connivance of the Burmese army. Thailand's recent prime minister, Chavalit Yongchaiyut, who is a former armed forces chief and minister of defense, has long cultivated ties—primarily commercial ones—with the Burmese army. The border areas provide important business opportunities for Bangkok, particularly since the Thai provinces in the northwest are still impoverished. An economic boom along the border would help ease chronic backwardness and its potential security problems. But Thai efforts to press ahead with construction of a "Friendship Bridge" across the Moie River plus efforts to, in effect, convert both sides of the border into a baht currency zone have angered the Burmese. Other irritants have included a fishing dispute and the long-running Burmese suspicion that the Thai have provided covert assistance to some of the ethnic separatists in Burma's border regions. When Chavalit visited Burma as deputy prime minister, the protocol he was accorded constituted a subtle snub.

In 1995 Burma closed all land border crossings with Thailand, suspended construction of the bridge, canceled all fishing contracts with Thailand, and protested alleged Thai logistical support for Khun Sa's Mong Tai Army (MTA). In 1996, Burma prohibited the use of Thai currency in its border provinces and encouraged a general boycott of Thai goods. Both countries have claimed the right of hot pursuit of hostile ethnic armed groups crossing the border. The joint commission established to deal with disputes has not met since 1994. From the Thai standpoint, the most disturbing development of all was the negotiated "surrender" of the MTA to the Rangoon authorities, thereby allowing the Burmese army to establish itself in former MTA camps along the border. For the first time in modern history, the ethnic buffer between the Burmese and Thai armies had been removed. The Royal Thai Army has responded by reinforcing its border garrisons with additional infantry, artillery, and aircraft.[11]

Thailand has tried to diffuse tension and restore commerce along the border with a number of conciliatory gestures including visits by the Thai foreign and defense ministers to Rangoon, the ASEAN Summit invitation, granting Burma most-favored nation status, assisting the Burmese tourist industry, and probably helping Rangoon squeeze the MTA by curtailing the vital flow of supplies through Thailand. These gestures culminated in a visit by then Prime Minister Chavalit to Rangoon in 1997. Thailand hopes this effort will produce a comprehensive new border agreement.

Thailand believes ASEAN has an important role to play. Burma is a difficult and sometimes threatening neighbor. Unlike its Thai counterpart, the Burmese army is tough, militarily capable, and battle-hardened. The Thai have no illusions that they can significantly influence the SLORC's behavior. Nor do they think sanctions and lectures from the West will be any more successful. But they do hope that subtle peer pressure from ASEAN as a whole will make a difference. Meanwhile Thai businessmen will pursue every opportunity for profitable commercial contact with Burma, and the Royal Thai Army will cultivate ties with its Burmese counterpart. The Thai ambassador in Rangoon will be the only ASEAN envoy to make a point of being present at every public event conducted by the NLD. Thailand has kept its independence and prospered in part by practicing an astute diplomacy that covers all the bases.

Malaysia

Malaysian policy toward Burma, like all Malaysian foreign policy, reflects the views of Prime Minister Mahathir Mohamed. His government has been outspoken in urging Burmese membership in ASEAN during 1997 so that the "completion" of ASEAN would occur under Malaysia's chairmanship and on the thirtieth anniversary of the founding of the association. Malaysian officials say the release of Aung San Suu Kyi from house arrest in 1995 was evidence that constructive engagement was having a positive effect. For Mahathir there is little doubt that Burma's admission to ASEAN has become another test of whether Southeast Asia will allow itself to be pushed around by the West, particularly the United States.[12] It was no accident that the first invitation to Than Swe for a state visit was from Kuala Lumpur.

The Malaysian government has no illusions concerning the harshness of the SLORC's rule. Demonstrations by Malaysian NGOs against Than Swe's visit were a sharp reminder. Kuala Lumpur has been particularly upset over mistreatment of the Rohingya Muslims in western Burma, which resulted in a refugee exodus into Bangladesh. Malaysian officials have reportedly urged Rangoon to facilitate their repatriation to Burma—with only modest success. Another less public concern involves the increased smuggling of narcotics and small arms into Malaysia as an apparent side effect of the agreements reached by the SLORC with ethnic separatists. In return for halting their armed rebellion, these groups apparently have been given a free hand to engage in any form of commerce they choose. Partly as a consequence, opium cultivation and heroin production have boomed. (See chapter 10, by Robert Gelbard, in this volume.)

Kuala Lumpur remains convinced that engagement is the most promising avenue to deal with these concerns. A powerful, probably decisive, impetus comes from Malaysia's growing economic stake in Burma. In the first ten months of 1996, Malaysian investment in Burma shot up to $446 million—triple that of a year before. Malaysia is now the fifth largest foreign investor in Burma and, if current trends hold, could be the largest in two or three years.[13] Malaysia also appears to be irritated with Aung San Suu Kyi—a sentiment that is present just below the surface elsewhere in ASEAN. The Nobel laureate is criticized and even resented because she is seen as too pushy, too confrontational (especially for a woman), too uncompromising, and too close to the West.

Singapore

Singapore's outlook toward Burma has several points in common with Malaysia. With official encouragement, Singaporean businesses lead the roster of foreign investors in Burma with $1.1 billion, followed by the United Kingdom, Thailand, France, Malaysia, and the United States. Much of Singapore's investment has gone into hotels and other facets of the tourism industry. Public reports have linked private investment from Singapore to prominent figures in the Burmese drug trade. News accounts also have suggested that Singapore has become the entrepot for a gray market in arms for Burma—including Portuguese arms exported to Burma in violation of European sanctions. In the process, Singapore allegedly has become the source of much of the more advanced military technology reaching Burma.

As with Malaysia, Singapore's economic involvement in Burma and its outspoken support for constructive engagement is mainly about making money. But the government shares the rest of ASEAN's concern about China's influence. Also, as the quintessential practitioner of balance of power diplomacy, Singapore views the addition of another member to ASEAN as a useful counterweight to Malaysia and Indonesia. And finally, as the region's most outspoken political "realists," Singaporean officials have not hesitated to declare that at the end of the day the only entity that can run Burma is the army, and the democratic opposition ultimately will have to accept that fact.[14]

Japan

Japan is clearly torn when it comes to Burma. On the one hand, Japanese banks and corporations are very anxious to gain a strong economic foothold there. Japanese businessmen are present in force in Burma assessing investment opportunities. The new Liberal Democratic Party (LDP) government with its traditional pro-business orientation will be strongly inclined to support such efforts. But Tokyo has not wanted to break step too sharply with the United States and has tried to play the role of friendly counselor to the SLORC, urging a more flexible policy toward the NLD. Tokyo has gone further to give its advice some teeth. When it appeared in 1996 that the SLORC was about to rearrest Aung San Suu Kyi, Tokyo publicly warned that the negative consequences of such a step would be severe. When the SLORC did crack down on NLD supporters, Japan suspended plans to restart development aid and withdrew from a major project to improve the Rangoon airport. The SLORC's 1996/97 decisions to impose further restrictions on Aung San Suu Kyi tested Tokyo's patience. How long and how successfully Japan can continue to juggle business interests and human rights concerns remains to be seen.

For each of the countries surveyed and for ASEAN as a whole, much of the impetus for constructive engagement comes from the perception of burgeoning economic opportunities in Burma. There is a certain irony in this, because it is not at all clear that the current flowering of the Burmese economy has any real roots or staying power. Recent market-oriented reforms have produced a short term economic stimulus with annual growth rates averaging above 7 percent for the past three years. But Dapice, whose chapter in this volume analyzes the economy in depth, argues persuasively that this "modest rebound is not likely to presage a period of Korea-style growth unless many other changes are made—changes that are not yet in evidence. Without [them] . . . the outlook is poor to grim."[15] Dapice argues that an economic relapse will have the pernicious effect of reinforcing the siege mentality of the junta, exacerbating its tendency toward police state methods. Such an economically hard-pressed regime will be likely to increase its collaboration in the narcotics trade and to turn to China. The result will be "more crossborder migration and increasing control of the economy by well-capitalized Chinese traders, at least in the northern parts of the country. More far-fetched, but not impossible, is even stronger absorption of some of the country along the lines of Tibet. For many ethnic groups, their historical experience with the Chinese has been better than that with the Burmans, and the de facto territorial integrity of a poor, weak, and divided nation cannot be taken for granted."[16]

U.S. Policy

Where does all this leave American policy? Surely it is time for a reassessment.

Since the earliest days of the Republic, U.S. foreign policy has exhibited two, often conflicting, tendencies. The first is a normative, "idealist" impulse to use foreign policy to further deeply-held American political values—notably democracy and human rights. The second is a geopolitical "realist" approach that stresses the pursuit of national interest defined largely in terms of power and economic advantage. Recently, the tension between these two orientations has been clearly evident in policy toward China and most specifically in the recurring debate over granting most-favored nation (MFN) trade status to China. Both within the Clinton administration and Congress, the proponents of conditioning MFN on Chinese adherence to basic human rights standards have clashed with those who see MFN as a matter of American economic self-interest.

In the case of China, the "realists" seem to have carried the day—largely because the costs of trying to impose a normative agenda on China are seen as being too high. In the case of Burma the normative approach has governed policy for most of the last decade. Policy has been driven by a deep repugnance for the crude, brutally authoritarian character of the SLORC. After all, it is a government that has massacred prodemocracy demonstrators (including students and Buddhist monks), suppressed political dissent, engaged in large scale forced labor, probably collaborated in opium/heroin trafficking, annulled the results of a democratic election in 1990, and imprisoned Aung San Suu Kyi.

Not surprisingly, U.S. policy toward Burma has reflected moral outrage. Since 1988, the United States has regularly condemned the actions of the regime, has halted all bilateral economic and military assistance, has suspended General System Preference (GSP) and MFN privileges, has opposed lending by international financial institutions to Burma and has tried to rally support for such policies among other countries—including a proposed international embargo on arms shipments to Rangoon. In 1997, the Clinton administration, responding to congressional legislation, barred new U.S. investment in Burma while leaving existing investment projects undisturbed.

The other aspect of U.S. policy has been outspoken support for Aung San Suu Kyi and other champions of democracy in Burma. Even before the outrages of 1988, Washington had kept its dealings with the authoritarian leadership in Rangoon to a minimum. Congressional interest in Burma has been episodic at best, but has usually taken the form of urging harsher, more punitive policies toward Rangoon. Sen. Mitch McConnell (R-Kentucky) introduced legislation that would have expanded existing sanctions to include termination of all American trade and investment with Burma, including tourism. In its original form the McConnell bill would have imposed these restrictions on non-U.S. companies dealing with Burma that also have a commercial presence in the United States. Legislation that did pass gave the president latitude to impose harsher U.S. sanctions if events in Burma warranted it.

This highly normative policy agenda has reflected three underlying realities: (1) During most of the Cold War period Burma was, from a U.S. perspective, geopolitically irrelevant. Its geographic remoteness and self-imposed isolation reinforced this assessment. (2) The events of 1988 and 1990 coupled with the inspirational defiance of Aung San Suu Kyi have thrown the normative issues into high relief. (3) There have been no significant national interest costs to the United States of a policy of principle regarding Burma. For officials in Washington, Burma is something of a foreign policy free good comparable to Cuba, and in contrast with China or North Korea.

In recent years, however, the strategic landscape in Southeast Asia has begun to change in ways that demand a rethinking of U.S. policy. The major new reality is the emergence of China as a regional great power. China's economic and military capabilities have grown dramatically at a time when its traditional security concern, Russia, has faded. Japan remains a long term, but not an immediate security problem. This has left China free, in geopolitical terms, to shift its attention to the south. The most striking manifestation of this development has been a very assertive policy toward the South China Sea. Beijing has declared the entire sea and all the land outcroppings within to be Chinese sovereign territory. This has been accompanied by a number of statements from senior Chinese civilian and military officials that seem to presage a kind of Chinese Monroe Doctrine for Southeast Asia—a modern reprise of the historic preponderance of the Middle Kingdom. This plus China's bareknuckled military intimidation of Taiwan has reinforced a growing perception in Southeast Asia of

China as a major security factor—and perhaps a threat. The Philippine navy's 1995 discovery of Chinese facilities on a reef near to, and claimed by, the Philippines did nothing to dispel these concerns.

Any policy, if it is to be maintained, must meet two related tests. First, is it working? Does it have a reasonable prospect of doing so? Second, is it appropriate to changing circumstances and realities?

The current U.S. policy of isolation and sanctions fails both tests. The essentially repressive character of the Burmese regime has remained unchanged despite years of pressure. In some respects—notably narcotics production and trafficking—the situation has even deteriorated. The policy of quarantining Burma has failed because for most of the last three decades the regime has sought to isolate itself from foreign influences. Isolation is not an effective sanction on a government that welcomes it. The net effect has been simply to reinforce the junta's instinctive xenophobia. Nor is there any prospect that added hardships will produce a favorable regime change. The current junta has, in effect, ruled Burma since the early 1960s. Deeply unpopular and oppressive, it nevertheless holds apparently firm control over the army and Burman ethnic population. More recently, the SLORC has been accepted by ASEAN. Again, a policy of isolation is obviated—this time by a host of U.S. friends and allies that have adopted contrary policies.

Ironically, to the extent that U.S. policy does have an impact, it will do so in ways that are anathema to American values and interests. Successful sanctions will weaken a highly vulnerable economy, leaving the regime with little choice but to rely more heavily on Chinese support and on revenue generated from narcotics. Heroin may be an intractable problem. Still, it is hard to imagine how any effective attack on the industry can be mounted without the full and willing cooperation of the authorities in Rangoon. Stringent sanctions will also reinforce the regime's already powerful instincts to respond with a paranoid reinforcement of authoritarian controls. Contrary to the hopeful analogies suggested by some proponents of sanctions, Burma is not a Southeast Asian reincarnation of South Africa. The South African white elite was vulnerable to Western sanctions for a number of reasons including the fact that the surrounding black African states supported their imposition. No such regional support exists in Southeast Asia.

The alternative to isolation is a U.S. policy of limited engagement toward the Burmese regime that would involve sending an ambassador to Rangoon, supporting Burmese membership in ASEAN, and eschewing barriers to U.S. trade with and private investment in Burma. Limited engagement would be more of a threat to the SLORC than current U.S. policies. An American presence, whether commercial, academic, or official, tends to be a subversive influence to authoritarian regimes. A policy of limited engagement would establish channels of influence to the next generation of Burmese leadership and to the second echelon of the current leadership. Dialogue can establish potential areas of common concern (including China) and take advantage of the apparent desire of the younger military for outside contact. The United States can exploit any realization that the regime's policies have essentially failed at national construction and have increasingly captured Burma in a strategic web of its own making.

A policy of limited engagement does not require moral neutrality on the issues of human rights and democracy. Washington can and should remain outspokenly critical of abuses as they occur in Burma. But there are strategic and other national interests to be served. The first requirement of policy is that it do so. It is time to recognize that present U.S. policy is not working, has no serious prospect of working, and is no longer a free good. The costs of that policy are measured in an escalating heroin problem, a loss of strategic ground to China, and an estrangement from ASEAN. It is time to think seriously about alternatives.

Notes

1. The views expressed are personal and not necessarily those of the National War College or the U.S. Department of Defense.

2. See George M. Kahin, *The Asian-African Conference; Bandung Indonesia, April 1955* (Ithaca, 1956); Angadipuram Appodarai, *The Bandung Conference* (New Delhi, 1956); Peter H. Tang, *Communist China Today: Domestic and Foreign Policies* (New York, 1957); Werner Levi, *Modern China's Foreign Policy* (Minneapolis, 1953); J. Brimmel, *Communism in Southeast Asia* (London, 1959); Russell H. Fifield, *The Diplomacy of Southeast Asia: 1945–1958* (New York, 1958).

3. Andrew Selth, "The Burma Army since 1988: Acquisitions and Adjustments," unpub. ms. (Canberra, 1955), 15–17; Frank S. Jannuzi, "The New Burma Road (Paved by Polytechnologies?)," chapter 11 of this book.

4. Bertil Lintner, "Enter the Dragon," *Far Eastern Economic Review* (22 December 1994), 23.

5. Bertil Lintner, "State in the Middle," *Far Eastern Economic Review* (3 August 1995), 26.

6. Lintner, "Enter the Dragon," 23. See also Economist Intelligence Unit, *Country Report: Burma* (3rd Quarter, 1994), 37.

7. Economist Intelligence Unit, *Country Report: Burma* (1st Quarter, 1996), 12.

8. Impressions formed on a trip to Burma in December 1991 when the author met with senior and middle grade military intelligence officers of the Burmese army.

9. Michael Vatikiotis, "Seeds of Division," *Far Eastern Economic Review* (October 1996), 16–17.

10. *The Washington Post* (26 July 1997), 21.

11. Ibid. See also Economist Intelligence Unit, *Country Report: Burma* (2nd Quarter 1994), 37–38, and (1st Quarter, 1996), 10–11.

12. Economist Intelligence Unit, *Country Report: Burma* (3rd Quarter, 1996), 16–17.

13. Sulochini Nair, *New Straits Times* (Kuala Lampur) (18 November 1996), 27.

14. Economist Intelligence Unit, *Country Report: Burma* (3rd Quarter, 1996), 13.

15. David Dapice, "Development Prospects for Burma: Cycles and Trends," chapter 8 of this book.

16. Ibid. 6

Part Two

THE MILITARY

CHAPTER 5

The Armed Forces and Military Rule in Burma

Andrew Selth

EVENTS IN Burma in recent years have focused attention on the contest of wills being waged between Nobel Peace Prize laureate Aung San Suu Kyi, and the ruling State Law and Order Restoration Council (SLORC). On one side is Aung San Suu Kyi's enormous popular appeal and international standing, while on the other is the might of the Burmese armed forces, or *tatmadaw*. Both sides have appealed to the rest of the world for understanding and support. To a greater or lesser degree, both have been successful. Yet, for all the international pressure applied against the military regime since 1988, and all the assistance provided to the SLORC by regional countries like China and Singapore, it ultimately will be developments in Burma itself which will decide the country's future.[1]

In considering the outcome of this struggle, the attitude of the armed forces will be crucial. For, with its pervasive political influence and increased military strength, the tatmadaw is still the final arbiter of power in Burma. It not only underpins the SLORC's continued rule but actively prevents the pro-democracy movement from exercising the mandate it secured in the 1990 general elections. If the armed forces were to be weakened, however, either through a major loss of operational capability or serious internal divisions, then the current balance of political forces in Burma could change significantly. Other factors would also be important, but the outcome of the struggle between Aung San Suu Kyi and the military hierarchy will ultimately depend on the strength and cohesion of the tatmadaw.

The Armed Forces since 1988

As soon as the armed forces crushed Burma's burgeoning pro-democracy movement in late 1988, and formally resumed direct political control of the country, they took a number of steps to increase their military strength.[2] The SLORC immediately arranged for the importation of a range of small arms, support weapons, and ammunition to replenish the army's depleted stocks and help guard against further challenges to military rule. Even before all these arms had arrived, however, the regime had begun planning an ambitious ten year program to expand the armed forces and significantly upgrade their operational capabilities. The SLORC also increased the scope and output of Burma's indigenous arms industries.

At the time the pro-democracy demonstrations began in mid-1988, the Burmese armed forces numbered about 186,000, all ranks. As is often the case when dealing with Burma, exact figures are not available, but the army was by far the largest service, with about 170,000 men and women in uniform. There were some 9,000 in the air force and approximately 7,000 in the navy. In addition, there were reported to be an additional 73,000 armed personnel in the paramilitary People's Police Force (PPF) and People's Militia, although the capacity of the latter two forces to perform in a combat role was limited.[3] As a result of the SLORC's expansion program, these numbers rapidly increased. Once again, it is difficult to be precise, but by mid-1992 the tatmadaw had probably grown to about 270,000, and by mid-1995 the Thai government was stating that the number had reached 300,000. One official U.S. estimate around this time reportedly went as high as 400,000.[4] The latter figure seems to have been a little premature, but an SLORC spokesman admitted to a visiting Australian researcher in early 1995 that the regime's goal was a well-equipped military machine of some 500,000 men and women by the turn of the century.[5]

The Burmese army has benefited most from this dramatic growth, rising to an estimated 275,000 all ranks. The other services have also grown, however, with the Burmese air force now numbering at least 20,000 and the Burmese navy probably reaching about the same level. In addition, the PPF and militia are reported to have increased to more than 85,000. All of these figures are very rough, but by any estimation it was a remarkable expansion in a very short time.[6] Even without counting the PPF and People's Militia, the Burmese armed forces are now the second largest in Southeast Asia and, if Vietnam continues its planned troop reductions, Burma's may soon become the largest. At the same time as this expansion has been taking place, the SLORC has devoted considerable resources to increasing and upgrading Burma's order of battle. Few of the major weapons, or weapons platforms, purchased to date represent the state of the art, but they are a major advance on Burma's older inventory and hold out the promise of much improved capabilities in a number of areas. For several reasons, the regime's annual defense expenditures have always been very difficult to determine.[7] Considering the size and scope of arms and equipment acquisitions made since 1988, however, estimates of 4.5 percent of gross national product (GNP)—or 35 to 40 percent of central government expenditures—in recent years do not seem out of place.[8]

Before 1988, the army consisted mainly of lightly equipped infantry battalions, organized and deployed for internal security purposes. In addition to the army's self-appointed political role, this included the conduct of counterinsurgency operations against guerrilla forces representing the Communist Party of Burma, ethnic separatist organizations, and narcotics-based rebel groups. There were few heavy weapons or armored vehicles in the army's inventory, and those that existed suffered from age, a lack of spare parts, and ammunition shortages. The army's transport, communications, and logistics systems were all very weak, constantly hampering operations and making it difficult for the central government to make any real progress against the insurgents. The SLORC's massive procurement program, however, has resulted in a flood of new arms and equipment entering the army's inventories. Precise details are not available, but over the past eight years it appears that Burma has received about 80 main battle tanks, 105 light tanks, 250 armored personnel carriers, a number of armored bridge layers and tank recovery vehicles, field and anti-aircraft artillery, multiple rocket launchers, surface-to-air missiles, trucks and four-wheel-drive vehicles, mortars, recoilless guns, grenade launchers, small arms, and ammunition. China has supplied most of these acquisitions, but orders also appear to have been placed with Pakistan, Poland, Israel, Singapore, Portugal, North Korea, Russia, Belgium, and a number of other countries.[9]

The Burmese navy has also benefited from the SLORC's arms acquisition program. Before 1988 the navy was barely able to perform its prime functions of supporting the army's counterinsurgency operations and patrolling Burma's inshore waters against smugglers and poachers. Despite a few obsolete corvettes, the navy had no blue water capability, and relied on an aging fleet of small patrol boats and support ships. These vessels were thinly armored and lightly armed. They had no real offensive capabilities, nor any defenses against air, surface, or sub-surface attack. Under the SLORC, however, the navy has grown dramatically in size and acquired a wide range of more modern systems.

After an initial purchase of three PB 90 class inshore patrol boats from Yugoslavia, Burma obtained sixteen Hainan class coastal patrol boats and four Houxin guided missile patrol boats from China. Funding will be a major factor, but there are persistent reports that China will eventually provide Burma with up to three Jianghu guided missile frigates and a small number of minesweepers. At the same time, Burma's own shipyards have built, or are in the process of building, a number of fast attack patrol boats. In addition, a tanker and transport auxiliary have been added to the Burmese fleet and the SLORC has initiated an extensive program to improve the country's naval infrastructure.[10]

The expansion of the air force under the SLORC has been equally dramatic. Before 1988 the air force consisted mainly of old transports, and small training aircraft modified locally to perform a ground attack role. There were also a number of helicopters, mainly remnants of a United States–supported narcotics control program. All these aircraft suffered from age and a lack of spare parts. Their primary role was to perform transport and reconnaissance duties, and to provide fire support to the army during counterinsurgency operations. Burma had no credible air defense capability. Since 1988, however, the air force has introduced several new aircraft types into service. Once again, it is difficult to be precise, but acquisitions have probably included five squadrons of F-7 fighters, two squadrons of A-5 fighter/ground attack aircraft, and a number of FT-7 and F-6 trainers, all from China. The SLORC has also bought one squadron of G-4 counterinsurgency aircraft from Yugoslavia. In 1996 the SLORC took steps to acquire a number of MiG-29 interceptors from Russia, but the order had to be shelved due to a lack of funds. To expand its tactical airlift capabilities, the air force has obtained at least two, and probably three, squadrons of Mil Mi-2 and Sokol W-3 medium helicopters from Poland, and two squadrons of Mil Mi-17 utility helicopters from Russia. The SLORC has also expressed interest in obtaining attack helicopters from China and Russia. Heavier airlift capabilities have been improved by the acquisition of four Y-8 transports from China. In addition, Burma is significantly upgrading its network of civil and military airfields to provide the air force with greater flexibility and operational reach.[11]

The tatmadaw is now the largest and best equipped military force that Burma has ever mustered. Since the SLORC's takeover nine years ago, the regime has more than doubled the number of men and women in uniform, and recruitment is continuing. According to most estimates since 1988, annual defense expenditure has at least doubled. The SLORC has greatly increased the number and sophistication of major weapon systems in the country's order of battle, and has continued to place orders for new arms and equipment with external suppliers.[12]

These developments have prompted widespread criticism, both from within

Burma and among members of the international community. Critics tend to focus on three main issues: the military regime's continued abuses of human rights since the massacres of pro-democracy demonstrators in 1988; the allocation of scarce national resources to the defense sector when so many other parts of Burmese society are clearly desperate for government support; and the refusal of the armed forces to hand over political authority to an elected civilian government. While these criticisms are valid and demand attention, they have tended to overshadow consideration of the Burmese armed forces from a more conventional, military point of view.

It is important to study the tatmadaw's growth and modernization under the SLORC as a response to Burma's legitimate defense needs. For, despite all the criticisms which the tatmadaw's massive expansion program has attracted, some improvement of the country's military capabilities after 1988 was not entirely without justification. Judged against certain objective criteria, and compared with recent military developments in other regional countries, a number of the measures taken by the SLORC to modernize the Burmese armed forces do not seem unusual. Indeed, it could even be argued that some were long overdue. An examination of these issues not only contributes to a more comprehensive understanding of events since 1988, but can also assist in the consideration of several other critical questions. These include the tatmadaw's future role in Burma and the attitude of the armed forces toward an eventual transition to a democratically elected civilian government.

The Rationale for Expansion

In considering the tatmadaw's expansion since 1988, and the modernization of its equipment inventory, it first needs to be borne in mind that both started from a very low base. Ever since Burma received its independence from Britain in 1948, the central government in Rangoon has been forced to rely on manpower rather than machinery to fight its wars. Yet, despite the size of Burma's population, and the range of security problems which it has faced since independence, the armed forces have never been very large. This was still the case in 1988, when the proportion of Burmese men and women in uniform was at least comparable to Thailand, which, despite the challenges of its own insurgencies, has faced far fewer security problems.[13] This situation has now changed, but in terms of soldiers per head of population, Burma still ranks behind Singapore, Brunei, Cambodia, and Vietnam.[14] Also, Burma has never had the financial resources or technical expertise to purchase or operate most modern weapons systems. The army, for example, has consisted primarily of light infantry, while the air force and navy, both more technically demanding services, have always been very small.

There is evidence too to suggest that, in some respects, the tatmadaw's rapid expansion since 1988 has occurred more on paper than in reality. While the number of formed units has undoubtedly increased, the actual fighting strength of the Burmese armed forces may not be as great as appearances first suggest. Few army battalions, for example, seem to be up to full strength, and many new recruits appear to be children who are barely capable of combat operations.[15] There is a severe shortage of experienced pilots and trained ground staff in the air force, and the navy is finding it difficult to crew and maintain all its new ships. Also, the increased demands of government and administration since the armed forces resumed direct control of the country seems to have absorbed a greater proportion of the tatmadaw's resources than originally anticipated. This burden will increase further in the event that Burma adopts a comprehensive socio-political system of military government, similar to the Indonesian *dwi fungsi* or "dual function" model. This model emphasizes and institutionalizes both a security and a political role for the armed forces.

In addition, the Burmese armed forces have always operated very frugally. Before the SLORC took over government, for example, Burma's public expenditures per soldier were estimated by one researcher to be the lowest of any country in the Asia-Pacific region.[16] Military pay and privileges tended to be better than those enjoyed by most other sectors of Burmese society, but, for many personnel in the lower ranks, conditions were still spartan. Those benefits they did receive were balanced by the high risk of death or injury while on operations against the country's numerous insurgent groups and narcotics-based armies. While some other armed forces might envy Burma's high "tooth to tail" ratio, the average Burmese soldier usually went into battle on foot, armed with weapons that were often inferior to those of his opponents.[17] He could have had no confidence in the availability of ammunition resupply, regular rations, or medical evacuation if wounded. Heavy weapons support was frequently absent and air cover was unreliable. Given the examples provided by dry season offensives over the past several years, and anecdotal evidence from captured Burmese army personnel, this situation has not significantly altered, despite all the changes made under the SLORC. Since 1988, there have also been problems with inadequate training, low morale, poor leadership, and outmoded doctrine. All have been aggravated by the rapid expansion of the armed forces and seem likely to remain unresolved for some time.[18]

Before 1988, the tatmadaw's inventories of weapons and military equipment simply did not stand comparison with those of most other regional countries. Burma's policies of strict neutrality in foreign affairs and economic self-suffi- ciency were given a higher priority than the benefits of military assistance of the kind provided—often lavishly—to some of its neighbors. While the tatmadaw has always taken a large share of central government expenditures, Burma's perennial economic problems meant that arms imports remained very low. Most of the weapons and weapons platforms acquired before 1988 were second-hand, and many had to be modified in-country to meet specific operational require- ments. The difficulty of obtaining spare parts from abroad also meant that, at any time, a large proportion of Burmese military vehicles, combat aircraft and naval vessels was unserviceable. During the 1970s and 1980s, the Ne Win regime could only look on with envy as countries like Thailand, Malaysia, and Singapore, drawing on their superior economic resources, began to upgrade their armed forces with better arms and equipment.[19] Not only could they afford more sophisticated weapon systems but, to an increasing extent, they could support them with a more developed scientific and industrial base. In this sense, it could be claimed that the development of more capable and balanced armed forces in Burma after 1988 was simply in keeping with wider trends.[20]

Even so, the development of the tatmadaw under the SLORC has hardly matched that of most other regional armed forces, which have ordered or acquired some of the world's most modern weapon systems. Few of the arms and equipment purchased by Burma in recent years can be considered state-of- the art. With some notable exceptions (like the regime's unsuccessful attempt to purchase MiG-29 fighters from Russia) most of the tatmadaw's new weapon systems are based on 1980s or even 1970s vintage technology. While a marked improvement on Burma's older inventory, they still cannot match those of its larger neighbors, like China and India, or of more economically and technolog- ically advanced regional countries like Singapore and Thailand. In some respects, Burma is only now catching up with the armed forces of lowly Bangladesh. Also, given the complaints that are being heard about many of the vehicles, artillery, and aircraft which Burma has purchased from China, and the naval patrol boats which were obtained from China and Yugoslavia, questions can be raised about the combat effectiveness of even the SLORC's most recent purchases.

Even if these and other problems are overcome, additions to an order of bat- tle do not automatically translate into improvements in military capabilities. The acquisition of new arms and equipment needs to be based on a balanced and coherent strategic plan, something for which the Burmese leadership has not been noted in the past. Already, serious questions are being asked (including in the tatmadaw itself) about some aspects of the SLORC's procurement program. Also, it will take some time before all the new and diverse weapon systems can be fully absorbed into the tatmadaw's existing order of battle. Most of the new additions will depend for their full operational effectiveness on further improvements to Burma's command, control, communications, and intelligence resources. There will be a greatly increased requirement for training, and the development of new doctrines and operating procedures. Many of the new weapon systems require new facilities for storage, transport, maintenance, and repair. Unlike many other Southeast Asian countries, Burma's technical and industrial support base is not sufficiently developed to support more sophisticated weapons platforms and military equipment, meaning a greater dependence on foreign expertise and spare parts. Both will add to the demands on Burma's dwindling foreign exchange reserves. Given all these factors, it is likely to be some time before the tatmadaw's real operational capabilities match its new material strength.

Another factor underlying the SLORC's massive military expansion program appears to have been a deep-seated concern that foreign powers may try to use force to topple the regime and allow the pro-democracy movement to establish a civilian government. Not long after the 1988 massacres, for example, there were strong rumors circulating in Rangoon that the United States was sending the Seventh Fleet to Burma, and SLORC Chairman Gen. Saw Maung later accused the United States of trying to intimidate the regime with threats of military force.[21] Following the United Nations–sponsored landings of U.S. troops in Haiti, there were again rumors in Rangoon that the United States, or a coalition of U.N. members, would be sent to Burma to force the SLORC to accept the results of the 1990 general elections. Also in the early 1990s, there were renewed concerns about military intervention as the international community, and the Islamic countries in particular, criticized the SLORC for its harsh treatment of Rohingya Muslims in Arakan State.[22] There were even reports that Muslim extremists might launch a holy war (or jihad) against Burma. These fears may now appear ridiculous, but at the time they were genuinely held, and seem to have prompted the early purchase of several weapon systems (such as radar and anti-aircraft guns) which bore no relation to the SLORC's internal security problems.

Burma may not have faced any real external threats since 1988, but there was some basis for the SLORC's claim to have a strong strategic rationale for its efforts to improve the tatmadaw's capabilities. In the aftermath of the Cold War, the strategic environment in Asia has been changing. Most regional countries are concerned about the uncertain outlook, and many have been quietly taking military precautions against possible future threats.[23] In considering these issues,

Burma has been acutely conscious of its delicate position between the regional giants of China and India. Burma is also the largest state in mainland Southeast Asia, sharing long and porous borders with five different countries. In the nearly fifty years since it regained its independence, Burma has experienced difficult relations with all five of its neighbors, and in recent years at least three have in different ways assisted or sheltered armed forces hostile to the central government in Rangoon.[24] Burma also has a long and broken coastline, surrounded by extensive maritime claims, and its airspace covers several major east-west air routes. Yet Burma had never been in a position to defend its territory from external attack, guard its natural resources against unauthorized exploitation, or prevent intruders from crossing its borders. In these circumstances, some measures to improve the capability of the Burmese armed forces were only to be expected, regardless of who exercised power in Rangoon.

When questioned about Burma's arms procurement program, spokesmen for both the SLORC and some of its major arms suppliers have been quick to point out that the new weapons were for defensive purposes only.[25] In one sense, this is correct. For all its acquisitions (or orders) of armored vehicles, field artillery, interceptor aircraft, and naval vessels since 1988, Burma still does not possess any real power projection capability. Nor is one in prospect. As far as can be determined, Burma has no plans to acquire long range strike aircraft, an air-to-air refueling capability, major naval surface combatants or submarines, or ballistic missiles of any kind. Accusations by anti-Rangoon insurgent groups of Burmese chemical and biological weapons development and use, and therefore the potential for a proliferation of these exotic weapons in the region, are still unproven.[26] Although some of Burma's neighbors, notably Thailand and India, have expressed some reservations, the growth and modernization of the tatmadaw does not in itself significantly change the regional strategic balance, or pose a serious military threat to any other country.[27]

Despite all of the arguments that can be made in support of a larger, better equipped tatmadaw, it is still difficult to escape the conclusion that the SLORC has devoted so much of Burma's resources to the armed forces for purely domestic political reasons. All the regime's rhetoric aside, the rapid expansion and modernization of the tatmadaw since 1988 seems to have been based primarily on the fear that it might lose its monopoly of political power. The tatmadaw's increased recruitment campaign and massive arms procurement program seem aimed above all else at preventing, or if necessary quelling, renewed civil unrest in the main population centers. The regime recognizes that the pro-democracy movement led by Aung San Suu Kyi is the most powerful obstacle to its consolidation of power. Increased efforts to defeat or neutralize ethnic insurgent groups and narcotics-based armies in the countryside have also been part of the regime's continuing determination to impose its own peculiar vision of the modern Burmese state upon the entire country, regardless of the wishes of the Burmese population.

In addition to crushing all domestic challenges to military rule from Rangoon, and establishing the kind of stability it claims is necessary for national unity and economic growth, the SLORC's short-term goal seems to be the endorsement of a new constitution. This will lead in turn to the election of a "civilian" government more acceptable to the international community. Such a government may exercise administrative and ceremonial functions but it will still be effectively controlled by the armed forces, which is guaranteed a major role in its functions. As summarized by Silverstein, under the SLORC's plan:

> 25% of the seats in each house of the future legislature must be reserved for the armed forces; the future president must have long military experience as a major qualification for office; the Minister for Defense must be a member of the military and in times of emergency the head of the armed forces will have power to declare a state emergency and take power; the military budget will not be subject to approval by the elected/appointed legislature.[28]

In addition to these measures, the tatmadaw will extend its powers through a much wider distribution of military units around the countryside, and a more direct role in local political, economic, and social affairs.

The SLORC and Military Rule

There are a number of developments, however, which could disrupt the SLORC's steady progress toward its desired outcome of increased political control at home and greater legitimacy abroad. One would be a resumption of open anti-regime activity by Aung San Suu Kyi, who was released from house arrest in July 1995 after six years' detention without trial. If she chooses a more confrontational path she could quickly reawaken public demands for a return to democratic rule.[29] She has already questioned the validity of the regime's national constitutional convention process and directly challenged the SLORC's refusal to hand over power to an elected civilian government.[30] If the SLORC was concerned about its ability to manage a resurgence of popular protest, however, it is hardly likely to have authorized Aung San Suu Kyi's release. There is little doubt that, if it were felt to be necessary, the army would once again be called in to restore what the SLORC calls law and order, just as it did in 1988. While the regime may be more sensitive now to international criticism, and more vulnerable to economic sanctions, these realities are unlikely in themselves to prevent another crackdown. A much more worrying prospect for the SLORC would be the possibility of a major split in the armed forces, its sole power base and the instrument through which it governs.

The possibility of a split in the armed forces is a highly sensitive issue in Burma. Perhaps more than anything else, it arouses deep concerns on the part of former President Ne Win and the military hierarchy. Ever since large parts of the Burmese army mutinied in 1948, and even more so since Ne Win's military coup in 1962, considerable efforts have been taken to prevent such a problem from arising again.[31] The most potent and pervasive weapon in the regime's arsenal is the Directorate of Defense Services Intelligence (DDSI). Through its Military Intelligence Service and an extensive network of paid informers, the DDSI has always kept a close watch not only on the civilian population, but also on members of the tatmadaw itself.[32] Under the SLORC this capacity has been greatly increased. Also, senior officers are moved frequently to prevent them from building up personal followings or individual power bases in particular geographical areas. Some officers are kept away from power centers entirely, for example through diplomatic postings overseas, while others are co-opted into the regime's political structure where they can be more easily controlled.[33] The SLORC severely punishes any officers who are considered disloyal to the regime, or who overstep the bounds of permissible behavior. On the other hand, it bestows a wide range of rewards on loyal officers, in the way of promotions, comfortable postings, special privileges, business opportunities, and other perquisites. It is also relevant that many in the armed forces leadership are connected by family, financial, and other personal ties.

Despite all these measures, however, there have long been rumors of dissatisfaction and at times even active dissent within the ranks of the armed forces. In Burma's closed society accurate details are very difficult to obtain, but a number of broad themes keep recurring.

Ever since the 1962 coup, differences appear to have arisen in the tatmadaw over the proper place of the armed forces in Burmese society, and the degree to which they should exercise a political role.[34] Under Ne Win, purges of malcontents were frequent, with numerous senior officers posted abroad or forced into early retirement. Such measures were not always successful. There was a major shake-up of the military intelligence apparatus in the 1960s, for example, after Ne Win accused it of disloyalty. It apparently dared to question the tatmadaw's new political role. In 1976, the regime uncovered a plot by a number of disillusioned young officers to overthrow the president and take the army back to the barracks. In 1988 about 1,000 servicemen from all three services actually joined the pro-democracy demonstrations in Rangoon, calling for a return to civilian rule. At the time, one very senior and well-connected former tatmadaw officer told the British Broadcasting Corporation that the pro-democracy movement had the support of 60 percent of the army.[35] There was also considerable disquiet reported on the part of many soldiers who were later ordered to shoot down young demonstrators.[36] Two years later, the National League for Democracy's (NLD) landslide victory in the general elections was a severe shock to the regime, not least because the overwhelming vote for the opposition (including in some military cantonment districts) suggested a considerable sympathy for Aung San Suu Kyi and the democracy movement among the armed forces. There was thus the potential for a serious difference of view in the tatmadaw over its treatment of the NLD and its future role in Burma.[37]

Aung San Suu Kyi poses a particular problem for the SLORC. Her father, Aung San, was Burma's much revered independence leader who was assassinated in 1947. He was also the founder of the Burmese armed forces and, significantly, resigned his military position in order to pursue a political career. In the Burmese fashion, many in the tatmadaw now accord his daughter considerable respect, and she speaks about Aung San with some authority. Ne Win has consistently tried to share Aung San's mantle as a "co-father" of the armed forces. Yet he was in a different faction of the nationalist movement and was never nominated as Aung San's military successor. In July 1989, Aung San Suu Kyi referred publicly to serious differences between Ne Win and her father, a forbidden subject since the 1962 coup. She also declared that Ne Win had taken the tatmadaw down a different path from that mapped out by her father. Aung San Suu Kyi appealed over the heads of the SLORC to more moderate elements in the armed forces, asking them to honor her father's memory and support her demand for a return to democratic civilian government. This implicit call for members of the tatmadaw to question their own leaders seems to have been the trigger which prompted her immediate arrest. Another senior NLD figure imprisoned at the same time was Tin Oo, a former army Chief of Staff and Defense Minister who retained a considerable following in the armed forces.[38] The SLORC was determined to prevent any faction developing in the tatmadaw which might heed the call from these two respected figures to eschew politics and return to the barracks.

Since 1988 there has been considerable speculation over the internal dynamics of the SLORC itself. Various members have been characterized as either "moderates" or "hardliners," and been held accountable for perceived shifts in the regime's policies. Since early 1992, for example, there have been strong rumors of disagreements in the SLORC over the approach to be taken toward Aung San Suu Kyi, and how to respond to the pressures being applied against the regime by some members of the international community.[39] The so-called moderates, reportedly led by DDSI chief Lt. Gen. Khin Nyunt, were initially believed to have lost out to the hardliners who opposed their wish to soften Burma's image abroad. After Aung San Suu Kyi's unexpected release, however, the "moderates" were felt to be in the ascendant. The orchestrated attack on Aung San Suu Kyi's motorcade by hundreds of armed men in late 1996 was interpreted by many well-informed observers as a tactic by SLORC hardliners to curb her public criticisms of the military regime.[40] The apparent maneuvering of these factions has also been connected with the postings of particular senior officers to positions either of influence or obscurity. Such rumors abound in Burma's closed society, however, and are very difficult to confirm. Policy and personal differences no doubt exist in the SLORC, but it is unlikely that any major decision would be taken, or taken in such a manner, which might seriously threaten SLORC or armed forces unity.

Tensions also appear to have arisen in the armed forces over the level of Chinese influence which has been allowed to develop in the country. It is likely that the SLORC's decision to turn to China for diplomatic, military, and economic support after 1988 was unanimous. Indeed, given the widespread international condemnation of the Burmese regime at that time, the arms embargoes, and the withdrawal of aid and international finance, the SLORC probably felt that there were few other options if the military regime were to survive.[41] China also welcomed and facilitated the arrangement. Yet there are reportedly strong differences within the armed forces now over the degree to which Burma has come to rely on China for its arms, their indifferent quality, and the access that China has apparently been given to some Burmese military facilities. The social impact of China's increased presence in Burma under the regime's "open door" economic policies has exacerbated these concerns. The old capital of Mandalay, for example, is now described as a Chinese city.[42] While disagreements on this issue within the SLORC appear to have been contained for the time being, there have been reliable reports of serious dissatisfaction at lower levels of the armed forces. In 1992, for example, an assassination plot was apparently hatched against Khin Nyunt, the SLORC member believed to be the architect of Burma's pro-China policy.[43]

Other issues have arisen over the years which have had the potential to cause serious internal problems for the tatmadaw. Most common have been stories of resentment and antagonism between the (often younger) officers on active service in the field, and those officers assigned to more comfortable administrative or political duties in rear areas. While this may not be unusual in itself, the much greater hardships experienced by the front-line troops in Burma and the increased opportunities for personal profits in the rear, have given this issue added significance.[44] These concerns have been exacerbated since 1988. Under the SLORC, the level of official corruption has risen dramatically, increasing the obvious disparity in privileges and living conditions between senior and junior ranks. Other problems have been caused by the rapid expansion of the army. Not only has this process placed considerable strain on the junior officers and non-commissioned officers at line level, but the recruitment of thousands of young, poorly educated men from all around Burma has seriously weakened the tat-madaw's professional volunteer base. Many new recruits have been coerced into joining the ranks and bitterly resent the rigid discipline normally imposed upon them. Efforts are made to indoctrinate them with the SLORC's world view, but their loyalty to the regime must be considered suspect.

There have also been persistent reports of suspicion and rivalry between the graduates of Burma's prestigious Defense Services Academy (DSA) at Maymyo and the Officer Training School (OTS) at Hmawbi.[45] There has always been a degree of competition between these institutions, but in Burma these differences were made much worse by the 1976 plot against Ne Win. Although led by an OTS graduate, this plot was seen to have sprung from members of a particular DSA class. For a long time this view led to a reluctance by the tatmadaw leadership to appoint DSA graduates to senior positions. As Lintner in particular has pointed out, this discrimination was something which in itself led to further tensions within the Burmese army officer corps, as the military leadership was seen to give priority for promotions and prestigious postings to one career stream over the other.[46] The increased demand for experienced officers needed to manage the expanded Burmese army has helped overcome this problem to a certain degree, but it has not disappeared entirely. Since 1988, for example, particular figures in the SLORC have reportedly attempted to strengthen their personal power bases by appointing DSA or OTS classmates to positions of power and influence. As former Prime Minister U Nu once remarked, "in Burma, all politics are personal politics," and the armed forces is no exception.[47]

In addition, tensions appear to have arisen between those officers who owe their promotions primarily to their ties with former President Ne Win, and those who have followed a more professional career path. To a large extent, the aging Ne Win no longer exercises day-to-day control over the government and armed forces, and his standing among the younger generation in the tatmadaw is nowhere near as great as it may once have been.[48] As an historical figure prominent in Burma's early struggles against ethnic and ideological insurgents, however, and later chief of the country's armed forces, the "Old Man" still commands a degree of respect and loyalty in military circles. More importantly, he has for many years seeded the army with like-minded proteges. Many now hold powerful government positions, like Khin Nyunt, who is Secretary (1) of the SLORC as well as the Director of Defense Services Intelligence. It has often been suggested that many senior army officers, including some in the SLORC itself, resent the power currently held by Khin Nyunt, because of his political connections and lack of combat experience.[49] Ne Win is now old and infirm, and his power is on the wane. Until his death, however, he will continue to exercise influence over the SLORC's policies and act to protect his favorites from jealous rivals.

There are also antagonisms between the army and the two other services. Much of this ill feeling stems from their different historical traditions. In the 1930s, during the early days of the anti-colonial struggle, many Burmese nationalists saw the navy and air force as being on the wrong side. The two "technical" services tended to rely on the Anglo-Burmese community and ethnic minorities (notably the Karens) for their recruits. During World War II most Burmese members of the air force and navy supported the Allies, in direct contrast to the army, which was dominated by Burma's anti-colonial, and for a period even pro-Japanese, nationalist movement. Despite the efforts of the Burmese air force and navy to support the new Union government after independence in 1948, they retained many British characteristics and were viewed with suspicion by Ne Win and the other Japanese-trained army officers around him. It is relevant, too, that the navy and air force have tended to recruit better educated men from urban areas, and send them overseas for training, whereas the army has generally relied on more poorly educated rural youths trained entirely in Burma. The fact that the army has always been accorded priority in the distribution of scarce official resources has also caused misunderstandings and resentment. Since 1988 it seems an effort has been made to redress some of these problems, but the differences which remain go well beyond the inter-service rivalries which are traditional in the armed forces of other countries.

If all of these reports of tensions in the tatmadaw are true, then they constitute a potentially explosive problem in a country where the unity of the armed forces is deemed essential for political power and continued control over all the disparate elements of the Union. The air force and navy have been greatly expanded since the SLORC took power but, even now, they could do little on their own to shake the foundations of the state. A major split in the ranks of the army, however, would lead to serious problems for the military regime. Given the volatility of Burmese politics, this is not impossible, but there are a number of compelling reasons why a major split of this kind is unlikely to occur in the foreseeable future.[50]

Firstly, there are many in the armed forces, at all levels, who appear sincerely to believe the regime's oft-repeated claim that the tatmadaw alone has been responsible for maintaining Burma's unity and independence since 1948. The struggle to protect the fledgling Union government from communist and ethnic insurgents in the period immediately after independence, for example, is well known. Also, the danger of a breakaway by some of the ethnic minorities is still accepted by many in the army as justification for the military overthrow of U Nu's democratically elected government in 1962. In the minds of many officers and their men, the loss of control caused by a serious split in the armed forces would be disastrous for Burma. The possible consequences range from a resurgence of popular unrest in the main population centers to increased ethnic insurgent activity in the countryside. In extreme circumstances, a mutiny by a large part of the army (as occurred in 1948) could lead to another costly civil war, or even the fragmentation of the country. This message has been reinforced by the SLORC since 1988, with repeated appeals to nationalist sentiment and military tradition. The regime has also claimed that the NLD, supported as it is by ethnic parties and purportedly left-wing groups, would squander the country's hard-won independence and be unable to control its centrifugal political forces. Acceptance of these claims may not in itself prevent differences from arising within the tatmadaw, but it would be a strong factor militating against a serious breakdown in discipline.[51]

There also seems to be a serious concern that, under a democratically elected civilian government in Rangoon, the armed forces would lose the large share of the national budget which they have always enjoyed. For example, during the 1989–90 election campaign there were a number of indications given that, an NLD government would drastically reduce the size of the armed forces. Much greater emphasis would be placed on peaceful negotiations with various insurgent groups and the possible development of a federal style of political system which would give the ethnic minorities greater autonomy. It was suggested at the time that, by abandoning the military regime's policy of crushing all ethnic insurgencies and imposing a highly centralized political system on the country, the then 200,000-strong armed forces could be reduced to a border protection force as small as 20,000–30,000 men.[52] Since then, the SLORC has itself signed ceasefire agreements with most major ethnic insurgent groups, but has persisted in its expansion of the tatmadaw. This policy is in stark contrast to the NLD's continuing preference for a much smaller, well-equipped, and professional armed force responsible to an elected civilian government.[53] In addition, the long overdue economic rehabilitation of the country and improved social services demanded by the civilian population would be enormously expensive. Development projects starved of funds by the SLORC and its predecessors would be bound to get a higher priority by a democratic government. This would inevitably be at the expense of new arms, military equipment, and defense facilities.

While the feeling is difficult to quantify, many members of the Burmese armed forces appear to be afraid that, should they lose control of their own fate, they will be forced to face the consequences of their harsh rule over the past 35 years.[54] Since Ne Win seized power in 1962, the military regime has been repeatedly condemned for its gross violations of human rights, with many observers describing it as one of the most brutal in the region. In 1988, for example, the armed forces killed more than 3,000 pro-democracy demonstrators and imprisoned thousands more. Many were tortured. During the 1988 demonstrations and since, there have been repeated demands by Burmese dissidents and others for members of the military regime to be brought before tribunals of the kind convened to judge German and Japanese war criminals after World War II. More recently, there have been calls for members of the SLORC to be tried by the international community *in absentia*, as has occurred with respect to crimes against humanity perpetrated in the former Republic of Yugoslavia. Given the likely outcome of such trials, there is little chance that any members of the current armed forces hierarchy in Rangoon would willingly permit anything to occur which might put them in such a vulnerable position.

It is relevant too that many members of the Burmese armed forces (in particular its most senior officers) have long enjoyed considerable social and economic privileges, as the regime has tried to retain their loyalty and protect them from the results of its own economic mismanagement. Pay scales have been less of an incentive although, in August 1988, in an obvious attempt to purchase the support of the rank and file of the armed forces in the face of rising popular unrest, the government awarded the tatmadaw a 45 percent pay raise.[55] In addition, over the years a large number of officers appear to have profited from official corruption and the booming black market (including narcotics deals). The property holdings of many senior military figures in Burma, for example, are out of all proportion to their official incomes. More recently, many officers appear to have acquired strong financial interests in the various commercial ventures which the SLORC has negotiated with companies from Thailand, Singapore, Taiwan, South Korea, and elsewhere, under the regime's new open door economic policies.[56] The level of corruption in the armed forces is now greater than ever before. Any transfer of power to an elected civilian government would thus not only risk the loss of many customary privileges and benefits, but in many cases would occasion considerable financial costs as well.

The Future

For all their criticisms of the SLORC and the role of the armed forces in the past, Aung San Suu Kyi and many other senior pro-democracy leaders realized at an early stage of their campaign that they needed to overcome the tatmadaw's fears if they were ever to loosen its grip on power and form a viable civilian government.[57] Hence Aung San Suu Kyi's appeal to the more moderate and professional elements of the armed forces in 1989. Since her release from house arrest in July 1995, she has continued to seek a dialogue with the military regime, recognizing that under current circumstances a peaceful transition to democratic rule can only occur with its concurrence, if not active support.[58] Although her position has progressively hardened as the SLORC has continued to ignore her calls for dialogue and imposed restrictions on the NLD's activities, Aung San Suu Kyi has emphasized that it is not the NLD's intention to split the tatmadaw. Indeed, she has noted that "dissension within the army means trouble for the country."[59] To make progress, however, other assurances may need to be given, as has already occurred for example in places like South Korea, South Africa, and Chile. An accommodation of some kind with the armed forces, possibly including an amnesty for its past actions, may not be popular with some of the more radical elements in the democracy movement. Yet without it, little progress can be made towards the kind of society that the majority of the Burmese population so clearly wants.[60]

In recent years the world has seen some remarkable reversals of political fortune. Authoritarian regimes have been toppled and military juntas have been forced to cede power to civilian governments. It is possible that the same may happen in Burma, but that will depend to a large extent on the cohesion and loyalty of the armed forces. Its support is critical to the survival of any government in Rangoon, civilian or military. In that regard, the outlook is bleak. Personal rivalries may exist, policy differences within the leadership may become highly charged, and Ne Win's death could even lead to a realignment of senior positions, but it is unlikely that there will be a major split in the tatmadaw in the near future. The nature of the armed forces is changing, but at present the forces binding it together are stronger than those which might cause serious division. Also, as noted above, the potential consequences of a split are well known to the regime and will help inhibit any moves which might cause such an event to occur. Barring unforeseen developments, Burma's future seems to be one of increasing military strength and a tighter, if more subtle, exercise of political power by the armed forces.

Notes

1. This chapter is based entirely on open sources. It represents the author's views alone and has no official status or endorsement. When information has been drawn from personal interviews, and the individuals concerned have asked not to be named, then only the place and date of the interview have been given.

2. Some foreign observers have described the formation of the SLORC in September 1988 as a coup, or at least as an assumption of power by the armed forces. This is incorrect. Despite the creation of numerous "civilian" political structures after the 1962 military coup, former Gen. Ne Win and the armed forces have wielded effective power since then. All that happened in 1988 was that the retired military officers in public office stepped aside and permitted serving members of the armed forces hierarchy to assume direct control of the country (albeit under Ne Win's continuing guidance).

3. These figures have been drawn from *The Military Balance 1988–1989* (London, 1988), 159.

4. See Bertil Lintner and Robert Karniol, "Unrest Swells the Burmese Ranks," *Jane's Defence Weekly* (13 June 1992), 1020; *The Defence of Thailand 1994* (Bangkok, 1994), 15; *Burma Debate* II (1995), 16.

5. Interview, Rangoon, April 1995.

6. Full details of this expansion program are given in Andrew Selth, *Transforming the Tatmadaw: The Burmese Armed Forces since 1988* (Canberra, 1996).

7. See, for example, R.H. Taylor, "Burma: Defence Expenditure and Threat Perceptions," in Chin Kin Wah (ed.), *Defence Spending in Southeast Asia* (Singapore, 1987), 252–280.

8. *World Military Expenditures and Arms Transfers 1995* (Washington, 1996), 66. See also *Foreign Economic Trends Report: Burma* (Rangoon, 1996), 21–25.

9. Andrew Selth, "The Myanmar Army since 1988: Acquisitions and Adjustments," *Contemporary Southeast Asia*, XVII (1995), 237–264.

10. William Ashton, "The Burmese Navy," *Jane's Intelligence Review*, VI (1994), 36–37; *Jane's Fighting Ships 1995–96* (Coulsdon, 1996), 77–82.

11. See for example William Ashton, "The Burmese Air Force," *Jane's Intelligence Review*, VI (1994), 463–466; William Ashton, "Myanmar Turns to Russia for Arms," *Asia-Pacific Defence Reporter*, XXII (1996), 13.

12. In late 1996, for example, the SLORC signed an agreement with China for the provision to Burma of additional military training, intelligence, and arms at "friendship prices." See Rowan Callick, "China and Burma Strengthen Ties with Military Agreement," *Australian Financial Review* (24 January 1997).

13. With 186,000 in the armed forces and a total population of 39,395,000, Burma in 1988 had a ratio of 1 serviceman/woman to every 212 people. The International Institute for Strategic Studies has calculated that in 1988 there were 5,294,000 men between the ages of 18 and 32 in Burma, and 5,282,000 women. With its population standing at 53,931,000 and its active armed forces numbering 256,000, the equivalent Thai ratio was 1:210. See *The Military Balance 1988–1989*, 159–160.

14. U.B. Singh, "Growth of Military Power in South-East Asia," *Asian Strategic Review 1994–95* (New Delhi, 1995), 313.

15. See, for example, *"No Childhood At All:" A Report about Child Soldiers in Burma* (Chiangmai, 1996).

16. R.L. Sivard, *World Military and Social Expenditures, 1987–88* (Washington, 1987), 48.

17. See, for example, William Dowell, "Allies but not Friends," *Time* (29 May 1995), 32. Also interview, Sydney, October 1996. The "tooth-to-tail" ratio is the proportion of men and women in

front-line combat units compared with those in rear-echelon support roles. It is thus one measure of the fighting efficiency of a country's armed forces.

18. Interview, Sydney, October 1996.

19. Graeme Cheeseman and Richard Leaver, *Trends in Arms Spending and Conventional Arms Trade in the Asia-Pacific Region* (Canberra, 1995); Bilveer Singh, "ASEAN's Arms Procurements: Challenge of the Security Dilemma in the Post Cold War Era," *Comparative Strategy,* XII (1993).

20. Tin Maung Maung Than, "Neither Inheritance nor Legacy: Leading the Myanmar State since Independence," *Contemporary Southeast Asia,* XV (1993), 60.

21. At one stage there were even reports of U.S. soldiers landing in Burma. See "Washington Denies Interfering in Burmese Affairs," Agence France Presse (13 September 1988); Yindee Lertcharoenchok, "Burmese Leader Calls Thailand a 'True Friend,'" The *Nation* (13 April 1989).

22. In April 1992, for example, Prince Khaled Bin Sultan Bin Abdul Aziz, the commander of the Saudi Arabian forces during the 1990–91 Gulf War, made a visit to Bangladesh, during which he called upon the UN to do for Burmese Muslims "just what it did to liberate Kuwait." John Bray, "Ethnic Minorities and the Future of Burma," *The World Today* (August/September 1992), 147. See also Bertil Lintner, "The Secret Mover," *Far Eastern Economic Review* (7 May 1992), 21.

23. See, for example, Andrew Selth, "The Changing Strategic Environment: A Global and Regional Overview," *Current Affairs Bulletin,* LXX (1994), 17–27; Singh, "ASEAN's Arms Procurements," 207–216.

24. Until the collapse of the Communist Party of Burma (CPB) in 1989, China provided considerable material and diplomatic support to the CPB. India had supported anti-regime ethnic groups in Burma's northwest and after 1988 provided funds and refuge to pro-democracy activists. Thailand has long given at least passive support to ethnic insurgent groups, black marketeers, and narcotics traffickers based along its border with Burma.

25. Interviews, Rangoon, April 1995.

26. Andrew Selth, "Burma and Exotic Weapons," *Strategic Analysis,* XIX (1996), 413–433.

27. The Royal Thai Navy's claim that improvements in the Burmese navy warrant the acquisition of a Thai submarine capability is clearly a case of special pleading, but more serious concerns have been expressed from time to time. See, for example, M.G. Rolls, "Thailand's Post Cold-War Security Policy and Defence Programme," *Contemporary Security Policy,* XV (1994), 101–103. India's concerns seem to relate more to Chinese influence over the Burmese armed forces, rather than to any improvements in the tatmadaw itself. See William Ashton, "Chinese Bases in Burma—Fact or Fiction?" *Jane's Intelligence Review,* VII (1995), 84–87.

28. Statement by Josef Silverstein, before the U.S. House of Representatives Committee on International Relations, Subcommittee on Asia and the Pacific, hearing on "Recent Developments in Burma," Washington (7 September 1995).

29. See, for example, Bertil Lintner, *Aung San Suu Kyi and Burma's Unfinished Renaissance* (Bangkok, 1990); Josef Silverstein, "Aung San Suu Kyi: Is She Burma's Woman of Destiny?" *Asian Survey,* XXX (1990). Aung San Suu Kyi's own views can be found in *Freedom from Fear,* Michael Aris (ed.), (London, 1995).

30. See, for example, "Suu Kyi Pledges to Fight," *Canberra Times* (4 December 1995); "Suu Kyi Dismisses Fear of Arrest as Tension Rises," *Australian* (4 September 1996).

31. See, for example, Bertil Lintner, "Purges and Spies Make Army Ne Win's Hardest Asset," *Far Eastern Economic Review* (22 September 1988), 16; "Masses in Revolt against Authoritarian Grip," *Far Eastern Economic Review* (25 August 1988), 12–13.

32. While the formal structure of Burma's intelligence apparatus has changed over the years, its basic components and functions have remained much the same. See Andrew Selth, *Burma's Intelligence Apparatus,* Strategic and Defence Studies Centre, Working Paper 308 (Canberra, 1997); Bertil Lintner, "Myanmar's Military Intelligence," *International Defense Review* XXIV (1991), 39; Michael Fredholm, *Ethnicity and Insurgency* (Westport, 1993), 92–93.

33. Since 1988, for example, the number of tatmadaw officers appointed to government posi-

tions at deputy minister rank or above has expanded from twenty-one to sixty-five. While there are several explanations for this development, one is the perceived need to bring influential figures in from the field, where they enjoyed considerable power and independence.

34. For a useful discussion of the growth of professionalism in the tatmadaw, see Moshe Lissak, *Military Roles in Modernization: Civil-Military Relations in Thailand and Burma* (Beverly Hills, 1976), 155ff. See also Mary. P. Callahan, "The Origins of Military Rule in Burma," unpub. Ph.D. dissertation (Cornell University, 1996).

35. Admittedly, this was Gen. Tin Oo, who by that time was a senior figure in the opposition National League for Democracy. His claim, however, has been supported since by other members (and former members) of the tatmadaw interviewed by the author. See also Bertil Lintner, "Backdown or Bloodbath," *Far Eastern Economic Review* (22 September 1988), 14; William Stewart, "Now a Coup," *Time* (26 September 1988), 14; Martin Smith, *Burma: Insurgency and the Politics of Ethnicity* (London, 1991), 10.

36. Bertil Lintner, "Dissent in the Ranks," *Far Eastern Economic Review* (17 August 1989), 22.

37. "Statement on votes gained by candidates who represent parties, seats won by the respective parties and percentages," *Working People's Daily* (2 July 1990).

38. Bertil Lintner, "Sowing the Wind," *Far Eastern Economic Review* (3 August 1989), 11–12; Rodney Tasker, "Haunting Memories," *Far Eastern Economic Review* (13 July 1989), 30.

39. See, for example, "Statement by Dr. Josef Silverstein," 7 September 1995.

40. Interviews, Rangoon, November 1996.

41. Khin Nyunt, "The Tatmadaw as Preserver of the Union," *Business Times* (4 August 1995). See also Andrew Selth, "Burma and the Strategic Competition between China and India," *Journal of Strategic Studies,* XIX (1996), 213–230.

42. Mya Maung, "On the Road to Mandalay: A Case Study of the Sinonization of Upper Burma," *Asian Survey,* XXXIV (1994), 447-459.

43. "Killers Cooled?" *Asiaweek* (27 November 1992), 43; Bertil Lintner, "Murmur in the Ranks," *Far Eastern Economic Review* (18 February 1993), 20. See also Bertil Lintner, "Myanmar's Chinese Connection," *International Defence Review,* XXVII (1994), 23.

44. See, for example, "Reining in the Majors," *Far Eastern Economic Review* (17 September 1987), 14; V.G. Kulkarni, "Straining at the Seams," *Far Eastern Economic Review* (7 July 1988), 16–18.

45. The DSA was established in 1955 and gives a four-year degree course for cadets chosen from among the best high school pupils. Graduates are assigned to services depending on the tatmadaw's manpower requirements. The OTS (which was recently moved from Hmawbi to Bahtoo) conducts four-month courses for university graduates, and eighteen-month courses for selected enlisted men. See F.M. Bunge (ed.), *Burma: A Country Study* (Washington, 1983), 252–253; Bertil Lintner, "Burma—Struggle for Power," *Jane's Intelligence Review,* V (1993), 466–471; Bertil Lintner, "Simple Soldiers," *Far Eastern Economic Review* (1 July 1993), 24.

46. The most complete discussion of this issue is Lintner, "Burma—Struggle for Power," 466–471. See also Bertil Lintner, "Myanmar's Influential Chief May Be Losing Power," *Jane's Defence Weekly* (12 June 1993), 29.

47. U Nu made this comment to Australian diplomat Philip Stonehouse in Rangoon in February 1989. Interview, Canberra, November 1996.

48. One tatmadaw source is reported to have stated that less than 25 percent of the armed forces still feel any personal loyalty to Ne Win. See Lintner, "Dissent in the Ranks," 22.

49. See, for example, Bertil Lintner, "Cracks in the Rock," *Far Eastern Economic Review* (24 October 1991), 11–12; Lintner, "Dissent in the Ranks," 22.

50. William Ashton, "Fearful Army Blocks Transfer of Power," *Asia-Pacific Defence Reporter,* XVII (December 1990/January 1991), 52–54.

51. Interviews, Rangoon and Mandalay, November 1996.

52. Rodney Tasker and Bertil Lintner, "The Plot Thickens," *Far Eastern Economic Review* (21 June 1990), 21–22.

53. Interviews, Rangoon, November 1996.

54. See, for example, Alan Boyd, "Burma Junta Fears Probe of Massacre," *Australian* (30 May 1990).

55. Daniel Benjamin et al, "Out...In 17 Days," *Time* (22 August 1988), 21.

56. See, for example, John Badgley, "The Burmese Way to Capitalism," in *Southeast Asian Affairs 1990* (Singapore, 1990), 229–239.

57. Louise Williams, "Revenge Is Not Our Priority, Says Opposition," *Sydney Morning Herald* (4 July 1990). Also, interview with Sein Win, "prime minister" of the National Coalition Government of the Union of Burma, Canberra, September 1996.

58. See, for example, "A Careful Hero," *Asiaweek* (4 August 1995), 16–17; Gordon Fairclough, "Winds of Change," *Far Eastern Economic Review* (31 August 1995), 24–26; "Suu Kyi Talks Ruled Out," *The Age* (3 August 1996).

59. Aung San Suu Kyi, speaking at an NLD press conference in Rangoon on 29 November 1995. See also "Lost Illusions," *Economist* (2 December 1995), 24. Not surprisingly, Aung San Suu Kyi's views on this subject are shared by Sein Win, the exiled "prime minister" of the National Coalition Government of the Union of Burma. Interview, Canberra, September 1996.

60. The recent trial in South Korea of former President Chun Doo-hwan, however, for atrocities committed by the Korean armed forces fifteen years ago, will doubtless add to any concerns which members of the SLORC may have about an amnesty offer.

CHAPTER 6

Burma's Role in Regional Security—Pawn or Pivot?

J. Mohan Malik

BURMA HAS come to occupy center stage in Asian strategic concerns since the early 1990s. A series of developments, both internal and external, has caused concern about the long-term stability, security, and independence of mainland Southeast Asia's largest country. Burma, with an area of some 678,500 square kilometers and a population of 45 million, lies at the juncture of three regions within Asia—East Asia, Southeast Asia, and South Asia. It occupies a critical geostrategic position between the two Asian giants—China and India. It also shares borders with Bangladesh, an Islamic state, in the west and with Thailand and Laos in the east. It has a substantial coastline in the south along the Bay of Bengal and the Andaman Sea, which provides access to the Indian Ocean. It is located in a region which has experienced tremendous economic growth over the last two decades.

Burma's potential wealth, as well as its natural and human resources, and geostrategic location between South Asia and Southeast Asia, suggest that it has the *potential* to be a major Southeast Asian player. However, Burma today cuts a sorry figure. Internally, it is a divided nation. Externally, it is ostracized and regarded as a pariah because of the military regime's systematic, brutal oppression of its people, and involvement in the narcotics trade. To make matters worse, the military junta has abandoned the traditional policy of political equidistance between China and India, and is seen as becoming a puppet of China as well as a base for future Chinese military operations, thus upsetting the regional balance of power.

Several observers have examined the factors underlying changes in Burma's relations with China and their implications for regional security.[1] This chapter seeks to answer three key questions: What will it take to transform Burma from a pawn to a pivot?[2] Does Burma have what it takes to be a regional player? More importantly, will it be allowed to do so by its powerful northern neighbor, China, which is often touted as the next superpower?

In a recent article, Selth offers an optimistic view. He suggests that Burma can successfully manage its relations with its two largest neighbors, and that the regional security outlook may not be quite as uncertain or unstable as some observers have suggested.[3] He believes that the current Burmese leaders have played a dangerous but clever game. However, he argues that they now are ready to welcome countervailing overtures from India and the Association of Southeast Asian Nations (ASEAN).[4] India and ASEAN are now giving high priority to improving security, diplomatic, and economic relations with Burma in order to minimize the growing power and influence of China in that nation. This development is seen by Burma-watchers as being in the best interests of Burma, ASEAN, Japan, and India, and as an essentially stabilizing factor in the region. But there is reason to believe that the present and future Burmese leaders would find it very difficult to withdraw completely from China's sphere of influence. Nor would the Chinese government allow them to do so because Burma now occupies the same place in China's calculus of deterrence in South and Southeast Asia that Pakistan does in South and Southwest Asia.

This chapter examines the dilemmas and challenges facing Burma by undertaking a detailed analysis of its fast changing relations with China, India, and ASEAN. It also offers a prognosis of Burma's policy options given that country's place in China's grand strategy for the twenty-first century. It concludes with a pessimistic view on the prospects of Burma's transformation from a pawn in China's regional chess game into a pivotal player in the early twenty-first century.

Burma: Cockpit of Rivalry?

Though none of Burma's neighbors pose a security threat, the country suffers from centrifugal tendencies generated mostly by its own ethnic groups, which have obtained limited support mainly from China and Thailand in the past. Since independence in 1948, successive governments in Burma have battled around the country's periphery with half a dozen insurgencies and separatist movements based on ethnic identity. Not surprisingly, then, the sole preoccupation of the

Burmese armed forces, *tatmadaw*, has been the defense of the country's territorial integrity from threats within rather than without. Until recently, the isolationist policies pursued by the previous Ne Win regime helped to perpetuate Burma's status as a buffer state between India and China. Not any more. Since September 1988, when the military brutally suppressed pro-democracy protests and killed thousands of people (a precursor to the Tian'anmen massacre in Beijing), the country has been run by the military's State Law and Order Restoration Council (SLORC), which has effectively put an end to Burma's neutrality by moving closer to China. In 1990, the SLORC presided over an election in which the opposition National League for Democracy (NLD) won by a landslide but was never allowed to take office. Instead, the military junta placed the Burmese opposition leader, Aung San Suu Kyi, under house arrest, and arrested thousands of NLD supporters and leaders. This sparked worldwide condemnation of widespread human rights abuses and pressure to restore the democratic process.

Faced with increasing international isolation and pressure following the suppression in 1990 of the democratic movement, the SLORC's position became even more desperate. There were major concerns about maintaining political power, further domestic unrest, continuing ethnic insurgency, and a xenophobic fear of a possible United Nations–sponsored military coalition action similar to Operation Desert Storm. The SLORC desperately needed foreign exchange, capital equipment, and technical expertise to prevent the collapse of its ailing economy, and it needed assistance in defeating ethnic insurgency.[5] At this point, Chinese interests conveniently synchronized with a range of the SLORC's major concerns and the military junta in Rangoon moved to establish closer military, economic, and diplomatic ties with the communist regime in Beijing which had found itself in a similar predicament following the Tian'anmen massacre. Thus began Burma's slide into China's embrace.

China is reported to have so far supplied more than U.S.$1.5 billion worth of arms to Burma, including fighter aircraft, radar equipment, naval patrol boats, heavy artillery, tanks, anti-aircraft missiles, guns, and ammunition.[6] Rangoon has relied heavily on these weapons and equipment to end hostilities with insurgents in the border regions. The army strength increased by 50 percent between 1988 and 1992. Most of the Chinese weaponry (including the Chinese-made HN5 anti-aircraft missiles) is now reportedly deployed on the Indo-Burmese border.[7] The military regime has been spending more than 60 percent of its national budget on the military at a time when ethnic insurgent activity is at its lowest level for many years. Burma-watchers argue that the SLORC has created a series of imagined external threats to secure the military's grip on power, to preserve the cohesion of armed forces, and to provide the unity necessary for continued military rule.[8] During 1991-1992, as many as 200,000 Rohingya Muslims from Burma's Arakan state fled over the border into neighboring Bangladesh when a brutal offensive was launched by the tatmadaw against its Muslim minority. Thousands of refugees also poured into India and Thailand following the Burmese military's stepped up counterinsurgency (COIN) operations against Burmese insurgents.

Burma's economic decline and international isolation also led to an upsurge in opium production and cross-border smuggling. Indeed, many of the SLORC's peace agreements with ex-communist rebels, and other ethnic minorities in the northeastern border regions, allowed the former guerillas to remain active in the drug trade within the infamous Golden Triangle region across the Burmese frontier with China, Thailand, and Laos. Worse still, the SLORC's policies seemed to have made drug money an integral part of Burma's economy.[9] The drug trade is facilitated by endemic corruption on both sides of the border despite the spectacularly cosmetic control exercises, drug burnings, and public executions. As Bertil Lintner, a veteran Burma-watcher, has noted: "The unprecedented heroin explosion in Burma's north and China's increasing political and economic influence over the entire country . . . threatens the stability and social fabric of the entire region."[10] Drug money is reportedly used to finance military hardware purchases from China and elsewhere.

Though some of the Chinese arms supplied to Burmese military are almost obsolete, the purchases and troop buildup nonetheless represent a major boost to Burma's military capabilities, and so have the potential to change the regional military balance of power. In addition, high ranking Burmese tatmadaw and Chinese People's Liberation Army (PLA) officers have strengthened relations both at the personal and official levels. Tatmadaw personnel are also receiving advanced training from the PLA in China. Chinese Prime Minister Li Peng's visit to Burma in December 1994 was the capstone to his strategy of establishing closer ties with China's southern neighbor. He emphasized that the new ideological affinity (authoritarianism and free-market economy) provided further impetus to partnership between two countries with long historical ties. The political implications of a Chinese nexus with Burma are not lost on Burma's neighbors, who are especially wary of a military nexus and its impact upon regional security environment.

From New Delhi's perspective, it was not the Burmese military buildup in itself which caused concern, but the supplier. The growing military relationship between Beijing and Rangoon not only marked the end of Burma's traditional non-aligned orientation, it also aroused Indian apprehensions.[11] It forced New

Delhi, *for the first time*, to pay increasing attention to events across its eastern frontier with Burma. As one observer of Burmese affairs noted: "Just as China's support for Pakistan puts pressure on India to the west, so closer Chinese ties with Burma adds to India's strategic concerns in the east."[12] There is concern in Asian capitals that the regional security situation could deteriorate if the Burmese military regime comes to replace the Khmer Rouge as the new linchpin of Chinese strategy for the expansion of its influence in South and Southeast Asia.

This de facto military alliance between Burma and China in early 1990s coincided with a serious deterioration in relations between India and Burma. While China strengthened its political and security ties with the Burmese military regime, the Indian government publicly aligned itself with the democratic movement led by Aung San Suu Kyi and condemned the Burmese military regime for violations of human rights. With India providing refuge to several key Burmese opposition figures and giving clandestine support to Burmese opposition groups in the border regions of Thailand, Rangoon accused New Delhi of interfering in its internal affairs, and the two countries became increasingly suspicious of each other.

Furthermore, reports of Beijing's involvement in the development of a Burmese naval base at Hainggyi Island and radar station at Coco Island, southwest of the Burmese coast, have introduced a whole new dimension to India's threat perceptions from a powerful neighbor. The new facilities are close to the Indian territory of Andaman and Nicobar Islands in the Bay of Bengal, and raise the specter of possible military use by Beijing.[13] Articles in *Jane's Defence Weekly, Jane's Intelligence Review, Asia-Pacific Defence Reporter, Far Eastern Economic Review*, Indian defense journals, and other print media have mentioned a number of possibilities including the establishment of signal intelligence (SIGINT) facilities by China to monitor Indian missile launches conducted between Orissa and the Andamans, maritime reconnaissance or communication and naval facilities for Chinese naval vessels, listening posts, and a deep water port for Chinese nuclear submarines.[14] Hundreds of Chinese naval personnel are reportedly working as instructors and helping to build five new ports and upgrade others along Burma's coast, from Victoria Point in the south to Sittwe in northern Arakan.[15] Much to India's chagrin, its subcontinental archrival, Pakistan, has stepped in to provide military and diplomatic support to the SLORC, and joined China in protecting Burma from criticism in international fora. Pakistani military instructors are also reportedly helping the Burmese army familiarize itself with Chinese hardware operated by Pakistan.

China's inroads into Burma, when juxtaposed with China's ties with Bangladesh and Pakistan's Burma connection, are from New Delhi's perspective, serious encroachments into India's sphere of influence. Therefore, according to Indian strategists, China is now seen as constituting a threat in the north *as well as in the east*. As one analyst at the New Delhi–based Institute for Defense Studies & Analyses (IDSA) put it: "In dealing with China we have to consider what it is doing in the east rather than see it only as a northern threat."[16] China's forays into Burma have been variously described by India's China-watchers as "a further demonstration of China's long encircling arms,"[17] formation of yet another "Chinese satellite,"[18] "removal of a useful strategic buffer on India's eastern border," "Tibetanisation of Burma," and a demonstration of Beijing's "westward thrust into the Indian Ocean, well beyond China's traditional sphere of influence" which constitutes a direct challenge to New Delhi's strategic interests.[19]

Despite significant improvement in bilateral relations between India and China, a serious geopolitical rivalry for influence and dominance in the post–Soviet Union Asia is intensifying between the region's "natural rivals." While China is striving to emerge as the unrivaled, unchallenged, paramount economic and military superpower in the Asia-Pacific by the turn of the century, India is anxious to assert its power and expand its influence in order to counteract similar moves by China. Inevitably this introduces a more competitive aspect into the Sino-Indian relationship. Each remains suspicious of the other's long-term agenda and intentions, and both see themselves as newly-rising great Asian powers whose time has finally come.

Chinese Shadow over Burma: Key Objectives

Relations between China and Burma have never been closer than they are today. Despite growing regional concern about Chinese intentions, Beijing's reluctance to clarify matters has further complicated the situation.[20] However, observers of Chinese and Burmese affairs have attributed several motives to China's desire to expand its economic and strategic influence down to the Bay of Bengal. A major one, of course, is Chinese economic planners' desire to open the old Burma Road to link up the poorer, inland provinces such as Yunnan, which have lagged behind the booming coastal provinces, with the fast growing economies of Southeast and South Asia.[21] China apparently also seeks an overland route through Burma to a port from which it can export cheap consumer goods to mainland Southeast Asia, India, and other developing countries farther afield.[22] Such an outlet would also reduce transport time for some of China's trade and would avoid the Malacca Strait choke point in the event of a conflict in the South China Sea.

The significance of the old Burma Road for economic growth was outlined first by a former vice-minister of communications, Pan Qi, in an article entitled "Opening to the Southwest: An Expert Opinion" in *Beijing Review* of Sept. 2, 1985. The three decades of self-imposed isolation, or what the regime described as the "Burmese road to socialism," had turned the region's most prosperous country into an economic basket case. Since 1990, the Chinese have found Burma a ready market for their cheap consumer goods such as textiles, bicycles, cigarettes, beer, utensils, and agricultural products. The annual Sino-Burmese trade is estimated to be more than U.S.$1.5 billion, excluding a lucrative cross-border illicit traffic in drugs from Burma's side of the Golden Triangle.[23] To strengthen and increase its trade links with Burma, China is also providing its southern neighbor with economic aid and technical help in developing its physical infrastructure. Chinese authorities in the southwest province of Yunnan have plans to build a 1,350 km railway through Laos and Burma to Thailand which will link Kunming with Bangkok. Hundreds of Chinese experts are already working on major highway, railway, and bridge construction projects in Burma which will significantly increase the volume of trade between China and its Southeast and South Asian neighbors in the years ahead.

From the strategic viewpoint, arms sales and/or military cooperation have always been an important means of funding the PLA's modernization drive and of expanding China's influence abroad. For example, through its military assistance, Beijing has recently come to acquire considerable political influence over Burma and Laos. Arms sales also raised China's profile in South Asia, thereby affording Beijing the opportunity to mediate the conflict between Burma and Bangladesh over Rohingya Muslim refugees. (Beijing has already demonstrated its crucial role in the settlement of other key regional disputes in Northeast and Southeast Asian subregions: e.g., the Korean peninsula, Cambodia, and in the Spratlys.)

Closer Sino-Burmese ties are now seen as "of great significance to the national security of China." Arguing that China's sea lanes of communications are subject to military blockades or interruption in the East and South China seas, Chinese defense planners now routinely stress that "a route from Yunnan to Rangoon could become an important transport line for goods and materials."[24] Chinese forays into Burma are also a reflection of China's transformation from a continental power into a maritime power increasingly dependent upon external trade, on ever-growing volumes of imports and exports through oceanic routes, and on overseas markets for capital and investments. Eighty-five percent of China's external trade is transported by sea. This, in turn, necessitates the development of a blue-water naval capability to protect vital sea lanes of communications. A major hurdle in the Chinese ambitions to dominate the Malacca Straits and to ensure the safe passage of goods through the vital sea lanes was the lack of any maintenance bases in and around the Indian Ocean for its naval ships. With Burma offering its port facilities for repair and maintenance, a key strategic objective—that is, an opening to the Bay of Bengal/Andaman Sea via China's southwest frontier—has now been realized.

The Chinese defense establishment is concerned about India's ambitions to dominate the Indian Ocean and its increasing military capability to project power.[25] Despite a recent thaw in Sino-Indian relations, Chinese strategic literature continues to list India as one of China's most likely opponents in regional conflicts on China's southern borders in the 1990s and beyond (the others being Vietnam and Taiwan).[26] Chinese strategists are also increasingly questioning India's view of its status in the Indian Ocean. A high-ranking PLA officer and Director of the Chinese Academy of Military Sciences, General Zhao Nanqi, was quoted in 1993 as saying that China would extend its naval operations farther than the South and East China seas to check attempts by India to "dominate" the Indian Ocean and other regional waters. Accusing India of seeking to develop a navy to rival that of "large global powers," General Zhao said that "this is something which we cannot accept . . . we are not prepared to let the Indian Ocean become India's Ocean."[27] Having established its naval dominance in the Pacific, the Chinese navy's expansion into the Indian Ocean should be seen as "the realization of one of Beijing's dreams, which is that its navy can operate in two major oceans" and thus heralds China's emergence as a *truly global power*.[28]

Last but not least, China's naval surges into the Indian Ocean are a part of Beijing's grand strategy for the next century. With its present rate of economic growth, China will become a major importer of Middle Eastern oil in ten years.[29] Resource scarcity in the twenty-first century could see nations engaged in intense competition, confrontation, and conflict, and the navy will be called upon to protect vital sea routes. In fact, competition for resources has already provoked elbow-bashing in the region—witness, for example, the rush to extend claim and counter-claim to the oil and gas that lie under the South China Sea, Sea of Japan, East China Sea, and Central Asia. As Blainey points out, a major function of war is to "reallocate natural resources and living space, often taking them from a declining nation and allocating them to a rising nation."[30] And, China is both a rising and an expanding nation—expanding in economy, energy needs, population, military strength, national frontiers, and of course, expanding in determination. Growing demand for imported petroleum may well explain Beijing's naval interests in Burma regarding security of shipping routes through the Indian Ocean to the Straits of Malacca and the South China Sea. China's naval buildup is thus being undertaken with a view to securing the country's oil supply routes. Given the geostrategic significance of the Spratly Islands for sea-lane defense, interdiction, and surveillance, whoever dominates the Malacca Straits and South China Sea will determine the destiny of the whole region. And there is little doubt that Beijing—by developing a blue-water navy and naval bases in Burma—is positioning itself to dominate both. In addition to Burma, China plans to secure permission from other friendly countries, such as Pakistan and Iran, to establish naval bases in the Indian Ocean and the Persian Gulf.[31]

According to Wortzel, "China is embarked on a new 'Long March' to become the first among roughly equal great powers that can enjoy freedom of action through a strong military presence and posture in a neo-imperial manner. . . ."[32] China's goal more often than not is not conquest or direct control but freedom of action, dominance, and influence through coercive presence in its foreign relations. Beijing's growing economic and political ties with the outside world have not weakened the hold of traditional notions of hegemony, cultural supremacy, and sovereignty. According to a noted China-watcher, Beijing is seeking to "place itself at the top of a new hierarchical pyramid of power in the region—a kind of new 'tribute system' whereby patronage and protection is dispensed to other countries in return for their recognition of China's superiority and sensitivities. International relations scholars recognize this as a classic benevolent hegemonic system, although China adheres to a more coercive definition of hegemony (*bachuanzhuyi*)."[33]

Apparently, both geo-economic and geo-strategic calculations lie behind China's long march into Burma.

India's Concerns

History shows that peace prevails when large nation-states of the size of China and India maintain and respect buffer states between them. War erupts when one or the other continental-sized nation annexes the buffer state (as China did in Tibet in 1950) or converts it into a client state (as China seems to be doing in Burma in the 1990s). Tibet and Burma were long seen as the two buffer states between India and China. Tibet fell in the 1950s and its annexation led to a war in 1962. Will Burma also fall into China's embrace? That is the major concern of the Indian government and defense planners in the 1990s and beyond.

Given India's long adversarial relationship with China, anything that promotes China's interests in its immediate neighborhood or expands China's influence worries India. New Delhi is reportedly *not* opposed to the reopening of the old Burma Road if the only purpose is to promote trade and economic links between southwest China and South Asia.[34] What worries Indian strategists is the growing military connection between China and Burma and its implications for India's broader strategic objectives in the northern Indian Ocean region. New Delhi's desire is for a stable, neutral, and peaceful buffer state of Burma between India and China. A Tibetanization of Burma is seen as detrimental to India's security interests because Burma also provides a potential invasion route for the Chinese. The Chinese naval activity in the Bay of Bengal has dramatically soared in recent years. In August 1994, the Indian navy seized in its waters one Chinese ship equipped with modern electronic monitoring gear and three cargo vessels flying the Burmese flag with a total of fifty-five Chinese crew.[35] Though the issue was quietly resolved, it had the potential for a major flare-up. The Indian naval establishment is of the view that Burma is in danger of becoming an unwitting stalking horse for China's strategic ambitions in the Indian Ocean. Given India's growing dependence on the Persian Gulf oil and the fact that 97 percent of India's trade is carried by sea, "the Chinese presence at [India's] doorstep could be a constant irritant."[36]

Despite a thaw in Sino-Indian relations since the late 1980s, mutual suspicion and basic insecurities continue to bedevil the bilateral relationship. Of particular concern to New Delhi is the challenge China's growing economic and military power might pose for India's own aspirations for regional leadership.[37] While China has sought economic and political engagement with India, it has continued its policy of military containment and strategic encirclement of India by seeking a ring of regional strategic alliances with India's neighbors. This has involved "the building of Pakistan as a counterweight to India, employing Burma as a strategic observatory and base and gaining a foothold in India's other neighbors—Bangladesh, Nepal, and Sri Lanka."[38] In the future, the chances of an economically and militarily powerful China taking greater interest in India's neighborhood are assured, particularly if its designs are frustrated in its backyard, Southeast Asia, by Japan and/or ASEAN.

Indian analysts believe that there are only two alternatives before the Asian countries: either accept Chinese hegemony or take steps to contain and balance Chinese power. New Delhi hopes and believes that the latter alternative would be more acceptable to China's neighbors. Sooner rather than later, the region will have to evolve counterweights to China. And India, which has the size, might, and numbers of China, is seeking to maneuver itself into a dominant position in order to offer itself and, more importantly, be seen as a military counterweight to the Chinese power in Asia. After a hiatus of six years, which saw major cuts in defense spending, India has recently signed a $3 billion weapons deal with

Russia which includes Su-30 long-range fighter bombers, two Kilo-class sub-marines, and possibly the purchase of an aircraft carrier.[39]

Foreign policy analysts are now optimistic that a shared interest in containing China's growing economic and military influence would cement Indian-American, Indian-Japanese, and Indian-ASEAN ties. Indian policy makers would like New Delhi, Tokyo, Hanoi, Jakarta, and Manila to cooperate on policy toward the world's fastest-rising power. To this end, India is seeking to establish closer ties with rapid-growing East Asian countries. New Delhi has already become a member of the ASEAN Regional Forum (ARF) and has repeatedly expressed its desire to join the Asia-Pacific Economic Community (APEC). Evidence suggests that ASEAN and Japan share India's concerns about the Chinese navy's access to Burmese bases.[40] True, it will be some time before China can take full advantage of its burgeoning military ties with Burma. Monitoring sites and refueling capa-bilities in the Bay of Bengal/Malacca Straits will undoubtedly have the effect of extending China's reach into the Indian Ocean.

India's Counter-Strategy

For New Delhi, the security implications of China's arms supplies to Burma coupled with instability and insurgency movements in India's northeast, and an increase in drug trafficking on the largely unguarded Indo-Burmese border became too serious to ignore. Consequently, since early 1993 India has been pur-suing a two-pronged strategy to counteract Chinese moves.

On the one hand, there has been a significant shift in New Delhi's Burma pol-icy to counterbalance China's influence there. Much like ASEAN, New Delhi has now decided to follow a policy of "constructive engagement" with Rangoon, thus abandoning its earlier stance of isolating the Burmese military regime. A working relationship with the Burmese government is no longer seen as under-mining India's support for the "democratic aspirations of the Burmese people." From the long-term perspective, "fighting for restoration of democracy in Burma is [still seen as] a fight for India's security," but in the short term, India's strate-gy is to promote economic links both to obtain a share of the Burmese market for Indian goods, reduce Burma's economic dependence on China, end Burmese support for ethnic insurgents in northeast India, and to counter China's influ-ence.[41] The reversal in India's Burma policy since March 1993 is a clear sign that India is willing to come to terms with the SLORC without renouncing its sup-port for the pro-democracy cause.

The second prong of India's strategy is to find a complementarity of interests with those Southeast Asian countries which share New Delhi's perception of "the China threat." Historically, Southeast Asian countries have seen "the China threat" as emerging from the east through Indochina and the South China Sea. However, Chinese expansion into the Indian Ocean amounts to the opening of a new front for Southeast Asian countries in the west as well. To assuage Southeast Asian countries' fears about India's own military buildup, New Delhi has established defense ties and conducted joint naval exercises with Malaysia, Indonesia, Singapore, and the Philippines. Already, indications are that New Delhi's new "Look East" policy has paid off. A senior Indonesian military official told *Far Eastern Economic Review* that his country was "worr[ied] about the close relationship between Burma and China."[42] Jakarta, always wary of Beijing's extraterritorial ambitions, has established a joint India-Indonesia ministerial council, conducted joint naval exercises not far from Coco Island, and exchanged high-level military visits. Meanwhile, India has moved further to strengthen its military and economic ties with its old Southeast Asian ally, Vietnam. During Indian Prime Minister Narasimha Rao's visit to Vietnam in September 1994, the two sides decided to forge closer political and economic ties and signed a defense accord to cooperate in defense areas such as training and servicing Soviet-made equipment used by both countries.[43] India welcomed Vietnam's membership in ASEAN in 1995, and Burma's 1997 induction into an enlarged ASEAN as it may result in curbing the latter's dependence on China.

Interestingly, "even those ASEAN nations not traditionally close to India have been more accommodating to New Delhi in recent years."[44] Thailand is a case in point. A close ally of China during the Cambodian conflict, Bangkok is now uncomfortable with Beijing's arming of its western neighbor and the Chinese military presence in its western maritime littoral—so much so that the then Indian Prime Minister Rao is said to have raised the issue of "India as a possible strategic counterbalance to China in Asia" during talks with Chuan Leekpai, his Thai counterpart, in Bangkok in April 1993.[45] The reasons are obvious. The ethnic conflict in Burma has spilled over into Thailand, exacerbating tensions between the two countries and making the existing border dispute more difficult to resolve. The dramatic expansion of Burma's armed forces has caused concern in Bangkok where armed forces are pressing for an increased defense budget and the acquisition of submarines. In 1994, a Thai military delegation visited India and expressed an interest in purchasing military equipment. There is some evidence to suggest that the region's smaller nations, Singapore and Brunei, are also increasingly viewing India's powerful military as a useful counterweight in maintaining a geopolitical balance of power.[46]

Clearly, China's forays in Burma have brought about a strategic consensus between India and the Southeast Asian countries on the need to counter Chinese expansion into the Indian Ocean. Most observers agree that Beijing seems to be motivated more by economic reasons (i.e., the maintenance of open sea lanes of communications) and the benefit of a secure flank, and less by the need to develop a base for aggression. Whatever the case, the fact remains that in recent years Burma has moved too close to China for India's or ASEAN's comfort. It does not matter whether China's expansion is dictated by economic interests or by strategic interests. What matters is that Beijing's Burma policy is a manifestation of a Chinese *desire* to dominate both the Pacific and Indian oceans. It is also demonstration of the *potential* for Chinese naval presence in the Indian Ocean, should it ever wish to establish one in the future. The net result is that Burma, occupying as it does a critical strategic position between the two Asian giants, has become a source of friction in the Sino-Indian equation. What is more, Burma has added a maritime dimension to traditional Sino-Indian rivalry, which could have troubling implications for Southeast Asia. Even if some accounts of China's military connection with Burma are untrue, the fact that they are so easily believed in New Delhi (and in Southeast Asian capitals) despite significant improvements in bilateral relations, shows the degree of residual distrust and suspicion.

ASEAN's Dilemma: How to Turn a Pariah into a Player?

Just as China and India are closely monitoring each other, so are regional Asian neighbors who share strategic concerns over the future intentions and developments in Burma. From ASEAN's perspective, Vietnam in the southeast and Burma in the southwest serve as two pillars in shoring up the regional defenses, and as a bulwark against major power expansion in the long term. Instead of getting drawn into a strategic competition between India and China or between China and Japan, the ASEAN countries' interests lie in playing one regional power off against the other in order to maintain the delicate multipolar balance of power. Geostrategic realities also ensure that ASEAN will never ostracize Burma. Unlike outsiders, neighbors have to live with one another, forever. Arguing that ganging up on Rangoon is counterproductive, as it would push the Burmese further into China's strategic orbit, ASEAN has pursued the policy of "constructive engagement." ASEAN has sought to encourage reform in Burma by maintaining commercial and political contacts, and resisting Western pressure for sanctions. Likewise, Japan has attempted a carrot rather than stick method of enticing Rangoon away from Beijing by reopening the aid pipeline, in the form of modest grants for humanitarian purposes. New Delhi has also lent its support, belatedly though, to ASEAN's efforts to draw Burma closer into its orbit. In July 1994, Burma was invited to join the ASEAN Post-Ministerial Conference as an observer, and it signed the Treaty of Amity and Cooperation, an essential prerequisite for becoming a member of ASEAN. Vietnam was admitted into ASEAN in 1995, and Burma and Laos became full members of ASEAN in July 1997. An expanded ASEAN grouping, which includes all of the ten Southeast Asian nations, is expected to provide "a robust barrier against any greater assertiveness by China."[47] Burma and Vietnam as ASEAN member-states thus figure prominently in the regional grouping's strategy to neutralize any potential threat of "Finlandization" of Southeast Asia by a powerful China. Turning a regional pariah, Burma, into a regional player is thus the first step in that direction.

The ASEAN's "constructive engagement" policy coupled with economic difficulties and the need to assuage regional concerns about Rangoon's pro-China foreign policy orientation forced Burma's military junta to open the door to foreign investment and renew contacts with its Southeast Asian neighbors. Indonesian, Malaysian, and Singaporean leaders have paid official visits to Rangoon, and SLORC officials have visited a number of ASEAN countries as well as India. Singapore is now Burma's largest trading partner after China and among its top ten foreign investors.[48] The Burmese government has expressed its desire to align their country with the booming economies and tourist industries of southern China, Vietnam, Thailand, Malaysia, Indonesia, and India. Economically, this policy has certainly enabled the ASEAN countries to take advantage of economic opportunities (in the form of a large market for goods and investment) offered by the SLORC's economic liberalization program.

Politically, however, apart from possibly securing the release of opposition leader Aung San Suu Kyi, "constructive engagement" has produced neither national reconciliation nor the restoration of the democratic process. On the contrary, there are signs that as its hold on power becomes firmer, the military regime intends to seek greater international ties and legitimacy on its own terms. As regards ASEAN's policy of seeking the SLORC's cooperation in addressing non-military threats to regional security, such as the cross-border drug trade, smuggling, prostitution, the AIDS epidemic, and environmental problems caused by indiscriminate logging and mining, not much progress has been made. If anything, the construction of a transport infrastructure between Burma and Yunnan province has made things worse by greatly facilitating the drug and illicit goods trade, along with the burgeoning official trade between the two countries. A rapidly growing AIDS epidemic, fueled by the region's major drug and sex industries, is having an effect from India's northeastern provinces across northern Burma and into Yunnan.[49] There is no end in sight to these problems while the SLORC avoids addressing the underlying issue which caused the insurgents to take up arms in the first place and then turn to drugs—that is, the need for a pluralist and democratic regime in Rangoon.

In fact, by raising regional concerns about Burma's strategic alignment and offering some economic inducements, the SLORC has used ASEAN's "constructive engagement" policy to its own advantage.[50] The military junta has extracted significant economic and political concessions from its erstwhile critics which, in turn, has helped fuel economic growth over the last few years, and helped it entrench itself in power. The SLORC has so far withstood all the criticism and pressure. Its refusal to change its ways not only caused a rift between the ASEAN states in late 1996 that at one stage seemed to derail the controversial policy of constructive engagement, but also put ASEAN's cherished consensus diplomacy under pressure. For the first time in ASEAN history, an open split developed within ASEAN. Pro-democracy states (the Philippines and Thailand, supported from the outside by South Korea and Taiwan) cautioned against rushing Burma into ASEAN's fold and wanted Burma's induction into ASEAN made conditional on the restoration of the democratic process. Anti-democracy states (Indonesia and Malaysia) cautioned against waiting, while Singapore was somewhere in between, at times tilting toward the military regime. Also, with the domestic tensions in that country and the international attention that will accompany Burma's entry into ASEAN and the ARF, the possibility of intra-regional tensions in the future cannot be ruled out.

Burma: From Pawn to Pivot?

As noted earlier, Burma is richly endowed with vast natural and human resources, including one of the largest forest reserves in Asia and soils that once produced a considerable proportion of the world's rice. Little of its potential wealth has been exploited. This is a fact not lost upon many of its neighbors. Its size and geostrategic location mean that it certainly has the *potential* to be a key regional player. A nonaligned, neutral, democratic, and prosperous Burma will certainly be a stabilizing factor in Asia. This section addresses the problems and prospects of Burma's transformation from a pawn to a pivot. More specifically, it looks at Burma's role in regional security and Sino-Burmese relations, especially from the perspective of China-watchers and Chinese strategists, and concludes with serious doubts about Burma's ability to be an independent regional player over the short to medium term.

Burma's Options

Seen from Rangoon's perspective, too much dependence on China is not in Burma's national interests. While the Chinese embrace might ensure the SLORC's survival, it also entails significant costs. It restricts Burma's freedom of action and results in a significant dilution of national sovereignty. Burma gave obeisance to China in exchange for respect for its independence and minimal intervention in Burma's internal affairs. However, arms transfers and economic ties have dramatically increased China's influence within Burma. In fact, a few years of trade and military aid have turned the non-aligned state of Burma into China's closest ally—an objective which the three decades of Beijing-supported insurgency and Burmese Communist Party's armed struggle failed to achieve. Not surprisingly, then, dissatisfied groups have accused the SLORC strongman and powerful intelligence chief Khin Nyunt of selling out to the Chinese.[51] *Far Eastern Economic Review* has reported the growing discontent in northern Burmese towns over a massive influx of ethnic Chinese, mainly from the border province of Yunnan, who have taken over houses, hotels, and businesses and forced the local inhabitants to move to the outlying areas.[52] Burma's markets are flooded with cheap Chinese consumer goods. "Road construction in the north, private investment in north-central towns and cities, and consumer products of every sort all reflect the embrace of the classic big brother-cum-enemy."[53] Obviously, all is not well between Burma and China. Growing Burmese opposition to Chinese domination of the economy and military, the plunder of the country's raw materials, large-scale Chinese immigration, and drug trafficking on the Sino-Burmese border are sources of friction.

A major reason why the Burmese regime turned to China was that it was spurned by its Asian neighbors. Now that it is no longer spurned, attempts are underway to wean Burma away from China's influence. In the long term, Burma's strategic interests lie in counterbalancing China's influence and power through its ties with India and ASEAN. Indeed, there have been indications that the SLORC has started looking toward India as a bargaining chip in its dealings with China. The Indian Army Chief, Gen. B. C. Joshi, visited Burma in May 1994 and unconfirmed reports suggest that "Burma may even purchase some Indian weapons for its armed forces."[54] Economic liberalization policies in India and Burma are laying the foundations of stronger economic ties between the two. Both have agreed on joint economic developments on their border, to build a bridge across the river Tiau, to supply Indian electricity to several remote Burmese villages, and to take joint security measures against insurgents and drug dealers. Furthermore, sustained economic growth, greater involvement in regional affairs, and membership of ASEAN and the ARF will provide the Burmese regime with powerful leverage and strong incentives to desist from making policy choices which arouse regional concerns.

Indeed, the Burmese leadership, extremely sensitive about the country's sovereignty and independence and always suspicious of Beijing's long-term intentions, sees its current closeness with China as "a temporary measure only."[55] Rangoon cannot be happy with a situation which allows Chinese dictation of the important aspects of Burma's foreign policy. The SLORC remains adamant that it will not allow foreign troops on its soil.[56] Some critics point out that by exaggerating the *potential* Chinese threat to the region, India and ASEAN have already put pressure on the SLORC regime to modify its hardline political stance and distance itself from China.[57] Despite all the hyperbole about Chinese incursions into the Indian Ocean, objective observers concede that given the limited amphibious, sea endurance, and sealift capabilities of China's navy to perform sustained operations in the Indian Ocean, China still has a long way to go before it can even think of dominating the Indian Ocean. The lack of supply ships and poor Burmese infrastructure also mean that such naval operations will be logistically difficult for a similar period. In the short to medium term, the South China Sea will remain the focus of the Chinese navy. At most, only a symbolic presence of the Chinese navy in the Indian Ocean can be expected over the next five to ten years.

The continuation of the political status quo within Burma also cannot be taken for granted. Aung San Suu Kyi and the remnants of the NLD continue to focus international media attention toward the SLORC's lack of a popular mandate. Remote though it may seem, one cannot rule out the possibility of the SLORC being overthrown by a popular movement for a democratic regime. In the information age, days of authoritarian, militaristic regimes are numbered. The ever-shrinking ranks of authoritarian regimes in Asia show that time is on the side of democratic forces worldwide. Political changes in Rangoon in the near future, for example the coming to power of an Aung San Suu Kyi-led democratic government, could also lead to a situation where China is denied access to the very naval facilities it is now building.

For its part, ASEAN needs to consider whether the time has come to replace the policy of "constructive engagement" with "comprehensive engagement"— one which seeks to engage the SLORC as well as the Burmese opposition forces. "Comprehensive engagement" would also offer the Burmese regime the opportunity to develop a fuller range of diplomatic, security, and economic contacts with Asian and Western countries. It would not only be able to seek new trading, investment, and financing opportunities in the West and East, but also develop a more balanced policy toward China and India.

If all these conditions are met, and that is indeed a big "if," the destabilizing implications of Burma's recent pro-Beijing tilt in foreign policy can be contained and managed. However, events over the last two years do not lend much confidence to the SLORC's ability to walk a fine line on issues of national and international importance. Aung San Suu Kyi is quoted as saying that the SLORC leaders "are like a chess player who only thinks one or two moves ahead."[58] This assessment is reinforced by Lee Kuan Yew, Singapore's elder statesman, who has been active in the growing commercial relations between Singapore and Rangoon. He said, "ASEAN cannot rescue Burma even if it wants to, and I have the awful feeling rescuing Burma is beyond the capacity of even the United States."[59] Given Burma's dependence on China for the military hardware, training, spare parts, financial assistance, and industrial equipment, Beijing can apply considerable pressure on the regime, be it military or civilian, to prevent its defection from China's camp. ASEAN's "constructive engagement" policy notwithstanding, China still remains Burma's main trading partner, arms supplier, and a steadfast supporter in international fora.

Chinese Checkers

I believe questions about Burma's future role in regional security cannot be answered satisfactorily without a proper understanding of Burma's place in China's grand strategy for the twenty-first century. China aspires to become the unchallenged and unrivaled superpower of the Asia-Pacific region. It is also destined to become the world's biggest economy well before the twenty-first century reaches its midpoint. This will make China a genuine global great power— something that the former Soviet Union never was. As such, it will exercise enormous influence on the international stage, most notably on its Asian neighbors and its major trading partners. Even when it was weak, China always played a hard game whenever its interests were threatened. In its territorial disputes, the political, military, and economic pressure that China is prepared to apply discomforts neighbors such as India, Vietnam, the Philippines, Malaysia, Indonesia, and Japan. Beijing will not abandon or compromise its claims to the Spratlys, Senkaku, and Taiwan, nor its hopes for a leading role in Southeast Asia, a decisive role in Northeast Asia, and a military presence in the Indian Ocean. And when it can dominate the whole Asia-Pacific region on its own, China has no intention of sharing the leadership role in either of these subregions with any other power, whether the United States, Japan, or India.[60] This could result in great power rivalry and competition in Asia which may not be much different from the U.S.-Soviet rivalry of the Cold War years. If China steps into the shoes of the erstwhile "evil empire," it is likely, over time, to precipitate a split within ASEAN into pro-China and anti-China states. Even if China plays by internationally-accepted rules of the game, a wealthy and powerful China will assert itself in world affairs as every other powerful nation has done because being a superpower is essentially about dominance, and the projection of power and influence.

Sooner rather than later, Beijing's quest for superpower status will pit it against Tokyo's ambitions for a status-quo in Northeast and Southeast Asia. China's rapid rise as an economic and military power will force Japan in the not-so-distant future to assume a greater security role by taking a keen interest in multilateral security processes and forming bilateral defense agreements with other nations in the Asia-Pacific region. A similar contest between China and India over dominating South and Central Asia, Burma, and the northern Indian Ocean (Malacca Straits) will intensify in the early part of the twenty-first century. Any move by China to prosecute more forcefully its maritime claims in the South China Sea or extend its reach into the Indian Ocean via Burma will force the Japanese to seek cooperation with ASEAN and India to counter China.

China's rise as a great power has already resulted in shifting alignments and a reorientation of the regional balance of power in Asia. Figure 6-1 shows the overall orientation of Asian countries vis-à-vis China on a ten-point scale from one (pro-China) to ten (anti-China). History shows that new, fast-rising great powers usually have very few friends and China is no exception to this rule. There has been a continuous decline in the number of pro-China states since the end of the Cold War. China's emergence as a superpower will make it very difficult for its Asian neighbors to stay neutral. India, Indonesia, Vietnam, the Philippines, Japan, the United States, and Australia are all deeply suspicious of China's motives, and, to varying degrees, appear willing to attempt to limit China's influence in the Asia-Pacific region. In fact, an informal anti-Chinese coalition has already started to take shape: a reaffirmation of the U.S.-Japan security alliance, the Sydney Declaration on Australia-U.S. alliance in 1996, the Australia-Indonesia security agreement, Vietnam's membership of ASEAN, and India's membership of the ASEAN Regional Forum in 1995, have all helped to counter China's influence and power.

Beijing views any formal alliance (such as between the United States and Australia or Japan) or any tacit alliance (such as between ASEAN and India or Japan) as a threat to its security, and it is determined to take countermeasures. China is seeking to establish a balance of power favorable to its national inter-

Figure 6-1. China's Rise and the Shifting Balance of Power in the Asia-Pacific Region

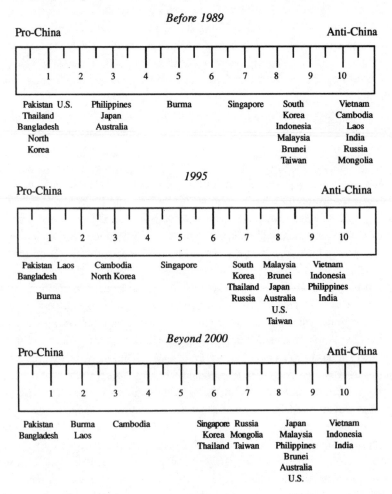

Before 1989

Pro-China   Anti-China

| 1 | 2 | 3 | 4 | 5 | 6 | 7 | 8 | 9 | 10 |

Pakistan U.S.	Philippines	Burma		Singapore	South		Vietnam
Thailand	Japan				Korea		Cambodia
Bangladesh	Australia				Indonesia		Laos
North					Malaysia		India
Korea					Brunei		Russia
					Taiwan		Mongolia

1995

Pro-China   Anti-China

| 1 | 2 | 3 | 4 | 5 | 6 | 7 | 8 | 9 | 10 |

Pakistan Laos	Cambodia	Singapore		South	Malaysia	Vietnam
Bangladesh	North Korea			Korea	Brunei	Indonesia
				Thailand	Japan	Philippines
Burma				Russia	Australia	India
					U.S.	
					Taiwan	

Beyond 2000

Pro-China   Anti-China

| 1 | 2 | 3 | 4 | 5 | 6 | 7 | 8 | 9 | 10 |

Pakistan	Burma	Cambodia		Singapore Russia	Japan	Vietnam
Bangladesh	Laos			Korea Mongolia	Malaysia	Indonesia
				Thailand Taiwan	Philippines	India
					Brunei	
					Australia	
					U.S.	

ests, and therefore actively dangling the carrot of economic, military, and diplomatic support to bring Asian countries closer to its world view. This inevitably involves an expansion of its political and military influence and footholds in countries stretching from Pakistan to Burma to Laos. China's interest in staking out a presence in Burma, and thereby on the Indian Ocean, is based on an assessment of China's strategic needs in the twenty-first century. As Lintner observes: "The Chinese have keyed the development of their outlying regions both in terms of economic development and security concerns to establishing symbiotic relations with adjacent territories."[61] The strategic context in which China views its relationship with Burma is as a client state both for southward expansion and to counteract the moves of its rival powers. China has also encouraged the Burmese military to develop closer ties with Pakistan. Strategic alliances with Pakistan in the southwest and Burma in the southeast constitute the linchpin of Beijing's strategy which serves two key objectives. One, it ties New Delhi down south of the Himalayas in order to prevent India's rise as a real rival to China. Two, through its friends and allies like Burma and Laos within ASEAN, Beijing can thwart the evolution of ASEAN into an anti-China or pro-Japan regional grouping.

Furthermore, China's and other Asian countries' dependence on the Middle East for energy needs is rapidly deepening. The geopolitical implications of closer economic interdependence between the volatile Middle East and dynamic Asia could be unsettling, to say the least. This means that the sea lanes from East Asia to the Gulf, together with such intermediate states along that path as Burma, are assuming increasing strategic importance.[62] The growing energy needs of Asian economies can be used both as an instrument of coercion and as a means of consolidating regional dominance. As Bodansky explains: "By controlling and facilitating the availability of oil/gas, Beijing will be able to coerce the Pacific Rim states into recognizing Beijing's hegemony and leadership, as well as supporting China's economic development."[63] To this end, Beijing has been coordinating efforts with Iran, Pakistan, the Central Asian republics, and Burma to ensure dominance and control over energy resources in the event of a regional conflict or an energy crisis worldwide. Therefore, the important role that allies like Pakistan and Burma will play in fulfilling China's ambitions of regional supremacy and in thwarting the ambitions of China's rival powers should not be underestimated.

Clearly, Beijing has taken advantage of Rangoon's isolation to satisfy its own great power ambitions, particularly its desire to counter India in the Indian Ocean and the approaches to the South China Sea, and to ensure the control of vital sea lanes by drawing Burma tightly into its sphere of influence. From China's perspective, Burma should be satisfied to gain a powerful friend, a permanent member of the UN Security Council, and an economic giant, who comes bearing gifts of much needed military hardware. Since influence over Burma is the key to China's future strategy for South and Southeast Asia, Beijing can be expected to use all means available to keep Burma within its orbit. Clearly, Beijing did not provide diplomatic protection, arms, aid, and finance—all on very generous terms—to the SLORC in its hour of need for nothing. China's prospects for economic growth depend on finding raw materials, markets for its goods, and investment for its economy. Self-interest motivated the Chinese to use their influence in cutting off aid to the Burmese rebels in an effort to gain better access to the resource-rich border region and accompanying trade benefits.

Proximity and complementarity also work in China's favor. China needs Burma's raw materials, timber, and minerals. At the same time, it offers cheap consumer goods, machinery, electronics, textile products, light manufactures, and capital goods that fit Burma's level of development and spending power. Tens of thousands of Chinese are moving into northern Burma every year. If Burma's attempts to steer an even-handed course undermine China's economic and security interests in the region, Beijing could even threaten to resume assistance to ethnic insurgents fighting for independence on the Sino-Burmese border. China has a reputation for using threats and bluff to force other states (friends and foes alike) to accede to its will. With the weight of cash and population on the Chinese side, it is likely that first capital transfers and then population transfers will keep Burma highly dependent on its northern neighbor. By choice or by necessity, Sino-Burmese trade relations are going to follow a pattern of Chinese domination.

Finally, ideological affinity between the two may also act as a constraint on Burma's future policy options. The ruling junta's world view is influenced and shaped by its ties to the old men of Beijing. Both have a siege mentality and adhere to the nineteenth-century notion of state sovereignty. Both remain strongly opposed to political pluralism in any form. The SLORC's bloodbath when it seized power in 1988 was matched, less than a year later, by the Tiananmen massacre in June 1989. Leaders in both countries combine appeals to nationalism and xenophobia with "cultural" arguments that claim, unpersuasively, that Asians are not receptive to Western-style concepts of human rights and democracy. To further consolidate its hold over power, the SLORC-dominated constituent assembly has adopted guidelines which grant the military "a leading role in the future political life of the state," and eliminate the possibility that Aung San Suu Kyi could hold office.[64] It may not be in China's interests to see Burma becoming a liberal-democratic state. China is already encircled by a large number of democratic states such as Russia, Mongolia, South Korea, Japan, Taiwan, the Philippines, Thailand, Nepal, and India. At the most, it would wish to see another Pakistan-like quasi-democratic state where civilians hold power so long as the military tolerates them. China would also prefer a Burmese military that is xenophobic and, therefore, remains heavily dependent on China for weapons, training, and support. According to noted China-watchers, politically subservient, weak, and compliant regimes on its borders add to Beijing's sense of security because most Chinese strategists believe that "China is more secure if other states are weaker and thus less secure."[65]

A realistic assessment of China's strategic and economic needs and Burma's predicament shows that Beijing is unlikely to easily give up what it has already gained in Burma. The increasing Chinese domination of northern Burma's economy has cultural, economic, security, and political repercussions. China's neighbors know too well that Beijing's bark can be worse than its bite. As Shambaugh observes: "Beijing is a ruthless and hard bargainer that intensely guards its sense of sovereignty and national interests. It bends only when the *quid pro quo* is financially worthwhile (such as reform policies that bring World Bank and IMF loans) or when the penalties of not compromising or complying are unacceptably high."[66] It is obvious that over the next five to ten years at least, neither the SLORC, ASEAN, India, Japan, nor the United States is capable of imposing "unacceptably high" penalties or offering "financially worthwhile" rewards sufficient to make Beijing give up what it has already acquired in and through Burma. Even a Burma optimist like Selth seems to agree: "The transition back to a more neutral and economically independent Burma will be neither quick nor easy, *particularly if this shift is opposed by China*. The latter's hold over Burma is already strong, and its strategic weight is steadily increasing as its economy grows and its defense forces are modernized. Also, *the bilateral relationship is developing a life of its own*, and is already affecting areas which may be beyond either the SLORC's, or China's, ability to control."[67]

Over the long term though (that is, beyond 2010), as China changes, Burma's political and economic standing improves, Burma's economy becomes more integrated with ASEAN's, and as regional organizations evolve into an effective multilateral security forum, Rangoon could find greater freedom of action and move slightly farther away from Beijing. But it still would not go very far for fear of antagonizing the superpower on its doorstep (see figure 6-1). This means that given its role in China's grand strategy for the next century, Burma is unlikely to play the role of an independent or pivotal player in regional security affairs.

Notes

1. Andrew Selth, "Burma: 'Hidden Paradise' or Paradise Lost," *Current Affairs Bulletin* (Sydney), LXVIII (1991), 4–11; P. Stobdan, "China's Forays into Burma: Implications for India," *Strategic Analysis* (New Delhi), XVI (1993), 21-38; David Steinberg, "Myanmar as Nexus: Sino-Indian Rivalries on the Frontier," *Studies in Conflict and Terrorism*, XIV (1993); J. Mohan Malik, "Sino-Indian Rivalry in Myanmar: Implications for Regional Security," *Contemporary Southeast Asia*, XVI (1994) 137–155; "China-India Relations in the Post-Soviet Era: The Continuing Rivalry," *The China Quarterly*, CXLII (1995) 317–355.

2. Some Burma watchers may not approve of the use of the term "pawn" to describe the recent pro-China tilt in Burmese foreign policy. However, the fact remains that Burma's neighbors do see

the SLORC as a Chinese puppet and, in international relations, perceptions are more important than realities.

3. Andrew Selth, "Burma and the Strategic Competition between China and India," *Journal of Strategic Studies*, XIX (1996), 213.

4. Ibid., 226.

5. Ibid., 214. Also see William Ashton, "Burma's Chemical Weapons Status," *Jane's Intelligence Review* [hereafter *JIR*], VII (1993), 284; Bertil Lintner, "Burma: Centrifugal Forces," *Far Eastern Economic Review* [hereafter *FEER*], (27 February 1992), 16.

6. William Ashton, "Chinese Bases in Burma—Fact or Fiction," *JIR*, VII (1995), 84.

7. Stobdan, "China's Forays into Burma," 35; Bertil Lintner, "Burma: Arms for Eyes," *FEER* (16 December 1993), 26.

8. Ashton, "Burma's Chemical Weapons Status," 284.

9. Bertil Lintner, *Burma in Revolt: Opium and Insurgency since 1948* (Boulder, 1994), 314–329. Also see Stobdan, "China's Forays into Burma," 25, 27.

10. Lintner, *Burma in Revolt*, 84.

11. *FEER* (28 November 1991), 11.

12. Selth, "Burma: 'Hidden Paradise' or Paradise Lost," 7.

13. *Jane's Defence Weekly* [hereafter *JDW*] reported that "about 70 Chinese personnel have been attached to the Burmese Navy as instructors and technicians. China is helping to build a new naval base at Hainggyi Island and to upgrade facilities at Sittwe (Akyab), Mergui, and Great Coco Island." See *JDW* (27 November 1993), 11.

14. Tai Ming Cheung, "Smoke Signals," *FEER* (12 November 1992), 29–30; William Ashton, "Chinese Naval Base: Many Rumors, Few Facts," *Asia-Pacific Defence Reporter* [hereafter *A-PDR*], (June-July 1993), 25.

15. Bertil Lintner, "Chinese Arms Bolster Burmese Forces," *JDW* (27 November 1993), 11. "An agreement has reportedly been reached with Burma that will allow PLA naval vessels 'facilities' at Burmese ports." See Clare Hollingworth, "Japan's Defence Worries Grow," *A-PDR* (April-May 1994), 9–10.

16. Nirmal Mitra, "Coming Closer," *Sunday* (Calcutta), (23–29 August 1992), 59. Emphasis added.

17. Surjit Mansingh, "An Overview of India-China Relations: From When to Where," *Indian Defence Review* (New Delhi), (April 1993), 75.

18. Hamish McDonald, "Mutual Benefits," *FEER* (3 February 1994), 14.

19. Stobdan, "China's Forays into Burma;" Daljit Singh, "The Eastern Neighbour: Myanmar," *Indian Defence Review*, (October 1992), 29–35.

20. As is their wont, the Chinese vehemently deny that they are "up to anything" whenever ASEAN and Indian leaders and officials have raised the topic of Chinese arms flows into Burma and the buildup of naval facilities. See *Sunday* (23–29 August 1992), 58–59. Also see Jeffrey Parker, "Top-Level Visit from China Triggers Navy Buildup Fear," *The Age* (Melbourne) (27 December 1994), 14; *FEER* (16 September 1993), 13.

21. Stobdan, "China's Forays into Burma," 34; Ashton, "Chinese Naval Base: Many Rumors, Few Facts," 25.

22. The *Economist* (23 January 1993), 27.

23. Bertil Lintner, "Rangoon's Rubicon," *FEER* (11 February 1993), 28.

24. See Chu Ko-Chien et al, "China's National Security in the Year 2000," in Larry M. Wortzel, "China Pursues Traditional Great-Power Status," *Orbis*, XXXVIII (1994), 164. Gen. Li Jiulong, commander of China's Chengddu military region, which is the command headquarters and major supply base for Chinese troops in Tibet, visited Burma's naval facilities in July 1994 and reportedly pressured Rangoon to allow greater Chinese access to three islands off the Burmese coast for signals intelligence—Ramree Island south of Sittwe in Western Arakan state, Coco Island in the Indian Ocean, and Zadetkyi Kyun or St. Matthew's Island off the Tenasserim coast in the southeast, which

is close to the northern entrance to the Straits of Malacca. See "Snooping Around," *FEER* (4 August 1994), 12.

25. Wortzel, "China Pursues Traditional Great-Power Status," 161–162; Desmond Ball, "Arms and Affluence: Military Acquisitions in the Asia-Pacific Region," *International Security,* XVIII (1993/94), 87.

26. Ye Zhengjia, "India's Foreign Policy in Restructuring International Relations," *International Studies* [Guoji Wenti], III (1992). A banned Chinese book authored by a serving PLA official sees the United States, India, Vietnam, and Taiwan as potential military enemies. *Weekend Australian* (20-21 November 1993), 16.

27. "China's Plan to Buildup Navy," *Hindustan Times* (13 January 1993), 14. Also see *Time* (10 May 1993), 39.

28. "Beijing Expands its Navy," *Inside China Mainland* (Taiwan), (April 1993), 67. Emphasis added. At a seminar at the Australian National University in May 1991, Hua Di, a Chinese strategist, said that China cannot claim to be a truly global superpower unless it has the capability to dominate two oceans, the Pacific and the Indian. He argued that the cases of the Soviet Union and the United States show that to be a superpower, an essential prerequisite is the ability to dominate at least two oceans—the Atlantic and the Pacific.

29. Several articles on the energy needs of China and Asia have concluded recently that China's thirst for oil will turn its attention to the Middle East and Southeast Asia, and this turn will become a source of potential Asian conflict in the coming decades. Martin Walker, "China and the New Era of Resource Scarcity," *World Policy Journal*, XIII (1996), 8–14; Mamdouh G. Salameh, "China, Oil and the Risk of Regional Conflict," *Survival*, XXXVII (1995–96), 133–146; Kent E. Calder, "Asia's Empty Tank," *Foreign Affairs*, LXXV (1996), 55–69; Yossef Bodansky, "Asia Prepares for a New Energy Crisis," *Defense & Foreign Affairs Strategic Policy*, (June-July 1996), 1, 8; Michael Richardson, "Oil Lies at the Bottom of China-Japan Dispute over Islands," *International Herald Tribune* (17 September 1996), 4.

30. Geoffrey Blainey, "Past and Future Wars," in Ramesh Thakur (ed.), *International Conflict Resolution* (Boulder, 1988), 98.

31. *South China Morning Post* (9 March 1993), 10.

32. Wortzel, "China Pursues Traditional Great-Power Status," 158, 159.

33. David Shambaugh, "Containment or Engagement of China?" *International Security*, XXI (1996), 187.

34. Jasjit Singh, "Future of Sino-Indian Relations," *Strategic Analysis*, XVI (March 1994), 1512.

35. Bertil Lintner, "Burma: Enter the Dragon," *FEER* (22 December 1994), 23.

36. Ruben Banerjee, "China: Worrying Approach," and Sunil Dasgupta, "The Navy: In Troubled Waters," *India Today* (30 April 1994), 70–71.

37. C. Uday Bhaskar, "Role of China in the Emerging World Order," *Strategic Analysis*, XVI (1993), 3–19; Singh, "Future of Sino-Indian Relations," 1509.

38. Brahma Chellaney, "The Dragon's Chicanery behind the Smile," *Pioneer* (New Delhi) (23 October 1996), 7; Timothy Mapes, "Nervous Neighbours," *FEER* (12 December 1996), 16–17.

39. "Major Defence Deal with Moscow on the Anvil," *Indian Express* (14 November 1996), 1.

40. "China's Buildup Draws Japan's Attention," *Aviation Week & Space Technology* (5 August 1996), 25. Japanese officials told *FEER* that "they are particularly concerned over the presence of the Chinese near Mergui, some 400 kilometers north of Penang and the entrance to the Strait of Malacca." See Bertil Lintner, "Burma: Arms for Eyes," *FEER* (16 December 1993), 26; Clare Hollingworth, "Japan's Defence Worries Grow," A-PDR, (April-May 1994), 9–10.

41. Stobdan, "China's Forays into Burma," 37; Rita Manchanda, "Reasons of State," *FEER* (6 May 1993), 12.

42. *FEER* (3 March 1994), 27.

43. Just as the Chinese routinely stress the fact that their military ties with India's South Asian

neighbors are not aimed at any third parties, an Indian official also pointed out that the Indo-Vietnamese defense pact "is very low-key, and it's not aimed at any third parties" (read, China). See "Liaison Agreed over Defence," *South China Morning Post* (8 September 1994), 18.

44. Sandy Gordon, "South Asia after the Cold War," *Asian Survey*, XXXV (1995), 889. Michael Richardson, "China's Push for Sea Control Angers ASEAN," *Australian* (23 July 1996), 6; "China-Burma Ties Upset Neighbors," *International Herald Tribune* (7 April 1995), 4.

45. *FEER* (22 April 1993), 9.

46. See M. Ohashi and J. Takanosu, "Southeast Asians Eye Western Frontier," *Nikkei Weekly* (17 May 1993), 24; Ranjan Gupta, "Singapore Buys Indian Protection as Old Friendships Cool," *Australian* (7 February 1994), 14.

47. Gordon, "South Asia after the Cold War," 890.

48. Bertil Lintner, "The Road to Mandalay," *FEER* (14 April 1994), 7.

49. Selth, "Burma and the Strategic Competition between China and India," 227.

50. See William Ashton, "Charm Offensive Working," *A-PDR*, XXI (1995 Annual Reference Edition), 41–42.

51. Bertil Lintner, "Murmur in the Ranks," *FEER* (16 February 1993), 20.

52. *FEER* (6 May 1993), 9.

53. Badgley, "Myanmar in 1993," 158.

54. Cited from Selth, "Burma and the Strategic Competition between China and India," 226.

55. Ibid., 224.

56. "Myanmar and China: But Will the Flag Follow Trade?" The *Economist* (8 October 1994), 32.

57. Ashton, "Chinese Naval Base: Many Rumors, Few Facts," 25; Sandy Gordon, "Sino-Indian Relations after the Cold War," *SDSC Newsletter* (Canberra) (March 1993), 1,4.

58. Aung San Suu Kyi quoted in "A New Game in Myanmar," The *Economist* (1 June 1996), 27.

59. Lee Kuan Yew, quoted by R. Tasker, "Fear of Loathing: ASEAN Keeps Soft Line on Rangoon Junta," *FEER* (20 June 1996).

60. See Greg Sheridan, "Caught in the Middle," *Weekend Australian* (16–17 November 1996), 25. Sheridan writes: "China wants the United States military out of Asia, according to a new U.S. assessment of Beijing's intentions."

61. Lintner, "Burma: Enter the Dragon," 23.

62. Kent Calder, "The Power of Seven," *Australian* (16 July 1996), 23.

63. Bodansky, "Asia Prepares for a New Energy Crisis," 1, 8. According to Li Desheng, a Chinese geologist, China's oil reserves will last only another twenty years.

64. Mary P. Callahan, "Burma in 1995," *Asian Survey*, XXXVI (1996), 159.

65. Banning N. Garrett and Bonnie S. Glaser, "Chinese Perspectives on Nuclear Arms Control," *International Security*, XX (1995/96), 75.

66. Shambaugh, "Containment or Engagement of China?" 207.

67. Selth, "Burma and the Strategic Competition between China and India," 226. Emphasis added.

CHAPTER 7

Ethnicity and Civil War in Burma
Where Is the Rationality?

Ananda Rajah

BURMA HAS the unenviable reputation of having the largest number of ethnic insurgencies together with one of the longest-running communist insurgencies of any country in the world. To say that it is a "country" is also to imply that it is a "state" but these insurgencies indicate that it is less of a state than the term conventionally suggests. It is only a state in the juridical rather than empirical sense.[1] To put it another way, it is a "weak" state because the very institutions of the state are contested to the point of violence, to use Buzan's criterion, and the state is distinguished by "contingent sovereignty" rather than absolute sovereignty.[2]

The civil war in Burma erupted almost immediately after Burma gained independence from the British in 1948 with the Communist Party of Burma (CPB) electing to go underground while ethno-nationalist movements, such as the Karen, resorted to armed conflict in order to pursue their goal of self-rule. They opposed the Burman nationalist aim of a unitary state.

Ethnic insurgent movements continued to proliferate in ensuing years, fueled by Prime Minister U Nu's attempt in 1960 to make Buddhism the state religion. The military's enforcement of a unitary state after seizing power from U Nu in 1962 further fueled the ethnic insurgencies. It is ironic that one of the justifications the military advanced for seizing state power was to quell ethnic unrest and save the state from dissolution.

The political and economic mismanagement of Burma under the military regime, especially during the years of Gen. Ne Win's "Burmese Way to

Socialism," culminated in a massive pro-democracy uprising in 1988, a political watershed in the post-colonial history of Burma. Political life in Burma was never the same again. Although the uprising was brutally crushed by the State Law and Order Restoration Council (SLORC), the junta which constituted itself in reaction to the uprising, that suppression has immeasurably complicated the civil war in Burma. Ethnic Burmans, constituting an incipient civil society united by, if nothing else, a shared alienation from the military regime, have now found common cause with the ethnic insurgents, though not the communist movement. The number of ethnic insurgent movements and ethnic Burman opposition groups in existence in 1989 attests to the indisputable empirical fragility of Burma as a state. There were twenty-five such organizations whose strength varied considerably.[3]

One of the tragedies of the 1988 crackdown on democracy activists was the spawning of a new ethnically based insurgent group, the Chin National Front (CNF). It consisted mostly of students enrolled in urban high schools and institutions of higher learning. Through their day-to-day contact with ethnic Burman and other students, Chin students came to share an antipathy toward the military regime. After the crackdown, however, the students dispersed, with the majority seeking refuge with the Karen. The Chin students, on the other hand, went north to seek support from the Mizos in Mizoram (eastern India), assuming that they would be welcomed on account of ethnolinguistic affinity. They received only moral support and thus turned to the Kachin Independence Organization and Army for military training.[4]

Almost immediately after the implosion of the Communist Party in 1989, the SLORC launched an unexpected initiative. It successfully sought out cease-fire agreements with the breakaway Kokang and Wa factions of the Communist Party. These agreements were followed by similar agreements with other ethnic insurgents and by the end of 1995, the only insurgents who had not entered into cease-fire agreements with the SLORC were the Karen and Mon. The unity of the Karen resistance was broken, however, with Buddhist Karen insurgents capitulating to the SLORC and turning on their mainly Christian former comrades-in-arms. The Mon were dispersed by a massive Burmese military presence related to the construction of a gas pipeline from the Yadana gas fields into Thailand. The New Mon State Party (NMSP) subsequently entered into a cease-fire agreement with the SLORC. Also noteworthy was the capitulation of Khun Sa, the commander-in-chief of the Mong Tai Army, in January 1996.

The military regime has, since the mid-1980s, shown a remarkable ability to react to changing situations; it currently retains the initiative in the civil war. This has been made possible by a sustained military buildup beginning in 1988.

Nevertheless, it has not brought the conflict to a conclusive end. The current situation remains enormously complex. Despite the cease-fires with the SLORC, the various insurgent movements have expressed support for Daw Aung San Suu Kyi and a willingness to work with her political party, the National League for Democracy (NLD). There is, however, an unresolved issue: while the insurgents favor a federal system, Aung San Suu Kyi has not indicated whether or not she believes that such a system represents an acceptable solution to Burma's political problems.

The protracted social conflict as well as the political conditions in Burma which led to the emergence of ethnic conflict and civil war have been the subject of very thorough and systematic studies.[5] This chapter focuses on hitherto unconsidered aspects of ethnic insurgency and civil war in Burma. The Shan and Karen insurgencies provide two cases.

An Absence of Rationality?

One of the most perplexing aspects of the post-colonial history of ethnic conflict in Burma is the contradictions, inconsistencies, and paradoxes which have characterized the positions and actions of the various ethnic insurgents. Examples include the existence of different insurgent movements which have strenuously avoided unifying themselves while claiming to represent the same ethnic group, the existence of ethno-nationalist insurgent leaders whose ancestries are known to be ethnically mixed, the frequent and bewildering changes of name of many of these movements, their factionalism and fissioning, the alliances between erstwhile enemies (e.g. insurgent with insurgent, insurgents with the military regime) resulting in improbable arrangements in the political economy of insurgency and the state, and the failure of the ethnic insurgents to establish a durable, united front against their common foe, the military regime which has ruled Burma since 1962.[6] Running throughout is a common thread: the goal of a federal state on the part of most insurgent movements and the insistence by the military on a unitary state.

The military regime itself has not been free of contradictions and inconsistencies either. Among the more bizarre are the demonetizations of the kyat in 1964, 1985, and 1987. The military regime first demonetized 100 and 50 kyat notes, replacing them with new notes of similar denominations, following the nationalization of banks in 1964. This wiped out the savings of ordinary people and contributed to a new wave of ethnic uprisings.[7] In 1985, the 100 and 50 kyat notes were again demonetized and replaced with 15, 45, and 75 kyat notes, once more wiping out private savings. In 1987, military rulers demonetized 25, 45, and 75 kyat notes, and introduced a 90 kyat note. The government justified these measures on the grounds that they were necessary to break the black market economy of the insurgents and black marketeers.[8] It is widely believed in Burma that policies were based on numero-astrological calculations important to Ne Win. The 75 kyat note was introduced on his seventy-fifth birthday while the number nine was said to be his lucky number, thus giving rise to the belief that the timing of significant events was based on a "sum-of-nine" formula. This formula apparently underlay even the scheduling of major national events such as the 1990 elections which were held on May 27, the fourth Sunday of the fifth month.[9] These patterns seem to defy rational explanation.

Although these contradictions and inconsistencies are evident, and in some cases well documented in existing studies, they have not received the analytical attention that they deserve. This oversight may be attributed, generally, to approaches in the analysis of ethnic conflict which place considerable importance on nationalism and ethno-nationalism in relation to post-colonial nation-state formation. Such approaches have produced understandings of the politicization of ethnicity, ethnic relations, and civil war in Burma, but these understandings are incomplete as long as they contain unexplained contradictions.[10] At first glance, these contradictions may appear to be partly ideological and partly the consequence of pragmatic strategies. A sociological and anthropological perspective suggests, however, that the contradictions reflect more fundamental conditions—social, economic, and political—and related modes of thought. In considering ethnic conflict in relation to the political and economic reconstruction of Burma, it is important to understand how the actors involved *think* about their problems. As Hildred and Clifford Geertz once said, "a way of seeing is also a way of not seeing."[11]

The Shan and Factionalism

Shan State has been one of the most troubled in Burma. The absence of civil order and the conflicts in the state following independence involved a complex intermeshing of ethnic insurgencies with the struggle of the Communist Party of Burma, the activities of Kuomintang forces with American, Taiwanese, and Thai support, and opium trading. Apart from being motivated by a mixture of ethno-nationalism and a sense of having been betrayed by the British, the Shan insurgencies began with the actions of government forces sent to contain the Kuomintang troops (1948–52), which alienated the Shan populace.

Brutalization of civilians (whether non-Burman or Burman) by the Burmese armed forces has been systematic. This brutalization has been standard operating procedure in various areas (e.g. Karen, Mon, and Arakan states) in more recent times. It has been well-documented by various groups such as Amnesty International, the Karen Human Rights Group under Kevin Heppner, the Southeast Asia Information Network, and EarthRights International.[12]

There were several insurgent groups which claimed to represent the Shan: the Noom Suk Harn established in 1958; the Shan State Independence Army (SSIA) in 1960; the Shan National United Front (SNUF) in 1961; the Thailand National Army (TNA) in 1963; the Shan State Army (SSA); the Shan State Progress Party (SPP); the Shan United Army (SUA, set up by Khun Sa); the Shan United Revolutionary Army (SURA); the Tailand Revolutionary Army (TRA); and the Mong Tai Army (MTA) subsequently established by Khun Sa.

Despite attempts, from time to time, to form a Shan united front against the military regime, these efforts were remarkable for their failures rather than successes. According to Chao Tzang Yawnghwe, a Shan exile, the failure of the Shan insurgencies to unify themselves was the product of a complex structure of interests (including non-political ethnic Chinese business interests involved in arms and opium trafficking), the invidious pursuit of power on the part of some insurgent leaders, an absence of rational political approaches, and the policies of division and co-optation on the part of the Burmese military regime.[13]

Chao Tzang attempted to rationalize the SSA and organize the First Military Region as a quasi-state run along rational, bureaucratic lines. His account of that effort is significant because it highlights the ubiquity in insurgent areas of "premodern-non-rational" modes of thought and political control. Chao Tzang received a modern, secular education at Rangoon University and applied it in a spirit of bureaucratic rationality and zeal. Perhaps even more important, Chao Tzang spoke hardly any Shan, at least in the beginning when he first went underground, and this must have profoundly influenced his ideas about the shape of Shan nationalism.[14]

Khun Sa, who began mobilizing the Shan in 1962, is part Chinese and part Shan.[15] Smith records that Khun Sa's family migrated to Loimaw in Shan state from China in the eighteenth century.[16] The Shan population is ethnically mixed. To say that it is ethnically mixed is not to assert, however, that it consists of Shan and Chinese with occasional intermarriage between the two, which is our present understanding. Smith seems to say the situation amounts to a form of "creolization" brought about by long-term historical contact between the two, with significant demographic and cultural consequences.

Khun Sa's stepfather was Myoza (literally "town eater" in Burmese) of

Loimaw, Muang Yai, Shan State. According to Chao Tzang, after the coup by Ne Win in 1962, Khun Sa turned against Rangoon and formed the Anti-Socialist United Party. In 1963, the Burmese military allowed Khun Sa and his Loimaw followers to retain their arms, and police and tax local trade as long as they did not join the separatists.[17] This was part of the military regime's more general policy to co-opt local bosses and militias to assist in the maintenance of local law and order. The local trade came to include opium trafficking in the 1970s and 1980s which also involved members of the Burmese military in, for example, the 99th Light Infantry Division.[18] In 1973, however, Khun Sa's militia took on Shan nationalist colors and named (or renamed) itself the SUA.

Khun Sa was captured in 1970 and released in 1973. He did not immediately return to the SUA; instead he regularly commuted between Rangoon and Mandalay on business and acted as a middle-man acquiring jade, rubies, and other precious stones for Burmese military officers. He left Rangoon in 1976 and rejoined the SUA.[19] He subsequently based himself at Ban Hin Taek in Chiangrai Province, Thailand, but was forced to flee into Shan State in 1982 when his base was attacked by the Thai army.[20] In 1984, on being made "Supreme Commander" of the MTA (an amalgamation of Shan groups not allied with the CPB), he announced that he would have nothing further to do with the trade in narcotics.[21] His submission, in 1996, to the SLORC was not a repetition of 1963. Khun Sa's headquarters in Ho Mong are now occupied by Burmese troops, and his own troops have surrendered their weapons.[22] He has also gained a newfound respectability. Whereas he was previously referred to simply as "Khun Sa" by the official media in Rangoon, his name is now prefixed with the honorific "U." This is extraordinary when we consider that it is common practice in the Burmese media to refer to convicted criminals by prefixing their names with the derogatory or condemnatory *nga*.[23]

Khun Sa's involvement in the narcotics trade with participation of Burmese military personnel, the military regime's apparent amnesia with regard to its previous antagonism toward him, its enthusiasm to grant him respectability while condemning the opium and heroin trade, and his espousal of Shan nationalism are all astonishing. It is possible to discern a certain logic at work: while Khun Sa has been motivated primarily by financial self-interest, the military regime on the other hand is prepared to tolerate all (including the possession of arms) as long as Khun Sa acknowledges the military government, does not confront it, and assists in maintaining order where his militia has effective control. Such an analysis, however, still begs the question—what is it that makes it possible for Khun Sa and the military regime to *see* their successive arrangements as "reasonable" solutions but not the contradictions they pose? What exactly is its rationality?

The Karen and Federalism

The Karen movement contrasts with the Shan insurgencies in that it has been far more unified. The unity of the Karen movement was by no means easily forged.[24] One of the remarkable things from 1948 onward, however, is that, despite their differences, the leaders of various Karen ethno-nationalist organizations have frequently attempted to work out these differences within rational organizational structures. This is not to say that there have not been any political intrigues, but even these intrigues occurred within the framework of such structures. Gen. Saw Bo Mya rose to power by displacing Mahn Ba Zan as president of the Karen National Union (KNU). Ba Zan's Maoist-inspired line of political thought was strongly resisted by the vigorously anti-communist Bo Mya. This was only in part a legacy of Saw Ba U Gyi, an Oxford-trained lawyer and the father of Karen nationalism. It is also related to the fact that many Karen involved in the movement in the beginning were urban-based and had acquired both military and administrative experience under the British. For many years, Kawthoolei, the "state" established by the Karen nationalists, was indeed a quasi-state and was governed in ways and along principles not unlike Chao Tzang's Shan First Military Region.

In the 1970s, a succession of political-*cum*-military fronts were formed consisting of various ethnic insurgent movements including the KNU. These fronts were a reaction to disillusionment with ethnic Burman opposition parties, the 1973 referendum in Burma and the 1974 Constitution of Burma which established a one-party state, and the rule of the Burma Socialist Program Party (BSPP) which was led by the military in civilian guise. One such front, the Revolutionary Nationalities Alliance (RNA) was formed in 1973 at Kawmoorah, a Karen stronghold. The aim of the RNA was the overthrow of the military regime as the term "revolutionary" suggests and the establishment of a "genuine federal union of independent national states based on the principle of equality and national self-determination."[25]

The RNA and other fronts were eventually replaced by the National Democratic Front (NDF), formed in 1976 at Manerplaw, the new Karen general headquarters. The principal purpose of this alliance was, again, to form a united front consisting of ethnic insurgent organizations and to develop greater coordination, political and military, in their confrontation with the military regime. The NDF came to have a significant impact on the conflict in Burma but it was initially plagued by differences over several issues including federalism and the right of secession. Here again, federalism was a goal of many of these organizations. An inherent problem in the past was that these fronts did not include any Burman parties. This, of course, changed after the 1988 pro-democracy uprising.

As a result of the uprising and the SLORC crackdown, several Burman opposition groups, including student activists, sought refuge in Kawthoolei, where the Karen played host to the National Coalition Government of the Union of Burma (NCGUB), the National League for Democracy (Liberated Area) (NLD-LA), the All Burma Students Democratic Front (ABSDF), and representatives of the Committee for the Restoration of Democracy in Burma (CRDB), among others. These groups established the Democratic Alliance of Burma (DAB) in late 1988. The DAB was not as cohesive as it may have appeared. Democracy activists who participated in the pro-democracy uprising were unhappy over the appointment of two representatives from the then Peoples Patriotic Front (PPF) and CRDB to the DAB Central Executive Committee. The alliance was, nonetheless, significant not because Burman and non-Burman opponents of the military regime finally recognized a common interest but because the *Burman* opposition groups recognized it and sought out a working relationship with the ethnic insurgents. This was, of course, by force of their own circumstances in Burma, i.e. their brutal suppression by the military. Were it not for these circumstances, it is unlikely that these groups would have actively searched out a modus vivendi with the ethnic insurgents under the auspices of the KNU.

With these developments, the Karen under Bo Mya were concerned with consolidating their pre-eminence. Bo Mya was not only chairman of the DAB; he came to be president of the National Council of the Union of Burma (NCUB) which was established in 1992.[26] An important feature of the resulting modus vivendi was the explicit recognition of the rights of the various ethnic groups and parity of their political status. It would be fair to say that the Burman opposition groups have, in principle, recognized these rights but they have been either against or ambivalent about the idea of a federal political system. Until 1992, their main concern was opposition to the military regime. Their recognition of group rights was expressed more formally and explicitly in the Manerplaw Agreement of July 1992.

The agreement states, among other things, that the signatories would "draw up a true Federal Union constitution in accordance with the desires of indigenous nationalities and all peoples" and that they will "follow the principle that no nationality shall have special privileges and no restrictions will be imposed on the basic right of any nationality or minority in the Union." Article 5 of the agreement reveals something of the basic structure of the Federal Union as the signatories proposed it. The Union was to incorporate the Kachin, Karen, Karenni, Chin, Mon, Burman, Arakan, and Shan peoples, each of whom would have "national states." These states would *"assign* certain powers to the Federal Union and the remaining powers will be exercised by the National States including legislative, administrative and judicial powers" (emphasis added); the Federal Union would consist of two Houses of Parliament: the National Assembly (Upper House) and the People's Assembly (Lower House). Furthermore, "in accordance with the principle of civilian supremacy over the military the Federal Union and State armies will be put under the direct supervision of the elected governments," "the legislative, administrative and judicial branches of the Federal Union Government will be checked and balanced in power, and the judiciary will be independent," and "the Constitution will be designed to prevent any re-emergence of chauvinism and fascist dictatorship in the future."

The agreement is quite remarkable on three grounds. First, what would constitute a *Burman* "national state?" Second, there is no mention of what to do about the military regime. Third, there seems to be an enormous amount of faith in words. Needless to say, the sentiments and intentions expressed in the Manerplaw Agreement are anathema to the military regime. The agreement was signed by almost all opposition and ethnic insurgent groups through various umbrella organizations. The signatories were: the NCGUB, the NLD-LA, the DAB, and NDF.

The Manerplaw Agreement was significant to the Karen in terms of their political position in relation to the Burmese state and other insurgent movements. As a member of previous fronts, the KNU had previously favored a federal system. Earlier, in 1984, Bo Mya had announced the independence of the "Republic of Kawthoolei."[27] Two months later, however, the NDF stated that it intended to "establish a unified federal Union with all the ethnic races including the Burmese."[28] This entailed rescinding any demands on the part of NDF members, including the KNU, for the right to secede. The NDF decision to establish a Federal Union represented a considerable compromise on the part of the Karen. The Karen position on federalism has been inconsistent.

When the KNU was part of the RNA, its stated aim was to form a "genuine federal union of independent national states based on the principle of equality and national self-determination." Thus, when the KNU (and other members of the NDF) talk of a federal union, they are concerned about retaining a very high degree of sovereignty or autonomy within their own "national states." The inconsistency is, however, more adequately explained in terms of the KNU's appreciation of the importance of uniting the various insurgent movements in order to confront the military regime more effectively. The compromise was in fact rational.

The alliance of Burman opposition groups and the ethnic insurgents made the destruction of Kawthoolei a high priority for the SLORC. The window of opportunity which unexpectedly presented itself to the military regime and which drastically altered the contours of ethnic conflict to the regime's benefit was the collapse of the CPB in 1989, following the revolt of its Kokang and Wa elements.

Within a week of the Kokang revolt, SLORC representatives went to the area to open negotiations. The SLORC and the various ex-CPB factions developed a form of conflict management which resulted in a cessation of hostilities. The agreement is somewhat uneasy, but it has persisted. Despite the claim that the agreement provided for the SLORC's extension of sovereignty and the understanding that the local ex-CPB militias would not engage in "dissident activities," the other aspects of the agreement indicated that the idea of an extension of the sovereignty of the unitary Burmese state was a compromised one. The administrative pre-eminence of local commands was one clear indication. The recognition of the claim of national sovereignty which the SLORC extracted from the ex-CPB elements hardly reflected the realities on the ground.

The point is that these realities are recognized in the conflict management strategy. The strategy included specific mechanisms which conflict management theorists have identified, such as "open channels of communication." Burmese military, Kokang and Wa units, for example, established signals communication down to platoon level to ensure that hostilities did not break out during the passage of troops. What emerged was, in effect, a localized, limited security regime. This regime is a relatively stable one. One of the principal factors contributing to the relative stability of the regime was the economic benefits deriving from a cessation of hostilities. The Burmese, Kokang, and Wa units have had a vested interest in various activities such as opium and heroin production and trafficking, as well as other commercial activities. These arrangements antedate the 1996 arrangements with Khun Sa, but they raise the same question of rationality.

Cease-fires followed throughout the country, and were extended to include almost all ethnic insurgent groups.[29] The most notable exceptions have been the Karen and Mon. The SLORC strategy has been extremely successful, at least with regard to the disarray of the Karen, the remaining major political and military force.

The military regime in Burma has effectively subdued these movements, but its insistence on territorial sovereignty and its willingness to concede to the insurgents the right to hold weapons, the administrative pre-eminence of local commands, and unrestricted commercial activities are clear evidence that national sovereignty in the sense associated with a unitary state has been compromised. The resulting cease-fire arrangements amount to a federalist structure for all intents and purposes: after all, the insurgents can bear arms, administer areas under their control and engage in economic activities, legal or otherwise. The Karen aside, it seems clear that these other insurgent leaders are not greatly troubled by the fact that they endorsed the idealistic vision of the DAB and the Manerplaw Agreement but thereafter happily entered into a pact to have an ongoing supper with the devil.

But what of the Karen intransigence with regard to accepting a cease-fire with the SLORC? The Karen position has been essentially modern-rationalist. Despite its compromise with regard to federalism, there has been one consistent position: never to sup with the devil.

Substantive and Formal Rationality

It is a basic assumption in the social sciences that human beings are *rational* in their own terms, but we also often tend to assume that they are rational in their own terms *and ours*. This is probably a mistake. Weber made an important distinction between formal and substantive rationality. When he employs the term without qualification he is in fact referring to formal rationality as opposed to all the other kinds.[30] Formal rationality is associated with intellectualization and rationalization and that "one can, in principle, master all things by calculation."[31] It implies a mode of thought which is quite different from modes of thought associated with all other forms of rationality which he labels as "substantive" or what I have called the "premodern-nonrational." In other words, while both kinds of rationality are concerned with means-ends relations, formal rationality entails a very different kind of outlook and cognition.

Gellner has brilliantly elaborated on this Weberian distinction and has provided us with extremely powerful concepts which enable us to make sense of the kinds of inconsistencies, contradictions, and paradoxes which have been explored in this chapter. Gellner argues that there has been a "cognitive path" consisting of a movement away from a type of conceptual system to another which, for present purposes, coincides with Weber's substantive rationalities and formal rationality respectively. According to Gellner, "The world *we* inhabit, and treat seriously, is single-stranded *and* referential. The world inhabited by primitive man was many-stranded and largely, though by no means wholly, non-referential."[32]

Multi-strandedness and the non-referential may be found in many societies, including our own. Not all societies are urban, industrial-capitalist. Indeed, many are agrarian or have large agricultural sectors (such as Burma), and others are hunter-gatherers. Furthermore, many states (which we often unthinkingly call "societies") contain within them people who occupy these three niches, often with movements from the agrarian to the urban, industrial-capitalist.

Multi-strandedness and the non-referential dominate in Burma for it is only in such terms that we may explain that society's contradictions, inconsistencies, and paradoxes. The dominance of this mode of thought was, in many ways, preserved and guaranteed by the autarkic, isolationist policies of the military regime, particularly during the period of the "Burmese way to socialism." The contradictions and so forth which we identify are not seen to be such by the social and political actors there because of multi-stranded thinking. But we identify them as such because we tend to think in single-stranded, referential ways. The cease-fires between the insurgents, Khun Sa, and the military regime were possible because they all think in the same way. The Karen, on the other hand, are rather more Western, preferring to adhere to a principle single-mindedly, and in the process bringing upon themselves their present misfortune.

Apart from the cease-fires and the intransigence of the Karen, a Gellnerian view enables us to understand other seemingly bizarre aspects of political and economic processes in Burma. The demonetizations of the kyat and the employment of the numero-astrological "sum-of-nine" formula referred to earlier are examples. It is possible to point to the timing of other events which have not followed the formula. The timing of military offensives by the Burmese armed forces against the ethnic insurgents is not guided by any direct reliance on the numero-astrological formula. But this is what we would expect, given that military organizations in conflict in post-colonial times are forced to operate in rather more formally rational, or at least *empirical,* ways, however much their leaders may be predisposed to pre-modern modes of thought. The inconsistency, in other words, is another instance of multi-strandedness at work.

No less significant is what I earlier termed "an enormous faith in words" in relation to the Manerplaw Agreement. This is yet again a clear instance of the non-referential use of language: the significance of the terms employed lies in their "essence" and a belief that their employment will produce the sought-after political reality seemingly without regard to the thorny problem of what to do with the military regime. Another example is the names of the various insurgent movements containing terms such as "democratic," "liberation," "progress," "revolutionary," "independence," and "united," all of which are at variance in one way or another with what actually goes on in these movements. This is no less true of the military regime's use of language, the most outstanding example of which is to be found in the idiosyncratic employment of Marxist and Buddhist terminology in the two internally and mutually inconsistent and contradictory documents, *The Burmese Way to Socialism* and *The System of Correlation of*

Man and His Environment, produced by the military regime soon after the 1962 coup.[33] A more recent manifestation of this is the conferment of respectability on Khun Sa through the use of the honorific "U" and the condemnation of Bo Mya through the term *nga.*

Conclusion

Multi-strandedness and the non-referential are common to the military regime and the ethnic insurgents. The two groups also have one common preoccupation, modern state formation, even if they have rather different definitions of what such a state should be. Yet, because they share similar modes of thought it has been possible for them to arrive at cease-fires despite disagreements over a unitary *versus* federal state system. Connor has argued convincingly that "most members of national minorities are prepared to settle for something less than separation" and that "ethnonational concerns, by their very nature, are more obsessed with a vision of freedom from domination by nonmembers than with a vision of freedom to conduct foreign relations with states."[34] The federalist aims of the insurgents in Burma and their willingness to enter into cease-fire arrangements with the SLORC (whatever the proximate causes) confirm the acuity of Connor's analysis.

There is now a divided system in the ethnic states (i.e. Shan State, Mon State, Karen State, Kayah State, etc.) consisting of territories under the effective control of the military and under the insurgents who have entered into cease-fire agreements with the regime. Nevertheless, the military is dominant because of its significantly superior numbers or "force advantage." The containment of armed conflict has enabled a resumption of economic activities (legal or otherwise), although not to pre-cease-fire levels where the insurgents are concerned. At the same time, however, there is ongoing exploitation of local ethnic populations through forced labor. The continuing presence of the Burmese military means that local communities are subjected not only to forced labor but to other exactions of food and money.

Although hostilities have ceased, local communities constitute "soft targets." They are "targeted" partly *because of their ethnicity* and partly because Burmese soldiers have been indoctrinated into thinking that they are in hostile territory and among hostile populations. Burmese army commanders have failed to impose restraints on soldiers' behavior. Indeed, it would appear that commanders condone, if not encourage, such behavior. However resentful the civilian populations and the insurgents may be, a return to protracted armed conflict is extremely unlikely for two reasons: first, the military's force advantage; second, the inability of the insurgent movements to acquire arms in Thailand, partly as a consequence of Thailand's rapprochement with the regime in Burma. The insurgents are also constrained because of reduced sources of revenue. They cannot rely on overseas Burmese communities (which are largely ethnic Burmans in any case) to finance arms purchases because these communities are ideologically committed to seeking a political solution. Even if they were not so committed, they lack the necessary funds to help the insurgents. These constraints, however, do not rule out sporadic clashes between the military and insurgents over territory and access to resources or commercial activities.

The principal challenge will be to alleviate the suffering of the civilian ethnic communities currently subject to the systematic predations of the military in the name of "development" as the SLORC defines it.

Notes

1. Robert H. Jackson and Carl G. Rosberg, "Why Africa's Weak States Persist: The Empirical and Juridical in Statehood," in Atul Kohli (ed.), *The State and Development in the Third World* (Princeton, 1986), 259–282.

2. Barry Buzan, *Peoples, States, and Fear* (Brighton, 1983); Rajah, "Contemporary Developments in Kawthoolei: The Karen and Conflict Resolution in Burma," *Thai-Yunnan Project Newsletter*, XIX (1992), 7–15.

3. Martin Smith, *Burma: Insurgency and the Politics of Ethnicity* (London, 1991), xiii. The following twenty-five ethnic insurgent movements and opposition groups existed in 1989: the Chin National Front (CNF, 200); Chin National Liberation Party (CNLP, twenty); CPB (15,000); Communist Party of Burma–Red Flag (CPB–RF, thirty); Kachin Independence Organization/Kachin Independence Army (KIO/KIA, 8,000); Karen National Union/Karen National Liberation Army (KNU/KNLA, 6,000); Karenni National Progressive Party (KNPP, 500); Karenni State Nationalities Liberation Front (KSNLF, 150); Karen/Kayan New Land Party (KNLP, 200); Lahu National Organization (LNO, 200); Naga National Socialist Council (NNSC, 400); National Mon Democracy Organization (NMDO, 100); New Mon State Party (NMSP, 1,500); National Unity Front of Arakan (NUFA, 260); Palaung State Liberation Party (PSLP, 500); Pao National Organization (PNO, 500); People's Patriotic Party (PPP, seventy); Shan State Nationalities Liberation Organization (SSNLO, 500); Shan State Progress Party (SSPP, 2,500); Thailand Revolutionary Council (MTA, 3,000); Wa National Organization (WNO, 200); Wa National Council (WNC, 500); and the All-Burma Students Democratic Front (ABSDF, 1,000).

4. Bertil Lintner, *Outrage: Burma's Struggle for Democracy* (London, 1990), 160–161.

5. The definitive works are Robert Taylor's *The State in Burma* (London, 1987), Martin Smith's *Burma: Insurgency and the Politics of Ethnicity,* and Bertil Lintner's coverage in the *Far Eastern Economic Review,* his *Land of Jade: A Journey through Insurgent Burma* (Edinburgh, 1990), and *Outrage: Burma's Struggle for Democracy.*

6. These inconsistencies and contradictions are not peculiar to the ethnic insurgencies in Burma. They seem to be general characteristics of political movements whatever their ideologies, whether separatist, rebel, or revolutionary and of political parties and regimes associated with the creation of post-colonial nation-states. These are in fact characteristics of collections of societies and cultures in transition. While this may appear obvious enough, the central question is *what kind of transition* is

involved? Such transitions are often viewed as being essentially political (or political and economic) in nature but there are good grounds for taking a broader perspective which focuses on transitions in cultures and modes of thought in the context of long-term human history.

7. Smith, *Burma: Insurgency and the Politics of Ethnicity*, 219.

8. Lintner, *Outrage: Burma's Struggle for Democracy*, 67.

9. Smith, *Burma:Insurgency*, 25–26. Smith also provides a revealing remark made by one of Ne Win's former foreign friends: "The trouble is he is no longer capable of rational thought. He only believes in omens and there are only two kinds, good ones and bad ones."

10. It might appear useful to focus on the roots of ethnic conflict on the grounds that an understanding of the sources of conflict would be helpful in formulating ways to end the conflict. The difficulty with this approach is that depending on one's perspective or preference, any number of sources of conflict may be identified. Should we, for example, trace the roots to British colonial policy, practice, and the conditions surrounding the Treaty of Panglong? Or, are they to be found in U Nu's attempt to make Buddhism the state religion of Burma in 1960–61? Or should we say that they have everything to do with Burman nationalism and ethnic nationalisms and the incompatibility of their respective desires for a unitary state as against a federal state? On the other hand, we could assert that all of these—together with numerous sets of associated circumstances and conditions— account for the protracted social conflict in Burma. To do so, however, is to admit to infinite historical regress and an infinite series of proximate causes. For these reasons, the search for the roots of ethnic conflict in Burma is in many ways a futile exercise. See Rajah, "Contemporary Developments in Kawthoolei: the Karen and Conflict Resolution in Burma," 7–15. See also Rajah, "Burma: Protracted Social Conflict, Displacement and Migration," paper presented at the International Conference on "Transmigration in the Asia-Pacific Region," Indochinese Information Centre, Chulalongkorn University (Bangkok, 1–2 December 1994).

The identification of root causes is also associated with conflict resolution approaches, but precisely because they focus on historically constituted sources of fundamental political differences between parties to conflict, these approaches have not produced many solutions. Conflict management approaches which are rather more modest and realist, on the other hand, attempt to identify specific conditions of conflict, the containment or amelioration of which *may* form the preconditions for longer-term solutions. See Gabriel Ben-Dor and David B. Dewitt, "Conflict and Conflict Management in the Middle East," in G. Ben-Dor and D.B. Dewitt, (eds.), *Conflict Management in the Middle East* (Lexington, Mass., 1987), 297–309. My discussion of the politicization of ethnicity and ethnic relations and their associated contradictions and inconsistencies will, accordingly, be guided by the kinds of practical considerations that conflict management theorists advocate.

11. Hildred and Clifford Geertz, "Teknonymy in Bali," *Journal of the Royal Anthropological Institute*, XCIV (1964), 105.

12. Where ethnic conflict is specifically concerned, the reports by the Karen Human Rights Group must be considered the most comprehensive, detailed, and meticulous. These reports are compiled by Karen "monitors" who have been trained to record the testimony of refugees and others in scrupulous detail. The information thus gathered includes the dates of incidents, the places where they occurred, the Burmese military units involved and where possible the names of the military personnel and commanders, as well as the nature of the abuses such as rape, torture, arbitrary killing, portering, food deprivation, and exactions of money. The Karen Human Rights Group reports are archived at the Free Burma website at URL: http://sunsite.unc.edu/freeburma. On Burmese military operations in Arakan State and the plight of the Rohingyas, see for example George Lombard, "The Burmese Refugees in Bangladesh: Causes and Prospects for Repatriation," *Thai–Yunnan Project Newsletter*, XIX (1992), 19–22.

13. Chao Tzang Yawnghwe, *The Shan of Burma: Memoirs of a Shan Exile* (Singapore, 1987), 112.

14. Gehan Wijeyewardene, "Rethinking the Frontiers of 'Burma,'" *Thai-Yunnan Project Newsletter*, XIX (1992), 5.

15. The case of Khun Sa and the military regime is of great interest in itself, but in the history of ethnic conflict in Burma it also represents a type of political and economic relations, temporary

or of longer duration which may be found among various ethnic insurgent groups and some of these groups in association with the CPB.

16. Smith, *Burma: Insurgency and the Politics of Ethnicity*, 95.

17. Yawnghwe, *The Shan of Burma*, 189; Smith, *Burma: Insurgency*, 95.

18. Smith, *Burma: Insurgency*, 314–315, 478; Chapter 18, note 18.

19. Ibid., 335.

20. Yawnghwe, *The Shan of Burma*, 189.

21. G. Wijeyewardene, "Thailand and the Tai: Versions of Ethnic Identity," in G. Wijeyewardene, (ed.), *Ethnic Groups across National Boundaries in Mainland Southeast Asia* (Singapore, 1990), 66.

22. Bertil Lintner, "Drug Triangle Handshake: Khun Sa Surrenders, but on His Own Terms," *Far Eastern Economic Review* (25 January 1996), 15–16.

23. Gen. Saw Bo Mya, leader of the Karen National Union and Karen National Liberation Army, is referred to as "Nga Mya" in the official media. See also *Whither KNU?* (Rangoon, 1995). The author of this publication is anonymous; the title page simply states "by: A resident of Kayin [Karen] State." The book is a collection of thirty-three articles which were previously published in Burmese newspapers, evidently as an exercise in anti-Karen propaganda. The real authors of the articles are thought to be a team of three officers from the Directorate of Defence Services Intelligence (DDSI). Bo Mya has consistently refused to agree to a cease-fire with the military regime. The vilification of Bo Mya and the granting of respectability to Khun Sa can hardly be coincidental. It is clearly intended to signal that co-operation with the regime has its rewards. Where Khun Sa is concerned, this includes the regime's present refusal to give in to U.S. demands that he be handed over for trial in the U.S.

24. A detailed and nuanced account of the origins and history of the Karen insurgency may be found in Smith, *Burma: Insurgency*, 82–87; 137–154.

25. Ibid., 294.

26. *News and Views* (a publication of the Committee for the Restoration of Democracy in Burma [Australia]), (October 1992), 7.

27. Smith, *Burma: Insurgency*, 478; Chapter 19, note 3.

28. Ibid., 386.

29. The situation is, in analytical principle, not unlike that of Khun Sa and the military regime. It might be argued that these insurgent leaders had no *choice* because, as Smith suggests, they were running out of ammunition as in the case of the KIO 4th Brigade, the PNO, and the PSLP. But of course, there were other insurgent groups which were not desperately short of ammunition. Even if they were, there *was* yet another choice: to leave and reside in Thailand. This was precisely what Chao Tzang did but not only that, he subsequently migrated to Canada where the Mahadevi had much earlier exiled herself as a consequence of her failure to unify the Shan movements. Chao Tzang's departure from the Shan nationalist movement in Burma and the insurgent scene was dictated by the utter impossibility of dealing with premodern-nonrational modes of thought.

30. Geoffrey Benjamin, "Rationalisation and Reenchantment in Malaysia: Temiar Religion 1964–1995," *Department of Sociology Working Papers* 130, National University of Singapore, 35.

31. Max Weber, "Science as a Vocation," in Hans H. Gerth and C. Wright Mills, (eds.), *From Max Weber: Essays in Sociology* (London, 1991), 139. I am extremely grateful to Geoffrey Benjamin for drawing my attention to Weber's distinction and Ernest Gellner's elaboration of this distinction.

32. Ernest Gellner, *Plough, Sword and Book: The Structure of Human History* (London, 1988), 78.

33. Rajah, "Buddhism and Secularisation in Burma from Parliamentary Democracy to Military Rule: An Anthropological Reconsideration." Revised version of a paper presented at the Conference on "Disenchantment and Reenchantment: Religion in Southeast Asia Today" (Canberra, 14–15 March 1996).

34. Walker Connor, *Ethnonationalism: The Quest for Understanding* (Princeton, 1994), 82–83.

Part Three

ECONOMIC
CONSIDERATIONS

CHAPTER 8

Development Prospects for Burma
Cycles and Trends

David Dapice

I F E V E R there were a nation in which politics clearly conditioned the chances for economic growth, it is Burma.[1] Coming out of World War II with many advantages and having enjoyed a decade of rapid growth in the 1950s, it slid into a prolonged period of isolation that left it far behind its previously lagging neighbors. Unsustainable policies brought a burst of modest growth in the 1970s, but this was followed by a period of negative per capita growth. The less isolationist and somewhat market oriented policies of the State Law and Order Restoration Council (SLORC) have sparked another period of rapid growth since 1989. Some see this as a sign that Burma is finally breaking out of its long-term pattern of isolation and dismal economic policy and performance.[2]

There can be no reasonable doubt that the policies currently followed are an improvement over "The Burmese Way to Socialism," which had been official policy under Gen. Ne Win from 1962 to 1988. It is much less clear whether these policies are sufficient to allow sustained growth. This paper argues that policies will probably not be good enough to sustain economic growth similar to that of Burma's successful Southeast Asian neighbors. More likely is a period of narrowly focused and short-lived growth that will not spread widely enough to create a "takeoff." The probable result will be something like the growth experience of several resource-rich African or Latin American economies that managed a decade or so of rapid growth and then faltered badly (see appendix B). A moderate level of foreign direct investment (FDI), some aid, and a growing level of gas production and exports is factored into this estimate of future growth. This

Table 8-1. Real Annual GDP Growth of Selected Asian Nations
Percent

Country	1950–60	1960–70	1970–80	1980–90	1990–96[a]
Burma	6.3	2.6	4.7	1.5[b]	6.4
Indonesia	3.8	3.5	7.2	5.5	7.0
Thailand	5.7	8.2	7.1	7.6	8.3
Philippines	6.4	5.1	6.0	0.9	3.0
India	4.2	3.6	3.4	5.3	4.3

SOURCE: World Bank calculations from World Tables or various issues of World Development Report.
a. Average of 1991–1996 annual GDP growth rates, except for Burma which is 1991–1995.
b. 1981–1990 for Burma.

prognosis assumes a continuation of the SLORC, but even if the government were to change, many of the same issues would remain, though perhaps they would be more tractable due to larger aid flows.

Past Trends and Comparisons

Table 8-1 shows the growth experience of Burma and some of its neighbors. Burma was among the fastest growing Asian nations in the 1950s, but the next three decades were marked by very sluggish growth, with annual gross domestic product (GDP) growth averaging less than 3 percent and population growth more than 2 percent. In contrast, all other nations in this table managed to do much better, from around 4 percent per year for the Philippines and India to more than 7 percent for Thailand. Burma again began to experience measured economic growth in the 1990s, but given problems of inflation and rising trade and budget deficits, it is uncertain how solid the underpinnings are of this most recent growth spurt. Alternatively, one can ask if, or how, the growth might be sustained by a series of economic reforms.

The economic data for Burma are even more unreliable than is normal for poorer countries. Narcotics appear to be the largest single export, probably accounting for a half-billion dollars a year in sales, an amount which exceeds official taxes collected.[3] Many private activities and payments are certainly unrecorded. The full scope of many state transactions may not be properly recorded. There have been suggestions that at least some of the recent measured gain in GDP may be due to the recognition of previously produced but unrecorded output. Economic data often have only a tenuous link to that which they purport to measure.

Creating an Environment for Sustained Growth

The countries that have succeeded in growing at high rates over several decades have all, to some degree, shared certain common policy approaches. The basic strategy has been to increase the accumulation of physical and human capital and to deploy it effectively. Mere accumulation (as the old Soviet model implied) will only work for a while. Market forces are needed to ensure efficiency, adaptive use of technology, and product quality and development. Within this general framework, certain other policies also seem universal. The list is long and can be presented in several ways, but the following would certainly be included.

1. Promote a healthy rural sector: All fast-growing countries (the city-states aside) have invested in rural areas. This means ensuring secure land titles, leaving family farms free to plant and sell what they want, and providing rural roads, schools, health posts, accessible credit at market rates, and reasonable prices for output. Indonesia, for example, has invested heavily in its rural areas and maintained an annual agricultural growth rate of over 3 percent, even in the 1980s when budget cutbacks were the rule.[4] This ability to create job opportunities in rural areas, and not just in farming, slows migration of workers to the cities until reasonably productive urban employment can be created. Rural growth also boosts export earnings, creates local markets, and provides savings. A dynamic rural sector provides a firm base for urban growth.

2. Promote a healthy macroeconomic environment: All successful countries have moved towards systems where the exchange rate reflects the scarcity of foreign exchange, the inflation rate is low enough not to interfere with investment decisions, and the financial system is able to mobilize savings and allocate them efficiently. Strong growth in domestic savings means less foreign debt is taken on. By creating a degree of stability in prices and exchange rates, firms are able to focus on their businesses and do not need to hedge with holdings in gold, dollars, real estate, or unproductive speculative inventory.

3. Promote manufactured exports: However rich in natural resources a country may be, the only sustainable source of exports and growth is manufactured exports. These exports take advantage of labor, create opportunities for enhancing skills, and initially use little capital. The ability to become "outward looking" does not depend on subsidies, but on a business environment free from currency controls, trade permits, and other red tape. It benefits from low cost and high quality services such as banking, insurance, freight, telecommunications, electricity, etc. (These services are not subsidized. They charge enough to make

a profit. But they are competitive and well enough run to make a profit and still charge a reasonable price while providing good service.)

These three aspects of economic development are not controversial. It is fairly well established that they are necessary for rapid growth to continue. Certain countries may manage to grow quickly with only partial implementation of these policies. They may do this by shifting to somewhat more efficient policies and away from very bad ones (such as Vietnam and Burma have) or by saving and investing very high amounts relative to GDP. But, eventually, either approach runs out of gas and the need to increase efficiency becomes clear. There is either further reform or stagnation.

Recent Gains Reflect Recovery . . .

How far along is Burma with respect to creating the conditions for sustained growth? The last few years have clearly seen rapid growth, but most of it is more accurately seen as a recovery from previously depressed levels than as growth from a normal base. In the ten years from 1986 to 1995, real output declined in four of those years, the economy grew at around 3 percent for two years, and it grew at 6 percent or more for four of those years (1992–95). Real output per capita in 1995 was essentially equal to that in 1985.[5] Partial recovery is welcome, but is far short of long-term growth. Recent problems of rising inflation and high deficits threaten continuation of growth after 1997.

And Agriculture Faces Many Problems . . .

Burma's agricultural sector is struggling, in spite of the much improved policy regime which no longer seeks to impose low prices, fixed inputs, and mandatory crops on farmers. These changes have sparked a reported rise in output of paddy by nearly one-third from 1992–93 to 1995–96, and 37 percent above 1985.[6] (Population rose 20 percent in the last decade, and there is a real possibility of over-reporting gains in farm output.) Levels of farmer indebtedness are high and a lack of effective formal credit institutions means most farmers must pay 10 percent a month for their loans. There are severe ecological problems in the Dry Zone (depleted soils and forests), the Ayeyarwady Delta (mangrove depletion and erosion), and many hilly areas (deforestation and soil mining). Extremely poor roads and other infrastructure problems also hamper progress, along with a decapitalized and poorly operating agro-processing industry.[7]

As if this were not enough, arbitrary local taxes sap the ability of many farmers to improve their farms or mechanize. Obligations for corvee labor hit many poor farm and landless families, contributing to poverty and lower levels of input use. The government imposes monopoly controls on rice exports, and periodic restrictions on other exports. These depress farm-gate prices, and tend to create a "two-tiered" system in which a few larger farmers control increasing amounts of land, irrigation, machinery, and credit.

This process of concentration is moving in the opposite direction of the "unimodal" model which land reforms in Korea and Taiwan encouraged, and instead resembles land distribution patterns in Bangladesh, the Philippines, and Latin America. This second group of nations has not had nearly so dynamic a rural sector. While it is always possible that a less "urban-biased" set of policies will be adopted, the fact remains that after the efficiency gains from abandoning socialism run out in a few years, more investment and better policies will be required to sustain rural growth. These changes include better price, credit, and infrastructure policies, as well as investments within the agricultural sector. These necessary changes do not appear to be near.

Macro-Policies Are Very Poor, in Spite of Improvements . . .

Burma is unique in that its share of taxes has recently been only 8 percent of GDP, and is falling. Even the 8 percent ratio is half the level of Indonesia, Thailand, the Philippines, or even Burma in the early 1980s.[8] Indeed, few countries in the world have a tax ratio so low. Reported expenditures by the government are much higher than the amount of taxes collected, and actual spending and taxes (including informal taxes) are higher still. The lack of effective review of much spending and taxation means that the burdens and benefits of the government sector fall very unevenly. With high military spending, there is very little left for investments. Civil servants are badly underpaid, leading to corruption and inefficiency. (Fuel subsidies are used to increase their pay, but this leads to shortages and other problems.)

In addition, the primary macroeconomic prices such as interest rates and exchange rates remain out of kilter. The official exchange rate of about 6 kyats to $1 bears little relationship to the market rate of more than 165 kyats to $1 (as of April 1997).[9] While many prices are being set by the latter rate, there are still subsidies throughout the economy based on the lower rate. The complications arising from lack of currency convertibility and distorted prices damage the economy. The interest rates for both loans and deposits are well below the inflation rate. Bank deposits are about $8 per person, compared to over $400 in the Philippines.[10] Again, there is no immediate sign of any change away from the large, inflationary government deficits or the rapid increase in money supply and the resulting inflation; or toward an adjustment of interest rates, or the long over-due unification of the exchange rate. Indeed, these counterproductive practices seem to be intensifying.

Unless these policies change, it is not likely that businesses will want to invest enough to sustain rapid growth or that the needed supply of funds will be available to finance them even if they did. Even if gas production rises to 500 million cubic feet a day, the resulting tax revenues will amount to less than 2 percent of GDP, far too little to change fundamentally the existing situation.[11] (The current budget deficit is 8 percent of GDP.) Even higher levels of gas production would accomplish little unless there were accompanying reforms.

And Business Does Not Face a "Level Playing Field"

Underlying all of the problems facing investors is a lack of certainty about procedures, rules, and regulations. Even investors from other Asian nations who are very familiar with negotiating with government bureaucracies find it hard to do business in Burma. There are few clear rules, a lack of predictability, a high degree of arbitrary government action, and the danger that a good business or business idea will be taken over by someone better placed. In many ways, the economy is run more on a wartime footing than a normal commercial one. The result is that cumulative approvals for foreign investment in the period through February 1997 amounted to $6.1 billion.[12] Actual cumulative FDI inflows from 1990–91 to 1994–95 were $946 million according to the balance of payments data. This average of under $5 per capita per year, about two-thirds of it in oil and gas, is welcome but not large. (Vietnam approved investments of over $3 bil-lion in the last *half* of 1995, and its annual actual FDI inflow is $30 per capita.) A large portion of the remaining one-third of FDI is in hotels and tourism ($78 million realized in five years). In manufacturing, $45 million was realized, with even smaller amounts in other sectors.

When underlying uncertainty is combined with astronomical phone charges, unreliable electricity supplies, rising inflation, currency inconvertibility, and poor transportation in a small market, the result is that both the quantity and quality of non-energy FDI suffers badly. Those who hope to profit from a land deal, or overprice their capital equipment, or benefit from a selective reduction (for themselves only) in import tariffs tend to flock to these situations. They offer the country little and often do not intend to build up operations in the nation and improve the economy.

At least some who might be tempted to enter in spite of the difficulties—including U.S.-based Pepsi and Levi-Strauss—are put off by the political troubles. They face external pressure which is not worth the cost, and they fear being treated poorly if the government changes. This adds one more layer of negativity to a situation that is already viewed as difficult, and is hard to explain to most boards of directors or bosses who find other pastures to be greener. Management time is limited and investors in Burma need to pack a lot of patience in their suitcases.

Burma without Development

If the current impasse remains and the government continues to implement reforms in a half-hearted way, it is likely that there will be a period of rapid but narrow growth followed by mounting debt and stagnation caused by high cost industries, the exhaustion of rural growth, and continued lack of domestic savings and investment. (Recent World Bank estimates put the share of savings and investment around one-eighth of GDP, well under half the levels in ASEAN countries.) The collapse of growth in the Philippines would be one example of this pattern, though other nations (Nigeria, Brazil) have gone through similar cycles. (See Appendix B.) The flow of opium-based money may cushion the decline in some urban sectors, but this would only accelerate internal migration into cities that would not be prepared for the numbers that would be likely to come.

Some have suggested that in spite of its many difficulties, it should not be hard to maintain growth in Burma because it is so poor to start with, suffered so much from poor policies in the past, and is in such a dynamic region, close to China and ASEAN. This argument could also apply to Bangladesh, Burma's neighbor, which is poor, similarly located, and arguably has a better set of economic policies than Burma—and a 2 percent per capita growth rate. It is likely that measured growth will remain high for a few years if the partial reforms and modest amount of foreign investment allow urban services and some manufacturing to grow. However, the growth reported in agriculture is suspect since apparent per capita consumption of rice is unbelievably high (215 kg of rice per capita, even with a very low ratio of rice extracted from paddy), and rice exports are under half of their 1956 level. Thailand's villages at their peak consumed less than 180 kg of rice per capita. Villagers in Thailand had higher levels of income than those in Burma, though not so high as to displace rice with other foods.

With 80 percent of the population living in rural areas, few signs of healthy rural or manufactured export growth, and manifold problems of political stability, businesses bought with narcotics money, and an economy run on a wartime footing, it is not likely that Burma's growth will remain either rapid or widespread.

If growth remains narrow and sporadic, it is likely that the environmental problems would worsen, the plight of landless and low-income farmers would intensify, and the centrifugal forces that caused internal political conflict among non-Burman ethnic groups and even within central Burma would return and intensify. Urban population growth, as suggested above, would accelerate, and with it would come shanty-towns with large underemployed populations. Crime, especially that related to narcotics, would logically assume a growing role in those areas, as well as expanding in several ethnic states. HIV and AIDS, already growing at alarming rates, would probably worsen and affect substantial parts of the population.

The issue of narcotics alone makes Burma of concern to the United States. Heroin exports have risen under the SLORC and are said to approach 200,000 kg per year, at a local price of several thousand dollars per kilogram. This issue probably could be resolved only slowly with rising levels of development. As other legitimate parts of an economy grow, interested groups see that there is more to lose than gain with continued drug production. With roads and better income-earning alternatives, it is easier for farmers to change crops. The slow changes just across the border around Chiang Mai have shown how development can reduce opium cultivation. Such a future is possible within Burma but not within sight, and it is certainly impossible so long as sanctions and isolationist policies are imposed.

It is unlikely that any future government will find it attractive or be in a position to limit the exports of narcotics. If the regime remained connected with the military and without popular legitimacy, it probably would rely increasingly on China for support. There is already a large and growing economic and political relationship between China and Burma. Further access to islands on the approaches to the Straits of Malacca for the Chinese navy is one possible further development. Another would be more cross-border migration and increasing control of the economy by well-capitalized Chinese traders, at least in the northern parts of the country. More far-fetched, but not impossible, is even stronger absorption of some of the country along the lines of Tibet. For many ethnic groups, their historical experience with the Chinese has been better than that with the Burmans, and the de facto territorial integrity of a poor, weak, and divided nation cannot be taken for granted. Long-running civil wars might reignite unless sustained economic growth can put an end to the zero or negative sum mentality that now poisons possibilities of compromise and cooperation. Such growth would require external support as well as internal reforms.

Even if a more representative government somehow emerged, many of the same pressures would still exist. The military would not disappear and would need funding; the interested and wealthy groups would want to continue with their narcotics activity; and there would be well organized urban pressure for preferential treatment, leading to policies disadvantageous for rural areas. It would be a herculean task to reorient the politics and economics of the country toward a peaceful, less repressive, and sustainable course of economic development.

Most of the suggested outcomes are dismal and pessimistic. They are not predictions as such but rather extrapolations based on the current tendencies. The purpose of this paper is not to predict, nor to outline in any systematic way what needs to be done to reverse these tendencies. It is rather to point out that the 1992–95 rebound, and subsequent growth is not likely to presage a period of Korea-style growth unless many other changes are made—changes that are not yet in evidence. Without a good dose of further fundamental reform, and much more legality and legitimacy to those ruling the nation, the outlook is poor to grim. This should not delight the United States or many Asian countries. The best responses to these dilemmas may be debated, but without better communication and some combination of carrots and sticks it is hard to see how the chances for a better future can be improved.

Appendix A: Data Pertaining to Burma

Table 8A-1. Real GDP, Population, GDP per Capita, Exports, and Imports
Index, 1985 = 100

	1980	1985	1990	1991	1992	1993	1994	1995	1996
Real GDP[a]	44.4	56. 0	50.3	49.9	54.6	57.8	61.5	67.5	71.4
Population[b]	33.6	37.1	41.0	41.8	42.6	43.4	44.2	45.1	45.9
GDP per capita[c]	89	100	82	79	86	89	92	100	103
Exports[b,d]	472	303	325	464	591	696	810	750	769
Imports[b,d]	353	283	270	851	1,010	1,302	1,547	2,010	1,909

SOURCES: *1995 Key Indicators of Developing Asian and Pacific Countries, Volume xxvi*, Asian Development Bank. For trade, the IMF is used for 1980–1990 and The Economist Intelligence Unit *Country Report* for 1991–1996.

a. Real GDP valued in billions of 1985/86 kyat.

b. Millions.

c. Per capita GDP is probably about $200, if valued at market prices. Investment estimates vary widely and are generally placed at between 10 percent and 15 percent of GDP in recent years.

d. Neither exports nor imports include substantial unrecorded amounts.

Table 8A-2. Major Trading Partners, 1995
Percent

Export destinations		Import origins	
Singapore	12.9	China	31.3
China	11.8	Singapore	23.0
India	11.0	Malaysia	12.6
Japan	7.4	Japan	7.9
United States	7.0	Thailand	5.6
Hong Kong	5.1	Hong Kong	3.2
Malaysia	3.1	Indonesia	2.3

SOURCE: Economist Intelligence Unit, second quarter 1997.

Table 8A-3. Major Exports and Imports, 1996
Millions of U.S. $

Exports		Imports	
Rice	60	Cement	41
Pulses, beans	214	Base metals and manufactures	179
Fish, prawns	116	Edible oils	81
Rubber	29	Electrical machinery	168
		Machinery & transport equipment	268

SOURCE: Economist Intelligence Unit, second quarter 1997.
Manufactured goods are recorded as 11 percent of total exports.
Heroin exports are estimated at 200,000 kg, and the border price is several thousand dollars per kilogram, so total heroin exports are about $500 million.

Table 8A-4. Comparative Statistics for Burma and Other Asian Nations

Country	Fertilizer use[a]	Commercial energy consumption[b]	Bank deposits[c]	Exports[d]
Burma	17[e]	56[f]	8[g]	21
Burma	13[h]	39	—	—
Thailand	54	678	1,737	942
India	72	242	124	—
Philippines	—	—	—	257
Indonesia	115	321	224[i]	234
Vietnam	135	77	28	70

SOURCES: World Development Report, various years, World Bank and International Financial Statistics Yearbook, 1996, International Monetary Fund.
a. Per hectare of agricultural land, 1992 except as noted.
b. Kg oil equivalent per capita, 1993 except as noted.
c. Per capita, 1994 U.S. $ or as noted.
d. Per capita, 1995 U.S. $.
e. 1982.
f. 1971.
g. 1995.
h. 1994.
i. 1992.

Appendix B: Fast-Growing Countries That Slowed Down, 1980–1993

Percent

Country	Period of growth	Spurt GDP	GDP Growth
Brazil	1969–76	10.0	2.1
Cameroon	1972–81	9.3	0.0
Ecuador	1969–79	9.5	2.4
Egypt	1974–83	9.6	4.3
Ivory Coast	1969–76	7.7	0.1
Kenya	1969–74	8.7	3.8
Mexico	1969–81	6.8	1.6
Paraguay	1971–81	9.1	2.8
Philippines	1972–79	6.8	1.4
Tunisia	1969–80	7.4	3.7
Turkey	1970–77	7.2	4.6
Average	8.5 years	8.4	2.4

SOURCE: International Financial Statistics Yearbook 1996, International Monetary Fund.

Notes

1. Burma was the nation's official name in English until it was changed by the SLORC, the current de facto government. Partly for reasons of inertia, and partly to support the National League for Democracy, which continues to prefer the name Burma, many outside the country still refer to the nation as Burma. Because it is more familiar, this paper will refer to Myanmar as Burma. In Burmese, the name of the nation was and is still Myanmar.

2. The author made several visits to Burma from 1994 to 1996 for the United Nations Development Program to evaluate the Human Development Initiative programs. He is also a Faculty Associate at the Harvard Institute for International Development, but neither the UNDP work nor this paper is in any way connected to HIID. This paper does not necessarily represent views of the UNDP or of Tufts University. This paper is a reworked and revised version of one given earlier in 1996.

3. This calculation is based on estimates from the U.S. State Department of heroin exports (about 200 tons) and on estimates from Paul Stares, *Global Habit* (Washington, 1996), 53, of heroin prices close to those of northern Thailand ($3,000/kg). The Economist Intelligence Unit (EIU) *Country Report* for the second quarter of 1997 put Burmese government revenue in 1996–97 at 38,033 million kyat, or $230 million at the market exchange rate.

4. *World Development Report* (Washington, 1992), 220.

5. Data on Burma's real GDP and population from 1967 to 1996 can be found in *The International Financial Statistics Yearbook* (Washington, 1997), 610–611.

6. Agricultural data can be found in the Burmese government's *1996 Statistical Abstract* (Rangoon, 1996), 124.

7. The interest rates and ecological problems were directly observed during 1994–95 field research.

8. The IFS and EIU, 21, provide supporting data.

9. EIU, 31.

10. *1996 Statistical Abstract*, 87; IFS, 685.

11. Thailand may pay about $2-$2.50 per 1,000 cubic feet, and perhaps $1 of this will remain as taxes, or $180 million per year compared to a GDP of about $10,000 million.

12. EIU, 24.

CHAPTER 9

Drugs and Economic Growth
Ethnicity and Exports

Bertil Lintner

FOR DECADES Burma has been a major producer of both opium and its deadly derivative heroin, but until a few years ago very little drug money stayed in
the country. The north of Burma supplied the raw material—sticky, brown
opium gum—but the farmers, who grew the poppies, earned a pittance from
months of laborious work in the fields.

Historically, local merchants bought opium and sent it down to the Thai border. Ethnic rebels, who controlled remote parts of Burma, taxed opium growers
and the drivers of convoys who passed through their territory. Officers from the
Burmese army, who were supposed to fight the rebels and suppress the opium
trade, happily looked the other way if bribes were offered. But this was only "tea
money," and usually consisted of small amounts of cash, fancy furniture from
Thailand, golf clubs, and foreign liquor.

The real money was made when the drugs entered the Thai frontier, where
the opium was refined into pure, number four heroin, and shipped on to the
world market. The refineries were owned and operated by ethnic Chinese crime
syndicates that collaborated with local warlord armies. Those armies included
remnants of nationalist Chinese Kuomintang (KMT) forces or troops loyal to
Zhang Qifu, alias Khun Sa, a local Sino-Shan drug lord. Profits from those operations were laundered in banks in Thailand, Hong Kong, and Singapore, and
reinvested in often legitimate regional businesses such as hotels, real estate,
department stores, and similar operations which showed an almost undetectable,
fast turnover.

Over the past few years, however, this long-established pattern has undergone fundamental changes. Khun Sa and other Thai-based operators lost ground to a new generation of more influential and better-connected heroin barons in northern Shan State, adjacent to the Yunnan frontier. Beginning in 1989, those new heroin barons established a new string of refineries in Kokang and the Wa Hills, conveniently located near the main growing areas and, equally important, close to the rapidly growing Chinese drug market and easier smuggling routes through Yunnan to the outside world. The operators of those refineries were officers of the former Communist Party of Burma (CPB), who in early 1989 had mutinied against the party's aging, ideologically motivated but extremely orthodox leadership.

The party subsequently split along ethnic lines into four local groups which made peace with the government in Rangoon. In exchange for not fighting the central authorities, former CPB military commanders were granted unofficial permission to engage in any kind of trade, which, in the mountainous parts of the CPB's former "liberated area," inevitably meant developing the local drug industry. Opium production shot up dramatically, and the refining of raw opium into pure, number four heroin began in the northeast.

Khun Sa's old network was effectively undermined, and was further affected when, in December 1993, several divisions of government troops encircled the headquarters of Khun Sa's Möng Tai Army along the Thai border, placing an effective stranglehold on his operations. In January 1996, Khun Sa surrendered to the authorities in Rangoon, enabling him to restructure his organization, which was essential if he wanted to survive and stay in business. Since then, Khun Sa has been enjoying the same benefits and privileges as the former CPB commanders. In February 1996, ten new companies were registered at an obscure address in Rangoon, a virtually empty room in a townhouse with little more than a sign and a mailbox outside. The registered owner of the premises is a company called "The Good Shan Brothers International Ltd.," which is engaged in "export, import, general trading and construction," according to the 1995-1996 Myanmar Business Directory.[1]

The Burmese government openly admits that it has awarded an official contract to Khun Sa to run buses between major cities in Burma. Private business sources say that Khun Sa and his organization have been allowed to mine rubies and sapphires in the Mogok area, northeast of Mandalay, while Thai intelligence sources assert that shortly after Khun Sa's surrender, 600 million Thai baht (U.S.$24 million) were transferred to Rangoon from various financial institutions in Thailand.[2]

Since 1990, trafficking organizations based in Kokang and the Wa Hills have also invested millions in "export, import, general trading and construction" in Burma. Drug-related investments have been so extensive that a recent report from the U.S. Embassy in Rangoon concluded that Burma's "export of opiates alone appear to be worth as much as all legal exports," which amounted to U.S.$922 million, at the official exchange rate, for the fiscal year which ended March 31, 1996. The report also said that the Burmese government "makes no perceptible effort to bar investments funded by the production or export of narcotics."[3]

Privately, many Rangoon-based diplomats worry that Burma is becoming hostage to drug barons, as have some Latin American countries. The absence of any major serious foreign investment apart from American and European commitments to oil and gas exploration, has had the inevitable, and undesirable, outcome of making Burma increasingly dependent on investment by drug traffickers.

This fact, in turn, raises a question facing any outside power which is interested in the political and economic reconstruction of Burma: Will sanctions, as proposed by many opponents of the present regime, eventually force the Burmese generals to step aside and give way to democratic reforms and effective drug enforcement? Or will economic isolation just deliver the Burmese economy into the hands of the drug lords? This chapter does not attempt to answer those questions, but to discuss the present state of affairs.

Background

The dramatic changes in the pattern of opium production, the location of heroin refineries, and the opening of new smuggling routes have emerged in the wake of two recent political events in Burma: the crushing of a popular uprising against military rule in 1988, and an unrelated mutiny the following year among the rank and file of the country's most powerful insurgent army, the CPB. In August and September of 1988, millions of people from virtually every town and major village across Burma took to the streets to demand an end to twenty-six years of stifling military rule and the restoration of the democracy which existed in Burma before the army took over in a coup d'etat in 1962. The protests shook Burma's military establishment, which responded fiercely. Thousands of people were gunned down as the army moved in to shore up a regime overwhelmed by popular protest. The crushing of the 1988 uprising was more dramatic and much bloodier than the better publicized events in Beijing's Tian'anmen Square a year later.

In the wake of the massacres in Rangoon and elsewhere in the country, more than 8,000 pro-democracy activists fled the urban centers for the border areas near Thailand, where a multitude of ethnic insurgencies, not involved in the narcotics trade, were active. The 1988 urban uprising had shaken the military establishment in Burma, which had been in power since 1962, and it now feared a renewed, potentially dangerous insurgency along its frontiers: a possible alliance between the ethnic rebels and the pro-democracy activists from Rangoon and other towns and cities.

But these Thai-border-based rebel groups—Karen, Mon, Karenni, and Pa-O—were unable to provide the urban dissidents with more than a handful of weapons. None of the ethnic groups could match the strength of the CPB, whose 10,000 to 15,000 troops then controlled a 20,000-square-kilometer territory along the Sino-Burmese frontier in the northeast. Unlike the ethnic insurgents, the CPB had vast quantities of arms and ammunition, which were supplied by China from 1968 to 1978, when it was Beijing's policy to support communist insurrections in Southeast Asia. Although the aid had virtually ceased by 1980, the CPB had enough munitions to last for at least ten years of guerrilla warfare against the central government in Rangoon.

Despite government claims of a "communist conspiracy" behind the 1988 uprising, there was at that time no linkage between the anti-totalitarian, pro-democracy movement in central Burma and the orthodox, Marxist-Leninist CPB. However, given the strong desire for revenge for the bloody events of 1988, it is plausible to assume that the urban dissidents would have accepted arms from any source. Thus, it became imperative for the new junta, the State Law and Order Restoration Council (SLORC), to neutralize as many of the border insurgencies as possible, especially the CPBs. A situation which was potentially more dangerous for the SLORC arose in March and April 1989 when the hill-tribe rank-and-file of the CPB, led by the military commanders who also came from the various minorities of its northeastern base area, mutinied against the party's aging, mostly Burman political leadership.[4]

On April 17, 1989, ethnic Wa mutineers from the CPB's army stormed party headquarters at Panghsang on the Yunnan border. The old leaders and their families—about 300 people—escaped to China while the former CPB army split along ethnic lines and formed four different, regional resistance armies:

—The United Wa State Army (UWSA), led by Pao Yochang and—until he suffered a stroke in 1995—Chao Ngi Lai, comprised the bulk of the old CPB's fighting force, or 8,000–10,000 men at the time of the mutiny. This figure was soon to increase as the UWSA began procuring more weapons from China and Thailand to strengthen its forces. The Wa Hills form the center of what used to be the CPB's base along the Yunnan frontier and are a major opium growing area.

—The Myanmar National Democratic Alliance Army (MNDAA), first led by two brothers, Peng Jiasheng and Peng Jiafu, became the new unit in Kokang, a small district north of the Wa Hills, which is inside Burma but dominated by ethnic Yunnanese. Kokang traditionally produced the best opium in Southeast Asia. The strength of the MNDAA is approximately 1,500 to 2,000 men, and it is now led by Yang Moliang and Yang Moan.

—The National Democratic Alliance Army, Eastern Shan State, in the hills north of Kengtung where the borders of Burma, China, and Laos meet, was the name of a third ex-CPB grouping led by Lin Mingxian (Sai Lin) and Zhang Zhiming (Kyi Myint), two former Red Guards from Yunnan who had joined the CPB as volunteers during the Cultural Revolution and stayed. The area under their control is also very rich in opium. The strength of the army is estimated at 3,500 to 4,000 men.

—The New Democratic Army (NDA) with fewer than 1,000 men is the smallest of the former CPB forces. It is led by Ting Ying and Zalum and its area of operation is around Kambaiti, Pangwa, and Hpimaw passes on the Yunnan frontier in Kachin State. Although some poppies are grown near Kambaiti, this is not a major drug producing area.

The SLORC worried about potential collaboration among these four groups and the ethnic minority groups along the Thai border, as well as the urban dissidents who had taken refuge there. The ethnic rebels sent a delegation from the Thai border to Panghsang to negotiate with the CPB mutineers soon after the breakup of the old party—but the authorities in Rangoon reacted faster, with more determination, and with much more to offer than the ethnic rebels. Within weeks of the CPB mutiny, the chief of Burma's military intelligence, Maj. Gen. (now Lt. Gen.) Khin Nyunt, traveled up to the border areas to meet personally with Peng Jiafu, Chao Ngi Lai, and other leaders of the mutiny.[5]

Step by step, alliances of convenience were forged between Burma's military authorities and various groups of mutineers. In exchange for promises not to attack government forces and to sever ties with other rebel groups, the CPB mutineers were granted unofficial permission to engage in any kind of business to sustain themselves. Rangoon also promised to launch a "border development program" in the former CPB areas. Lo Hsing-han, the uncrowned "King of the Golden Triangle" in the early 1970s, played a major role in negotiating the cease-fire deals with the former CPB forces. Lo was arrested in Thailand in 1973 and extradited to Burma, where he was sentenced to death in 1976. But he was released during a general amnesty in 1980, and returned to Lashio in northeastern Shan State, where he became a small-scale entrepreneur, running bus companies, video parlors, and liquor franchises. The CPB mutiny provided Lo with a golden opportunity to rebuild his former drug empire, which he had lost to

Khun Sa and others following his arrest in 1973. Lo is a native of the Kokang region and was well placed to act as a go-between for the SLORC and the mutineers in Kokang.[6]

Ironically, at a time when almost the entire population of Burma had turned against the regime, thousands of former insurgents thus rallied behind the ruling military. The threat from the border areas was thwarted, the regime was safe, but the consequences for the country, and the outside world, were disastrous. The border development program progressed slowly, with a few showcases for foreign visitors. But the heroin trade took off with a speed that caught almost every observer of the Southeast Asian drug scene by surprise.

Chemicals, mainly acetic anhydrite, which is needed to convert raw opium into heroin, were brought in by truck from India, and within a year of the CPB mutiny, intelligence sources claimed that there were at least seventeen new heroin refineries in Kokang and the adjacent former CPB territory west of the Salween: four near the former CPB's Northern Bureau headquarters at Möng Ko; six at Möng Hom, about 20 kilometers to the south; two at Nam Kyaun; one at Loi Kang Möng south of the Hsenwi-Kunlong road; and four inside Kokang proper, east of the Salween.[7]

Six refineries were located in the Wa Hills, and their processing rate reportedly doubled during the first half of 1990. In Lin Mingxian's area in eastern Shan State, new heroin refineries went into operation near the Man Hpai headquarters of the former "815 War Zone," and at Loi Mi mountain near the border town of Möng La opposite the Yunnanese market town of Daluo. Burma's sector of the Golden Triangle has always produced the bulk of the region's supply of opium. Even so, the annual production of opium went from 1,100 tons in 1986 to 2,560 tons in 1996.[8] The area under poppy cultivation has also doubled over the past decade, and is still increasing; the 1996 figure is estimated to be 9 percent higher than that in 1995, and there are no signs to indicate that the government is making any serious efforts to curb the production and exportation of Burmese narcotics. On the contrary, the druglords, who are allied with the government, have expanded production to include synthetic drugs such as methamphetamines and ecstasy.

With the collapse of the communist insurgency in 1989, several smaller ethnic rebel armies gave in. The 2,000-strong Shan State Army, which for decades had waged a war for autonomy for Shan State, made peace with Rangoon on Sept. 24, 1989, and was granted timber concessions in the Hsipaw area in northern Shan State. Urban dissidents, who had been staying with the Shan State Army, either surrendered or moved to the Thai border. Other ethnic groups that have ended their struggle against the central government include:

—The Kachin Democratic Army (KDA), the former 4th brigade of the Kachin Independence Army (KIA), which operated in northeastern Shan State. It broke away from the main KIA to make peace with Rangoon on Jan. 11, 1991.

—The Pa-O National Army (PNA), whose 600–700 men were active in the Pa-O area in the hills around the Shan State capital of Taunggyi, concluded a peace agreement with the government on Feb. 18, 1991.

—The Palaung State Liberation Army (PSLA) in northern Shan State made peace with Rangoon on April 21, 1991. Its strength is estimated at 700-800 men.

—The Kayan Home Guards, a small, perhaps 100-man breakaway faction of the Kayan (Padaung) army in southern Shan State, made peace on Feb. 27, 1992.

—The Kachin Independence Army (KIA) with 8,000 men in arms was once one of Burma's most powerful ethnic rebel armies. It entered into an agreement with the SLORC in October 1993, and signed a formal cease-fire agreement with Rangoon in February 1994. As a result, several pro-democracy activists, who had fled to the KIA-controlled area in the north, surrendered in early July 1994.

—The Karenni Nationalities People's Liberation Front (KNPLF), a CPB-allied Karenni faction with perhaps 300 to 400 men in arms, made peace with Rangoon on May 9, 1994.

—The Kayan Newland Party (KNLP), a 100-strong Kayan (Padaung) rebel group in southern Shan State, made peace on July 26, 1994.

—The Shan State Nationalities People's Liberation Organization (SSNPLO), another Pa-O faction with 800–900 men active in the hills around Taunggyi, made peace with Rangoon on Oct. 9, 1994.

—The Karenni National Progressive Party/the Karenni Army (KNPP/KA), a non-communist Karenni group with 600–700 men, made peace with Rangoon on March 7, 1995. It operated in the hills of Kayah State, opposite Mae Hong Son, Thailand.

—The New Mon State Party/the Mon National Liberation Army (NMSP/ MNLA) followed in June 1995 and many of its leaders moved to Rangoon.

—The Möng Tai Army (MTA) of notorious opium warlord Khun Sa gave itself up in early 1996. Thousands of soldiers laid down their arms—machine guns, automatic rifles and even surface-to-air missiles (SAM-7s)—at a grand ceremony at the army's Homong headquarters on January 6, and, within a month, more than 12,000 men out of a total of 18,000 had "returned to the legal fold," as the government-controlled press usually puts it when a former insurgent group makes peace with the SLORC. Khun Sa himself moved to Rangoon and the former drug king, once demonized by the authorities in Rangoon, was seen shaking hands with Burmese generals and being greeted respectfully as "U Khun Sa."

Only a handful of groups along the Thai border remained in armed opposition to Rangoon in 1997, notably the Karen National Union and the All-Burma Students Democratic Front, with a combined strength of perhaps 4,000 troops. There are also remnants of the MTA which have refused to surrender and are roaming the hills of northern Shan State. Their number is estimated at 2,000–3,000 men who now call themselves the Shan State Army (SSA).

Despite the cease-fires, there existed in 1997 another 20,000-30,000 armed personnel in Burma who were not under any governmental control. According to the terms of the peace agreements, the groups have not only been allowed to engage in various kinds of businesses, but also to retain their arms and control over their respective areas. The cease-fires have frozen rather than resolved Burma's decades-long ethnic conflict. Some groups, such as the Was, have even strengthened their forces since they made peace with the government.

China: The Return of Drug Abuse

The CPB mutiny in 1989, and the subsequent cease-fires with the government in Rangoon led to the opening of new trading routes across the border into Yunnan, and on to ports along the coast of southern China. Officially, several former CPB commanders were barred from entering China because of their known involvement in the drug trade. But the fact that all of them had been operating for years along the Sino-Burmese border meant that they had long-standing working relationships with Chinese security authorities. These personal friendships enabled them to visit China regularly and own property across the border, including hotels and houses.

Within a year of the CPB mutiny, China had become a major transshipment route for Golden Triangle heroin destined for the West. China also soon developed into a lucrative market for the traffickers. The communist government almost wiped out opium cultivation and drug abuse in the 1950s; it is now back in full force, and China now has more addicts than most countries in the region. It officially counts 500,000 drug addicts, with Yunnan having the highest rate of addiction. The U.S. State Department's narcotics bureau estimates the real figure is two to three times larger. Some sources estimate the number of drug users in China at four million.[9]

The degree to which the influx of drug money had affected politics and society in Yunnan became evident in late 1992 when thousands of Chinese troops supported by tanks were forced to besiege a border town which had been taken over by drug traffickers. According to the Chinese journal *People's Armed Police News,* a major military operation had been carried out against drug traffickers in Yunnan in 1992 for "over two months beginning 31 August."[10] The target was Pingyuan, a town near the Vietnamese border, which served as a major smuggling center for Chinese contraband entering Vietnam before the border was opened to legal trade in late 1991.

The economy of the area was in the hands of the ethnic Yunnanese Muslims—Panthays or "Hui," as they are called in China—who have dominated the caravan trade in Burma for more than a century. Through their contacts throughout the Golden Triangle, Panthay drug smuggling rings had built up an extensive network of routes from Burma through southern China, and beyond. By 1992, Pingyuan had become a "country within the country," giving safe haven to outlaws and bandits from across China, the unusual report in the *People's Armed Police News* stated. Thousands of heavily armed paramilitary troops from the People's Armed Police (PAP), supported by armor, eventually moved in.

When the fighting, which lasted for eighty days, was over, the Chinese commanders found that drug barons were living in luxury villas with dancing girls and entertaining themselves in karaoke bars. Among them was Ma Siling, who owned a fortified villa in Pingyuan despite having been officially sentenced to death for drug trafficking by a local court in Yunnan. Significantly, knowledge of the operation in Pingyuan was kept secret from low-level officials in Yunnan. The net haul after the operation included 854 people arrested and 981 kilograms of drugs seized along with 353 assorted weapons. More than 1,000 PAP officers and privates received awards for "meritorious service in the operation," according to the *People's Armed Police News.*

Another drive against drug trafficking in Yunnan was launched in mid-1994. It followed the arrest on May 9 of Yang Moxian, a younger brother of Yang Moliang, Pheung Kya-shin's successor as commander of the Kokang-based MNDAA, one of the cease-fire groups that had been afforded status as local militia by the government in Rangoon. Yang was apprehended in Zhenkang, a small Yunnanese town just across the border from Kokang, and charged with smuggling hundreds of kilograms of heroin into Yunnan. Yang was executed in Kunming, the provincial capital of Yunnan, in October along with sixteen accomplices. Two of them were local police officers and another two came from the coastal province of Fujian. The involvement of the police reflected official complicity in the trade while the presence of the Fujianese showed links with organized crime: the Chinese Triads have always been strong among the Fujianese who also dominate Chinatowns in Burma, Malaysia, and the United States. An estimated 150–200 local border officials—police, customs, and security personnel—were also detained in the wake of Yang's arrest, emphasizing the magnitude of official complicity in the trade in Yunnan. Again, it appears that the central authorities have used the PAP to carry out the campaign. The deployment of the PAP, which could be described as the strike force of China's powerful internal security apparatus, to deal with the traffickers indicated that local authorities were unable, or even unwilling, to confront the drug problem.

The situation on the Burmese side, where government-recognized militia forces are involved in large scale drug trafficking, was raised by the Chinese when Lt. Gen. Khin Nyunt, Burma's powerful intelligence chief, visited China in September 1994. Despite an otherwise close and cordial relationship between the Burmese junta and the government in Beijing, the Chinese were said to be furious with Rangoon's connivance with the trade. Khin Nyunt was asked to take firm action against the traffickers. It remains to be seen if pressure from Beijing will have any impact on Burmese policies toward the gangs in Kokang and elsewhere, but in China the situation is becoming extremely serious and the authorities feel compelled to do something about it. It is estimated that 80 percent of the crimes committed in areas of Yunnan bordering Burma are perpetrated by drug addicts.

With the drug explosion in China, organized crime is also back with a vengeance. There is significant involvement by what are termed "outside elements," especially in border areas. In Shenzhen in Guangdong province, one of China's four special economic zones, drug trafficking involves the Triads, who are based across the border in Hong Kong. As early as 1991, the Shenzhen municipal government issued a special "Circular on Banning Drugs and Suppressing Triad Organizations."[11]

Organized crime may be China's biggest obstacle in its war against drugs. The PAP has performed well against certain groups in Yunnan, but sinologists warn against counting on the force to fight illegal drugs. They point out that Public Security Minister Tao Siju—who is also the PAP's political commissar—made headlines in 1992 when he said some Hong Kong-based Triads are comprised of "patriotic" and "good people" who are welcome to do business in China.[12] Tao mentioned especially the Xiang Brothers, Triad leaders who are deeply involved in the heroin business in Hong Kong.

Other Markets

After opening the China route, traffickers looked elsewhere for additional outlets for their drugs. In late 1991 and early 1992, trucks loaded with raw opium and heroin began heading from the poppy growing areas in the northeast down to the central plains around Mandalay, a town which is quickly emerging as the hub of the drug traffic in northern Burma; its many new restaurants, hotels, big shops, and luxury cars are ample evidence of this fact. This is where substantial amounts of drug money from Kokang and the Wa Hills are laundered and reinvested in real estate and the tourist business.

In early 1992, a string of six new heroin refineries was identified along the Chindwin river, close to the Indian border: north of Singkaling Hkamti, near Tamanthi, Homalin, Moreh, Kalemyo, Tiddim, and Paletwa on the western edge of Chin and Arakan states.[13] For the first time, refineries were established in traditionally "white," or insurgent-free, areas, close to major Burmese army installations. There are even reports of heroin refineries in the vicinity of Mandalay, run by mainland Chinese drug traffickers and protected by the Burmese authorities in exchange for fees.

Drug addiction has become rife in the northeastern Indian states of Nagaland and Manipur. The latter state had 600 addicts in 1988. A couple of years later, there were at least 15,000, and by 1997 the estimate had climbed to 30,000–40,000 addicts, many of whom are infected with the AIDS virus.[14] India reportedly has 7 million to 8 million addicts. Most of them use "brown sugar" (number three heroin) smuggled from Pakistan and Afghanistan, but Burmese heroin (white number four) is also becoming readily available in India. Most Indian drug addicts are between the ages of 15 and 35.[15]

The drug trade along the Indian border, and in Kokang and the Wa Hills, is "free" with many private traffickers and peddlers. By contrast, Lin Mingxian and Zhang Zhiming—the old Red Guards in the former CPB area near Laos—have established the best organized drug syndicate in northern Burma. The trade in the hills north of Kengtung, where they are ensconced, is strictly controlled by a committee of thirteen people, headed by Lin.

Lin's syndicate remains one of the best connected in Burma, with massive investment in Rangoon and elsewhere. During the recent political crisis in Burma in September and October 1996, Lin's deputy, Chinese-born Zhang Zhiming, was actually brought forward at an SLORC-sponsored press conference in Rangoon. He was introduced as "Kyi Myint," a "Shan leader" pleading for "economic progress" and non-confrontation with the authorities in Rangoon.[16] Few, if any, of the foreign correspondents who were present at this unusual press conference probably had any idea who Kyi Myint actually was.

A major refinery complex was set up a few years ago near the China-Burma border opposite Man Tang Shan village in China's Xishuangbanna (Sipsong-panna) region. Lin's group collects raw opium from his own area as well as from

Loung Nam Tha province in Laos across the Mekong border river. Their refinery is capable of turning out 1,000 to 2,000 kilograms of pure number four heroin a year.[17]

Through Laos, a new route has been opened down to Cambodia, where the island of Koh Kong has emerged as a major drug trafficking center. Lin has a wide network of contacts in Laos, dating back to the late 1970s and 1980s when right-wing Laotian guerrillas and Hmong hill-tribe fighters transited his area en route to Chinese training camps in Yunnan.

The first documented case of Burmese heroin turning up in Laos occurred in August 1991, when Laotian security forces pursuing a group of unidentified rebels who had crossed the border from Burma captured two of them and seized fifteen kilograms of pure heroin.[18] After this abortive attempt to open a route through Laos, Lin and his group are said to have approached corrupt elements within the Laotian military instead.

In Cambodia, drugs pass through Khmer Rouge as well as government-controlled areas, at one stage under the noses of the UN police who were stationed there in 1992–93 to supervise general elections.[19] The failure of the United Nations to restore peace in Cambodia, and the continuing chaos in that country, is seen as the reason why it has turned into a haven for the illegal trade in narcotics and arms as well as money laundering.

In a surprisingly candid interview with the Hong Kong–based magazine *Asiaweek*, Sam Rainsy, Cambodia's ousted but well-respected finance minister, stated:

> Land prices [in Cambodia] are very high because of speculators from Thailand, Hong Kong, Singapore, Malaysia and the many Chinese people in the region, who I think are related to the Mafia because they want to launder money. They launder money in three ways: property development, banking and gold smuggling . . . the money comes mainly from Hong Kong and Thailand—mostly from drugs and arms trafficking . . . trafficking in heroin from Laos is increasing. From Thailand and Burma the drugs go to Laos, and from Laos they go through the whole of Cambodia to Phnom Penh, then to Vietnam and to Sihanoukville . . . there are 29 banks in a small country like ours. [Some] are laundering money, making deposits and sending funds to another country and saying the money comes from Cambodia.

Intelligence sources also emphasize that it is not only Burmese groups that are buying weapons from the Thai-Cambodian border; other customers include the Tamil Tigers in Sri Lanka, the Naga rebels in India's northeast and armed opposition groups in the Philippines. The Liberation Tigers of Tamil Eelam (LTTE) especially seem to have been able to cash in on both the anarchic gun market in Cambodia—and the booming Burmese drug trade.[20]

While the border remains an important marketplace for arms, a new route for weapons from Cambodia was discovered in February 1994 when a ship carrying twenty tons of munitions was detained along the Mekong River while on its way to Vietnam.[21] Only 20 percent of the weapons were functional, but the investigation showed that private arms dealers in Vietnam buy old weapons from Cambodia, repair them, and resell them. Before they surrendered to the Burmese authorities, Khun Sa and his Möng Tai Army were reported to have bought large quantities of refurbished Soviet weapons at very low prices through middlemen in Singapore.

In addition to its role in the illegal trade in weapons, Vietnam is becoming an important transit country for drugs and a market for Golden Triangle heroin. The *Bangkok Post* reported in 1993: "One of Vietnam's most pressing social problems is rising availability of illicit drugs, and a concerned Hanoi government is spending great effort to combat the problem."[22] The first death sentences of drug traffickers were meted out later that year, but the situation today is believed to be worse than ever. Vietnam is believed to have at least 200,000 addicts.[23]

The Vietnamese authorities have stated that "international drug traffickers in Bangkok and Hong Kong have chosen Vietnam as a transit point for destinations such as France, Germany and East Europe."[24] Narcotics from Burma also pass through Laos en route to Danang and other seaports from which they are smuggled to North America and Australia.

In 1997, Vietnam was shaken by its most serious drug-related corruption scandal in recent history as a major heroin-trafficking network was unearthed through the confession of a smuggler from Laos, who had been arrested along the border. Twenty-two of those involved in the ring were sentenced by Hanoi's People's Court. Half of them were officials, including several senior police and Interior Ministry officials, and Ministry of Defense border guards.[25]

The drug invasion of Taiwan coincides with the surge in heroin production in Burma after 1989—and the rise of new drug gangs, which, unlike many of the older groups, have no historical or emotional ties to Taiwan. Sources in the Golden Triangle say the remnants of the KMT as well as Khun Sa's MTA always refrained from selling heroin if the destination were Taiwan. The new dealers, many of whom are former Burmese communists or Yunnan-based syndicates, may have no such qualms; to them, Taiwan is only a lucrative market for their produce.

A brochure issued in the mid-1990s by the government in Taipei states:

"Drugs were not a serious problem in the ROC [Republic of China] until five years ago. Now drug abuse has reached major proportions. . . . Recent drug busts have pointed to Thailand and the Chinese mainland as the major sources. ROC police estimate that 3,000 kilograms of heroin . . . finds its way across the mainland into Taiwan each year, but only one-tenth of this amount is seized by the police."[26] Another ROC government publication states that the amount of heroin seized in Taiwan did not exceed ten kilograms annually before 1990. In 1990, the amount jumped to twenty-two kilograms and increased to seventy-six kilograms in 1991 and 320 kilograms in 1992.[27]

In 1993, Taiwanese law enforcement agencies seized a record 1,110 kilos of heroin, morphine, and marijuana (96 percent of the kilos were heroin), and 3,357 kilos of methamphetamine (1,253 kilos were finished product; the rest were half-products and ephedrine, the raw materials), up 133 percent and 17 percent respectively from the previous year.[28]

Several recent reports from northeastern Burma indicate that the former CPB areas along the Chinese border are also becoming havens for producers of methamphetamines, which are sold mainly in neighboring China and Thailand, but also re-exported to countries such as Taiwan, Korea, and Japan.[29]

How Important Are Drugs to the Burmese Economy?

Given the magnitude of Burma's drug production, and the rapid expansion of markets in Asia where Burmese heroin and methamphetamines are readily available, it is not far-fetched to conclude that narcotics have become the country's single most important export. Burma's drug explosion has also had a tremendous impact on a number of related problems, ranging from the spread of AIDS in Burma, China, and Thailand to a surge in organized crime and gun running in the region.

Post-1989 developments have enabled the traffickers to invest their laundered drug money in Burma more easily than elsewhere in the region, creating a situation in which only oil can generate the same kind of revenue as illegal narcotics. The U.S. State Department reports that the former CPB drug armies have "benefited immensely from their good relationship with the Rangoon regime; their businesses—legitimate and illegitimate—have prospered . . . during the past six years there has been no progress in reducing opium cultivation or in stopping the heroin-trafficking activities of ethnic armies now considered part of the 'legal fold.'"[30] The report also identifies Lin Mingxian, Peng Jiasheng, Pao Yochang, Li Ziru of the former CPB, and Mahtu Naw of the KDA, as major traffickers.[31]

All of these traffickers have invested heavily in the booming construction business in Rangoon, Mandalay and other major towns. Robert S. Gelbard, then-U.S. assistant secretary of state for international narcotics and law-enforcement affairs, said:

> Consider these facts: Rangoon's *New Light of Myanmar* reported on August 3 [1996] the purchase of a new Rangoon office tower by Pao Yu-chiang [or Pao Yochang], head of the United Wa State Army, East Asia's largest heroin-trafficking organization. A photograph showed him shaking hands with Rangoon mayor U Ko Lay . . . eight SLORC cabinet ministers and numerous subordinates rubbed elbows with the who's who of Burma's drug trade at a lavish wedding last March of narco-trafficker Lo Hsing Han's son, who has taken over management of his father's business. SLORC is protecting the drug trade and flaunting its defiance of international concern, including that of its neighbors.[32]

Even the current Myanmar Business Directory of the Union of Myanmar Chamber of Commerce and Industry reads like a who's who in the drug trade. Khun Sa's "Good Shan Brothers" is listed there along with the Lo family's Asia World Group—Burma's biggest private business conglomerate today—as well as the various World companies associated with the Wa State Army, and the "Peace Myanmar Group," which is owned by the Yang brothers from Kohang.[33]

The Asia World Group has invested at least U.S.$200 million in various hotel and infrastructure projects in Burma.[34] A company profile, prepared by the Asia World Group itself, mentions investment in the Traders Hotel, the Shangri-La, and the Equatorial in Rangoon and the Sedona Hotel in Mandalay; a local Tiger Beer Factory project, garment industries, paper mills, palm oil, and the construction of office towers in Rangoon as well as a new road from Lashio to Muse on the Chinese border in northeastern Burma.[35] The main shareholder in this unusual group of companies is the Lo family's Kokang Import Export Co. Ltd., which lists Lo Hsing-han as its chairman and his son Steven Law (or Lo), or Htun Myint Naing, as general manager.[36] Their involvement with prominent businessmen in the region, including the powerful Robert Kuok, a Malaysian-born, Hong Kong–based multibillionaire, became major news in Southeast Asia when Steven Law was denied a visa by the United States in August 1996 for his suspected links with the Burmese drug trade. Law was on his way to negotiate a partnership with Wente Vineyard in California, which seems to have been unaware of the true identity of the Burmese businessmen who had offered to sell its products in Burma. The company subsequently terminated its plans to export wine to Burma.

The World group runs supermarkets and office towers in Rangoon, and is involved in the construction of condominiums. Another company funded by interests from the former CPB, Loi Hein Co. Ltd., has taken over the formerly state-run People's Ice and Softdrink Factory, and manufactures lemonade and orangeade in cooperation with personnel from the Ministry of Defense. Four similarly obscure companies are involved in the construction of a new toll road from Rangoon to Mandalay. As the U.S. State Department's March 1996 drug report concludes, "The lack of vigorous enforcement efforts against money laundering leaves Burma vulnerable to the growing influence of traffickers, who will use drug proceeds in legitimate business ventures, thereby gaining influence over investment and commercial activities."[37]

A major conduit for money laundered in that manner is the Union of Myanmar Economic Holdings Ltd. (UMEH), which was officially registered in February 1990 as a "special company" under the guidance of the Directorate of Procurement under the Ministry of Defense, with which it shares its offices. UMEH's authorized capital was stated as ten billion kyats divided into ten million shares of 1,000 kyats each.[38] Four million "A" shares are held by the government, specifically, the Directorate of Procurement, and six million "B" shares are to be held by active and retired military personnel and veterans organizations. It is in partnerships with the latter that drug lords have invested in this lucrative undertaking, which has set up joint ventures with a number of foreign companies. UMEH also controls the Myawaddy Bank which claims assets of U.S.$40 million, presumably including land. The bank promises in advertisements in the Burmese press "prompt, accurate, secure and secret" services for its clients.[39]

According to former U.S. Secretary of State Warren Christopher, "As the rule of law deteriorates in Burma, the threat its heroin trade poses to our nations is growing. Major drug traffickers receive government contracts and launder money in state banks. The warlord, Khun Sa, remains unpunished. The longer the political impasse continues, the more entrenched the drug trade will become."[40]

That impasse is unlikely to be broken so long as the SLORC's present policy of refusing to negotiate with the country's political opposition continues. The opposition manifested its strength in 1988–89 and won a landslide victory in a general election in May 1990, capturing 392 out of 485 contested seats in a parliament which, however, was never convened. More disturbingly, the SLORC's policy of neutralizing all opposition at any cost has turned the narcotics business into the country's main growth industry. How to deal with this growing problem—and its many extremely dangerous side-effects—remains a challenge to any administration in the United States, a major recipient of Burmese heroin, as well as to the countries in the Southeast Asian region, which are also suffering from a deluge of Burmese heroin.

Appendix: Top Four Countries in World Opium Production and Drug Production in the Golden Triangle

Table 9A-1. Top Four Opium-Producing Countries, 1989–1996
Metric tons

Year	Burma	Afghanistan	Laos	Pakistan
1986	1,100	300	250	200
1987	1,200	600	260	250
1988	1,250	700	260	250
1989	2,450	600	300	150
1990	2,250	400	250	200
1991	2,300	480	250	210
1992	2,270	650	250	200
1993	2,600	700	210	200
1994	2,100	950	80	200
1995	2,300	1,250	200	180
1996	2,560	n.a.	200	n.a.

Table 9A-2. Southeast Asia: Opium Cultivation and Production 1991–1996

Country	1991	1992	1993	1994	1995	1996
Net cultivation (hectares)	192,625	181,360	194,720	167,230	175,470	190,520
Burma	160,000	153,700	165,800	146,600	154,070	163,100
Laos	29,625	25,610	26,040	18,520	19,650	25,250
Thailand	3,000	2,050	2,880	2,110	1,750	2,170
Potential production (metric tons)	2,650	2,543	2,797	2,132	2,545	2,790
Burma	2,350	2,280	2,575	2,030	2,340	2,560
Laos	265	230	180	185	180	200
Thailand	35	24	42	17	25	30
Potential heroin production (metric tons)	221	211	234	177	212	233
Burma	196	190	215	169	195	214
Laos	22	19	15	7	15	16
Thailand	3	2	4	1	2	3

SOURCE: U.S. Department of State.

Notes

1. Union of Myanmar Chamber of Commerce and Industry, *Myanmar Business Directory* (Rangoon, 1995).

2. Bertil Lintner, "Drug Buddies," *Far Eastern Economic Review* (14 November 1996).

3. U.S. Embassy Rangoon, *Foreign Economic Trends Report: Burma* (July 1996), 92–93. The report also says that the cease-fire with Khun Sa has "allegedly resulted in large cash inflows into the legal economy," 82.

4. For an account of the CPB mutiny, see Bertil Lintner, *The Rise and Fall of the Communist Party of Burma* (Ithaca, 1990).

5. *Working People's Daily* [Rangoon] (31 May 1989). See also Bertil Lintner, *Burma in Revolt: Opium and Insurgency since 1948* (Boulder, 1994), 297–299.

6. For an account of Lo Hsing-han's past and present activities, see Lintner, *Burma in Revolt*, 213–230, 361–368.

7. Bertil Lintner, *The Politics of the Drug Trade in Burma* (Nedlands, Australia, 1993). This paper is based on information this writer collected in Yunnan in May 1989, January 1991, and January 1992.

8. See appendix.

9. For a succinct account of China's growing drug problem, see Dali L. Yang, "Illegal Drugs, Policy Change, and State Power: The Case of Contemporary China," *The Journal of Contemporary China*, No. 4 (1993).

10. *People's Armed Police News* (13 December 1992).

11. Yang, "Illegal Drugs," 23.

12. Bertil Lintner, "A Piece of the Action," *Far Eastern Economic Review* (22 December 1994).

13. "Burma-India: A Fourth Side to the Golden Triangle," *The Geopolitical Drugwatch* [Paris] (December 1992).

14. Harbinder Baweja and Arun Katiyar, "The Indian Face of AIDS," *India Today* (30 November 1992).

15. *The Nation* [Bangkok] (23 November 1996).

16. Stephen Brookes, "Former Rebel Leaders Talk with SLORC," *Asia Times* (3 October 1996).

17. "Cambodia: Mekong Pipeline," *The Geopolitical Drugwatch* [Paris] (February 1993).

18. The U.S. Department of State, Bureau of International Narcotics Matters, *International Narcotics Control Strategy Report*, Lao Chapter, (Washington, 1 March 1992).

19. "Cambodia: Mekong Pipeline," *The Geopolitical Drugwatch* [Paris] (February 1993).

20. "Tamil Tigers Shopping for Arms in Cambodia," *Phnom Penh Post* (20 September–3 October 1996). See also "Tigers Inc.," *Asiaweek* (26 July 1996), cover story which mentions LTTE involvement in the drug trade from Burma.

21. *Phnom Penh Post* (11–24 February 1994).

22. Alan Dawson, "Government Battling the Growing Trade in Illicit Drugs," *Bangkok Post* (3 August 1993).

23. Lintner, "Drug Buddies," (14 November 1996).

24. *The Nation* [Bangkok] (30 April 1993).

25. *The Nation* [Bangkok] (7 July 1997).

26. Government Information Office, *The War on Drugs in Taiwan, ROC* (Taipei, December 1993), 2-3.

27. The Ministry of Justice Investigation Bureau, *Prevention of Economic and Drug Crimes Yearbook, 1992* (Taipei, 1993).

28. Ying-Jeou Ma, Minister of Justice, Republic of China, "War on Drugs: The Experience of the Republic of China on Taiwan" (Taipei, January 1996).

29. The U.S. State Department's Bureau for International Narcotics Matters and Law

Enforcement Affairs, *International Narcotics Control Strategy Report: Burma* (Washington, March 1996).

30. Ibid.

31. Ibid. The spellings of the names of these traffickers vary depending on which system for Romanizing Chinese names is used.

32. Robert S. Gelbard, "SLORC's Drug Links," *Far Eastern Economic Review* (21 November 1996).

33. For a detailed account of Burma's narco economy, see Anthony Davis and Bruce Hawke, "Burma—the country that won't kick the habit," *Jane's Intelligence Review*, March 1998.

34. See a recent TV documentary from the Australian Special Broadcasting Service (SBS). Titled "Singapore Sling," it first aired on 12 October 1996 in Australia.

35. "Myanmar Business Update," Irrawaddy Advisors Ltd., Hong Kong (25 June 1996).

36. "Asia World Company Ltd.," a twelve-page document issued by the company, and various name cards seen by this writer.

37. See the report, which also is quoted in "Foreign Economic Trends Report: Burma," 93.

38. Ministry of Trade notification no. 7/90 (19 February 1990).

39. *The Nation* [Bangkok] (7 July 1997).

40. Quoted in "Drug Buddies," *Far Eastern Economic Review* (14 November 1996).

CHAPTER 10

Burma: The Booming Drug Trade

Robert S. Gelbard

Since the State Law and Order Restoration Council (SLORC) took power in Burma in 1988, the world's attention has been focused on the repression of the democratic opposition and the broader denial of human rights. The fundamental problem at the root of this crisis is the breakdown of the rule of law. This problem has also led to Burma's rise as the world's leading producer of opium and heroin. From 1989, the first full year of the SLORC's rule, through 1997 Burma was one of only four countries consistently denied certification by the United States for a failure to undertake adequate measures in the fight against narcotics. The others are Iran, Syria, and Afghanistan. Not without coincidence, all of these countries share a common bond of poor human rights records and lack of governmental accountability, factors that have contributed to the burgeoning drug trade.[1]

A convergence of factors has allowed drug production and trafficking to flourish in Burma: low political commitment to counternarcotics efforts, widespread poverty and underdevelopment, low and declining education levels, corruption, and the lack of governmental accountability. The SLORC's failure to address these problems has contributed to untold suffering not only in Burma, but in the region and around the world.

Burma has been the main source of heroin imported into the United States since the late 1980s and it is now spreading the scourge of amphetamines throughout East Asia. American interests in ending the abuse of Burmese citizens' most basic human rights and stopping the massive hemorrhage of drugs from Burma are complementary, not contradictory. Only a responsible government that has the mandate of its people can bring about reforms in both key areas through consistent application of the law to protect law-abiding citizens and punish drug traffickers.

Commercial Opium Cultivation Takes Off

Opium cultivation figures dramatically highlight the SLORC's failure to take action against narcotics. Opium production in Burma almost doubled from an estimated 1,280 metric tons to 2,430 metric tons in the first year after the SLORC took power. Production has remained at about this level in the intervening years, and in 1996, Burma produced an estimated 2,560 metric tons of opium gum, the raw material from which heroin is derived. The record outputs make Burma the world's unrivaled leader in opiates production. By comparison, Afghanistan, which is the second-largest producer in the world, produced an estimated 1,230 metric tons in 1996.

While poverty and underdevelopment have historically been key factors in sustaining opium cultivation in the highlands of Burma's Shan and Kachin states, these factors alone cannot account for the country's drug output. Reporting in recent years has shown that drug traffickers have encouraged the commercial cultivation of opium to provide stocks for the heroin refineries owned and operated by drug armies such as the United Wa State Army (UWSA) and Eastern Shan State Army (ESSA). This commercial cultivation of opium involves harvesting multiple-acre plots of planted poppy, and an organized effort on the part of both traffickers—who frequently give advance money, seeds, and fertilizer to farmers—and the farmers who must provide enough manpower for the labor-intensive task of scoring poppy bulbs to extract the lucrative gum. Farmers involved in this large-scale production of opium gum are earning revenues far beyond a subsistence level.

The SLORC's lax policies toward opium cultivation and drug trafficking have allowed this massive expansion in drug production. The ruling junta has made minimal efforts to eradicate the crop on the Shan Plateau. Until 1988, the U.S. government had funded and advised an aerial eradication program, which at its height was able to destroy more than 12,000 hectares of poppy cultivation annually. This program was limited in geographic scope and undermined by corruption and the absence of a meaningful program of development on the ground. Nevertheless, in retrospect it is clear that the eradication helped keep expansion of the crop in check. Following the Burmese military's bloody suppression of peaceful democracy protesters and staging of a military coup, the United States ceased counternarcotics assistance to Burma. The SLORC could have continued eradication efforts, but, in an early indication of its lack of commitment to fight narcotics, it instead halted the eradication program. Since 1988, opium cultivation has dramatically expanded from the traditional growing areas east of the Salween River, areas in the past not under the central government's control, to areas west of the Salween long subject to Rangoon's authority.

Faustian Bargains

Another sign of the near collapse of counternarcotics efforts in Burma since 1988 has been the SLORC's political accommodation with most of the country's armed drug trafficking groups. Through cease-fire agreements, the SLORC has seemed to sacrifice drug control objectives for security and economic objectives, which are of foremost concern to the ruling generals. In essence, the SLORC has agreed not to interfere with these groups so long as they honor their cease-fire agreements with the Burmese army. The original agreements were devoid of any drug control provisions, although the SLORC later obtained public antidrug pledges from some of the groups. Thus far, these pledges have not led to any tangible signs of effective drug control. In reality, these agreements have given the Wa, the Kokang, and the ESSA a free hand in developing their drug businesses.

In 1989, the SLORC forged cease-fire agreements with the ethnic drug armies formed from the Burmese Communist Party's (BCP) demise and made additional accommodations with other drug armies—such as the Shan State Army (SSA), the Kachin Defense Army (KDA), and the New Democratic Army (NDA) in 1990 and 1991. That left only one major narco-insurgent force which the Burmese army continued to fight: Khun Sa's Mong Tai Army (MTA). The SLORC seemed to differentiate between the other drug groups and the MTA, referring to the latter as a terrorist or criminal group. The SLORC spared no effort in vilifying the MTA and its leader Khun Sa, a key target of U.S. drug enforcement investigations, in its official media. This public effort as well as the Burmese army's counterinsurgency efforts against the MTA intensified in 1993, when Khun Sa declared his territory independent of Burma.

By mid-1995, the Burmese army's campaign against the MTA, coupled with U.S. and Thai law enforcement successes against elements of the MTA's drug trafficking network in Thailand, began to show success in the form of large-scale defections of MTA forces and the increasing financial problems of the MTA organization. It appears that sometime in early 1995, Khun Sa, through his representatives, began negotiating with SLORC officials for an eventual peace agreement. It is important to note that the MTA has always been composed of two separate entities: the large insurgent force of some 15,000 ethnic Shan troops, and a small core of leaders, largely ethnic Chinese, making up Khun Sa's business organization. The latter group, comprised of about twenty to forty people, was the money-making element of the MTA, involved in the drug trade.

On Jan. 18, 1996, Khun Sa appeared before the SLORC-run media and formally surrendered a large portion of the MTA's fighting force, along with weapons and military facilities, including the MTA's headquarters at Ho Mong near the Thai border. The SLORC touted this surrender as both a military and a counternarcotics victory; many Western analysts agreed that this signaled a setback to the Shan State drug trade. At first, reports of rising heroin prices and even shortages of the drug in northern Thailand seemed to confirm that the drug trade in that part of the Golden Triangle had been disrupted by the MTA's demise.

However, the SLORC's claims that the surrender of the armed Shan insurgent force was "unconditional" have been contradicted by reports that Khun Sa was assured by the government that he would not be extradited to the United States or punished under Burmese law in return for his cooperation. Burmese officials, who are well aware of the importance the U.S. government attaches to the prosecution of Khun Sa, have not responded to repeated U.S. requests for cooperation in bringing this indicted drug trafficker to justice.

Evidence strongly suggests that, while the military organization of the MTA surrendered to the Burmese, the much smaller business cell of Khun Sa associates has been spared a similar fate and continues to operate quietly. Several reports suggest that Khun Sa, through his sons and ethnic Chinese business partners, runs drug production and trafficking operations in the Shan State from his new residence in Rangoon. Though this peace agreement with the SLORC is distinct from earlier cease-fire pacts in that the MTA surrendered en masse, it follows the SLORC's predictable pattern of obtaining security gains at the expense of drug control.

Despite initial predictions that Khun Sa's surrender could have a long-term impact on the drug trade, it has not significantly disrupted the flow of narcotics from Burma to the rest of the world. The United Wa State Army has continued its business without interruption and is now the leading trafficking organization in Burma. The Wa, who maintain headquarters on Burma's borders with Thailand and China, are now increasingly shipping heroin through China in response to increased Thai law enforcement efforts. One of the largest seizures of Burmese heroin worldwide in 1996 was in China, indicating the increasing importance of the China route to drug traffickers.

Heroin reaches the world market from Burma through several routes. One is from north Burma across the border into China's southwestern Yunnan Province. From there, the heroin is shipped to China's southeastern coastal provinces and onward, often through intermediate stops in Asia, to the international market, including the United States. Another route is through central Burma, often from Lashio, through Mandalay to Rangoon or other seaports. There is also some trafficking through Kachin and Chin states to India.

The Kachin Independence Army (KIA) is the one ethnic group traditionally involved in the narcotics business that has reversed policy and developed effective measures against opium cultivation and narcotics trafficking. Tellingly, it has registered successes as a result of its own initiative and efforts, and not those of the SLORC. In 1991, then Kachin leader Brang Seng announced that no opium would be grown in his area and took strong measures against farmers violating the ban. Brang Seng had rightly come to the conclusion that the trade was hurting his own people as he saw addiction rates rise. He was concerned as well for the international reputation of the Kachin. The result was a decrease in the area of cultivation. The KIA also reduced trafficking through areas under its control. As the Burmese army moved into areas that had been held by the KIA following the 1994 cease-fire agreement, however, trafficking again began increasing. Burmese army personnel reportedly have turned a blind eye to trafficking in return for bribes.

As the ethnic armies began to reach agreements with the SLORC in the late 1980s, they also increasingly emphasized narcotics trafficking as a goal in and of itself and were less driven by ideological and separatist objectives. Before its dissolution in 1989, for instance, the Burma Communist Party (BCP) had funded its activities partly through drug trafficking, but it saw its main goal as fighting for the communist cause. Drug trafficking was a means to an end. The groups spawned from the break-up, however, put narcotics trafficking first. In the case of the Wa, those who had been in charge of trafficking in the BCP—including Peng Chia-sheng and Chao Ngi Lai—took charge of the organization, which has become Burma's leading drug trafficking group.

Turning to Legal Business

More than thirty-five years ago, a young ethnic Chinese resident of northern Burma was cutting his teeth in the heroin trade as a junior lieutenant in a government-sponsored drug trafficking militia known as the Kokang Ka Kwe Ye (Self-Defense Forces). Today, Lo Hsing-han, the pioneer of contemporary

Burma's druglords, lives in luxury in Rangoon, playing golf with senior Burmese generals and overseeing a large and growing empire of businesses which are prospering with the active assistance of SLORC officials.

Shortly after Lo helped the SLORC bring about the demise of the Burmese Communist Party, by far the largest insurgent threat to the central government throughout the 1970s and 1980s, he was instrumental in negotiating the first cease-fire agreement with the Kokang militia, one of the three main armed ethnic factions which emerged from the ashes of the BCP. This role earned Lo special status in the eyes of the SLORC generals, who felt indebted to him. Lo moved to Rangoon and, with government approval, began building an empire of legitimate businesses. Today these businesses are involved in a number of enterprises, including tourism and infrastructure projects of crucial importance to the modernization of Burma's economy.

Other traffickers have followed Lo Hsing-han's footsteps in gaining acceptance and clout in SLORC-run Burma. Shortly after the BCP's breakup and the conclusion of cease-fire agreements between the SLORC and the Kokang militia, the United Wa State Army and the Eastern Shan State Army, the drug traffickers who led these armed groups began showing up in Rangoon to share in the economic benefits of the cease-fires. This process of being "laundered" or having their images refurbished included their admittance into the government's National Constitutional Convention as "special invitees," highly publicized audiences with top SLORC generals including Khin Nyunt, and the right to open legal businesses in Rangoon and Mandalay.

Harnessing the Drug Trade

Denied access to the loan packages which international financial institutions normally make available to developing countries, Burma is hard-pressed to find sources of large investment to upgrade its woefully inadequate infrastructure. Those infrastructure improvements are vital to sustain economic growth in the country. The Lo family has invested in a key Rangoon container port facility and has a contract to build and operate a highway between the northern Shan State town of Lashio and the Chinese border (on the route of the old "Burma Road"). Unconfirmed reports suggest that Khun Sa's money is financing a new highway between Rangoon and Mandalay. These reports suggest to many observers that the SLORC may use drug money to fuel economic development.

With the new permissive business environment introduced as a result of the SLORC's desperate need for investment, the Burmese drug business is gradually shifting from its traditional site in the hinterlands of the Shan State to central Burma, particularly Mandalay and Rangoon. Drug proceeds which had heretofore been earned and banked outside Burma can now be repatriated and deposited in banks controlled by the military. The SLORC's 1993 introduction of Foreign Exchange Certificates (FEC) denominated in U.S. dollars allowed Burmese citizens to possess and use foreign currency for the first time. Drug traffickers now have a vehicle by which to repatriate off-shore foreign exchange holdings.

Traffickers Diversify

Burmese traffickers in the Shan State are diversifying their sources of income. Major trafficking groups in Burma have begun producing and trafficking amphetamines, relying on essential chemicals from China for the refining process. In many cases, amphetamines are produced side-by-side with heroin at refineries in the Shan State run by groups such as the ESSA and UWSA. Unlike the huge Shan State heroin trade which has been supported largely by demand in the United States and Europe, this new trend in amphetamine production is geared almost exclusively for the regional market. Amphetamine use is growing at an alarming pace in Thailand, Taiwan, China, and Malaysia.

Given the role that the Shan drug trafficking armies play in trafficking in both heroin and amphetamines, there is a new imperative for governments in the region to address the Burmese drug problem.

Burma at the Crossroads

Today Burma's drug trade is in a state of flux as the drug trade is becoming more closely integrated into the central Burmese economy. So far, the SLORC has sat back and watched or even encouraged this dangerous transition. There is no suggestion that the government is prepared to confront the worsening drug abuse problems in Burma's urban centers—problems that are the direct consequences of the government's laissez-faire attitude towards the armed groups that peddle drugs to Burmese youths in cities such as Rangoon, Mandalay, and Myitkyina.

Clearly, a heavy reliance on drug money would have a large distorting effect on the economy. Within the next few years Burma could join the likes of Colombia, where drug trafficking reaches the highest political levels and distorts economic incentives. Traffickers, with their considerable clout, can crowd out legitimate Burmese business people, who may be intimidated or unable to match the sizable financial resources available to traffickers when bidding for key contracts and business deals. Traffickers can easily elbow aside the legitimate entrepreneurs, just at the time when Burma is beginning to develop its infrastructure.

Traffickers have been allowed to shroud their drug operations with layer upon layer of legitimacy. As drug traffickers move into legal businesses, they will have easy cover for the movement and laundering of the large sums of money produced by the heroin and amphetamine trades. Traffickers' success in legal investments may create a dangerous cycle in which the government becomes increasingly reliant on them for additional capital investments to finance Burma's economic development.

Rule of Lawlessness

Over the past few years, the SLORC's repressive rule over Burmese citizens has been lawless and arbitrary. The military arrests political dissidents and even common Burmese who dare to listen to the speeches of Burma's main opposition leader, Daw Aung San Suu Kyi. Those arrested are often held indefinitely without charges, and are denied their rights to due process under the law. When the regime has bothered to cite laws in suppressing political dissent, it has been highly imaginative, trumping up charges for various insignificant infractions. However, when it comes to dealing with the country's many major drug traffickers—who operate openly and within reach of Burmese drug enforcement authorities—the regime has for years overlooked its drug laws and allowed traffickers with whom it has forged peace agreements to operate freely. In 1996, the government failed to bring Khun Sa to justice, and instead accepted him into the "legal fold," the SLORC's phrase for reaching an accommodation or peace agreement with an individual or an insurgent ethnic group. Such obvious disregard for international norms of law enforcement illustrates the arbitrary fashion in which the SLORC applies Burma's laws.

Though Burma is a signatory to the 1988 UN Convention on Illicit Traffic in Narcotic Drugs and Psychotropic Substances and the SLORC has upgraded the country's drug laws to add provisions to combat money laundering in accord with the criteria of the UN Convention, the government has done little to enforce its new laws and fulfill its obligations under the UN pact. The SLORC's failure to enforce these laws adequately suggests tolerance of the investment or laundering of ill-gotten gains.

The general breakdown of consistent law enforcement has also fostered a new wave of corruption. Though there is no evidence that the SLORC is sponsoring drug trafficking or is engaged in the drug trade in a direct and institutional fashion, mid- and low-level military and police officials are increasingly involved in drug-related corruption. It has been reported that Burmese army officers at the battalion commander level are implicated in the drug trade through, for instance, accepting bribes to allow the free passage of narcotics or collecting heroin or opium as a form of taxation. The SLORC seldom takes action against corrupt officials and, when it does, it usually confines punishment to the transfer of the guilty officer.

The Effect on the United States and the Southeast Asian Region

Burma is the largest source of heroin for the U.S. market. Partly as a result of the doubling in Burmese opium output since the SLORC took power, the purity of heroin on the streets of the United States has increased, the price has generally remained stable, and the number of abusers has risen. A decade ago, the average purity of retail heroin nationwide was about 7 percent. In 1991, the figure had risen to 26.6 percent and, by 1995, it had increased to 39.7 percent. Spurred by increasing availability, and by higher purity at generally stable prices, the abuser population has grown. A decade ago, the estimated number of hard-core heroin users was 500,000. Today it is about 600,000. From 1989 to 1994, the number of heroin-related hospital emergency room episodes has increased dramatically from about 42,000 to 64,000.

The method of abuse has also changed. With lower levels of purity, only injection could deliver an effective dosage. Today, inhalation and smoking are viable options that do not carry the stigma and some of the health risks, including HIV infection, of injection. As users shift away from injection, heroin usage is becoming "chic."

The tragic effects of Burma's expanding opium cultivation are all too clear in the United States. The effects are no less clear in Burma's neighboring states, where the drug abuse problem will complicate long-term social and economic development. China—which in the 1950s had proudly, if ruthlessly, eliminated the opium scourge—has seen a rapid resurgence of addiction in the last decade. Initially, Burmese heroin passed through China on the way to consumers in other countries, but, following the usual pattern, trafficking led to abuse. Addiction is especially well-entrenched along the trafficking route from Yunnan to

Guangdong. China's increasing rates of HIV infection can also be attributed largely to heroin injection.

In Thailand, with a population of about 60 million, the number of heroin addicts is estimated at more than 200,000, a higher per capita rate than in the United States. Initially a problem of the cities, heroin addiction in Thailand has spread to the hill tribes in the north and the fishermen in the south. Thailand also is increasingly concerned about extensive stimulant abuse.

Malaysia in 1995 experienced its highest number of new addicts and relapse cases since 1988, despite enforcement of harsh penalties for drug trafficking and a strong national counternarcotics policy. Malaysia's rehabilitation centers, where treatment for addicts is mandatory, now house about 15,000 people.

Much heroin is transported through Vietnam and Cambodia, and both countries are seriously concerned about the effects of trafficking on their own populations. Allegations of drug-related corruption in the Cambodian government have intensified Phnom Penh's concerns, and, before the leadership shake-up of July 1997, the government had worked closely with the U.S. Drug Enforcement Agency to strengthen Cambodia's law enforcement capabilities.

Laos, which is the world's third largest producer of opium, has initiated crop substitution programs, which have been successful in their limited areas of operation. There was, however, an overall increase in opium output in 1996. In addition, there are indications that trafficking through Laos from Burma has increased as routes through Thailand have been disrupted and as elements of the MTA reportedly have relocated to the Laos-Burma border.

Advancing Drug Control Interests

The outflow of heroin from Burma has terrible consequences for the U.S., but under present circumstances, U.S. influence on Burma's drug control policies is limited. Because drug trafficking and human rights violations in Burma are, as President Clinton has stated, "two sides of the same coin," a political dialogue is the key to the problem, and the United States will not take any steps in pursuing counternarcotics objectives that could compromise progress in human rights and democracy. In recognition of these considerations, Congress has also passed legislation placing strict conditions on counternarcotics assistance.

Multilateral programs, such as those run by the United Nations Drug Control Program (UNDCP), might be able to encourage alternative development strategies in traditional drug-growing areas. As experience in Thailand and elsewhere has shown, the economic and social needs of the farmer must be addressed if opium cultivation is to decline over the long term. Burma, however, has raised obstacles that have slowed implementation of UNDCP programs.

Given the limitations on U.S. and multilateral approaches, efforts by countries of the region are of great importance. The United States has encouraged Burma's neighbors to join in urging Rangoon to take effective action to reduce and eventually end cultivation of opium, production of heroin, and drug trafficking. The countries of the region are increasingly affected by Burma's laissez-faire approach to drug trafficking, and they are increasingly concerned by the problem. China is perhaps one of the countries most adversely affected by the outflow of narcotics from Burma. As one of Burma's leading trading partners and its prime weapons supplier, China has the leverage to press for an effective counternarcotics program.

The SLORC's interest in maintaining cease-fires with narcotics trafficking groups, and the growing involvement of drug traffickers in economic development projects, suggest that the SLORC is unlikely to take effective action soon against producers or traffickers of drugs. Thoroughgoing change will come only when Burma's government can offer ethnic minorities a legitimate means of sustenance through increased national prosperity, can undertake effective law enforcement measures, and can encourage national reconciliation. The U.S. government has long called on the SLORC to engage in dialogue with the opposition in order to help realize these goals. Failing national reconciliation, Burma will not be able to address systematically its drug problem, which poses a threat to the Burmese people, the region, and the world.

Note

1. The information in this paper came from U.S. State Department sources and analysts.

CHAPTER 11

The New Burma Road
(Paved by Polytechnologies?)

Frank S. Jannuzi

VISITORS TO Mandalay cannot help but notice that after a long slumber, the city has awakened and resumed its role as a jumping-off point to China.[1] Chinese restaurants and karaoke bars dot the city, and Mandarin can be heard in its banks, apothecaries, and retail shops. The settlement of the Kachin insurgency and improvements in road, rail, and air links have resulted in a boom in cross-border trade, and Mandalay serves as the hub. Products from landlocked Yunnan Province are flowing into Burma, some destined for re-export through Burmese ports. Chinese investment is growing rapidly, particularly in northern Burma. In exchange, Burmese raw materials—timber, jade, and agricultural products (notably opium)—are flowing into China.[2]

Big Brother, Little Brother

The expansion of economic links parallels improvements in political and military relations since China ended its support to the Burmese Communist Party (BCP) and began improving ties with Rangoon's military leaders in the late 1980s. China has become the primary supplier of weapons to the State Law and Order Restoration Council (SLORC). The relationship enjoys high level support in both capitals, although Rangoon remains wary of Beijing's intentions and harbors doubts about the wisdom of becoming too dependent on China. Burma's push to join the Association of Southeast Asian Nations (ASEAN)—an objective realized at the organization's thirtieth anniversary in July 1997 in Kuala Lumpur—was motivated not only by the SLORC's desire for international legitimacy, but also by its interest in establishing alternatives to Beijing as sources of investment trade, and even munitions.

China understands that the performance of the SLORC in the political/diplomatic arena—particularly its reputation for human rights violations and indiscriminate counterinsurgency campaigns—makes Rangoon a potential international liability for any friend. Nonetheless, China sees sufficient political and economic benefit from its "big brother" relationship with Burma to endure moderate international criticism. In heart-to-heart discussions in Beijing, Chinese leaders have advised the Burmese to keep dissident political activity under wraps so as to demonstrate for international consumption that Rangoon's military government is in complete and legitimate control. They have assured the Burmese that Beijing has no disagreement with the SLORC's stated plans for a "lengthy" process of constitution drafting leading "eventually" to an elected civilian government. Drawing on personal experience from Tibet and even Tian'anmen Square, however, Chinese leaders have also reportedly admonished the SLORC to play down the martial law basis of its rule and seek negotiated settlements with opposition groups.[3]

For its part, Burma still harbors old resentments about China's support for the BCP, and anti-Chinese sentiment occasionally bubbles to the surface. On Dec. 25, 1996, a bomb went off in Rangoon, killing five and wounding nineteen, during an exhibition of a Buddhist tooth relic on loan from China. The SLORC subsequently blamed the BCP, among others, for this terrorist act, an accusation which Beijing must have found galling. China supported the BCP in the 1970s and early 1980s, but its support tapered off in the mid-1980s and is now—like the BCP itself, which was formally disbanded in 1989—a thing of the past. Yet senior SLORC officials, including Khin Nyunt, continue to use the BCP as a convenient target for otherwise unattributable acts of sabotage. Government-controlled media occasionally contain references to BCP members "living inside China."

Guanxi

Burma's modern partnership with China has been built gradually through a series of reciprocal visits by trade, military, and political officials. The SLORC reached out to China at a time when it was internationally isolated and in need of weapons with which to prosecute more than half a dozen counterinsurgency campaigns. A loosely-enforced U.S. and European Union arms embargo precluded significant contributions from Burma's traditional arms suppliers. Beijing then, as now, was motivated by a desire to increase its *guanxi* (connections/influence) with Rangoon, building a "mutually beneficial" relationship in accordance with Beijing's longstanding foreign policy objectives. Beijing was also keen to find new buyers for its arms in the wake of the Iran-Iraq war, a war in which Beijing had profitably armed both sides.

SLORC Chairman Senior Gen. Than Shwe, accompanied by then Brig. Gens. Khin Nyunt and Kyaw Ba, laid the foundation for the current Beijing-Rangoon partnership when he traveled to Beijing in October 1989. Than visited state-run Norinco munitions factories and a Shanghai naval shipyard.[4] Than was hosted by People's Liberation Army (PLA) Maj. Gen. Song Wenzhong, but his access to top level Chinese officials appears to have been limited, based on muted treatment of his visit in the Chinese press. A request to meet with Chairman Deng Xiaoping and Premier Li Peng reportedly was denied.[5]

Nonetheless, Than's visit was an important milestone in Burma's relationship with China and marked a departure from Rangoon's past practice on arms imports. Pursuant to a policy of neutrality, Burma throughout the 1950s and 1960s eschewed large arms purchases and even turned down offers of U.S. military assistance. Weapons imports remained modest through the 1970s, despite an increase in the size and operational tempo of the armed forces. In 1989, confronted not only by the threat of popular uprisings in Burma's cities, but also by well-armed insurgent groups eager to exploit the regime's disarray, the SLORC set a new course. It launched an ambitious plan to enlarge and modernize the *tatmadaw* with heavy reliance on China.

Expanding Ties

A Burmese delegation led by Brig. Gen. Tin Oo traveled to Beijing in December 1989 and presented the Chinese with a shopping list of military hardware which reportedly was worth more than $1 billion.[6] Beijing agreed to reverse its policy of not providing military goods to the SLORC, initiating an arms trade relationship that has grown steadily ever since.[7] China's decision to support the SLORC reflects a blend of national interests: a shared 2,000 km border, counternarcotics efforts, market access for Chinese manufactured goods, and energy security.

Trade officials from prestigious and well-connected Chinese firms visited Burma in the early 1990s, gradually expanding Chinese investment in Burma's telecommunications, mining, automotive, aviation, and oil industries. The companies involved read like a "Who's Who" of Chinese industrial conglomerates, including China International Trust and Investment Corp., Beijing Automotive Industrial Corp., and the Machine Manufacturing and Electronics Industry. Chinese arms industry officials, including the chairman of Bao Li Technologies (a.k.a. Polytechnologies), also made numerous trips to Burma during this time, supervising the delivery of arms and signing new contracts worth tens of millions of dollars. Chinese arms carriers traded in their charts of the Persian Gulf for guides to Rangoon Harbor and Monkey Point.[8]

Beijing dispatched Foreign Minister Qian Qichen to Rangoon in early 1993 for meetings with Than Shwe and Khin Nyunt. Greeting each other as *lao pengyou* (old friends), Chinese and Burmese delegations discussed strategic issues, including opening up trade links with Yunnan Province and intelligence sharing. The Chinese apparently got a green light to proceed with the construction of a maritime reconnaissance/signals intelligence facility on Great Coco Island, just north of India's Andaman Islands.[9] China has also assisted with upgrades to the small Burmese navy patrol boat base at Hainggyi Island at the mouth of the Bassein River. Contrary to some press reports, however, neither facility appears to be a precursor to a Chinese naval base.[10] Moreover, China's interest in the Indian Ocean is clearly subordinate to more pressing maritime security concerns in the disputed Spratly Islands and the Taiwan Straits.

Maturing Relationship

Defense contacts continue to mature, with Tin Oo and other senior SLORC officers treading the now well-beaten path to Beijing. Tin Oo reportedly signed a $400 million arms package in November 1994, including helicopters, artillery, and armored vehicles.[11] In January 1996, Than Shwe made an official state visit to China, consolidating a relationship that has become critical to the SLORC's efforts to expand, modernize, and professionalize the Burmese army. Than Shwe's trip reciprocated a 1994 visit to Burma by Li Peng. During his visit to the "middle kingdom," Than Shwe and his Chinese counterparts tried to put the Rangoon-Beijing strategic relationship on a more solid foundation. Discussions led to broad agreements on political, cultural, and economic links. Both countries agreed to expand cultural ties and trade—now estimated at $1.5 billion annually[12]—and pledged not to interfere in each other's internal affairs. China also agreed in principle to provide additional development loans to Burma, although the details (i.e. whether the loans will be earmarked for specific projects using Chinese companies/equipment currently operating in Burma) remain to be worked out.

The emphasis on economic issues during Than Shwe's visit reflects China's priority of expanding trade with Southeast Asia and the SLORC's increasing confidence in its position vis-à-vis a host of ethnic insurgents who have waged low-level guerrilla struggles for greater autonomy since World War II. That confidence was sorely lacking in 1988, when Rangoon found that China was among a select group of nations willing to conduct business with Burma following the SLORC's brutal suppression of public dissent. The impetus for the rapid improvement in Sino-Burmese relations came from the SLORC's urgent need for weapons and Beijing's eagerness to parlay guns for cash, raw materials, and political influence.

Military Build-up and Counterinsurgency Successes

SLORC generals in 1988 began an ambitious program of expansion and modernization of the armed forces to cope with organized insurgents, such as the Karen National Union and the Kachin Independence Army; drug armies, such as Khun Sa's Mong Thai Army (MTA); and paramilitary political dissidents, such as the All Burma Student Democratic Front (ABSDF).[13] Since World War II, as many as forty ethnic insurgencies effectively thwarted Burmese efforts to establish firm control over large swathes of the country. Although they have not directly threatened the existence of the state since 1950, the insurgents exercised control over lucrative trade routes and rich timber and gem resources. The thought that these ethnic insurgents—numbering only about 35,000 to 40,000 effective combatants in the late 1980s—might link up with Burmese political dissidents lent urgency to the SLORC's army-building.

Through aggressive recruiting and conscription, the Burmese army grew from 180,000 troops in 1988 to about 300,000 in 1994.[14] The class size at Maymyo Defense Services Academy was increased from 600 to 800 students to help accommodate the troop build-up. Expansion allowed the army to put pressure on several of the more potent ethnic insurgencies simultaneously. Before the late 1980s, the Kachin, Karen, Karenni, Arakan, Shan, and Mon could count on at least a brief respite following any concerted army offensive. Beginning in 1991, the interval between "rounds" became shorter, and the recuperative powers of the insurgents were sorely tested.

The expansion of the armed forces created a large demand for infantry weapons. Burma probably would have preferred to negotiate for Soviet and Soviet-Bloc equipment, but economic conditions in those nations mandated hard currency transactions. In contrast, China stood ready to provide soft finance options, including barter and long-term loans, which the SLORC found impossible to refuse.

Bountiful Chinese Arms Basket

Of approximately $1 billion in arms purchased by Burma from 1991–1995, about $740 million came from China. China has sold Burma fighter aircraft (including at least twenty-four F-7 fighters and more than a dozen A-5 ground attack aircraft), Hainan-class corvettes, tanks, armored personnel carriers, and small arms. Hungry for export opportunities following the end of the Iran-Iraq war, Chinese defense industrial giants Norinco and Polytechnologies were quick to build bridges to Burma (quite literally, in the case of the Shweli River bridge completed in the fall of 1992).

The Burmese army has been the primary recipient of Chinese arms. The SLORC has purchased at least eighty T-69II main battle tanks and more than 100 light tanks from Beijing, and has also taken delivery of about 250 Type-85 armored personnel carriers. Beijing reportedly has sold more than 100 large-caliber artillery pieces over the past seven years, including 122mm field howitzers and 107mm Type 63 multiple launcher rocket systems. The army has also upgraded its transport capacity, importing about 1,000 Chinese trucks of various sizes since 1988.[15]

New weapons for the air force, though limited in number, have attracted considerable regional attention. Burma's Chinese-made F-7 fighters (a copy of the 1970s era Soviet MiG-21) do not pose much of a threat to Thailand, but they are a big improvement over Rangoon's old Swiss Pilatus ground-attack planes. Khun Sa's forces actually shot down two of the air force's Pilatus PC-9s in 1994, underscoring the vulnerability of lightly armed propeller-driven aircraft to insurgents equipped with shoulder-fired surface-to-air missiles. Burma's new Chinese A-5 ground attack aircraft, moreover, could pose a greater threat to Rangoon's neighbors, although limited training and poor maintenance standards probably will limit their effectiveness.

Naval upgrades have also received considerable attention, sometimes bordering on alarm.[16] Indian concerns about Chinese naval activity in the Bay of Bengal are reminiscent of Cold War descriptions of the Soviet invasion of Afghanistan as a strategic thrust to capture a warm water port, presumably in Pakistan. In fact, there is no evidence to suggest China hopes to establish naval bases in Burma, or that arms sales to Burma, Bangladesh, and Pakistan are part of a containment policy toward India. Beijing's emerging interest in the Indian

Ocean probably reflects its growing reliance on Mideast oil, particularly from Iran. Burmese navy acquisitions are fairly modest, with most geared toward coastal and riverine security patrols. In addition to its ten Hainan-class patrol boats, the navy recently took delivery of two Houxin-class guided-missile patrol boats (PGM) equipped with C-801 surface-to-surface missiles. Rangoon probably hopes that the Houxin-class PGMs will discourage Thai fishermen from encroaching on Burmese waters; Thai fishing boats were involved in several deadly clashes with Burmese navy vessels in 1996.

The Keys to Rangoon's Success

For all of its reliance on China as an arms supplier, the Burmese army's success against insurgent groups in the early 1990s had less to do with Chinese weapons, *per se,* than it did with improved logistics and the political fragmentation of the opposition. Accordingly, suspension of Chinese military assistance probably would do little to undermine the SLORC's counterinsurgency efforts. Japanese trucks and Polish helicopters have done more to consolidate Burma's hold over remote mountainous regions than have Norinco tanks. The primary insurgent threats to the Burmese army are found almost exclusively in mountainous or swampy regions ill-suited to tank warfare.

Similarly, Beijing's export of F-7 fighters to the SLORC may have raised eyebrows in Bangkok, but Karen insurgents know the jets are of little value in a guerrilla war. Most of the F-7s have never seen battle. Chinese A-5 ground attack aircraft should have improved the ability of the Burmese air force to provide close air support to its light infantry divisions, but in practice the A-5s overfly the battlefield too quickly to put metal on target, especially given limited Burmese air force pilot training and poor coordination between army and air force units. Air force readiness is further limited by maintenance problems and shortages of spare parts. Chinese jets may have boosted the morale of Burmese pilots, but they have played only a minor role in the government's counterinsurgency efforts.

Emphasis on Logistics

Before 1992, Rangoon placed little formal emphasis on logistics support to the army, counting on it to live off the land and husband scarce ammunition supplies. Traditionally, the army traveled light and fast, an advantage in Burma's

mountainous terrain where long baggage trains are an invitation to ambush. Each
dry season, regional commands, supplemented by battalions drawn from a central complement of light infantry divisions, undertook raids on insurgent strong-
holds. Each spring they fell back to secure positions, making little effort to hold
on to any captured turf. Unfortunately for the army, the insurgents anticipated
many of the thrusts and simply moved out of the way, quickly reasserting themselves once the monsoon rains made the army's advance posts untenable.

Beginning with its 1991–92 dry season offensive, the army undertook a concerted effort to improve roads and airports, build heliports, and expand ware-
houses adjacent to insurgent-held territory, shortening supply lines and permit-
ting year-round operations. With dozens of new battalions to draw on, the army's
Tactical Operational Commands were able to commit regional units and light
infantry battalions to action while maintaining adequate mobile reserves. The
army demonstrated patience, consolidating gains before probing for additional
weakness.

Defeating the Karen National Union

The army's offensive against the Karen National Union (KNU) from 1992 to
1995 demonstrated the impact of logistics upgrades and improved counterinsurgency techniques. Although KNU elements continue to resist Rangoon's efforts
to consolidate its hold on the Thai-Burma border, they no longer have any realistic chance of wresting control away from the SLORC and its allies in the
Salween River valley. At the end of April 1992, major elements of three light
infantry divisions finally drove the KNU off Sleeping Dog Mountain, high
ground which commanded the western approaches to the KNU stronghold of
Mannerplaw. From Sleeping Dog Mountain, artillery could range Mannerplaw,
although shelling the village proved difficult given the intervening terrain.
During its advance on Sleeping Dog Mountain, the army used helicopters extensively to supply forward positions, evacuate wounded soldiers, and scout enemy
troop concentrations. Chinese Y-8 Cub transports also provided logistic support.
The SLORC even forced convicts from Insein Prison to serve as porters, light-
ening the load carried by soldiers and thereby improving their mobility. As wet
weather approached, the army fortified its outposts on the mountain and built lat-
erite roads linking these positions with forward bases of supply.

To the south, the army approached the KNU stronghold of Kawmura in a
similar way. Kawmura was guarded on three sides by the Moi River, and the sole
land approach was heavily fortified. Approaching slowly and always retaining

the high ground, the army drew a noose around Kawmura. Army engineers worked for two years to improve road access to these forward positions before the army felt confident enough to proceed.

After effectively isolating Mannerplaw and Kawmura, the SLORC moved to undercut the morale and cohesion of its adversary. The army succeeded in convincing the Thai to restrict the flow of arms and supplies from Karen refugee camps along the Salween to KNU insurgents operating inside Burma. Still, the army would have faced a difficult and bloody final campaign against the KNU were it not for the fragmentation of the insurgency in December 1994. Rangoon exploited differences between Karen Buddhists and Christians, encouraging the formation of the pro-SLORC Democratic Kayin Buddhist Organization (DKBO) and its military arm (the DKBA). This breakaway group, although comprising only a few hundred combatants, played a key role in the fall of Mannerplaw. They provided valuable intelligence on the location of mine fields and other obstacles and conducted a series of cross-border raids to force Karen refugees in Thailand to return to Burma. Rangoon continues to rely on the DKBA to keep pressure on the KNU and to launch periodic attacks—most recently in January 1997—on Karen refugee camps just across the Thai border.

Future Challenges

In the short run, expanding and modernizing the military has given the SLORC an edge in coping with ethnic insurgents. Over a longer timeframe, the SLORC probably calculates that its new tanks and armored personnel carriers will prove effective in deterring anti-government protests, or in any case will enable the army to quickly crush them. Ultimately, however, the massive buildup may prove counterproductive. Burma's debt to China will prove difficult to pay. Salaries and pensions for the bloated military will make much-needed investments in education, health, and transportation infrastructure difficult to finance. Newly acquired weapons have put a strain on the army's maintenance and supply system; Chinese armored vehicles are unreliable and difficult to service. Operational readiness levels in Burma's air force and navy are low. Both services are expensive to operate and require large numbers of personnel with technical expertise, rare in Burma even before the closing of its universities.

Paradoxically, efforts to address these difficulties could spawn new ones. Burma's military leadership recognizes that its new weapons need to be melded into a force that is capable of conducting combined arms/joint service operations. However, little has actually been done to begin the process of training and evaluating that would be necessary to build competence in joint operations. Given the limited depth of the officer corps' experience, it is doubtful that greatly improved capability by any branch of the Burmese armed forces will be demonstrated soon. Moreover, field commanders comfortable with the tatmadaw's traditional light infantry counterinsurgency role may come to resent the prominence of a new generation of "desk jockeys" and foreign-trained specialists who are essential to the functioning of a modern military. There is already some evidence that Chinese-trained officers and graduates of the prestigious Defense Services Academy are being viewed with suspicion by less well-schooled fellow officers. The expansion and modernization drive eventually may threaten cohesion in the military, opening fissures which could be exploited by opposition groups.

Epilogue: Whose Army Is It, Anyway?

On March 27, 1996, the fifty-first anniversary of the day on which the Burmese openly joined the resistance to the Japanese, the Burmese military celebrated what is now commemorated as Armed Forces Day. Than Shwe reviewed about 4,000 troops drawn from the three branches of the armed forces on a closed parade ground near the parliament building. Organized groups of supporters, including ethnic minority representatives in native costume, were on hand, as were foreign military attaches.

Than Shwe praised the military for its role against the Japanese and stressed the closeness of the military to the Burmese people. He spoke of the unique savior role repeatedly played by the armed forces since the end of World War II and heralded the success of the SLORC in bringing fifteen ethnic groups back into the "legal fold." In a pointed challenge to the National League for Democracy, Than Shwe criticized foreign and domestic "deconstructionists" out to undermine the good work of the Burmese military.

Across town, about a thousand persons attended the NLD's lecture held under the rubric of the earlier designation of the holiday, namely Fascist Resistance Day. NLD Vice-Chairman Tin Oo, among others, praised Burmese army founder Gen. Aung San and the popular resistance to Japanese rule. The subtext of his speech was that the SLORC is a fascist regime which has betrayed the traditional role of the Burmese military as a "people's army."

The two presentations could not have contrasted more sharply. They foreshadowed the steady retreat in 1996 from the national reconciliation both sides once spoke of wanting. As is often the case with such opposing polemical remarks, the true nature of the Burmese army and its role in Burmese society must lie somewhere in the middle ground; neither a benign savior of the people nor a fascist oppressor, but rather an instrument of Burmese nationalism and territorial integrity currently in the hands of authoritarians unwilling to bow to civilian, democratic rule. China's continuing support for the SLORC, particularly its role as Rangoon's arms merchant, helps to insulate the regime from mounting international pressure for reform. It also complicates Beijing's relations with its ASEAN neighbors and conjures unflattering comparisons between the SLORC and China's own post-Tiananmen leadership.

Notes

1. The views expressed here are solely those of the author, and do not necessarily represent the judgments or policies of the U.S. Government or the Department of State.

2. Personal observations, October 1994. See also Mya Maung, "On the Road to Mandalay: A Case Study of the Sinonization of Upper Burma," *Asian Survey,* XXXIV (1994), 447–459.

3. Observations drawn from personal interviews with Chinese Ministry of Foreign Affairs Southeast Asia hands in meetings in October 1994. In October 1996, analysts from the China Institute for International and Strategic Studies in Beijing confirmed to the author that senior Beijing officials had often offered Rangoon advice on how best to resolve its insurgency problems.

4. Bertil Lintner, "Lock and Load," *Far Eastern Economic Review* (13 September 1990), 28.

5. Author's interview with knowledgeable Chinese government authorities in Beijing, October 1994.

6. Precise estimates of the value of Chinese arms exports to Burma are difficult to make. Often the monetary value of the deal is masked by terms of payment which may include a mix of loans, barter, and hard currency. For the best "guesstimate" of the value of recent Burmese arms imports, see *World Military Expenditures and Arms Transfers*, Arms Control and Disarmament Agency (Washington, 1995), 104.

7. Bertil Lintner, "Myanmar's Chinese Connection," *International Defense Review*, XXVII (1994), 23–26.

8. Chinese defense industries rely on PRC merchant vessels to transport most of their arms shipments. These vessels made frequent visits to the Persian Gulf during the Iran-Iraq war, and began to make port calls in Burma in the early 1990s.

9. Robert Karniol, "Chinese Puzzle over Burmese SIGINT Base," *Jane's Defence Weekly* (29 January 1994), 14.

10. Such reports probably originate in Indian defense circles, where officials are eager to stave off budget cuts. Beijing reportedly has given assurances to Rangoon that it has no intention of building bases in Burma; see Surjit Mansingh, "An Overview of India-China Relations: From When to Where," *Indian Defense Review* (New Delhi), 285–300. In October 1996, the author was told emphatically by PRC analysts associated with the Ministry of State Security that Beijing had no intention of abandoning its policy against basing troops or naval units overseas, although this assurance begs the question of navy port calls.

11. Bertil Lintner, "$400M Deal Signed by China and Myanmar," *Jane's Defence Weekly* (3 December 1994), 1.

12. Bertil Lintner, "Rangoon's Rubicon," *Far Eastern Economic Review* (11 February 1993), 28.

13. For an in-depth analysis, see Andrew Selth, "Burma's Arms Procurement Programme,"

Strategic & Defence Studies Centre Working Paper No. 289, Australian National University, 1995.

14. Bertil Lintner and Robert Kamiol, "Unrest Swells the Burmese Ranks," *Jane's Defence Weekly* (13 June 1992), 1020.

15. Reliable figures on Burma's precise imports of Chinese weapons systems are hard to come by. Some of the more authoritative reports have been filed by Bertil Lintner. See especially "Chinese Arms Bolster Burmese Forces," *Jane's Defence Weekly* (27 November 1991). See also Lintner "Arms for Eyes," *Far Eastern Economic Review* (16 December 1993).

16. See Ruben Banerjee, "China: Worrying Approach," *India Today* (New Delhi) (30 April 1994), 71; Brahma Chellaney, "The Dragon's Chicanery behind the Smile," *Pioneer* (New Delhi) (23 October 1996).

CHAPTER 12

Foreign Direct Investment in Burma
Trends, Determinants, and Prospects

Mark Mason

FOREIGN DIRECT investment (FDI) is once again entering Burma.[1] Following the virtual absence of such investment during some three decades of self-imposed isolation, this Southeast Asian country has attracted modest inflows of FDI from Asia and the West since 1989. On an approvals basis, the energy sector has received more FDI than any other industry, but significant quantities of FDI have been approved in the hotels and tourism, and mining sectors as well.[2]

This fresh infusion of FDI has in turn raised important questions about its characteristics, the location-specific advantages and disadvantages of Burma as an investment host, and the future prospects for such investment in this frontier Southeast Asian economy. To answer these and related questions, this chapter examines recent FDI trends in Burma, the current position of such investment in the country, and its principal features. The major determinants of Burma's investment record and the ways in which FDI in Burma likely will evolve in the foreseeable future are also analyzed.

FDI in Burma: An Overview

Foreign direct investors have participated in the economy of Burma for centuries. Portuguese interests operated factories in the country as early as the 1500s, as did Britain's East India Company in the 1600s. Among Western interests, the Dutch also had established operations in Burma well before the end of the 1700s. These European investors procured and exported Burma's teak and other natural resources.[3] The country's foreign investment and other international economic relations with its two largest regional neighbors, China and India, extend back still further.[4]

British and other FDI increased substantially beginning in the latter half of the nineteenth century. Firms based in Great Britain and elsewhere in the British Empire in particular invested aggressively following the British annexation of Lower Burma in 1852, and extended their investments northward after the colonization of Upper Burma in 1886.[5] These firms participated actively in the trade of timber, rice, petroleum, and other products. (Indeed, Burma was the world's largest rice exporter before World War II.) Accumulations of FDI in Burma probably peaked during the years immediately preceding World War II. British, Indian, and Chinese investments predominated, with total stocks of FDI in Burma calculated to have reached some £155 million by 1941.[6] It has been estimated that no less than one quarter of the nation's capital stock was by then owned by foreign investors, and profit, interest, and dividend remittances together amounted to some 6 percent of gross domestic product (GDP).[7]

Foreign direct investors returned to Burma shortly after the end of World War II, and were permitted to operate in the country through the early 1960s. After the country achieved independence from Great Britain in 1948, foreign companies once again came to occupy important positions in the petroleum, teak, and other industries.[8] These FDI inflows received official encouragement following issuance of the Burmese government's 1955 Investment Policy Statement as well as its subsequent (1959) passage of the Union of Burma Investment Act, the latter of which provided significant tax and other incentives for approved investment projects together with limited guarantees against nationalization.[9]

In the wake of a military coup in 1962, however, Burmese authorities abruptly changed their policy toward inward FDI. Under the slogan "The Burmese Way to Socialism," the newly installed military government run by Gen. Ne Win pursued a national strategy of central economic planning and international economic isolation. The state nationalized virtually all major business enterprises and strictly regulated most forms of economic activity, including international trade and foreign investment.[10] With the exception of a few offshore foreign oil and gas concessions and a joint venture between the new government and Fritz Werner, a West German engineering firm, to manufacture arms, the government prohibited FDI in Burma for more than a quarter of a century thereafter.[11]

Recent Trends

In recent years, however, Burma once again has begun to receive significant inflows of direct investment from abroad. Following a change of government in the latter part of 1988, the newly installed military regime controlled by the so-called State Law and Order Restoration Council (SLORC) enacted a Foreign Investment Law (FIL) to facilitate the entry of approved FDI. Passage of the FIL was one of the SLORC's very first legislative initiatives, and marked a major policy departure from the country's previous stance towards the international economy.

Official government statistics on approvals of FDI applications under the investment law offer some insights into recent trends and other features of this new investment.[12] The value of FDI approvals under the law, which took effect in 1989, has varied considerably during the subsequent years of recorded activity.[13] (See table 12-1 for annual approvals [and disbursements, discussed below] by source country for fiscal years 1989/90 through 1995/96).[14] Following fairly modest approved inflows immediately after enactment of the law, foreign investment fell off sharply in 1991/92, but then regained momentum beginning in 1992/93 and peaked in 1994/95. Approval of FDI in a major offshore natural gas project—perhaps the country's single most ambitious infrastructural development project to date—accounts for most of the exceptionally large quantity of approved FDI in 1994/95.[15] On this approvals basis, accumulated inflows of FDI between 1989/90 and 1995/96 totaled roughly U.S. $3.24 billion.[16]

On a disbursements rather than approvals basis, however, the inflow record looks different. Disbursements measure quantities of FDI actually invested in the local economy rather than amounts of such investment approved by the authorities. According to official Burmese government statistics made available to the International Monetary Fund, FDI inflows from 1989/90 through 1995/96 using this alternative measure have been far more modest than the approvals figures would suggest. At the same time, these disbursements-based inflow data point to a smoother, less erratic year-to-year pattern of FDI entry. On this disbursements basis, accumulated inflows of FDI between 1989/90 and 1995/96 totaled roughly $1.21 billion (or about 37 percent of the approved total for that same period).

Official Burmese data on FDI approved under the foreign investment law reveal additional information. By country, these data indicate that the United Kingdom ranked first in total quantities of approved FDI as measured by the Burmese authorities through 1995/96 (with $792 million), followed by

Table 12-1. FDI Inflows to Burma by Source Country, 1989/90–1995/96

US $Millions

Country	1989/90		1990/91		1991/92		1992/93		1993/94		1994/95		1995/96	
	Approved[b]	Actual[c]	Approved[b]	Actual[c]	Approved[b]	Actual[c]	Approved[a]	Actual[b]	Approved[a]	Actual[b]	Approved[a]	Actual[b]	Approved[a]	Actual[d]
Australia	25.2	5.0	—	18.0	—	13.2	2.0	0.6	—	—	1.0	—	1.8	2.8
Austria	71.5	—	—	—	—	—	—	—	—	—	—	0.1	—	—
Bangladesh	—	—	3.0	2.9	—	—	—	—	—	—	—	—	—	—
Canada	22.0	6.6	—	8.3	—	11.9	—	10.8	—	0.1	4.4	—	3.0	0.7
China	—	—	—	—	—	—	0.4	—	0.7	—	455.0	0.1	—	2.5
France	—	—	—	—	—	—	10.0	27.1	—	24.7	—	25.0	0.2	90.4
Hong Kong	1.0	—	11.4	1.3	0.6	—	14.3	3.3	30.9	1.5	6.1	6.5	0.2	5.7
Japan	40.0	5.8	60.0	32.3	0.7	31.0	0.5	5.7	—	1.0	—	0.5	18.7	0.4
Republic of Korea	50.1	7.1	3.3	40.9	4.0	38.0	—	7.3	3.1	2.0	0.2	0.6	—	1.5
Macau	—	—	—	—	—	—	2.4	—	—	1.6	—	0.4	—	—
Malaysia	80.0	10.5	—	26.0	—	—	8.6	1.4	45.2	1.8	15.8	0.5	157.7	6.5
The Netherlands	—	—	—	—	—	40.2	—	25.0	—	—	3.0	0.1	—	2.0
The Philippines	—	—	—	—	—	—	—	—	—	—	6.7	3.0	—	3.1
Singapore	3.5	0.9	5.3	2.2	—	3.5	23.2	1.2	228.8	6.1	55.1	29.8	288.0	53.3
Sri Lanka	—	—	—	—	—	—	—	—	—	—	1.0	—	—	0.2
Thailand	64.1	—	96.9	19.6	0.6	—	8.9	1.0	41.3	9.0	199.8	15.0	10.2	32.4
United Kingdom	12.1	4.3	7.5	12.9	—	10.0	4.0	13.4	8.1	10.5	599.8	16.6	160.4	90.6
United States	80.0	15.8	93.2	60.7	—	87.3	29.5	52.2	19.5	33.4	4.0	16.4	14.8	30.8
Total	449.5	56.0	280.6	225.1	5.9	235.1	103.8	149.0	377.6	91.7	1,351.9	114.6	654.8	322.9

SOURCES: Data provided by the Burma/Myanmar authorities, as reported by the IMF and the ADB.

a. It should be noted that the term "country" does not in all cases refer to a territorial entity that is a state as understood by international law and practice. The term also covers some territorial entities that are not states but for which statistical data are maintained and provided internationally on a separate and independent basis.

b. Projects approved by the Myanmar Investment Commission under the provisions of the 1988 Foreign Investment Law; those permits that have been withdrawn or canceled are adjusted. Exclusive of drawback items.

c. Investment actually disbursed on projects approved under the Foreign Investment Law. Foreign direct investment on projects not approved under the Law is excluded from this table but included in the authorities' balance of payment accounts.

d. Preliminary

Singapore ($604 million), France ($465 million), and Thailand ($422 million) (see table 12-1). Summary data provided still more recently by Burma to the International Monetary Fund, however, suggest that Asian FDI had become proportionally more significant by late 1996 (see below). It should be noted, however, that official Burmese methods for assigning FDI to a particular source country surely overstate the position of the United Kingdom but probably understate those of Japan and the United States.[17]

Official data also provide some insight into the sectoral distribution and ownership structure of FDI in Burma. Such data suggest that the oil and gas sector accounted for the largest amount of approved FDI between 1989/90 and 1995/96, as noted above, followed by hotels and tourism, and mining (see table 12-2). However, these proportions have changed somewhat since 1989/90. Most importantly, recent data point to growing relative shares of FDI in sectors outside the oil and gas field.[18] On the other hand, small or negligible shares of FDI consistently have been approved in agriculture and transportation, among other sectors.

Available official data point to considerable diversity in the ownership structure of approved FDI projects. Production-sharing arrangements (the lion's share of the FDI in the category "other" in table 12-3) ranked first in terms of FDI approvals and disbursements for the period 1989/90 to 1995/96. Solely foreign-owned ventures placed second on an approvals basis during these same years, but joint ventures ranked second in disbursements terms.

These government statistics on inward FDI approved under the foreign investment law do not, however, capture all such investment in Burma. In addition to capital inflows approved under the foreign investment law, a significant amount of FDI has entered the country through investments in local firms registered under the Burma Companies Act.[19] As of March 31, 1995, for example, it was reported that there were some 452 registered firms in which foreign capital was invested. Slightly more than 400 of these firms were 100 percent wholly owned corporations or branches formed under the Act; the remainder were joint ventures generally undertaken in concert with government interests.[20] The total value of such FDI was estimated by the Burmese authorities to be worth about $500 million by 1995.[21] Trading, sales, and distribution reportedly have been the primary sectors into which this investment has entered.

Finally, there are indications that additional significant quantities of FDI have entered Burma in recent years through illicit or other informal means. Although there are no reliable estimates of the total value of such investments, various reports suggest that a substantial proportion of such FDI originates in China and is concentrated in Mandalay and elsewhere in northern Burma. Here again, trading, sales, and distribution seem to have attracted majority shares.

Table 12-2. FDI Inflows to Burma by Recipient Sector, 1989/90–1995/96

US $Millions

Sector	1989/90 Approved[b]	1989/90 Actual[c]	1990/91 Approved[b]	1990/91 Actual[c]	1991/92 Approved[b]	1991/92 Actual[c]	1992/93 Approved[a]	1992/93 Actual[b]	1993/94 Approved[a]	1993/94 Actual[b]	1994/95 Approved[a]	1994/95 Actual[b]	1995/96 Approved[a]	1995/96 Actual[b]
Agriculture	--	--	--	--	--	--	2.7	--	--	0.1	--	--	--	--
Manufacturing	15.9	0.9	42.7	18.0	5.9	0.8	13.3	9.5	18.2	4.3	76.3	11.9	21.3	31.3
Oil and gas	298.0	55.1	19.1	178.1	--	228.4	44.5	128.7	19.5	66.5	1,039.5	47.4	14.8	196.5
Mining	54.1	--	55.1	18.3	--	3.2	33.4	0.4	20.9	0.2	0.5	9.9	155.8	10.6
Fishery	--	--	77.3	3.0	--	--	5.9	--	7.6	0.5	148.2	6.8	13.1	2.7
Hotels and tourism	81.5	--	86.4	7.7	--	2.7	3.0	9.4	311.4	20.1	86.1	37.6	79.2	70.7
Transport	--	--	--	--	--	--	1.0	1.0	--	--	1.3	1.0	--	--
Total	449.5	56.0	280.6	225.1	5.9	235.1	103.8	149.0	377.6	91.7	1,351.9	114.6	284.2	311.8

SOURCES: Data provided by the Burma authorities, as reported by the IMF and the ADB.

a. Projects approved by the Myanmar Investment Commission under the provisions of the 1988 Foreign Investment Law; those permits that have been withdrawn or canceled are adjusted. Exclusive of drawback items.

b. Investment actually disbursed on projects approved under the Foreign Investment Law. Foreign direct investment on projects not approved under the Law is excluded from this Table but included in the authorities' balance of payment accounts.

Table 12-3. FDI Inflows to Burma by Ownership Structure, 1989/90–1995/96

US $Millions

Type of ownership	1989/90 Approved[b]	1989/90 Actual[c]	1990/91 Approved[b]	1990/91 Actual[c]	1991/92 Approved[b]	1991/92 Actual[c]	1992/93 Approved[a]	1992/93 Actual[b]	1993/94 Approved[a]	1993/94 Actual[b]	1994/95 Approved[a]	1994/95 Actual[b]	1995/96 Approved[a]	1995/96 Actual[b]
Solely foreign-owned venture	10.0	--	78.5	7.7	--	0.3	--	0.3	238.2	13.1	246.1	24.7	471.9	65.0
Joint venture	87.4	0.9	131.2	21.2	5.9	6.4	25.9	19.8	99.0	11.9	65.0	32.6	181.3	52.7
Production sharing	352.1	55.1	70.9	196.2	--	228.4	77.9	128.9	40.4	66.7	1,040.0	57.3	15.0	205.2
Total	449.5	56.0	280.6	225.1	5.9	235.1	103.8	149.0	377.6	91.7	1,351.9	114.6	668.2	322.9

SOURCES: Data provided by the Burma authorities, as reported by the IMF and the ADB.

a. Projects approved by the Myanmar Investment Commission under the provisions of the 1988 Foreign Investment Law; those permits that have been withdrawn or canceled are adjusted. Exclusive of drawback items.

b. Investment actually disbursed on projects approved under the Foreign Investment Law. Foreign direct investment on projects not approved under the Law is excluded from this Table but included in the authorities' balance of payment accounts.

The performance of FDI in Burma remains difficult to gauge. Government officials indicated that, at least by mid-1995, most foreign investors had not realized net profits from their projects. On the other hand, most of these investments were (and still are) generally young, and in many cases would not normally become profitable in their early stages of development. There are, in addition, a number of cases in which foreign investors terminated enterprises and withdrew from the country—in most instances presumably at a loss. On the other hand, these same Burmese government officials cite a number of FDI projects, particularly in the consumer products sector, which by mid-1995 apparently had achieved reasonably high levels of profitability.[22]

Nor is there much concrete information currently available on the trade behavior of foreign affiliates in Burma, although in 1995 government officials indicated that a number of foreign manufacturing concerns approved under the investment law had made commitments to export sizable shares of their total output.[23] Approved FDI proposals often include statements of intent to transfer technology to Burma, although here again precise data are lacking. Information on local content and value-added of foreign affiliates in Burma also is not currently available. Despite the renewed influx of FDI to Burma, in comparative regional terms these investment inflows have remained quite modest. FDI inflows to other members of the Association of Southeast Asian Nations (ASEAN) such as Thailand, Malaysia, and Indonesia, for example, have for years far exceeded those entering Burma.[24] Even recent ASEAN entrant Vietnam has managed to attract far greater FDI inflows than has Burma. Indeed, although the figures are not strictly comparable, approved FDI inflows to Vietnam for the 1995 calendar year alone as reported by that country's Ministry of Planning and Investment exceeded official Burmese figures on total accruals of approved FDI inflows to Burma over the six fiscal years from 1989/90 through 1994/95 by a factor approaching three.[25]

Despite their far smaller populations, even neighboring countries such as Cambodia and Laos have received FDI inflows of the same rough magnitudes as has Burma in recent years. Lao authorities, for example, report that total accrued FDI inflows on an approvals basis from 1988 through 1995 amounted to some $4.6 billion—even though the population of land-locked Laos is roughly one-tenth that of Burma. Even Cambodia's recent (and short) experience as host to FDI compares favorably with that of Burma: according to the Cambodian Investment Board, the war-torn country of roughly 10 million people attracted about $2.6 billion in FDI approvals for the period from August 1994 through July 1996.[26] Whether or not Burma will receive substantially greater levels of FDI in coming years depends on several critical developments.

Determinants

What are the principal factors which have shaped the recent development of FDI in Burma? Clearly both economic and non-economic forces have played critical roles. Some of these forces have served to stimulate FDI inflows whereas others have worked to discourage such investment. Still other factors have influenced additional characteristics of this investment. The following section briefly sets forth some of the main factors which help explain the nature of recent FDI.

Attractions

Numerous aspects of Burma's economic environment constitute important attractions to prospective foreign direct investors. Perhaps most notably, Burma possesses vast quantities of valuable natural resources. In the energy sector, for example, the country has large proven reserves of natural gas located principally in offshore fields such as those in the Gulf of Martaban, as well as limited quantities of onshore oil. Burma also has vast forest preserves containing valuable species of timber, which in some recent years have generated important export revenues. The country possesses an estimated three-quarters of the world's teak forests, for example, which reportedly include some of the highest quality varieties found anywhere, together with other valuable tropical hardwoods.[27]

In addition to the energy and forestry sectors, Burma also possesses considerable natural resources in the fields of agriculture, fisheries, and mining. The agricultural sector produces edible crops such as rice, beans, pulses, and oilseeds as well as industrial crops including cotton, jute, rubber, and tobacco. There also exist huge tracts of fertile land suitable for livestock breeding as well as the production of cash crops. The country's extensive coastal waters contain major stores of shrimp and other tropical seafood. Added to these saltwater resources are considerable freshwater fish reserves in the country's interior.

Finally, among natural resources Burma also possesses extensive reserves in the mining sector. Mineral resources include metallic minerals such as lead, zinc, tin, copper, silver, and gold, as well as industrial minerals such as coal, gypsum, and limestone. Also notable are the country's reserves of precious stones, including rubies, sapphires, jade, and diamonds. However, large areas of the country's most promising mineral tracts have yet to be systematically surveyed or explored.[28]

Moderately strong economic growth in recent years constitutes another important attraction for foreign investors. Following almost three decades of generally disappointing economic performance beginning in the early 1960s, official data suggest that the country's real GDP grew at an average annual rate of roughly 8 percent between 1992/93 and 1995/96—although these rates are calculated from a relatively low absolute base.[29] More difficult to estimate, however, are real GDP growth rates in the informal or unofficial sectors of the economy.

The country's significant potential for tourism likewise has created inducements for foreign investors. The cultural and other attractions of cities such as Pagan, Mandalay, and Rangoon—locales largely inaccessible to most overseas travelers for decades—together with the unspoiled beauty of Burma's tropical beaches and inland terrain, create enormous opportunities for touristic development. Although this sector remained dormant under the previous regime, the new government has actively promoted the development of hotels and related tourism infrastructure.

Aspects of the domestic labor market likewise are attractive to many foreign investors. Prolonged economic stagnation has kept wage rates far below those of dynamic neighboring economies such as Thailand and Malaysia and, indeed, Burma's wages are now among the lowest in the world.[30] Burma's sizable population also includes large numbers of educated job seekers, and English is still widely spoken in the principal urban areas. Low wage rates in particular prove attractive to labor-intensive manufacturing industries, such as textiles.

Finally, Burma lies close to several fast-growing regional economies, including ASEAN members Malaysia, Singapore, Thailand, and Vietnam, as well as the economies of India and China's Yunnan Province. (Indeed, the reconstruction of the old Burma Road promises to reconnect the historically important trading link between Yunnan's capital of Kunming and Burma's northern commercial center of Mandalay.)

Certain non-economic factors also have proved attractive to foreign investors. Perhaps most importantly, the SLORC fundamentally altered Burma's longstanding restrictions on FDI shortly after taking power. The cornerstone of this new policy was implemented through promulgation of the foreign investment law on November 30, 1988, and the issuance of related procedures in late 1988 and early 1989.[31]

The law offers a number of FDI incentives. First, it provides guarantees against nationalization during the term of the contract.[32] Second, it guarantees that, at the end of the contract period, the foreign investor may repatriate capital and net profits in the foreign currency in which the investment was originally made.[33] Third, the law guarantees significant tax incentives for approved projects. These public incentives also generally include income tax exemptions for at least the first three years of operation of a foreign investment project, and may also include tax breaks on profits, accelerated depreciation, and various other forms of tax exemption or relief.[34] Wholly owned foreign subsidiaries as well as joint ventures are permitted under this legislation. To qualify for these advantages, however, prospective investors must first gain official approval. (On approval criteria, see below.)

At the same time, the SLORC has taken steps to dismantle the central economic planning apparatus established during the Ne Win era. This shift in national economic policy is being cautiously implemented through a series of policy reforms.[35] First, the SLORC initiated a limited program of economic deregulation. To promote such deregulation, beginning in late 1988 the government removed a range of restrictions on private-sector trade (domestic as well as foreign), decontrolled the prices of a range of goods and services, relaxed regulations on domestic private investment, and permitted in principle the establishment of local private banks. Second, and related, the SLORC gradually began to privatize parts of the large state-controlled sector of the economy—although the process has been carried out very slowly and unevenly. And third, the government has begun to lay plans for the creation of the country's first domestic capital market in concert with Daiwa Securities, the Japanese financial services firm.

At least three other aspects of Burma's environment have proved attractive to foreign investors. For one thing, the investment approval process is highly centralized. In filing an application under the foreign investment law, a prospective investor need only obtain the approval of the central government to undertake investment and receive incentives provided under the law. These central government decisions proceed through a fairly simple approvals process. At the initial stage, the prospective foreign investor contacts the Office of the Myanmar Investment Commission and negotiates terms of entry with the relevant ministry (see figure 12-1). The scope of planned activities, expected rates of profit, performance criteria, and other specific matters are examined in this first step. A preliminary meeting of the commission, composed of relevant ministers and other concerned officials, then evaluates the proposal. If successful at this stage, the application is then submitted to the full membership for a formal vote of approval in principle, and then to the cabinet for final authorization.[36] The results of this screening process are communicated to the applicant through the commission offices. According to an official at the Myanmar Investment Commission, as of early 1995 it had approved roughly 95 percent of all proposals received and formally voted upon.[37]

Such centralization of decision-making authority can simplify considerably

Figure 12-1. The Approval Process under the Foreign Investment Laws

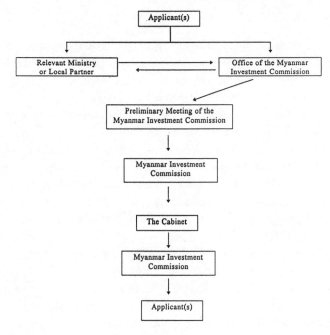

SOURCE: Myanmar Investment Commission (MIC).

the entry process for foreign firms.[38] This aspect of the entry process contrasts starkly with that encountered in certain neighboring East Asian countries also seeking FDI, such as Vietnam, where permission to invest often requires numerous official approvals at the local and provincial as well as national levels.

Second, components of the British legal and accounting systems remain operative in Burma. First established in the country during colonial days, these systems provide a useful framework for the establishment and operation of business enterprises often not found in developing countries. This aspect of the business environment in Burma again contrasts with that of Vietnam, among other neighboring countries, where the conduct of foreign business often is hampered by the absence of such established legal and accounting norms.

Third, Burma acceded to full membership in ASEAN in July 1997. Admittance to ASEAN should enable Burma increasingly to integrate its markets with those of its numerous economically dynamic neighbors. For this and other reasons, Burma within ASEAN should create still additional attractions for foreign companies to directly invest.[39]

Disincentives

Despite the considerable attractions of Burma as an investment host, a number of major factors have greatly limited foreign business interest. Far and away the most important of these factors stems from the internal political situation. For one thing, the persistent and increasingly bitter standoff between the SLORC and the National League for Democracy (NLD)—the political party which won a clear majority in the country's democratic but unimplemented elections of 1990—has raised issues of political legitimacy and contributed to growing fears about the country's political stability. In addition, the United Nations, many foreign governments, and other organizations allege widespread violation of human rights in Burma. And Daw Aung San Suu Kyi, Nobel Peace Prize winner, daughter of Burma's founding father Gen. Aung San, and leader of the NLD, has specifically called upon foreign companies to withhold investments from Burma until there is a fundamental change in domestic political circumstances.

These internal political developments have in turn encouraged various groups based abroad to press for foreign economic disengagement from Burma. Activist groups based in the United States and elsewhere, for example, have become increasingly forceful advocates for divestment and other measures to economically isolate the country. Such activism has included boycotts of foreign companies operating in Burma, shareholder resolutions at annual meetings of such companies, and, in the United States, adoption of selective purchasing and other laws at the municipal and state levels to limit economic interaction with Burma.[40]

In addition, recent political developments in Burma have led a number of major Western governments to contemplate or enact various measures to limit economic relationships with that country. The European Union, for example, voted in March 1997 to suspend Burma's generalized system of preferences (GSP) trading benefits with the Union. Australia for some time has deliberated various measures to limit economic interaction, and, in July 1997, Canada reportedly was set to impose economic sanctions.[41] Perhaps most significantly, in late 1996 the U.S. Congress voted to empower the president to ban new American investment under certain circumstances. President Clinton exercised this power in April 1997 when he announced that new U.S. investment in Burma would be generally banned.[42] This ban supplements earlier American policy decisions to prohibit U.S. Export-Import Bank assistance to American firms doing business in Burma, limit U.S. imports from that country, deny U.S. overseas development assistance, and prohibit lending to Burma from the International Monetary Fund, the World Bank, and other international financial institutions.

These political factors have seriously curtailed Western business interest in Burma. Although many of the underlying economic fundamentals continue to attract the interest of foreign companies, actual or potential public criticism, boycotts and other actions by activist groups, limited official support at the national and, in some cases, international levels, actual or potential imposition of sanctions, and related factors have combined to discourage much potential FDI from the West.

Other non-economic factors also have discouraged greater FDI in Burma. The government's foreign exchange policies have acted as a powerful deterrent. Authorities maintain the official value of the kyat at an artificially high rate of exchange. Indeed, the kyat is officially valued at roughly six per dollar, whereas the prevailing market rate in mid-1997 exceeded 200 to the dollar. Although the government has recently adopted limited corrective measures, this gross disparity has greatly complicated (and, at least until the recent past, often severely penalized) foreign investors required to import and convert foreign exchange at the official rate. In addition to its artificially high rate, the kyat is not convertible. As a result, foreign investors generally must purchase and export domestic products such as beans and seafood or bear other significant transaction costs to convert local kyat earnings into hard foreign currency.[43] Beginning in mid-1996, too, the country's already limited reserves of foreign exchange dwindled to very low levels, which in turn led the authorities to limit severely approvals for requisite foreign exchange licenses to import. Finally, the market rate of exchange of the kyat has been highly volatile since mid-1996, falling suddenly in both the summers of 1996 and 1997.[44]

Second, the continued operation of a large state sector has rendered Burma less attractive to many foreign investors. Currently producing about one-fifth of Burma's GDP, the public sector remains far less efficient than the private sector despite limited recent reforms. Foreign investors often are required to purchase from or otherwise transact with state-owned firms—many of which hold monopolies in their respective fields. These transactions can substantially raise input costs and other expenses for foreign companies. In addition, the inefficiencies of the state sector constitute a serious drag on the local economy and thereby indirectly render the local economy less attractive to companies seeking entry into only the most dynamic emerging markets.

Third, the nature and operation of the government bureaucracy has discouraged many foreign investors. Bureaucrats in Burma often retain the interventionist habits and mindset molded by years of experience operating under the authoritarian, centrally planned economic system of the past. Licenses and other bureaucratic approvals are still required to undertake myriad domestic and international economic transactions. In addition, Burma's government ministries are overly large, highly nationalistic and tend to defer important decisions to the very top of the organization. There have also been widespread reports of sudden and seemingly arbitrary changes in bureaucratic regulations with little or no advance public notice. Corruption has also become serious, and has been credibly linked in the past to the illicit trade in drugs.[45] Finally, as in many other Asian countries, personal relationships remain vital to the smooth and efficient conduct of business with the bureaucracy, which may discourage foreign companies lacking such ties or unwilling to work to establish them.

Fourth, the legal rights of foreign investors remain limited despite the existence of the foreign investment law and other legislation. Foreign (and other private) firms, for example, still do not enjoy comprehensive protection of intellectual property rights.[46] And the investment law does not contain an explicit dispute settlement mechanism. Foreign investors do have recourse through the Burma Arbitration Act and the local courts, but to date that system has rarely been tested.[47]

Finally, government screening of foreign investment proposals has limited the number and in many cases altered the nature of approved projects.[48] For example, approval depends in part on the likelihood that a proposed foreign investment will fulfill one or more of the government's overall policy goals. In the foreign investment domain, stated goals include export promotion, natural resource exploitation, and other economic undertakings which require large investments, technology transfer, job creation, energy savings, and regional development. Some investment proposals which did not meet these (or other) policy objectives reportedly were rejected by the investment commission, whereas others were substantially modified before receiving requisite official permission.

Foreign investment applications must satisfy other critical conditions as well. The law specifies that the foreign capital contribution must constitute at least 35 percent of the total capital, for example, and that such foreign capital amount to no less than $500,000 in cash or kind.[49] Moreover, the government issues specific lists only of economic activities which *are* open to foreign investment— lists which *do not* cover many of the most potentially attractive opportunities. The Commission does, however, consider investment proposals for non-listed activities on an individual basis.[50] Yet even if the authorities approve foreign investments, they limit the duration of projects to an average of twenty years, and generally to a maximum of thirty years.[51]

Added to these non-economic disincentives are numerous economic factors which also have discouraged greater FDI in Burma. Although the economy has been growing significantly in recent years, failure to enact needed stabilization measures and comprehensive structural reforms could dampen current growth rates significantly. The International Monetary Fund, for example, estimates that real annual GDP growth could fall to 4 percent by the year 2000 if such measures and reforms are not soon adopted. In addition, despite its rapid growth, the absolute size of the Burmese economy remains small.[52] Moreover, the gross lack of modern infrastructure has rendered many potential investment projects unusually problematic. The underdeveloped state of the nation's airports, shipping terminals, railroads, and highways, for example, presents enormous challenges to foreign firms whose businesses depend critically on an efficient transportation sector. The poor state of Burma's domestic and international telecommunications systems creates added problems for foreign investors. And an aging and limited system of power generation can meet only limited energy needs and often develops outages and related problems.

Nor does the list of economic disincentives stop there. Burma's high inflation rate, estimated at 30 to 40 percent in mid-1997, continues to place downward pressure on the value of the kyat and thereby renders local currency earnings increasingly less valuable. The absence of developed capital markets has created additional challenges for potential foreign direct investors. Among other economic intangibles, supplies of skilled entrepreneurs and trained business managers remain relatively scarce, despite widespread literacy in English.[53]

Prospects

What are the prospects for FDI in Burma? In a number of Western countries, pressure is growing to further restrict already limited economic ties with Burma. An organized network of activist groups has proved increasingly effective both in dissuading individual Western firms from direct investments, and in pressing their calls for investment bans and similar measures at official Western policy levels. Movements such as these have also contributed substantially to growing official sentiment in many Western countries to further curtail economic engagement with Burma.

Largely as a result of these pressures, most Western-based firms not now participating in the Burmese economy as direct investors have become increasingly hesitant to enter, and a substantial number of those Western companies which had entered at an earlier stage have chosen to withdraw or are contemplating doing so. It is true that, as of early 1997, a number of major European multinationals, such as Alcatel (France), Siemens (Germany), and Standard Chartered

Bank (United Kingdom), continue to invest directly in Burma. Yet others, such as Carlsberg (Denmark), Heineken (Netherlands), and Philips (Netherlands), have recently elected to withdraw. Many other potential foreign entrants have put their plans on indefinite hold.

Most established American firms have become particularly cautious with respect to FDI in Burma. A handful of U.S. energy companies, including Unocal, remain committed investors in offshore natural gas projects. Yet recent developments have led to the withdrawal of a host of other major U.S. firms, including Apple Computer, Hewlett-Packard, Levi-Strauss, Motorola, and Pepsico. The pitfalls also have discouraged other American companies from undertaking initial investments. In the absence of major changes within Burma, these trends suggest that U.S. and other Western FDI will remain fairly modest in the foreseeable future.

In contrast, a number of Asian governments continue to support economic and other forms of engagement with Burma.[54] China, for example, remains firmly committed to a policy of engagement. The Indian government has demonstrated an increased willingness to interact with Burma. The Japanese government has cautiously resumed modest levels of development assistance to Burma, and Japan's Ministry of International Trade and Industry now offers trade as well as investment guarantees for interested Japanese companies.[55] Perhaps most importantly, ASEAN remains committed to a policy of engagement and admitted Burma (together with Laos) as a full member of this key regional economic grouping in July 1997.[56]

Official Asian support for continued economic ties with Burma has encouraged a growing number of Asian-based firms to directly invest. Burmese government data suggest, for example, that growing quantities of FDI are now entering Burma from Asian countries such as Singapore, Malaysia, and Thailand.[57] In addition, other evidence points to increased direct investments from a host of major Japanese multinationals.[58] Also significant are the growing economic links with China and, to a lesser extent, India. These trends therefore point to the increasing importance of Asian FDI as a proportion of total FDI in Burma.[59]

Indeed, these trends on the investment front point to a larger theme now emerging in Burma's developing international economic relationships. Whether measured in terms of international trade, technology transfer, overseas development assistance, or foreign direct investment, it is Asia, rather than the West, which is becoming increasingly central to the country's external economic interests. In short, recent trends underline the growing Asianization of the Burmese economy.[60]

That Asianization in turn carries important political implications for the West. Many American and European activists in particular argue that their governments should impose stronger economic sanctions on Burma to force internal political change within Burma. Growing economic ties between Burma and its Asian neighbors, however, may well restrict Western economic leverage over Burma and thereby significantly limit the effectiveness of such a sanctions strategy.

Notes

1. FDI denotes investment by a person or persons of one country in a business located in another country sufficient to wield significant managerial influence over that foreign entity. In the United States, the Department of Commerce currently places the minimum threshold for FDI at a 10 percent stake in the foreign entity. Foreign investments below this threshold are termed portfolio investments. As stipulated under Burma's Foreign Investment Law, all approved FDI in that country must have a minimum 35 percent foreign share.

2. On the limitations of official Burmese investment data, see below. Although foreigners are not permitted to own land in Burma, the category "Real Estate" apparently refers to land leases and related property arrangements.

3. Tun Wai, *Economic Development of Burma from 1800 to 1940* (Rangoon, 1961), 20–21.

4. Mya Than, *Myanmar's External Trade: An Overview in the Southeast Asian Context* (Singapore, 1992), 6–7.

5. The British administered Burma as a province of India until 1937, when it was designated a separate administrative state.

6. J. Russell Andrus, "Foreign Investments in Burma," *Pacific Affairs*, XVII (1944), 90–93. This estimate covers all forms of foreign investments, including those reflected in government and municipal obligations.

7. Tun Wai, "The Myanmar Economy at the Crossroads: Options and Constraints," in Mya Than and Joseph Tan (eds.), *Myanmar Dilemmas and Options: The Challenge of Economic Transition in the 1990s* (Singapore, 1990), 19.

8. On joint ventures in Burma during this era, see Tun Thin, William Paw et al. "Joint International Business Ventures in the Union of Burma," unpub. report (New York, 1959).

9. Mya Than, "The Union of Burma Foreign Investment Law: Prospects of Mobilizing Foreign Capital for Development?" in Mya Than and Joseph Tan (eds.), *Myanmar Dilemmas and Options*, 187.

10. The private sector, however, was allowed to engage in various economic activities in, for example, the forestry, livestock and fishery, and domestic trade sectors. Indeed, under the Ne Win regime more than half of GDP apparently was produced by (generally small-scale) private firms. In addition, the government undertook limited reforms in the early 1970s, which included acceptance of overseas development assistance and partial commercialization of the state-owned enterprises. (See Si Si Win, "Investment Climate in Myanmar," unpub. report [n.d.], 3). These reforms contributed to a modest increase in economic activity during the late 1970s and early 1980s. See Mya Than and Myat Thein, "Transitional Economy of Myanmar: Performance, Issues and Problems," unpub. working paper (n.d.), 4.

11. Hal Hill and Sisira Jayasuriya, *An Inward-Looking Economy in Transition: Economic Development in Burma since the 1960s* (Singapore, 1986), 1, 19.

12. As with many other developing countries, use of Burmese FDI and other official economic statistics requires considerable caution. Such statistics generally do not capture important economic phenomena which take place outside the official economy. The statistics also contain other serious measurement problems and are subject to considerable revision years after their initial announcement.

13. Official, publicly available inflow approval data in 1997 extend through the 1995/96 fiscal year.

14. The Burmese fiscal year begins April 1.

15. Valued at more than $1 billion, the so-called Yadana project aims to transport offshore natural gas from Burmese territorial waters to Thailand via a pipeline currently under construction. The principal partners in this joint venture are the Myanmar Oil and Gas Enterprise, the Petroleum Authority of Thailand, and the energy companies Total (based in France) and Unocal (based in the United States). The project is set for completion in mid-1998.

16. Unless otherwise stated, all dollar amounts cited in this chapter refer to U.S. dollars.

17. The authorities assign approved FDI for a specified project to that country whose firm officially submits the proposed project to the MIC. The nationality of the firm is determined by the country in which it is registered. The government assigns FDI to the original investor even in cases where foreign ownership subsequently changes hands, unless there is a change in the country in which the relevant firm is registered. MIC officials and United States Embassy, Rangoon, "Country Commercial Guide: Burma (Myanmar)," unpub. report (December 1994), 39.

18. Burmese data reported to the International Monetary Fund for the period through October 1996 indicate that FDI approvals by late 1996 had risen most markedly in the manufacturing and real estate sectors.

19. Burma Companies Act (India Act VII, 1913), April 1, 1914.

20. Interview with Hla Tun, Rangoon, March 1995.

21. Interview with Khine Khine, former Joint Secretary, Myanmar Investment Commission, Rangoon, March 1995.

22. Myanmar Singapura United Tobacco Co. Ltd., a 65 percent/35 percent joint venture between Ministry of Industry (1) and Singaporean interests, for example, reportedly earned a profit of some U.S.$5.8 million between April and December 1994, alone. Interview with officials of Ministry of Industry (1).

23. Indeed, Ministry of Industry (1) officials reported that many of the joint ventures in their sector exported between 80 percent and 90 percent of their production in the mid-1990s, selling just enough locally to cover domestic labor and other local kyat expenses.

24. See, for example, United Nations Conference on Trade and Development (UNCTAD), *World Investment Report 1996: Investment, Trade and International Policy Arrangements* (Geneva, 1996), Table 1.

25. In addition to measurement differences between the Vietnamese and Burmese methods for calculating FDI, there are significant differences in the underlying economies of the two countries. On the one hand, Vietnam's population is estimated at about 75 million people, whereas the estimated population of Burma is some 45 million. On the other hand, the relative lack of Western legal and accounting standards in Vietnam might be expected to moderate FDI inflows compared to a country such as Burma, which generally adheres to such conventions in major business dealings.

26. Figures supplied by the Cambodian Investment Board, as reported by the IMF.

27. See Union of Myanmar, Ministry of National Planning and Economic Development *Statistical Yearbook: 1993* (Rangoon, 1994), 5–6; U.S. Embassy, "Country Commercial Guide," 13.

28. More generally, Burma possesses the largest land area of any country in mainland Southeast Asia.

29. Burmese data analyzed by the staff of the International Monetary Fund and provided to the author.

30. In the state sector, for example, the minimum daily wage for an unskilled worker in 1994 stood at just 20 kyat per day, or well below 20 U.S. cents at 1994 market rates of exchange. Union of Myanmar, Foreign Investment Commission, *Investing in Myanmar* (Bangkok, 1994), 29.

31. See "The Union of Myanmar Foreign Investment Law" (The State Law and Order Restoration Council Law No. 10/88, Nov. 30, 1988) as amended; "Procedures Relating to the Union of Myanmar Foreign Investment Law" (The Government of the Union of Myanmar Notification No.

11/88, Dec. 7, 1988); "Types of Economic Activities Allowed for Foreign Investment" (The Union of Myanmar Foreign Investment Commission Notification No. 1/89, May 30, 1989).

32. Contract terms range up to thirty years under the FIL, but can be extended upon application to the MIC (see below). According to a Commission official, as of mid-1995 the average length of contract for approved investments was twenty years.

33. FIL, Chapter XI, "Guarantees," 12.

34. FIL, Chapter X, "Exemptions and Reliefs," 9–11. The corporate tax rate in Burma in 1997 was 30 percent.

35. The following discussion draws largely on Mya Than and Myat Thein, "Transitional Economy of Myanmar."

36. In mid-1995, the MIC met twice monthly, and two-thirds of its members had to be present to constitute a quorum. Decisions were made by majority voting of the members present. As of April 21, 1993, the MIC consisted of the following sixteen members: each of the two Deputy Prime Ministers (Chairman and Vice-Chairman), Ministers of Industry 1, Forestry, Agriculture, Hotels and Tourism, Trade, Mines, Transport, Livestock Breeding and Fisheries, Energy, Industry 2, Finance and Revenue, Cooperatives, National Planning and Economic Development (Secretary), and one person designated by the Chairman (Joint Secretary).

37. Those proposals which failed to gain approval often involved only small amounts of foreign capital or did not include significant transfers of technology. Interview with Khine Khine, Rangoon, March 1995.

38. On the other hand, the practice whereby all major (and many relatively minor) decisions are made by the central government can considerably slow down the decision-making process. In the realm of foreign investment, however, the speed of the process under the FIL to date reportedly has been relatively fast in most cases.

39. On Burmese accession to ASEAN, see, in particular, *Asia Week* (13 June 1997). *Financial Times* (2 June 1997) reports that Burma will not be required to meet the tariff reduction schedule of the ASEAN Free Trade Area (AFTA), however, until 2008.

40. By the end of 1996, one state—Massachusetts—and eight municipalities—Berkeley, Santa Monica, San Francisco, and Oakland, Calif.; Takoma Park, Md.; Ann Arbor, Mich.; Carborro, N.C.; and Madison, Wis.—had adopted such measures. On current legal debates over the constitutionality of such measures, see David Schmahmann and James Finch, "The Unconstitutionality of State and Local Enactments in the United States Restricting Business Ties with Burma (Myanmar)," *Vanderbilt Journal of Transnational Law*, XXX (1997), 175–207.

41. Associated Press (29 July 1997).

42. "Investment Sanctions in Burma," White House press release (22 April 1997). Details of the ban were spelled out in a subsequent executive order.

43. Indeed, there is now a sizable network of firms based in Burma which specialize in converting kyat into hard foreign currencies through trade conversion and other means.

44. *Financial Times* (22 July 1997).

45. The unusually low public sector wage rates also contribute to bureaucratic corruption.

46. There do exist legal protections for patents, copyrights, and trademarks, but other types of legal protection have yet to be provided.

47. According to the MIC, only one lawsuit involving a foreign investor had been adjudicated through the Burmese courts by mid-1995. In that case, which involved a hotel project, the issue was reportedly settled in favor of the foreign investor. In general, parties to such disputes are encouraged to settle the matter privately and informally. Failing this, the issue can be brought to a panel set up under the Burma Arbitration Act. If this, too, fails to produce a settlement, foreign investors can bring the matter before the township, city and, ultimately, Central Court of Burma.

48. In addition to the limits imposed by the FIL, the law is also unusually brief and lacks many specifics. This provides government officials with considerable discretion in applying the law in individual cases—which creates added uncertainties for prospective foreign investors.

49. Acceptable forms of in-kind investment reportedly include machinery, equipment, spare parts, intellectual property rights, and technical know-how.

50. A number of the sectors most potentially attractive to foreign investors are reserved *in principle* for state-owned enterprises (SOEs), and are included among the economic activities defined under Section 3 of the State-Owned Economic Enterprises Law. FDI in these activities, which include extraction and sale of teak; exploration, extraction, production, and sale of oil and natural gas; and exploration, extraction, and export of precious stones are subject to particularly rigorous government screening procedures based on unspecified criteria relating to the "interests of the state." For details, see "Procedures Relating to Permission to Carry Out Economic Enterprises under Section 3 of the State-Owned Economic Enterprises Law," as contained in Union of Myanmar, Foreign Investment Commission, *Guide to Foreign Investment in Myanmar: Parts One and Two* (Rangoon, 1990), Part Two, Appendix 4. Indeed, as of March 31, 1995, roughly 28 percent of the permitted foreign enterprises under the FIL were in the exempted fields of mining, oil and gas, and transportation. To gain permission for FDI in these economic domains, the government typically requires that prospective foreign investors agree to joint venture with SOEs.

51. Permitted duration depends upon the nature of the proposed project, the amount of capital, and other factors. Local rules also limit the duration of foreign-held land leases: land ownership by foreign firms or individuals is prohibited, but (extendable) 10- to 30-year leases are permitted. See Si Si Win, "Investment Climate in Myanmar," 14.

52. Indeed, Burma's highly underdeveloped economy led the United Nations to officially designate Burma a "least developed country" in December 1987. In the early 1990s there were some forty-seven countries so designated, of which thirty-one were located in Africa. UNCTAD *World Investment Report 1994,* 113, n. 38.

53. Other important aspects of macroeconomic performance which threaten sustained economic development (and can discourage potential FDI) include low levels of domestic savings, large current account deficits, high debt/service ratios (but small absolute amounts of outstanding external debt), large government deficits, and interest rates set at levels well below prevailing rates of inflation.

54. On Asian reaction to the U.S. decision to impose a ban on most new U.S. investments, see, for instance, "Burmese Sanctions Get Little Backing in Asia," *New York Times* (25 April 1997).

55. *Financial Times* (3 May 1995).

56. See, for example, *Financial Times* (30 January 1997), and the several articles in early 1997 by Barry Wain in *Asian Wall Street Journal.*

57. Burmese data analyzed by the staff of the International Monetary Fund and provided to the author.

58. See, for example, *Asian Wall Street Journal* (27 January 1997).

59. On a disbursements basis, for example, the United States was the largest single source country for FDI for the period 1990/91 through 1994/95 as a whole, but the U.S. figure peaked in 1991/92 and then declined in each of the following three years. Of total disbursements during these years, the Asian share accounted for roughly one-third. For 1994/95 alone, however, in disbursement terms Singapore ranked first (and the United States fifth). In that year, the Asian share rose to more than half of the total. Moreover, summary data on FDI approvals recently provided by the Burmese government to the IMF indicates that Singapore ranked first in total approvals from enactment of the Foreign Investment Law through October 1996, and that three of the top five source countries were Asian by that latter date. Yet these figures do not include FDI which entered Burma through methods other than the foreign investment law. Appropriately adjusting the above figures would probably increase the Asian proportion significantly, owing in particular to Chinese FDI which entered through non-FIL channels.

60. Consider, for example, Burmese trading relationships. With respect to imports, official Burmese data suggest that other Asian economies shipped between 70 percent and 87 percent of the value of total imports to Burma throughout the early 1990s. (In 1993/94, the major source countries for imports to Burma were, in rank order: Japan, China, Thailand, Singapore, and Malaysia. Imports

from the United States accounted for just 3.5 percent of the total value of Burmese imports.) With regard to exports, these same data suggest that Asia received between 83 percent and 94 percent of the value of Burmese exports during the early 1990s. (In 1993/94, the major recipients of exports from Burma were, in rank order: Singapore, Thailand, India, Hong Kong, and China. Exports to the United States accounted for a mere 3.7 percent of total Burmese exports.) Some share of this trade with other Asian countries involved transshipments involving non-Asian trading partners, yet the Asian ties apparently remain crucial even after making related adjustments.

Concerning overseas development assistance, Asia again proves central. Among member countries of the Organization for Economic Cooperation and Development (OECD), for example, Japan alone contributed some 89 percent of the combined (though relatively modest) bilateral assistance from all OECD countries in 1993, and an estimated 68 percent of all OECD multilateral as well as bilateral assistance that same year. To this amount should be added the substantial (though difficult to quantify) financial assistance provided by China in particular, for non-military as well as military purposes.

Finally, although the international transfer of technology is notoriously difficult to measure, anecdotal evidence suggests that in recent years a substantial if not majority proportion of such transfers has involved other Asian countries. With the important exception of the energy sector, many of the technologies transferred to Burma reportedly originated in South Korea, Singapore, Japan, Thailand, and China. It appears that these were often medium-level technologies in the construction and manufacturing sectors.

Part Four

HEALTH AND EDUCATION

CHAPTER 13

The State's Role in Education in Burma

An Overview

John J. Brandon

FOR THE PAST thirty-five years, Southeast Asia's economic growth has been nothing short of spectacular, particularly in those countries that compose the Association of Southeast Asian Nations (ASEAN).[1] Since the early 1960s, per capita income in the region has grown by an average of 6 percent a year, and the standard of living has increased markedly. This economic dynamism has translated into high levels of investment in the social sectors such as health and education. Consequently, the quality of life for many Southeast Asians has improved in numerous ways: life expectancy has increased by almost twenty years, infant mortality has been reduced by more than half, and educational opportunities have been expanded and improved.[2]

Unfortunately, the peoples of Burma have not benefited from the region's vibrant economic growth. Initially, this was due to a set of political and economic policies called the "Burmese Way to Socialism," which effectively isolated Burma from the rest of the world and destroyed the country's economy. In 1987–1988, however, Burma's military leaders discarded these policies, pursued an "open door" policy, and introduced economic reforms with the hope of lifting the country out of its economic morass by enticing foreign investment. Despite such reform, Burma's unresolved political crisis has neutralized these economic moves and has left the country in a dire state, both politically and economically.

Since the State Law and Order Restoration Council (SLORC) came to power in September 1988, military spending has increased dramatically. Estimates of the military's share of overall government spending range from 8.2 percent to 50 percent.[3] Despite the dubious nature of Burmese government statistics, defense spending has increased in real terms as a share of legal (non-drug-related) gross domestic product (GDP) and central government expenditures. According to a 1995 World Bank report, the SLORC spent 46 percent of its total expenditures on defense between 1989 and 1994 while spending in the social service sectors (which includes health and education) declined from 32 percent to 23 percent in real terms.[4]

The SLORC's diminishing financial commitment to Burma's health and education systems has politicized health and education issues. Since Aung San Suu Kyi was released from house arrest in July 1995, she has criticized the government for not spending enough on education and health care. In her weekly column for the Japanese newspaper *Mainichi Daily News,* Aung San Suu Kyi blamed the SLORC for the "unsavory conditions of our hospitals" and "the disgraceful state of our educational system."[5] These poor conditions have led to widespread corruption as teachers and doctors extort "donations" from people in order to receive service. Such corruption is exacerbated by the small, fixed income of civil servants working in these sectors. The average monthly salary for a government doctor is 1,500 kyat, or the equivalent of less than U.S.$10 at 1997's unofficial exchange rate.[6] Teachers' salaries are slightly lower.

The SLORC has been very sensitive to these charges and, using common code phrases such as "lackeys of neo-colonialists," has indirectly accused Aung San Suu Kyi of trying to undermine improvements in the country's educational system. In a speech to high school teachers, Lt. Gen. Khin Nyunt said the government spent $766 million on education in 1996.[7] This figure reflects spending at the official exchange rate. When using the more meaningful unofficial exchange rate, however, this figure is worth only a fraction of its official value.

The SLORC's inability (or unwillingness) to invest more money in its education and health care systems will greatly impede Burma's ability to develop economically and integrate into the regional economy. The inadequate quality of instruction and the government's skewed spending priorities have not allowed Burma to develop a talent pool of capable individuals to lead the country. Even if Burma were well endowed with bureaucrats and military officials wanting to serve the public interest, their lack of sufficient training would inhibit them from being able to govern competently and fairly. If Burma's leaders (be they members of the SLORC, a civilian government, or some combination of the two) are going to develop a productive society and economy, the Burmese people will need to be healthier and better educated.

Although health and education issues are closely intertwined, this chapter will only address how Burma's policies have contributed to the deterioration of the country's educational standards. Analyses of Burma's health care policies are addressed by David Chandler in chapter 14. This chapter concludes that Burma may wish to examine how two of its neighbors, Thailand and Indonesia, developed educational policies and allocated resources in such a way that both countries developed high literacy rates, which contributed to their impressive economic growth.

Education in Burma

Since Ne Win came to power in March 1962, Burma's educational system has suffered from thirty-five years of isolation, stagnation, and repression. Universities have been closed for approximately 20 percent of the time, particularly whenever the first sign of political unrest has appeared. In December 1996, most institutes of higher learning were closed after thousands of students took to the streets in the biggest anti-government demonstrations since 1988. Students were protesting police brutality, seeking to organize independent unions, and demanding greater freedoms. Since December 1996, some thirty colleges and universities suspected of being linked to student unrest have remained closed indefinitely under the SLORC's order.[8] Closures of schools have created an enormous backlog of students waiting to start and finish their degrees. As a result of such closings since the SLORC came to power, students who entered university in 1994 had finished high school in 1988.[9] Such a backlog, coupled with inadequate resources for education, presents a dilemma for the SLORC. While it strives to modernize the country and develop its economy, the SLORC also wants to restrict information that it views as harmful to its interest.

The SLORC appears willing to sacrifice the education of primary and secondary school students to keep trouble at bay. Primary and secondary schools were closed in March 1997 for vacation and were due to reopen in June, but the SLORC kept them closed to prevent possible protests before admission to ASEAN in July 1997. The schools were reopened on August 11, 1997, just after the ninth anniversary of the violent civil unrest that brought the SLORC to power in 1988.[10]

Historically, Burma has been viewed as having a high literacy rate. In fact, Burma touted its efforts to promote literacy and encouraged volunteers to go to rural areas and act as tutors. For these efforts Burma won two awards from the United Nations Education, Scientific and Cultural Organization (UNESCO) for promoting literacy in the 1970s. The country's literacy rate, however, has been cast in doubt. To get debt relief, in 1987 Burma ardently sought "least developed country" (LDC) status from the United Nations, thereby placing Burma in the same economic category as the world's poorest countries. To receive LDC status, a country's literacy rate must be below 20 percent. Thus, in 1987, Burma's officially reported literacy rate dropped from 78.6 percent to 18.7 percent.[11] Interestingly, the United Nations Development Program (UNDP) estimates that in 1993, 82 percent of Burma's peoples were literate despite the closing of all schools for almost three years and the SLORC's diminished expenditures on education.[12] The United Nations Children's Fund (UNICEF) believes that Burma's actual functional literacy rate is much lower, though official numbers are unreliable.[13]

Burma's 1966 Basic Education Law and the 1973 Union of Burma Education Law established the country's current educational structure. These laws mandate five years of primary education, from kindergarten through fourth grade. Children eligible and able to matriculate beyond primary school can attend four years of middle school and two years of high school. Students who score the highest in math, science, engineering, and medicine and aspire to attend an institute of advanced learning are eligible to take the government entrance examination. It is estimated that only 3 percent of all students who finish primary or secondary schooling now go on to some form of tertiary education, be it at a university, or a technical or vocational institute.[14]

In 1991, Burma became a signatory to the UN Convention on the Rights of the Child. Articles 28 and 29 of this convention state that a basic education should develop a child's fullest possible potential without any financial costs to parents. Two years later, Burma enacted its Child Law which stipulates that every child has the right to a free primary education at compulsory public schools. The Child Law further stipulates that every child has the right to cherish his or her own language, literature, culture, religion, traditions, and customs.[15] While such laws and guarantees are good in theory, putting them into practice in Burma has been another issue. The international community has not pursued enforcement of international treaties in the case of Burma, though human rights organizations have raised the issue. For example, the Child Law guarantees children the right to freely express themselves, but other laws give the state the right to punish anyone who says or writes anything that can be construed as negative about the state or the armed forces.

Government statistics portray a very positive picture of universal access to primary education in Burma. According to official statistics, Burma opened 12,000 new primary schools and recruited more than 70,000 new teachers between 1983 and 1993. Of the approximately 36,500 primary schools in Burma, 32,000 are located in rural areas.[16] In addition to these government-run primary schools, there are 930 monasteries that provide primary education for approximately 39,500 students, less than 1 percent of the primary school age population.[17] Buddhist monasteries, in the absence of other schools, have often been the main source of learning in rural villages.

In theory, primary education in Burma has been free of charge under both the Burma Socialist Program Party (BSPP) and the SLORC. Article 52 of Burma's second constitution, promulgated in 1974, states that "every citizen shall have the right to an education" and that such education shall be compulsory. In reality, primary schools in Burma are costly and fail to provide a basic education for many people. Parents incur significant costs for textbooks, paper, supplies, a yearly contribution to the Parent Teacher Association (PTA) fund, and other contributions for school improvement. Sending one's children to school can pose an economic hardship for most families in Burma. A UNICEF survey found that 39 percent of school age children have never attended primary school. This survey also found that 26 percent of parents said they could not afford the cost.[18]

Another major problem is that only 25 percent of children enrolled in school complete their primary education. It is believed that only 10 percent of all students entering kindergarten complete their five years of primary education without repeating a grade. Consequently, such a high repetition rate inflates school enrollment. On average, it takes 12.2 years to produce a primary school graduate rather than five years.[19]

There is also a major difference between the number of new teachers recruited and the number actually trained. Two-thirds of Burma's primary school teachers have no training because they must work for five years before they receive any formal training. Those who have had the good fortune of being trained have not likely received any additional training to improve and upgrade their skills. The situation is exacerbated in rural areas where there are only two or three teachers for all five grades.[20] Many teachers, no matter how committed, are being forced to leave their jobs because their salaries do not enable them to make a decent standard of living. Many teachers can earn ten times their government salary through private tutoring. In April 1994, to combat this problem, Khin Nyunt announced the establishment of an "Education Employee Cooperative" to help teachers who were experiencing financial difficulties, but he also threatened to make private tuition illegal.[21] Consequently, many parents who want to give their children an education must pool their money to pay the salaries of teachers and principals, thus adding to the parents' economic hardship.

As teaching methods in Burma are antiquated, so, too, is the physical infrastructure of the nation's schools. This problem is particularly acute in rural areas where resources are far more sparse. A 1991 survey found that 57 percent of primary schools were overcrowded and lacked adequate facilities, including basic furniture. Many schools need major repairs as one-third of the buildings have already exceeded their expected lifespan.[22] PTAs are principally involved in improving and maintaining schools, but with 39 percent of the children not enrolled and an economy in disarray, parents who can send their children to school find it difficult to provide the necessary resources to provide a nurturing learning environment.

Given the high dropout rate from primary school, few students continue their education at the middle school and high school levels. While BSPP statistics indicate a significant expansion of middle and high schools in the 1970s and 1980s, many secondary schools suffer from the same shortcomings as primary schools: poor funding and shortages of materials. The quality of secondary education also declined when the use of English was banned in 1966. Censorship delays did not permit timely translations of textbooks from English. In 1980, the government suddenly reintroduced English language instruction.[23] Skeptics believe that the decision to reintroduce English was made because Ne Win's daughter Sanda was rejected by a medical school in England because of her lack of English language proficiency.

Competitive entrance examinations to attend universities present yet another barrier to higher education. Even if a student passes, enrollment is limited by the number of places available each year. With the heavy backlog of students resulting from extended university closures between 1988 and 1992, competition has become even more keen. Such conditions have bred widespread corruption. To quote Aung San Suu Kyi: "Examination questions, advance information on grades achieved and the marking up of low grades can all be obtained for a price."[24]

Students in Burma's ethnic minority states have been poorly served by Burma's educational system. There is little educational spending in government controlled areas in the ethnic states. Literacy rate estimates range between 50 percent and 65 percent in those areas compared to a national rate of approximately 80 percent. The teaching or research of any ethnic minority language is not permitted in any secondary schools or tertiary institutes. The SLORC has promised to upgrade the ethnic states' regional colleges to universities but the necessary resources have not been forthcoming. In 1991, the SLORC upgraded the Academy for the Development of National Groups to a university. The Academy was originally established to teach the "Burmese Way to Socialism" in ethnic minority areas, but its critics charge that its real purpose is to train Burmese language teachers and promote a Buddhist culture.[25] Understandably, there is a great deal of resentment among ethnic minorities that government schools only teach Burmese and no other languages. Non-Burmans feel government schools are little more than tools for imposing discipline and control in government-controlled areas. Schools near conflict areas that teach in ethnic languages are allegedly the first to be "dismantled." Because of such conflict, many children are denied an education in their own language and culture.

Two other groups in Burma that have historically been denied educational opportunities are children of Chinese and Indian ancestry. Under a strict 1982 Citizenship Law, people of Chinese and Indian ancestry must be able to prove that their ancestors have resided in Burma since the first British annexation in 1824. This is virtually impossible. Those who cannot prove that their ancestral lineage goes this far back are given Foreign Registration Cards. As university entrance requires being a "Burmese national," this bars many from matriculating for a university degree despite having spent their lifetime living in Burma. Those who cannot prove their ancestral lineage in Burma predates the first British annexation are normally excluded from studying subjects such as technology and medicine despite high grades.[26] Some Chinese in Burma run their own primary and secondary schools because they believe that they can provide a better education than state-run schools.[27]

Successive leaderships have severely restricted educational opportunities and academic freedom in Burma. Martial law has been widely used to control the movement of both students and teachers, and an anti-intellectual ideology was spawned by the BSPP and now the SLORC. SLORC leaders are poorly educated as few have studied beyond secondary school. When students and intellectuals have tried to express their views, the military has responded violently. Thousands were killed during the civil unrest of August and September 1988 and many still remain unaccounted for. More than eight years later, it remains unclear who is dead, imprisoned, in exile, or in armed opposition against the government.[28]

The SLORC has neutralized teachers, professors, and students by: 1) breaking down the student population into smaller communities; 2) holding teachers responsible for students' actions; and 3) prohibiting teachers and students from engaging in political activity.

In July 1992 the SLORC announced a new correspondence course system called "The University of Distance Learning."[29] Ostensibly, the purpose of this program is to enable those who live far from universities and technical colleges to study for a degree by mail. The actual purpose of these correspondence courses is to keep students at home and prevent them from communicating with their fellow students from other parts of the country. After the civil unrest of 1988, all parents were required by the SLORC to sign forms acknowledging responsibility for the behavior of their children, regardless of the child's age. The inference was that if children misbehaved by engaging in activities not viewed as appropriate by the SLORC, the parents as well as children could be subject to prosecution. Students who attend universities on campus are required to remain in the same room all day for lectures to prevent them from organizing.[30]

Before returning to teach in 1991, teachers were required to answer a questionnaire on a broad range of topics, including Aung San Suu Kyi, communism, the United States, and the Central Intelligence Agency. Those who answered these questions favorably, in the SLORC's view, were permitted to keep their jobs. In 1991 and 1992, 7,000 teachers were believed to be dismissed from their jobs for holding views contrary to the SLORC's. Several hundred university professors were dismissed as well. In addition, the SLORC arbitrarily transferred thousands of teachers from one end of the country to the other, splitting up many families and teaching couples.[31]

When universities and regional colleges were closed at various intervals between 1988 and 1992, the SLORC required that all teachers participate in a "boot camp" and attend "re-education courses" at the Directorate of Defense Services Intelligence's psychological warfare school in Phayunggyii. There, teachers were required to wear military uniforms and attend courses that stressed the promotion of patriotism, upholding national unity, and managing student affairs.[32] "Managing student affairs" was a euphemism for teachers' new security duties, such as monitoring halls and bathrooms to ensure that students did not become unruly. To the chagrin of many who participated in the boot camp, the SLORC demanded that its college and university lecturers create a kindergarten type of atmosphere. Other teachers are required to attend "refresher courses." Anyone who fails a course loses his or her teaching job.

Teacher and student unions are banned in Burma, and SLORC Law 2/88 prohibits the assembly of more than five people without permission. In April 1991, SLORC Law No. 1/91 prohibited all civil servants, including teachers, from engaging in politics.[33] This decree does not, however, prohibit teachers from joining the Union Solidarity and Development Association (USDA). The USDA is a mass member organization, but not a political party. Civil servants and military personnel are not prohibited from joining. Quite the contrary, teachers are expected to join, and it is estimated that millions of Burmese have attended rallies throughout the country. The USDA is similar to what GOLKAR, the Indonesian government's political organization, was when it was established in 1967—a constitutionally justified apparatus that enables the military to have greater political influence.

There is little donor activity to help improve the quality of education in

Burma. UNICEF is the only international development organization working on primary education issues. From 1996 to 2000, UNICEF plans to spend $6.4 million to improve primary education. The Burmese government is expected to provide counterpart contributions amounting to $4 million. During this period, depending on the availability of funds, supplemental funds totaling $5 million may become available. One project this money will support is called All Children in School (ACIS). Its main purpose is to increase enrollment and raise the successful completion rate of primary schooling. This program will also strive to make primary education free for poor families. During this five year program, ACIS will be implemented in thirty to forty townships and affect an estimated 4,500 to 6,000 primary schools. A goal of this program is to raise the completion rate for primary education from 25 percent to 80 percent.[34]

As the ACIS program is less than two years old, it is too early to assess its success. While the ACIS project will likely benefit those school children which it targets, it does not address the larger, more chronic, problems that exist in Burma's educational system—the biggest being SLORC's political control over the schools. Given the government's budget priorities, it calls into question whether the SLORC will continue to contribute counterpart funding and make such projects sustainable. The SLORC's view may be that these projects generate good publicity, but future programs will likely be contingent on funding from international organizations. A comprehensive education policy needs to be developed that will provide basic literacy and numeracy skills for all of Burma's peoples and respect the languages and cultures of this ethnically diverse nation. Until greater priority is given to providing the financial resources necessary for a good education, and political interference abates, the general state of education is likely to remain unchanged.

Comparison with Other ASEAN Nations

No country can undergo a structural transformation of its economy without raising basic education standards. Burma is no exception. This will require the government to readjust its priorities, significantly reducing its spending on defense and allocating more financial resources to education and other sectors important in developing the country's human capital. Economic growth will fail to materialize unless the SLORC invests in Burma's human development.

To understand the benefits of economic growth, Burma needs to look no further than its backyard. While many of the ASEAN nations experienced a marked increase in defense spending (the exceptions being the Philippines and Vietnam), the percentage of defense spending as compared to total government spending has declined in recent years. This has allowed ASEAN members to spend more of their resources on education.[35] One way the ASEAN nations accomplished this increase was by reducing their military personnel between 1990 and 1995. Burma, on the other hand, has increased its armed forces personnel to 300,000 and analysts believe the SLORC aspires to expand its armed forces to anywhere between 400,000 and 500,000 troops.[36] Burma's increase in military personnel is occurring despite the absence of an external security threat. At the same time, Burma's expenditures on health and education have significantly declined. This, coupled with the country's poor economic performance, has caused Burma's educational system to fall into disarray.

In the early 1960s, Burma's stage of development was similar to Thailand's. The two began to diverge, however, when Burma chose to isolate itself from the world, and Thailand opened its economy. With U.S. economic assistance, Thailand significantly invested in primary education and made a concerted effort to ensure that primary schooling was extended beyond provincial towns and into virtually all villages. By the 1980s, all children completed the minimum four years of primary education.[37] In 1985, Thailand extended compulsory education to six years, and in 1996 further extended it to nine years with the goal of developing a force of knowledgeable and skilled workers needed to meet the demands of a rapidly industrializing economy. A benefit of Thailand's investment in human capital through primary and lower secondary education is that its per capita income is ten times greater than Burma's today.

Even Indonesia, a country that spends a good deal less on education than its ASEAN partners, has made important strides in making primary education available to its people. In 1961, more than two-thirds of Indonesia's population had no schooling and less than 15 percent had a primary education. Beginning in the mid-1970s, the Indonesian government endeavored to make primary education available to all children. By the late 1980s, more than 91 percent of children in rural areas were enrolled in primary school, only slightly less than the 92 percent enrolled nationwide.[38] Although regional gaps in enrollment ratios and literacy rates remain, the focus on primary education has been an effective way to make the most of limited educational resources. Like Thailand, Indonesia in 1987 expanded compulsory education up to the ninth grade. While the quality of education has declined, the Indonesian government continues to identify primary education as a key educational objective. The result is that despite its own political problems, Indonesia is viewed as one of the world's top emerging markets. Direct foreign investment has tripled in the past two years. Moreover, education helped reduce Indonesia's poverty rate from 60 percent to 14 percent between 1966 and 1993.

If Burma wants to attract investment like Thailand, Indonesia, and the other ASEAN nations have done, its peoples will need the literacy, numeracy, and discipline learned in primary and secondary schools—skills that give countries with well-educated people an advantage in exporting manufactured goods, and allow them to attain a higher quality of life. Education also helps farmers not so much because it provides them with information, but because it enhances their ability to learn from their experience or that of others. Burma's educational policies do not come close to meeting this need.

In any successful educational system it is important that parents play an active role in setting school policies. As taxpayers, parents have this right. A PTA is a forum where parents have the opportunity to learn about school policy and to support or question it. In Burma, however, PTAs are used primarily to raise funds to maintain school buildings. Parents and teachers have no voice in school policy and are unable to voice their concerns, aspirations, or discontent. Those who attempt to do so are dismissed from their jobs and risk imprisonment.

The Thai and Indonesian governments are trying to keep pace with the people's demand for education. In a number of cases private schools have proven to be better in developing the marketable skills that are needed in private industry. While this development has caused some underlying tension along racial and religious lines, Indonesia still appears to recognize the inevitability of such institutions. Private institutions and universities in Thailand have extended educational opportunities so that a small, yet growing, student population is comprised of the sons and daughters of farmers.

Both countries are also working closely with the private sector to develop the skills necessary to create a rapidly industrializing economy. In 1996, as part of its agreement to build a $750 million assembly plant, General Motors demanded that Thailand develop a training center to upgrade the skills of workers in Thailand's fledgling automobile industry. In addition to the $15 million that the Thai government has pledged to develop this center, General Motors and other automobile companies will be contributing to the center's development. Moreover, universities and private Thai foundations are eager to work with the automotive industry as well as other industries to help define the educational needs of Thai workers.[39] Burma's professors and students have not had the opportunity either to upgrade or learn skills important to the country's development because of the strict censorship imposed by the SLORC and the country's pervasive political repression.

If Burma does not link its future economic growth and human development to skillful and intelligent policy management, then economic development there will remain jobless, voiceless, rootless, and futureless. Until such policies come into being, Burma's peoples will continue to suffer through no fault of their own—and sadly, they will enter the twenty-first century poorer and less well educated than they were half a century ago when Burma achieved independence.

Notes

1. John Brandon is the assistant director for The Asia Foundation in Washington, D.C. The views expressed are his own and are not necessarily those of his employer or any other institution.

2. See United Nations Development Project, *Human Development Report* (New York, 1996), 209.

3. John Dori and Richard Fisher, *U.S. and Asia Statistical Handbook* (Washington, 1996), 35.

4. The World Bank, *Myanmar Policies for Sustaining Economic Reform* (Washington, 1995), 117. The U.S. Embassy in Rangoon's 1996 Country Commercial Guide estimates that Burma spends half of its state budget on the military.

5. Associated Press (14 October 1996).

6. The official exchange rate is 5.9 kyat to U.S.$1. This currency is highly overvalued. Unofficial exchange estimates vary from 120 to 170 kyats to U.S.$1. With the country's spiraling inflation, this writer is estimating that the kyat at the unofficial exchange rate is 150 to U.S.$1. Inflation is believed to be about 40 percent.

7. Associated Press (10 September 1996).

8. Susuma Chatterjee, "New Generation of Burmese Students Learns Politics of Protest," *Washington Post* (9 December 1996), A11.

9. Martin Smith, "Burma (Myanmar)," in *Academic Freedom 3: Education and Human Rights* (London, 1995), 100.

10. Reuters, "Burma Reopens Schools, but Not All Universities" (12 August 1997).

11. Martin Smith, "Burma (Myanmar)," in *Academic Freedom 2: A Human Rights Report.* (London, 1993), 23.

12. United Nations Development Program, *Human Development Report* (New York, 1996), 145.

13. United Nations Children's Fund, *Children and Women in Myanmar* (Rangoon, 1995), 57.

14. Smith, "Burma (Myanmar)," in *Academic Freedom 3*, 96.

15. UNICEF, *Children and Women in Myanmar*, 51, 52.

16. Ibid., 32.

17. Ibid., 54.

18. Ibid., 53.

19. Ibid., 33.

20. Ibid., 54, 55.

21. Smith, "Burma (Myanmar)," in *Academic Freedom 3*, 97.

22. UNICEF, *Children and Women in Myanmar*, 54.

23. Smith, "Burma (Myanmar)," in *Academic Freedom 2*, 25.

24. Associated Press (14 October 1996).

25. Smith, *Academic Freedom 3*, 102, 103.

26. Ibid., 104, 105.

27. Personal communication, December 1996.

28. For a more detailed discussion of the events of August-September 1988, see Bertil Lintner, *Outrage* (Hong Kong, 1989).

29. Article XIX (1992), *Our Heads Are Bloody but Unbowed: Suppression of Educational Freedoms in Burma* (London, 1992), 11.

30. Ibid., 11.

31. Ibid., 12, 13.

32. Ibid., 11.

33. Ibid., 12.

34. Telephone conversation with Xiaolin Chai, Country Officer for UNICEF, New York City, Nov. 25, 1996.

35. World Bank, *World Bank Development Report* (New York, 1995), 180, 181.

36. Andrew Selth, *Transforming the Tatmadaw: The Burmese Armed Forces since 1988*, (Canberra, 1996), Appendix C.

37. Robert Muscat, *The Fifth Tiger: A Study of Thai Development Policy* (New York, 1994), 239, 240.

38. Hal Hill, *The Indonesian Economy since 1966: Southeast Asia's Emerging Giant* (Cambridge, 1996), 206–212.

39. Gordon Fairclough, "Learning Curve," *Far Eastern Economic Review* (14 November 1996), 34.

CHAPTER 14

Health in Burma
An Interpretive Review

David A. Chandler

BURMA'S HEALTH STATISTICS are striking. The country has an infant mortality rate of 105 per 1,000, and a maternal mortality rate of 232 per 100,000. An estimated 16 percent of children are severely malnourished and 43 percent are mildly or moderately malnourished. Only 60 percent of Burmese have access to health services, and 59.7 percent have access to "safe and convenient" drinking water. HIV infection and AIDS are spreading rapidly in a country with very limited resources, little health resistance, and slow mobilization against the epidemic. Rates of malaria, tuberculosis, and dengue hemorrhagic fever are growing rapidly, although universal child immunization has been very successful.[1]

When dealing with issues of early childhood development, the Burmese still use traditional approaches. With large scale socioeconomic changes on the horizon, it is clear that new models and approaches must be developed. On the positive side, deprivation and discrimination against women and girls do not seem to exist on the same scale as in other countries in the region.[2] There have not been many studies in this area, however, and the nature of gender conflicts and issues is not fully understood. Because budgets, in real dollars, continue to be reduced, the capacity to address problems is being diminished, while the number of children requiring special services seems to be growing exponentially. The mechanisms are in place for programs to fulfill Burma's obligations under the United Nations Convention on the Rights of the Child. But the programs have not yet been effectively utilized, and their potential is not being tapped.

Burma's estimated annual per capita income is U.S.$216.[3] It is not sufficient to cover more than the most basic survival needs of food, water, cooking fuel, and transportation. There is a large "informal" economy, but it is difficult to estimate what percentage of the population participates in it. Qualitative evidence and experience indicate that many families are struggling just to provide daily meals.

The definition of poverty is a series of layered or multiple problems that are difficult or even impossible to separate and tackle singly. The vast majority of people in Burma face layers of problems. This reality is compounded by the fact that most people simply do not have the economic resources, education, or contacts to find appropriate and lasting solutions.

Service delivery systems have fallen behind. Years of double-digit inflation, the aftermath of thirty years of civil war, the beginnings of heavy urbanization, and pressures for Burma to become a part of the global community have taken their toll. Traditional approaches and solutions are no longer practical or effective. New ideas and methodologies are taking root slowly. They seem, however, to be taking root faster in the private sector than in the public sector.

There are indications of hope. Indigenous and international non-governmental organizations (NGOs), along with international organizations, are beginning to find creative ways to address these complex problems. In some instances, there has been effective cooperation between indigenous NGOs and various Burmese ministries. International organizations and international NGOs have helped to facilitate these linkages. In doing so, there is a role for well targeted and carefully implemented humanitarian assistance.

Reliable data that reflect the health realities in Burma are difficult to obtain. This chapter pulls together the most informative quantitative data available in an effort to describe accurately the health situation in Burma (see table 14-1).[4] The information is then combined with qualitative data and representative anecdotes to provide an overview of the health realities in Burma. This report uses as its base of information Article II of the *Myanmar–UNICEF Country Programme of Cooperation, 1996–2000, Master Plan of Operations* (MPO) and the *Union of Myanmar Monitoring Progress towards the Goals of the World Summit for Children through Multiple Indicator Cluster Survey* (MICS).[5] Table 14-1 shows basic health indicators for Burma.

For every birth, thirteen forms must be completed as part of various government reporting requirements. For every death, thirteen forms must again be filled out and filed. Thus, when an infant is born and then dies shortly afterwards, twenty-six forms must be completed and filed. In hospitals, it is likely that this record keeping is painstakingly maintained. In rural areas, however, records often are not kept. By forgoing the record keeping, rural residents minimize their

Table 14-1. Vital Health Statistics

Health indicators[a]	
Under-5 mortality rate (per 1,000)	150
Infant mortality rate	105
Maternal mortality rate	232
Crude birth rate-urban	28
Crude birth rate-rural	30.1
Crude death rate-urban	8.6
Crude death rate-rural	9.9
Population	44.7 million[b]

a. *The State of the World's Children 1997*, 80. United Nations Fund for Population Activities, *Maternal Mortality Survey, 1994*, 5. Central Statistical Organization, The Government of the Union of Myanmar, Ministry of National Planning and Economic Development, *Statistical Abstract 1996* (Rangoon, 1996), 13.

b. *Statistical Abstract 1996*, 9. This population projection for 1995 was based on the 1983 census. A growth rate was developed as a result of the data collected in the *Population Change and Fertility* Survey conducted by the Immigration and Population Department, and the United Nations Fund for Population Activities. Although these are the best data available, preliminary assessments indicate that population growth is slower than predicted in the above-cited projections. If this is true, then all coverage estimates will need to be revised upward.

workload and reduce negative feedback from the government (medical officers are often criticized for reporting high death rates in their area).

It is estimated that between 33 percent and 50 percent of public health workers' time is spent on data collection and management. This has a tremendous impact on the amount of time the public health staff can spend on service delivery.

Nutrition

It has been well documented that the death rate of mildly or moderately malnourished children is three times that of well-nourished children. The death rate for severely malnourished children is nine times greater. The long-term impact of malnutrition on the children of any nation is so significant that these data simply cannot be ignored.

There is the belief that no one starves in Burma because it is a fertile rice-growing country. This ingrained notion is very difficult to debunk. There is no question that Burma is a land of tremendous resources, with great food production capacity. However, the MICS data indicating that 15.8 percent of children were severely malnourished indicates a very serious problem (see tables 14-2 and 14-3).

In the townships where World Vision has projects, families say that they do not have enough to eat. They will drink rice water for nutrition, and they drink tea at night to stave off hunger pangs. It is not uncommon for families to eat meat only two times per week. There are ample data indicating that most families in Burma have limited socioeconomic opportunities, and they are experiencing great pressure in meeting their basic survival needs.

Table 14-2. Malnutrition in Children under Age Five
Percent

Category	Current value	1995 target
Severe malnutrition	15.8	8.8[a]
Mild or moderate malnutrition	42.9	29.6[b]

a. Multiple Indicator Cluster Survey, 2. Figures represent percentage of children under five who are more than three standard deviations below the median National Center for Health Statistics/WHO standard (classified as severely underweight).

b. Multiple Indicator Cluster Survey, 2. Figures represent percentage of children under five who fall below two standard deviations of the median weight for age of the NCHS/WHO standard (underweight moderate and severe).

Physicians state unequivocally that 80 to 100 percent of children in Burma have worms. This may have a tremendous impact on the level of malnutrition. Children are measured by weight-to-age ratios. This is the basis on which they are positioned on the standardized nutritional scale. The presence of worms must inhibit the amount of nutritional value children receive from the food taken in. In this way the true nutritional status of children has been masked.

Some argue that the MICS data overstate the problem. They suggest that the malnutrition is a reflection of multiple problems, including diseases, poor water supplies, worms, and lack of nutritional balance in meals.

The UNICEF/Ministry of Health's estimate of 11 percent for severely malnourished children is probably understated because of the way the data were collected.[6] Midwives, who are responsible for these data, are so busy that they cannot work outside of their assigned multi-village cluster, so they cannot assist the other midwives in the weighing of children. Midwives also rarely have time to weigh all the children in their cluster. Generally, they only reach the children in their home village. Consequently it is estimated that children are only weighed in one out of five villages. Furthermore, children are generally not weighed in the border areas. Auxiliary midwives are unable to assist outside of their multi-village cluster as well.[7]

Nutritional deficiencies affect mothers and children alike (see table 14-4). The percentage of mothers of children under 5 who know the signs of acute respiratory infection is 99.4.[8] The worst-hit areas for iodine deficiency disorder are the Chin, Kachin, and Shan states, i.e. the hilly region. The problem is increasing in the delta area because of floods.

Table 14-3. Breast-Feeding Practices

Age	Status	Percentage
Under 4 months	Exclusively breast-fed	30
6–9 months	Breast milk and complementary food	33.6
12–15 months	Breast-fed	81.1
20–23 months	Breast-fed	55.8
Under 1 year	Receive food or drink from a bottle	9.3
Under 1 year	Ever breast-fed	99.4

Table 14-4. Nutritional Deficiencies[a]

Deficiency	Percentage of population
Vitamin A (6 months to 6 years)[b]	0.4
Protein energy and malnutrition[c]	31.2
Anemia in pregnant women[d]	>60
Iodine (schoolchildren)[e]	33

a. Potential shortcomings of these vitamin deficiency data include the fact that the sample size of 14,000 may be too small for meaningful conclusions; there are high-risk areas of the country that have not been captured in the data.
b. United Nations Children's Fund, *Children and Women in Myanmar: A Situation Analysis, 1995* (Rangoon, 1995), 49.
c. Ibid., 47.
d. Ibid., 26.
e. Ibid., 49.

Burma's primary health care service and infrastructure are gradually improving (see table 14-5). Given this reality, UNICEF and the Ministry of Health estimate that 80 percent of the population have access to some basic health services. Typically, these include immunization and maternal care. Approximately 60 percent of the population has access to a broader range of primary health care services. In spite of the progress, many problems remain, including shortages of essential drugs, understaffed clinics in the border townships, and low salaries for government doctors, which causes many of them to engage in private practices on the side (see table 14-6).[9]

Some traditional medical practitioners are licensed by the government, but the vast majority are unlicensed, making it difficult to obtain an accurate estimate of the number of traditional medical practitioners.

Overall health coverage is low. Access to public health services is in the range of 60 percent. It is worse in remote areas, where services are provided on an outreach basis, perhaps once every four months. Constraints include limited access and availability of essential drugs, low wages, and shortages of manpower in certain locations. Even public health doctors run private practices to supplement

Table 14-5. Basic Health Coverage

Public health facilities	1992	1995
Government hospitals	693	737
Total hospital beds	27,334	28,372
Persons per bed	1,549	1,577
Rural health centers	1,375	1,427
Primary health centers	83	88
Maternal and child health centers	348	358
School health teams	80	85
Traditional medicine hospitals	2	3
Traditional medicine clinics	169	188

SOURCE: Department of Planning and Statistics, Ministry of Health, Myanmar Health Facts (Rangoon, 1996).

Table 14-6. Number of Health Practitioners

Type of practitioner	1992	1995
Total doctors	11,872	12,950
Public	4,726	5,404
Cooperative and private	7,146	7,546
Health manpower persons per doctor	3,571	3,455
Dental surgeons	794	860
Nurses	7,900	9,851
Persons per nurse	5,348	4,542
Dental nurses	103	113
Basic health staff	11,569	12,904
Lady health visitors[a]	1,616	1,683
Midwives	7,242	8,143
Health assistants	1,276	1,328
Public health supervisor	1,435	1,750
Persons per basic health staff member	3,659	3,467

SOURCE: Myanmar Health Facts.
a. Highly trained nurses.

their income. The net result is that the vast majority of health services are, in reality, provided by the private sector.

Table 14-7 gives data on government expenditures on health care. To provide some perspective on Burma's overall public health service coverage, table 14-8, with information on access to health services in other countries, shows how Burma compares with its neighbors.[10]

To address the problem of coverage, the government is providing incentive programs for doctors to go to remote areas. These include shorter assignments and immediate access to graduate study programs. The government also has nearly doubled its capital budget for health. In 1995-96, the capital budget for health was 1 billion kyats. In 1996–97 it was increased to 1.9 billion kyats.[11] These are all steps in the right direction. The next step would be to increase the budget for equipment, salaries, and consumable items such as essential drugs and dressings.

The potable water assessments published in the past are much lower than those developed by the MICS (see table 14-9). The reason is that the MICS includes private (commercial) facilities along with public clean water sources.

Table 14-7. Government Health Expenditures

Government health expenditure	1992	1995
Total health expenditure (million kyats)	2,007	2,776
Health expenditure as percent of GDP	0.83	0.45
Health as percent of government budget	7.3	6.9
Per capita expenditure on health (kyats)	49	62[a]

SOURCE: Myanmar Health Facts.

Table 14-8. Percentage of Population Covered by Public Health Service

Country	Percentage
Vietnam	90
Thailand	90
China	83
Indonesia	80
Philippines	76
Laos	67
Burma	60
Cambodia	53

Anecdotal experience indicates that the use of latrines is low, so potential for groundwater contamination is high. Without sufficient training, community members view latrines as unnecessary devices that must be kept clean for use by visiting VIPs. In addition, people tend not to boil water because the fuel costs are high. Finally, many communities are accustomed to the taste of river or pond water. Without appropriate training and adjustment time, they will often reject water from tube wells. Consequently, clean water is often available in principle, but not in practice. Through the implementation of projects such as long-term participatory community development projects, these are solvable problems.

HIV and AIDS

HIV and AIDS are rapidly increasing and have very high potential to destroy the lives of many people in all segments of the population (see table 14-10). By 1993, only 261 cases of AIDS and fewer than 7,500 cases of HIV had been confirmed. The World Health Organization estimated, however, that by the end of 1994 the number of HIV-positive cases may have been as high as 400,000 to 500,000 people (see table 14-11). Particularly at risk are men of reproductive age working as truck drivers, traders, day laborers, fishermen, and miners, as well as the women who are their wives or partners. National programs to combat HIV and AIDS have expanded rapidly since 1993.[12]

Table 14-9. Percentage of Households with Access to Water and Sanitation
Percent

Access to	Current value	1995 target
Potable water	59.7	49
Sanitary latrines	42.7	36.9

SOURCE: Multiple Indicator Cluster Survey, 3. "Timing of MICS during monsoon months may have contributed to slightly high value."

Table 14-10. Reported Cases of AIDS, March 1995

Division	Number of cases
Rangoon	304
Tanintharyi	140
Shan State	84
Mandalay	19
Sagaing	7
Bago	4
Ayeyarwaddy	2
Kachin State	6
Mon State	2
Yakhine State	1
Kayin State	1
Total	570

World Vision has anecdotal evidence that strongly supports the higher HIV infection estimates of WHO and other organizations. Four of the townships in which World Vision is working report that at least one person per day dies of AIDS. These deaths, however, are not reported as AIDS deaths. Admittedly, these townships (with populations ranging from 70,000 to 100,00) are in high-risk areas. It is believed that official numbers for HIV infection and AIDS are low because most patients avoid public health services in favor of private practitioners. Government figures are a reflection only of the usage of public health services.

In a focus group discussion in Kawthaung, general practitioners said that HIV-positive patients will exhibit symptoms of AIDS within six months to three years. This dormancy period, which is extremely short when compared to that in more developed countries, is comparable to that in Thailand.

The issue of social stigma remains a problem. There are indications that certain hill tribes will shun or disown those members who are confirmed as HIV-positive. One couple in a fishing village died of AIDS, and their three children died shortly thereafter due to neglect. It is clear that counseling and care programs

Table 14-11. Reported HIV-Positive Cases, 1988–95

Year	Cases
1988	1
1989	323
1990	1,034
1991	2,152
1992	1,641
1993	2,001
1994	2,361
1995 (March)	372
Total	9,885

need to be established, supplementing the awareness and prevention programs already underway.

There are sufficient data from a range of sources to indicate that the HIV/AIDS situation in Burma is on the scale of a national emergency. HIV infection has penetrated virtually all population groups and all geographic locations. The most common modes of transmission are heterosexual intercourse and intravenous drug use.

Other Diseases and Epidemiological Concerns

Burma's Department of Health ranks the top ten health risks in the following order of priority:[13]
1. Malaria
2. Tuberculosis
3. Acquired Immune Deficiency Syndrome
4. Diarrhea and dysentery
5. Protein energy malnutrition
6. Sexually transmitted diseases
7. Drug abuse
8. Leprosy
9. Abortions
10. Anemia

Malaria

Malaria is the most pressing public health concern in the country. Tables 14-12 and 14-13 show the extent of the problem.

Tuberculosis

The main problems associated with tuberculosis in Burma are its rising incidence, its prevalence among the working age group (15 to 39 years), the easy communicability of the disease, and the prolonged period of treatment required to cure it. Tables 14-14 and 14-15 show its prevalence and mortality.

Dengue Hemorrhagic Fever (DHF)

Epidemic outbreaks of dengue hemorrhagic fever tend to be cyclical. In

Table 14-12. Results of Blood Slide Examination in Burma

Year	Slides examined	Number positive	Annual parasite incidence	Annual blood exam rate	Number of *P. falciparum*	Percent of total
1982	769,763	42,021	1.29	2.37	34,768	82.7
1983	1,111,582	47,700	1.43	3.34	40,928	85.8
1984	1,136,624	60,488	1.78	3.34	52,235	86.4
1985	1,306,000	65,279	1.87	3.75	55,849	85.6
1986	1,160,394	62,917	1.68	3.10	54,068	85.9
1987	917,241	66,643	1.74	2.4	58,746	88.2
1988	948,235	94,736	2.43	2.43	84,032	88.7
1989	1,242,271	135,194	3.40	3.12	115,887	85.7
1990	1,147,570	133,049	3.28	2.82	112,570	84.6
1991	1,038,248	126,967	3.35	2.74	106,365	83.8
1992	898,237	125,710	2.97	2.12	106,030	84.3
1993	746,166	116,724	2.71	1.73	99,684	85.4
1994	600,252	111,672	2.54	1.36	94,670	84.8

SOURCE: Basic Health Division, Department of Health, Country Health Profile Myanmar, 38–39.

Burma, however, the overall rate is rising (see figure 14-1). The severity of dengue fever and dengue shock syndrome is described in four grades. Grades I and II can be effectively treated and cured. But Grades III and IV are much more serious, with mortality rates of 30 to 40 percent. Most Southeast Asian countries hospitalize patients with all grades of dengue fever. Burma, however, hospitalizes and reports only grades III and IV. Thus, the actual incidence of dengue in Burma is much higher than reported. Since the only reported dengue cases are

Table 14-13. Hospital Records of Clinical Malaria Cases and Deaths due to Malaria in Burma

Year	Clinically suspected malaria outpatients (thousands)	Outpatients (percent)	Clinically suspected malaria inpatients (thousands)	Inpatients (percent)	Malaria deaths	Mortality rate per 100,000
1982	773	3.9	104	15.6	1,980	6.1
1983	703	4.0	102	14.4	2,217	6.7
1984	702	4.7	116	16.4	3,236	9.5
1985	761	5.2	111	14.7	2,856	8.2
1986	764	5.3	114	15.9	3,102	8.3
1987	764	5.3	127	16.9	3,578	9.4
1988	823	6.2	184	19.7	4,072	10.4
1989	870	7.3	146	20.6	4,885	12.3
1990	835	7.8	155	20.3	5,127	12.6
1991	787	7.7	152	20.6	5,231	12.6
1992	657	7.5	132	19.1	4,739	10.0
1993	573	7.3	129	18.7	4,129	9.8
1994	569	7.7	132	19.0	4,380	10.0

Table 14-14. Tuberculosis among Hospital Inpatients from 1988–93

	1988		1989		1990		1991		1992		1993	
	#	%	#	%	#	%	#	%	#	%	#	%
M	11,645	64	22,292	65	23,784	66	20,310	67	19,202	66	10,002	62
F	6,614	36	11,996	35	13,131	34	9,799	33	9,704	34	6,088	38
T	18,259	100	34,288	100	35,915	100	30,109	100	28,906	100	16,090	100

SOURCE: Basic Health Division, Department of Health, Country Health Profile Myanmar, 40.

Table 14-15. Deaths due to Tuberculosis, 1988–93

	1988		1989		1990		1991		1992		1993	
	#	%	#	%	#	%	#	%	#	%	#	%
M	1,010	58	2,387	64	4,855	63	2,156	77	2,173	74	716	73
F	719	42	1,358	36	2,834	37	656	23	756	26	267	27
T	1,729	100	3,745	100	7,689	100	2,812	100	2,929	100	983	100

those that are most severe, it is not surprising that Burma has the highest case fatality rate among children in any Southeast Asian country. This problem is exacerbated by the fact that there is a severe shortage of appropriate treatment facilities, supplies, and equipment throughout the country.[14]

These data regarding the incidence and deaths due to malaria, tuberculosis, and dengue hemorrhagic fever reflect only those patients who received assistance from the public health service. It is not known how many more cases and deaths occurred outside the purview of the public health system. But it is estimated that the deaths from malaria are four to five times greater than the reported numbers. Referrals are a problem because of lack of transportation to hospitals. If the reporting system could incorporate data from the private sector and general practitioners, the overall reporting quality could be significantly improved.

Figure 14-1. Outbreaks of Dengue Hemorrhagic Fever, 1980–95
Number of cases

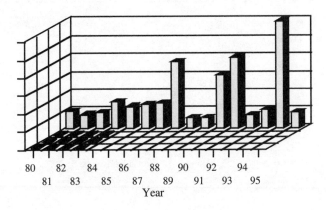

Year

Many strains of tuberculosis and malaria are resistant to drugs, and many patients fail to follow a full course of treatment. Typically, a doctor will prescribe a full course of antibiotics for a patient with a particular malady. However, due to the lack of availability, and/or the cost, the patient will stop taking the pills when he or she feels better. Consequently, the resistance issue is steadily worsening in Burma. There is a methodology called Directly Observed Chemo-Therapy Short Course (DOTS). It provides a means to insure that patients are fully treated and not just partially treated with a chemotherapy program. It is only now being introduced in Burma. The initial feedback from the pilot study is positive.

The resistance problem is further complicated by the fact that symptoms of AIDS often manifest themselves as tuberculosis and malaria. Some portion of the under reporting of AIDS is due to the fact that patients are identified as HIV positive, but the doctors are not informed in order to ensure that the patient continues to receive care. When the patients die, the death is officially registered as tuberculosis or malaria.

Universal Child Immunization

The immunization program is considered by many to be a success story over the past ten years. The death rate from immunizable diseases has gone down sharply in that time period (see tables 14-16 and 14-17). This includes the recent efforts toward polio eradication. In 1996, two sets of National Immunization Days were held. This effort was nationwide with extremely broad mobilization of resources and man-

Table 14-16. Cases and Deaths of Immunization-Targeted Diseases in Burma, Selected Years, 1978–95

Diseases	1978		1984		1990		1995	
	Cases	Deaths	Cases	Deaths	Cases	Deaths	Cases	Deaths
Diphtheria			353	37	181	10	34	1
Whooping cough	10,795	9	11,747	35	4,882	38	640	
Measles	5,867	7	13,580	95	6,243	71	905	6
Poliomyelitis	267	0	193	1	36	1	7	0
Neonatal tetanus							31	7
Other tetanus	1,732	249	2,343	358	769	150	293	47
Tuberculosis	10,215	0	11,045	612	12,416	519		

SOURCE: Central Epidemiology Unit, Department of Health, Ministry of Health, Cases and Deaths of EPI/Target Diseases in Myanmar 1978–1995 (Rangoon, 1996).

Table 14-17. Universal Child Immunization Coverage
Percent

Antigens	1985	1987	1989	1991	1993	1995
BCG	44	54	66	69	80	89.8
DPT3	17	27	50	67	73	83.5
OPV3	3	10	45	67	73	83.5
Measles		17	50	67	71	82.0
TT2	20	30	42	64	66	75.5

SOURCE: Central Epidemiology Unit, Department of Health, Ministry of Health, Universal Child Immunization 1985–1995 (Rangoon, 1996).

power. The effort achieved very wide coverage. Children five years old and under were targeted. Initial indicators suggest that more than 95 percent participated.

Early Childhood Development

The family is responsible for the stimulation, development, and education of very young children in Burma. Knowledge of child-rearing practices is considered traditional and is passed along within the family. For new parents, there are few other sources of information available on early childhood development and stimulation. With more women joining the work force, the traditional practices are being disrupted, and services such as day care are not generally available to fill in the gaps. Day-care programs sponsored by the Department of Social Welfare are located primarily in urban areas and only accommodate about 50,000 of the estimated 4 million children between the ages of three and five.[15]

Because the demand for child-care services far outstrips the supply, spontaneous services are springing up within the communities. A number of private or semi-private services are being provided. These providers include the Kachin Baptist Convention, the Myanmar Maternal Child Welfare Association, and the Young Men's Christian Association (YMCA). Furthermore, informal services are spontaneously emerging among the wards and villages of the very poor. One woman will volunteer to care for the children of other working women. A survey of early childhood care services has been recently produced by Save the Children Fund (United Kingdom) in an effort to understand the nature of these spontaneous programs and to determine the best way to provide appropriate assistance.

Anecdotally, it is known that in some suburban townships, parents commute long distances to work. They leave older children behind to care for younger siblings. Older children thus must drop out of school, and the younger children, receiving very loose supervision, are more prone to accidents and other trauma.

It is estimated that approximately 2 percent of the eligible children are receiving early childhood care services from publicly provided sources.[16] With work patterns changing, it is clear that the need for appropriate early childhood development programs is great and growing. Failing to address this need appropriately will add fuel to a growing and potentially large-scale street children problem.

Status of Women and Girls

Burmese women and girls do not experience as much discrimination and deprivation as their counterparts in other Asian countries. There are, however, significant problems that are made more difficult by the simple fact that gender issues are not so visible. Reaching the root of those problems will require extensive and sensitive research. Important areas to explore include access to nutrition and basic health services, and issues affecting social and economic development. Specific problems that need to be tracked include maternal health; enrollment, retention, and completion of primary education by girls; and education and employment for adolescent girls, particularly in the border areas.[17]

It is generally acknowledged that women do the domestic work as well as much of the income-generating work. Women also generally control the purse strings. In informal data collection exercises, men said that they wanted to get married so they could give most of the day-to-day concerns to their wives, enabling them to focus on a few things. Men are noted for the amount of time they spend in tea shops. Burmese women do not assume their husbands' names upon marriage.

The Multiple Indicator Cluster Survey indicates that primary school enrollment and graduation differentials between men and women are low.[18] More women than men attend and graduate from universities and medical schools. Although women do not hold senior level positions in the government (there are only two female directors general), women are prominent in medicine and on university faculties.

Another interesting fact identified in the Multiple Indicator Cluster Survey is that boys are slightly more malnourished than girls as indicated by weight among children under five.[19] Apparently, on the societal level, Burmese women experience less of the deprivation and discrimination that is so common in other countries in the region. What is not so clear is whether they enjoy commensurate opportunities for professional and other forms of development. Although it is not documented, it is suspected that women in lower socioeconomic categories experience a different reality than women from well-to-do families or those who are well educated.

Status of Children

In most developing countries, including Burma, the health and education of children in urban areas tends to be better than that of children in rural areas. Health, nutrition, and education statistics suggest that children in the central divisions of Burma are better off than children living in the peripheral states. This is noteworthy because most ethnic minority groups live in the peripheral states. Immunization data provide a good illustration. In 1994, 89 percent of children were immunized in the seven divisions and Mon State. In the remaining six states, the immunization coverage was 23 percent. There are ethnic communities scattered throughout the border areas that have had, for the most part, no public services due to armed conflict and impassable terrain. In 1992, government services began to reach some of these communities.

There are some exceptions to the generalization that urban children are better off than rural children. Because the poor are generally concentrated in suburban areas, the experience of children in resettlement areas around the cities or towns may well be significantly different than that of children living in the urban centers.[20]

The number of street children is increasing—especially in the suburban resettlement areas. Parents work, and consequently, many older children drop out of school to take care of younger children. They also seek ways to supplement family incomes.

In Kawthaung, most of the prostitutes (known as "hospitality girls") are younger daughters (out of five or six children) in families that have recently lost a working parent. Anecdotal evidence indicates that the majority of these girls come from townships in Rangoon that are suburban resettlement sites or urban slums.

Although still in its early stages, the number and range of Children in Especially Difficult Circumstances (CEDC) is another problem that exists on a massive scale. Almost all categories of CEDC (which include working children, street children, children of war and armed conflict, disabled children, HIV- and AIDS-infected children, sexually exploited children, and refugee and displaced children) must be addressed. Typically, children in "especially difficult circumstances" are an indication of families in especially difficult circumstances. In other words, the symptoms as manifested by the emergence of a CEDC problem indicate a number of underlying problems which first have to be under-stood before they can be systematically addressed. The first step in addressing this problem is to conduct assessments. Once the scope and range of the CEDC problem in Burma is understood, then models for effective programs can be developed and implemented.

The Union of Myanmar is a signatory to the U.N. Convention on the Rights of the Child. As such, the country is legally obligated to fulfill its mandate. In response to this mandate, laws have been enacted, and all the mechanisms are in place. Whether they are active and effective is not known. However, with the mechanisms in place, there is an opportunity to develop models to address the various identified needs. The challenge is to mobilize efforts at the township and ward levels.

Socioeconomic Status and Conditions

Estimated per capita average annual income was U.S.$216 for 99 percent of the population in 1995. This calculation is the result of combining UNICEF's estimate of the per capita income of rural populations with World Vision's data for urban poor. Since the rural population represents 75 percent of the country, a weighted average was used to determine the overall estimated number.

UNICEF surveyed rural populations and estimated the monthly wage at 2,000 kyats or U.S.$16, which is approximately U.S.$192 per year. World Vision surveyed the urban poor and found that in an urban suburb of Rangoon the aver-age monthly income was 3,000 kyats or U.S.$24. This works out to an estimat-ed U.S.$288 per year at the 1995 exchange rate.

Using the weighted average of the two population groups, the per capita income for the vast majority is U.S.$216. There are a few very rich people in Burma, whose incomes have not been included in these calculations. World Vision estimates that they may number approximately 50,000 (or 0.1 percent) of the entire population.[21]

Financial Pressures on the Family

WV-Myanmar estimates that daily laborers earn between $.40 and $1.60 per day. A survey conducted for WV of an entire ward (canvassing 277 families, or approximately 1,500 people) in one urban township verified this. The survey indicated that the average family income is $24 per

Table 14-18. Household Expenditure on Food and Beverages per Month in 1996

City	Percentage
Rangoon	64.7
Mandalay	71

SOURCE: *Statistical Abstract 1996*, 115–116.

month. The low among the survey group was $1.60, and the high was $36. This estimated average income of $.80 per day barely covers the minimum daily expenses incurred by a family. In Myanmar the average family size is estimated at five to six. WV has provided daily expense estimates for a family of three:

Food	$.32–$.40 per day;
Water	$.05–$.10 per day;
Transportation	$.05–$.10 per day; and
Cooking fuel	$.24–$.32 per day.

With the daily cash requirement between $.66–$.92 for a family of three, it is clear that the average family income for an urban poor family will barely cover the daily living expenses. If rent is charged; taxes are levied; a family member gets sick; clothes must be purchased; or school fees are required, then there is little or no margin with which to cover any emergencies or additional expenses.[22]

It is clear that the vast majority of the population in Burma faces a daily struggle to meet its basic survival needs. Food and water comprise most of the daily budgetary expenses (see table 14-18). Anecdotally, we know there is a large "informal" economy permeating the entire economy. What is not known is the percentage of the population that has access to it. Qualitative evidence and experience indicate that the majority of families are struggling just to provide daily meals.

In development, it is always important to know the survival techniques of the target community. Communities will always seek to preserve the future, until they reach the point of desperation. Then they will, of necessity, sacrifice the future to preserve the present. Much of the population of Burma is at this point of desperation.

Conclusion

Traditional solutions are not adequate to address Burma's modern problems. Such problems include a burgeoning HIV/AIDS problem, many children in dif-

ficult circumstances, and insufficient staff, supplies, equipment, and infrastructure to provide adequate public health services to the entire population.

There are obviously important roles that NGOs and international organizations can play in Burma, including delivery of services directly to the point of
need, accountability in spending, and the modeling of appropriate behaviors.
These data indicate that there is a clear need for humanitarian assistance.

Cumulative and layered problems need to be gradually reversed and unraveled. There are initial indications of hope. Indigenous NGOs, international
NGOs, and international organizations are beginning to implement programs in
Burma in an effort to find creative ways to address these complex problems. In
some instances, there has been effective cooperation between indigenous NGOs
and the various ministries.

These are tentative steps that have been taken against a backdrop of enormous
problems. But effective pilot programs are being implemented. Over time, when
communities develop an awareness that solutions are possible, the impact of this
change in attitude should be great.

Notes

1. United Nations Children's Fund, *The State of the World's Children 1997* (Oxford, 1997), 80.
United Nations Fund for Population Activities, Myanmar Maternal & Child Welfare Association,
Institute of Economics, Ministry of Education, Department of Planning and Statistics Ministry of
Health, *Maternal Mortality Survey, 1994* (Rangoon, 1994), 5. Department of Planning and Statistics
Ministry of Health, United Nations Children's Fund, *Union of Myanmar Monitoring Progress
Towards the Goals of The World Summit for Children Through Multiple Indicator Cluster Survey*
(Rangoon, 1995), 2, 3. Government of the Union of Myanmar, *Master Plan of Operations
1996–2000: Country Program of Cooperation between the Government of the Union of Myanmar
and the United Nations Children's Fund (UNICEF) for the Survival, Protection and Development of
Children and Women in Myanmar*, 2.

2. *Master Plan of Operations 1996–2000*, 3.

3. David A. Chandler, "An Introduction to World Vision Myanmar Update June, 1996," unpub.
report, 3–4.

4. Information for this chapter was collected with the Assistance of UNICEF-Myanmar, the
Myanmar Ministry of Health, World Vision International-Myanmar, and other organizations.

5. *Master Plan of Operations 1996–2000*, 2–3.

6. *Master Plan of Operations 1996–2000*, 2.

7. The data on "Deficiencies Vitamin A, Protein, Iodine, and Iron" cited in *Children and Women
in Myanmar: A Situation Analysis 1995* come from research conducted in 1990 and 1991. It is
important to note that these surveys typically have small sample sizes. Also the cluster selection is
made on the basis of the Township Medical Officer's (TMO) recommendation. Generally, the TMO
will make the cluster selection based on where the Ministry of Health is operational; this is a better
reflection of their efforts, whereas MICS cluster selection was random (adhering to strict WHO standards) and nationwide.

8. Ibid., 4.

9. *Master Plan of Operations 1996–2000*, 2.

10. United Nations Development Program, *Human Development Report 1996* (New York, 1996), 143–145. The figure for Burma includes general practitioners as well as Public Health Service doctors. The value provided in the 1995 publication of the *Human Development Report* was 41 percent because it included public health practitioners only.

11. Ministry of National Planning and Economic Development, *Review of the Financial, Economic and Social Conditions for 1995/1996* (Rangoon, 1996), 212.

12. *Master Plan of Operations 1996–2000*, 2.

13. Basic Health Division, Department of Health, *Country Health Profile Myanmar*, 18.

14. Ibid., 2.

15. *Master Plan of Operations 1996–2000*, 2.

16. Ibid., 112.

17. Ibid., 3.

18. *Multiple Indicator Cluster Survey*, 27–31.

19. Ibid., 35–40.

20. *Master Plan of Operations 1996–2000*, 3.

21. *Introduction to World Vision Myanmar Update* 3–4.

22. Ibid., 4.

Part Five

LOOKING FORWARD

CHAPTER 15

The Road to Political Recovery
The Salience of Politics in Economics

David I. Steinberg

"POLITICAL RECOVERY" is an ambiguous term. Depending on one's perspective, its meaning may imply process or product, permanence or evanescence. The path to such an amorphous goal is equally obscure. When applied to Burma, recovery clearly represents an external view, one proposed by outsiders who see alternative roads to a future they believe will be more in keeping with the long-term interests both of the Burmese people and of regional, and indeed global, actors for moral, economic, security, and political reasons.[1]

The State Law and Order Restoration Council (SLORC), however, might argue that the goal of political recovery is internal and has been reached already through the activities of the SLORC and the *tatmadaw* (armed forces). Indeed, such a view is inherent in the title of the council, and explicit in many of its announcements. From the SLORC's vantage point, the people's revolution—which it calls the "chaos" of the summer of 1988—represents the nadir from which it has attempted to raise the country. The future, the SLORC might argue, is not one of recovery, but rather of maintaining through other, military-directed constitutional, means the order that they have imposed on the state through martial law and political repression.

The SLORC might continue to contend that stability is the *sine qua non* of both governance and economic development. It has so declaimed in other contexts, and on many occasions. In an abstracted situation, many might agree. A state in ferment is a cause of regional, and sometimes worldwide concern, as rarely is political or economic chaos confined within national boundaries. Refugees, disease, revolutionary bases, and other impediments to regional stability spill over beyond the littoral of any state. Regional and global trade patterns are disrupted, investment is circumscribed, and markets and extraction of raw materials are thrown into confusion. Foreign and internal critics have argued, however, that immediate stability imposed by authoritarian rule eventually will unleash greater instability when the system collapses through attempted micro-management of the political and economic processes or through struggles for power.

The tatmadaw would assert that protecting the security of the state is its objective. This concept of security is based on a set of fears, both external and internal, although the latter is perceptually and objectively the more immediate and important of the two.

The external fears are based on the perceived threats to the integrity of the state from its more populous and powerful neighbors, and the support of dissidents within the country by Westerners. These fears, however irrelevant they may now seem to foreigners, are caused by historical analogies to previous authorized and unauthorized involvements by regional and global powers in support of insurgent regimes or groups. These include support for the Burma Communist Party by China on a "party-to-party basis," Thai involvement at various military and bureaucratic levels with a number of insurgent groups acting as buffer states along its western frontier protecting, in effect, a conservative Bangkok regime, British unofficial support for the Karens, and U.S. clandestine funding of the Chinese Nationalist forces within Burma. In addition, the SLORC has been worried that China, India, and Bangladesh have overwhelming populations and could be demographic threats to Burma. For this reason, Gen. Ne Win had a strong pro-natalist policy which outlawed birth control and abortion, except in rare cases. During the long, self-imposed night of Burmese isolation from the outside world beginning in 1963, the multiple insurgent groups had more political and economic contact with the external world than did the military governments of Burma, a situation that heightened the sense of insecurity. Part of the rationale for Burma's more open external policies may have been predicated on seizing this initiative from the dissidents and insurgents, as well as for economic development.

Internal threats, however, have been the primary focus of the tatmadaw. The protection of the regime has been of paramount importance, together with now explicit concern for ensuring the future role of the tatmadaw as the leading force in the state. A secondary unarticulated concern has been the tatmadaw's attempt to guarantee the dominance, in both military and civilian realms, of the Burman ethnic group, which comprises about two-thirds of the population. In spite of military pronouncements about the unity of the national "races" (ethnic/linguistic groups) through "weal and woe," to quote Aung San, to succeed in Burma even in the civilian era was to be Burman, or to play by the Burman rules of the power game.

To understand Burma requires understanding the SLORC's perceptions of its external and internal roles, and the functions it feels foreigners may perform. Whether there is continuity or change between power and authority of the SLORC today and the Burma of the civilian period is a subject of considerable debate. To attribute to the SLORC solely a continuity with the past that is both necessary and sufficient for the present, or to contend that the past is completely irrelevant to the contemporary concepts of power and legitimacy both probably obscure reality, which may be a particular mixture of the traditional and the modern.

The SLORC could, and has, defended its activities as beyond the appropriate concern of foreigners, who have had a predilection to interfere in internal Burmese affairs. The SLORC has argued for a redefinition of human rights in a specifically "Myanmar" or Asian context, based on culture and economic standing, to serve its parochial interests. Other states within the region—such as China, Indonesia, and Singapore—also have defended this general position, perhaps as much from anxiety that such inquiries in Burma might be a precedent for and justification of external examination of some of their own internal idiosyncratic and repressive political activities. This seems to have been the general position of the Association of Southeast Asian Nations (ASEAN), with the Philippines an obvious exception.

With few deviations, the military generally has resisted foreign surveillance of the economy except for some teams from the World Bank, Asian Development Bank, and International Monetary Fund. It generally has avoided expatriate advisory services in the economic policy and planning sector. The SLORC also has argued that foreigners have little regard for Burma, and do not "love" it as only "Myanmarese" (sic) can. The SLORC continuously has denigrated foreign individuals, cultures, and lifestyles in the press, all of which is state-controlled. Its assumption that there is a disconnect between patriotism and patrimony, which it upholds with vigor, and foreign concern and empathy, which it denigrates, obfuscates the real need for analyses and reality checks that under the present structure of hierarchical power only outsiders may be able to perform.

On Foreigners and Burma

There are many who would argue that change in Burma can only be accomplished by the Burmese themselves since they are the actors on the stage.[2] To continue the analogy, some foreigners might contend that they can be the stagehands behind the scene, assisting the production but remaining obscured. The SLORC might insist that foreigners are the audience divorced from the action who should view the scene through the lenses prescribed by the author and the director. The SLORC might hope that foreigners might also play the role of the financiers of the production, allowing the directors the freedom to stage the drama according to their "artistic" (political) preferences. Others might maintain that the foreign role is that of the drama critic, who assesses the performance. It is significant in this analogy that Aung San Suu Kyi is essentially portrayed by the SLORC as a foreigner, and thus is not deemed worthy to be an actor on the Burmese stage.

The solution, insofar as there is one, to the problems facing Burma must be resolved by the Burmese. This does not deny a role, in fact multiple roles, for foreigners, ones far more active than simply viewing the unfolding drama of Burmese events.

One essential part in a sense is forced on foreigners—those who have the interests of the Burmese people in mind. This is due to an inherent inability of those within Burma to provide the function of internal observer and potentially constructive critic. The leaders of the tatmadaw, both under the earlier Burma Socialist Program Party (BSPP) and the SLORC, are unwilling to ascertain from the lower ranks the actual conditions and problems affecting ordinary people within their state. There seems a pervasive reluctance to bring problems to the attention of the highest authorities when such issues may conflict with propaganda from above. The leadership thus cannot alleviate problems and their causes. This contradictory situation seems an anomaly in a state in which the government, through all its organs, including intelligence agencies, mass mobilization efforts, and the ubiquitous parastatal cooperative network, reaches down into the bowels of society. Yet a milieu of fear so pervades the polity that problems, some obvious to outside observers, cannot surface to the top of the intensely hierarchical and command-driven military structure from the bottom of the social, political, or economic ladder. This has been evident since the military coup of 1962 and is even more pronounced today. The BSPP had designed an elaborate feedback mechanism in which the BSPP officials, "elected" under a single-party mobilization system, would report back to their constituencies and learn about local problems, which they would in turn bring to the attention of the party's leadership. This system failed, and the leaders were unaware until too late of the problems of the periphery.[3]

The issue has been apparent during more than three decades of military rule. Ne Win in 1987, before his retirement in 1988, finally recognized it, and stated that it was time to stop lying about increased production with fabricated statistics. Yet such falsehoods were, in effect, politically required, and this requirement was prompted not only by the fears of the military throughout the country, but by Ne Win's own mercurial temper and personality. He brooked no disagreement from below. The evidence that the tatmadaw has been out of touch with the populace is demonstrated by its failure to understand the dynamics of popular sentiment and predict the results of the elections of 1960 and 1990.

The role of the foreigner is thus to provide in the modern world the functions of the traditional Imperial Chinese Censorate, which had access to the emperor and told him what was going wrong and the mistakes he was making. In democracies, the media provide this essential service; in Burma there is no censorate and no independent media. One role of foreigners, thus, is to help bring transparency to a state which is opaque, and in which power is personalized, fear is endemic, statistics whimsical, and where politics and power are the driving forces to which all else is subordinated.

There are also external roles for the foreign community, all of which seem anathema to the SLORC. The first is that of analyst—assessor of events internal and external, and predictor of future trends and needs.

A second function is to share and dispense information. Because information is power, the SLORC vigorously controls the media. Images presented both internally and to the outside world sift and winnow only those data that the SLORC wishes to present, and colors such information to attempt to shape public opinion. In a sense, the role of the foreigner (and foreign institution) in this regard is not only to provide other data to a broad audience, but to counter the official views with different perspectives because one of the most dangerous of circumstances is a regime that believes its own propaganda. This seems likely in Burma, where foreigners may dismiss many of the pronouncements of the SLORC as if they were insincere cant or simply campaign slogans in some democratic election. Instead, they may represent to the leadership very ardent and strongly held, if parochial and insular, tenets. Thus, the charge that foreigners are out to break up the country and that only the tatmadaw can protect the state are probably views that are tenaciously believed by the military itself. Since foreign intervention has historical bases in fact, the acceptance of such attitudes today becomes all the easier in spite of a complete change in the attitudes of both internal groups and external powers.

A more proactive role for foreigners is to advocate for reform. It is important, for example, that multilateral and bilateral donors continue to analyze and press for economic reforms and political reforms related to what is called "good governance" and human rights. Donors should conduct sectoral and other surveys of needs in the society, with SLORC approval, even if they do not have permission to implement programs. This has a dual function: it allows quick action by donors if and when general conditions prompt the resumption of lending and assistance, and it offers a potential incentive for reform even if it is left unstated. The potential for these studies to add legitimacy to the regime, is perhaps less important than their potential positive impacts.

Another foreign function is to support those affected by internal events, including political dissidents, students, refugees, and migratory workers. This support is especially important when neighboring states, such as Thailand, view such persons as threats to their perceived national interests. It is in providing support that the non-governmental community has an especially important role.

Contrary to what the SLORC may believe, there are multiple and legitimate roles for foreign observers. The foreigner, or the expatriate Burmese, must determine how to perform this external observer function most effectively. Is it essentially to rally the opposition supporters or influence policy changes? Although these positions are not necessarily contradictory, different emphases could produce different effects. One question is how public or private these observations should be. The dilemma is not easily resolved. Public criticism of any regime often creates a backlash of nationalism that makes local adoption of foreign suggestions even more difficult. This is especially true in Burma, where we have witnessed, through the controlled press, a form of xenophobia that is among the world's most vitriolic. This is especially prevalent in response to foreign media, while academic articles and advice receive more muted negative responses simply because they have far less circulation. Public critiques, however, may be effective in exhorting believers to rally around opposition organizations. On the other hand, private advice can be easily ignored without effect. Whatever the private conversations between authorities of ASEAN states and the SLORC under the guise of "constructive engagement," they seem to have had little, if any, impact.

The foreign business community performs a quite different set of functions in its engagement with Burma. Even the limited openings to the private sector that the SLORC has encouraged would, under normal political circumstances, have been viewed by the world community as the most important progress that Burma has made in several decades. Political factors retard the acceptance of these changes as an unlimited good. All internal political parties, including the National League for Democracy (NLD), welcome the encouragement of the private sector, but the NLD says that the time is not appropriate politically for foreign investment. Political reform must precede economic reform, or the present, illegitimate government will be strengthened and will be even more unwilling to sponsor political change. The SLORC and some foreign businesses claim that private sector investment will improve the lives of the people, even though the process is one of "trickle down," which has proven less than efficacious in many societies. There is no question that unemployment, at least in Rangoon and Mandalay, is down, and that wages for workers in the private sector have risen, although perhaps not sufficiently to keep up with inflation. Yet the economic impact of existing foreign investment has been concentrated geographically and socially, and has not reached the society as a whole. There is also the more generalized argument that economic growth through foreign involvement in the private sector will lead to political reform and democracy. This is perhaps the most questionable of assumptions. The demands of a vigorous private sector do increase the need for timely economic information, and create strains with which governments have to cope as businesses try to limit state interference in economic matters. But their effect on politics occurs over a very long time. In Korea and Taiwan, for example, economic development had an impact on the political power structure only after several decades. Growth in Singapore, China, Vietnam, Indonesia, and other states indicate that there is as yet no necessary corollary between economic growth and political pluralism. Those who rationalize that investing in Burma will force political changes had better be young enough to wait out the probable protracted impact of such investment and activities.

The Tatmadaw and Political Change

The SLORC argues that the tatmadaw is the only cohesive force in Burmese society. Factionalism and divisiveness have been hallmarks of the Burmese political process since political parties were introduced in the colonial period. Although the tatmadaw appears united, it is evident that the military fears internal splits. The most heinous crime, of which Aung San Suu Kyi has been accused, is of attempting to split the military. The SLORC goes to great and continuous pains to assure the world that it is united in its efforts.

The SLORC is correct that the military is a major cohesive force, although part of the reason is that it has participated in a self-fulfilling prophecy. The SLORC has attempted to divide the opposition, both ethnic and political, and has eliminated all vestiges of civil society in Burma. The existence of those organizations autonomous of government (rather than titularly "private" groups) that provided points of pluralistic power is past. Independent non-governmental organizations do not exist beyond village temple societies. The SLORC has registered and controlled the Buddhist *sangha* (priesthood). In its place, the SLORC, as the BSPP before it, has created its own "civil society"—a society that is alive and well and run by the government.

This pseudo-civil society is the Union Solidarity and Development Association (USDA), the mass mobilization organization with well over 5 million members (perhaps 20 percent of the adult population) that the military has designed explicitly to be its civilian support. It functions on the model of the Burma Socialist Program Party in its mass phase after 1972, and Golkar in Indonesia before it became an overt political party. Because it is registered as a social group, the military may, and is encouraged (perhaps required), to join along with civil servants. Both of those groups are prohibited from joining registered political parties. The USDA comes out at rallies to support the SLORC, and denounce Aung San Suu Kyi, and is thus a useful tool for the tatmadaw. When the time comes to approve a new military-mandated constitution produced from the workings of the heavily military-scripted National Convention, the USDA is expected to play a major role in drumming up approval.

If factionalism has been a problem in Burmese society, the military has had its own "faction," those who served under Ne Win in the Fourth Burma Rifles. Much of the military leadership evolved from that group. As Ne Win passes from the scene, and as younger officers take over, the cohesiveness of the military based on this association may begin to erode.

The problem of cohesiveness of political or other non-religious groups in Burma is one that observers should carefully consider. The primary cause of this problem, one that likely will continue to some significant degree, is that power is conceived as finite and personal. It creates hierarchies and factionalism and an unwillingness to share or delegate it either institutionally or personally, for such actions are a zero-sum game in which the sharer loses. This has profound implications for the future issues of leadership, federalism, or autonomy of any non-state actors, and is a primary reason why the Burmese state is likely to remain dirigiste, and not simply in economic terms. Even those institutions held together by the military structure may be expected to fissure over time.

The Anti-Fascist People's Freedom League (AFPFL), as its name implies, was united in opposition to foreign domination, but later split, allowing the first (legalized) Burmese military coup to take place in 1958. Before 1958, it may have been held together by the threats of the various and multiple rebellions that had mushroomed following independence. So too the military may be united today not only because of its vision of a new Burma and the role it will play, but because of the real fear of what might happen to it should power evolve into other hands. Observers should not, however, consider the military as monolithic, but rather subject to the same strains and potential fissures over time as other organizations. Fission is also a danger of which the political opposition in Burma is no doubt aware, for should it assume a governing role, divisions could prove a real threat.

Whatever the nature of the future governments of Burma over the next decade, whether overtly military, "civilianized" military in mufti, or a real civilian administration, the military may be expected to play the critical role that it has played since independence. It likely will hold veto power over pivotal state decisions even if the NLD or another civilian organization holds titular authority. In this sense, whatever future road political events follow in Burma, the military will at least be watching from the sidelines and ready to intervene again when it perceive its, or the country's, interests threatened.

Any planned path to the reform of political authority in Burma must somehow take this fact into account. To do so means not simply neutralizing the military from politics, which is virtually impossible to do at this stage without its expressed approval, but also persuading the military that there is little to fear from a civilian regime that peacefully evolves, rather than one born in the heat of popular revolution. The price of pluralism may be limited retribution for past, egregious, and brutal acts.

Such a result will be unpalatable to many on all sides of what could be a difficult debate. Following the 1990 elections, U Kyi Maung of the NLD said there would be no Nuremberg Trials, but this offer of conciliation to the tatmadaw by a former colonel and member of the Revolutionary Council of 1958 only resulted in his being jailed. Korean human rights activists are still dissatisfied with the results of the investigation into the Kwangju massacre of 1980 and the sentencing of two former presidents (one to death, since commuted to life) and a few others. So too any reconciliation with the Burmese military is likely to produce anguish among many who may want more drastic and widespread punishment.

Examples of the transition from military to civilian rule in Spain, Portugal, Chile, Brazil, Argentina, and other countries, none of which provide exact or even completely satisfactory models are still instructive. Change may occur in Burma through popular revolution, which cannot be dismissed and might be caused by some totally unrelated event that focuses pent up public political and economic frustration against the SLORC or a future military dominated government—as happened in 1988 in Burma and elsewhere under various dictatorships. Otherwise, change may come from within the military and its perceived need to reestablish the prestige and pristine patriotism of the tatmadaw by withdrawing from direct administration. To this end, some guarantees of the retention of military perquisites and protection against retribution may well be necessary, however unpalatable to many in civil society.

Although the SLORC has strong internal and external detractors, it also has some important external support. Chinese military sources, when asked about Chinese interests, discussed Burma's geopolitical importance to China's security. The sources said unequivocally that China would support the SLORC in the event of an internal military coup. When the question was posed about a popular uprising, the answer was that it would be more difficult, but that China would still support the SLORC.[4]

The commanding position of China in contemporary Burmese affairs may begin to worry some within the military, who are dissatisfied with the hold the Chinese seemed to have gained over the economy and who believe that the military equipment supplied by China is inferior. But if China has prompted internal concerns, the external issues have been more pronounced. Burma has seemed to become a surrogate for China in Southeast Asia and along the Bay of Bengal. India is concerned over a disputed border with China in its northeast, now outflanked by a Burma in economic thrall to China. Thailand is similarly concerned, and worries about its loss of cross-border trade prominence. Should China project its growing military capabilities into the Indian Ocean through Burma, the seeds of regional instability and concern could well germinate.

The increasing size of the Burmese armed forces interferes with the ability of the regime to deliver goods and services to the country. Burma spends one-third of the state's annual budget on the military but the real expenditures equal perhaps half of the national budget. This amount becomes increasingly important because the cease-fires with the minorities on the periphery have been based in part on the state's willingness and capacity to provide both a degree of local autonomy and basic needs, such as education and health facilities as well as an improved agricultural base, to those most deprived of peoples. If this delivery does not happen, then the truces may collapse.

The planned inclusion of the military in the *Pyithu Hluttaw* (National Assembly) as one-quarter of its members (plus those who run who are retired from the military), together with the provision that the military may perform administrative duties for the executive branch at any level of administration, as well as the complete autonomy of the military from civilian scrutiny, control, fiscal oversight, and authority all point to the continuing command of the military under its proposed, and likely, civilianized government. To do so effectively translates into the state's decision that loyalty to the armed forces and political reliability are far more important than competence or independence of views. With a dearth of civilian intellectual leadership, as evidenced by the legal and illegal exodus of about 1 percent of the population (mostly educated) from the country since military rule, the military, with its limited and fragmentary views of the major disciplines required for planning and administration, will be hard-pressed to develop competence in addition to enthusiasm and capacity in addition to loyalty.

Political change, let alone political recovery, under any of the scenarios that might be predicted, will in all probability involve the military to some significant degree. Aung San Suu Kyi has continuously expressed her respect for the Burmese military, which her father founded, and the desire for some modus vivendi with it through a process of dialogue, in which to date the military has expressed no interest. But to ignore the military or consider it insignificant in a future democratized state because of its outrageous acts against the civilian populations is to ignore Burmese reality, however emotionally unsavory.

Economic Recovery within the Political Context

Economic reconstruction is a concept about which most observers of Burma, both internal and external, would agree. Even with the spurious specificity of statistics that are often available, the opaque nature of the decision-making processes, and the extensive underground economy based on multiple exchange rates, quantifiable indicators demonstrate the degree to which the country has sunk, and some of the salutary changes that have been induced as a result of limited privatization efforts.

Although foreign investment is encouraged and the indigenous private sector approved, basic economic reforms have not taken place. Other chapters deal with those subjects. Here, consideration of some of the social and political aspects and ramifications of such developments is suggested.

Under the SLORC, or under whatever government replaces the SLORC, the role of the state in the economy will be profound. The historical evidence is extensive dating from the pre-colonial era. Burma is not likely to be an open market, a free economy, and one in which the private economic sector, whether domestic or foreign, will have a strong influence over the government or the regulatory regime. The economic sector will have little influence over politics.

The military currently has three roles in the economy: significant involvement in direct foreign investment and trade, control of direct production, and command of the economic decision-making process. Even if at some future date it were to give up the direct authority over economic decision-making, its influence would remain substantial.

The military has already established itself as a major economic actor under any future government, and even a completely civilianized regime will be unlikely to be able to diminish its established role. Through the Myanmar Economic Holdings Corporation, a wholly owned military venture, highly capitalized (10 billion kyat), and run by both the Defense Procurement Agency and active duty and retired military officers, the military has an extensive interest in the economy and has major contracts with foreign investors. In addition, the Burmese armed forces have established a broad network of military-owned factories to provide some of the necessities for the armed forces. The involvement of the Burmese military in the economy is neither a product of the SLORC nor the BSPP, but was begun in the 1950s under the Defense Services Institute, which started as a type of military post exchange, but developed an important grip over the economy during the military "caretaker" government period, 1958–60.

The military has historically been suspicious of the private sector, a suspicion that was shared by much of the population even during the civilian government because the modern economy was seen to be essentially in foreign hands. During the caretaker period, and under the SLORC as well, merchants were ordered to lower prices, and production costs had little to do with authorized sales prices. In the BSPP era, the regime simply tried to do away with the private industrial sector, but found that doing so was impossible and reluctantly allowed it to exist, although most major firms were part of the State Economic Enterprises; that is, the public sector, which itself had little autonomy in pricing or personnel policies.

The military in any administration is unlikely to allow private businesses to grow independently. The suspicion of that group remains strong, and is based in part on fear of the development of real internal economic or political pluralism, and fear that the economy may once again revert to foreign control. It seems likely that whatever modest capital is made available to the indigenous private sector through both state and "private" banking systems will be subject to political sensitivity checks and influences that will affect negatively the market operations of the economy as a whole. There are also advantages that such control gives to the governing elite, both through legal contracts and access to goods and services. It also provides opportunities for corruption, without which civil servants and the military, as well as pensioners, cannot exist because of the completely unrealistic exchange rate (about 1/25th of market value), and the rate of inflation that officially hovers in the 30 percent range, although it may well be higher. High-level civil servants and military officers receive about $10 monthly at the unofficial, accommodation exchange rate, and although they have extensive benefits, subsistence is difficult, if not impossible, without access to additional income. This then becomes an invitation to corruption.

Corruption is culturally defined, but its impact is felt in dual ways. As a country opens its economy to foreign participation, corruption becomes a matter of international scrutiny and concern. If it is predictable, foreign investors will calculate the advantages of investing and decide accordingly; if its levels and requirements are uncertain, they more likely will invest elsewhere where predictability is assured. Internally, a society will establish for itself the rules and degree of extra-legal remuneration, favoritism, or nepotism. When these rules are broken, or when it appears that there are unfair (a culturally determined concept as well) discrepancies in access to the fruits of legal or illegal activities, the regime may be in trouble, and political legitimacy may be withdrawn.

The issue of corruption must weigh in any prognostication of the future of Burma. Cynicism about governments and concern about their legitimacy are exacerbated by the perceptions that small, elite groups (together with their offspring) are unduly benefiting from such activities. Insofar as these groups are seen to be in league with foreign elements, about whom suspicions abound (Suharto and his family in Indonesia and the Chinese conglomerates), then their stability may be undercut.

During the BSPP period, the legal import of consumer goods was largely restricted to a small percentage of all imports. The gap between supply and demand was met through an extensive and well-organized smuggling operation along the Thai border. This changed with the third and most drastic of the demonetizations of the BSPP on Sept. 5, 1987. Urban dwellers did not want to hold kyat (to have foreign exchange was illegal then), so demand for consumer goods mushroomed at the same time that the Chinese liberalized their economy. The border posts with Yunnan opened and the Burmese Communist Party collapsed along that frontier. In November 1988, border trade was legalized by the SLORC, although such legalization had been planned in the last days of the BSPP, but the official figures probably understate to a highly significant degree the actual extent of the trade. The urban public's demand for consumer goods in lieu of cash was mirrored in the rural sector where peasants held paddy, and this demand then pushed the price of rice up in urban areas. This inflation was a significant cause of the 1988 uprising.

Two concerns for the future of Burmese politics are evident. The first is that those with access to funds, and thus to middle class status, are severely restricted. Capital for indigenous private investment through the newly formed private banking system (which is heavily controlled and in some cases owned by government entities, such as the Rangoon Corporation, the cooperatives, and elements of the military) is very limited. Funds for rural development are largely confined to seasonal loans to farmers. Those with access to money are from two groups: the higher officers of the tatmadaw and those civilians closely linked with them, and the Chinese community through external family, clan, and linguistic affiliations. Chinese have been allowed to enter Burma without visas, and through various subterfuges establish rights and buy property and invest in businesses. These investments do not show up in official national or international economic reporting because they do not go through the Foreign Investment

Board, and thus their magnitude is masked, perhaps even from the state's economic bureaucracy. Mandalay, the seat of Burman culture, is said to have become a Chinese city.

The second issue is more general—the question of the continuation of the private sector opening. Should these trends continue, then the danger to even the limited open economy now established as well as to the political order may come as the Burmans once again, as in the 1930s and 1940s, realize that the modern sector of the economy is no longer in their hands, and when the obvious inequalities of incomes, as manifested in the conspicuous consumption so evident in the present society, prompt a popular revulsion from the direction in which the economy has changed. Thus, state (Burman) ownership may be reintroduced. There were anti-Chinese riots in Rangoon in 1967, ostensibly caused by the cultural revolution but used by the military in Burma to direct economic frustration against the Chinese as scapegoats. A reversion to some form of statist economic control is conceivable.

The blatant xenophobia that the SLORC has carefully fostered internally through the media creates a dilemma; it needs foreign investment and tourists, but has portrayed foreigners as unmitigated devils incarnate, and thus excites a population to abhor those very elements on which a substantial part of its planned regime legitimacy will be based, and where foreign physical presence will be pronounced.

Whatever the merits of the Burmese Foreign Investment Law of 1988, the implementation of that law is dependent on a bureaucracy and military that is parochial and suspicious and fearful of making mistakes. Thus approval from the very apex of the power system is needed to ensure prompt action on requests. At lower rungs of the administrative system, frustration is likely. The economic failure of the socialist period may in part be attributed to an essentially incompetent bureaucracy, which had been purged of its professionals and replaced with enthusiastic but amateur military.

Thus, the politics of fear and personalization of power are likely to inhibit the attainment of the goals that the SLORC has set for itself. In any future government, the continuation of some form of highly dirigiste policies is likely. Politics will probably prevail over economic rationality or over the needs of the populace as a whole.

Politics, Power, and Legitimacy

Burma's political path will in part be determined by the degree to which any regime is capable of acquiring political legitimacy, first in the eyes of its population, and then to a less important degree in those of the outside world. There are four essential components of political legitimacy: shared norms and values of the leadership and the citizenry; conformity with the established rules of acquiring power; the proper and effective use of power; and the consent of the governed. These may be considered the normative, procedural, performance, and consensual aspects of legitimacy.[5] Legitimacy is not a static concept, although it may be reviewed at a single point in time. It changes with undulating concepts of power and authority, personalities of leaders of the regime and opposition, and the economic conditions inherited, fostered, or planned by the administration.

In this sense, then, the future of the regimes in Burma rests with the Burmese who will make this determination, and who may change their views as events unfold. This is obviously a complex arena. In Korea, Park Chung Hee initially was personally considered an illegitimate ruler, and his regime broadly despised. His abuses of human rights were legion. Today, however, he is regarded as an important and legitimate ruler because of his economic accomplishments—accomplishments that were attained through the sacrifices of the Korean workers. Moralists may disapprove of this change, but time has softened the excesses of that regime in the public's view. In part this is because he now appears abstemious in his personal life in comparison to his successors.

The role of foreigners in the process of legitimation is also in flux. At one time in Korea, the imprimatur of the United States was an important element of legitimation—a cross that the U.S. must still bear in its association with some previous regimes. Some have called Korea a "client state" of the United States during that period, even though in many ways the so-called "client" controlled the "patron."

In Burma, the situation is different. Burma is no state's client, although its relationship to China makes it more dependent on that country than on any other regime. The SLORC is not impervious to foreign criticism, but it evidently has succeeded in withstanding considerable foreign pressure. It apparently has altered some of its behavior, although not its control over power, in the face of criticisms that affect its perceived interests, such as on certain types of foreign investment and on the treatment of Aung San Suu Kyi. Foreigners read the SLORC-generated oracle bones to determine the future changes hinted at by minuscule acts. But it is unlikely that there will be a major diminution of power by the SLORC.

Does the SLORC today have legitimacy in the eyes of the populace? The answer to this observer must be no, although others could argue the opposite. My view is based not only on the elections of May 1990, but on the degree to which repression and mass mobilization continue to be used, indeed required, to attain the regime's ends. Will this change over time should the SLORC remain in power or transmit power to an administration of its choosing? The result will depend in part on the degree to which its economic programs succeed. It is unlikely to happen within the foreseeable future because the reforms undertaken by the regime are not sufficient to encourage the degree and continuity of growth and the diffusion of the benefits of such growth to a wide enough swath of the population to warrant a change in attitude.

What is the role of foreign observers and well-wishers? They cannot prescribe legitimacy, but conversely they probably can influence it negatively. The continued international designation by many states of Burma as a pariah regime has several effects. It gives solace to the organized opposition both within and without the country. It indicates sympathy for the plight of the Burmese internally who remain unorganized or who are forced to submit to the SLORC's organizational pressures. It retards foreign economic assistance from both multilateral and bilateral donors and lenders. And it discourages investment in Burma, although the lure and smell of profits will nevertheless prompt many to seek quick returns, such as in trade, or major profits, such as in extractive industries. These activities add a modicum of legitimacy to the SLORC, but to no profound degree.

Are these negative foreign activities enough to topple a government? This is not evident, but they do prompt the SLORC to consider carefully the degree to which it can ignore international criticism. Such comments may influence those within the country, and especially within the military, to consider whether the reputation of the tatmadaw might in the long run be enhanced through withdrawal from direct administration.

But the opposition's negative hyperbole helps no one. Neither does the SLORC's and its apologists' positive hyperbole, such as that from some of the ASEAN states. Both diminish the accurate assessment of regime capabilities and the opposition to it, and thus may prompt inappropriate responses. One allows the state to vilify more easily those internally who want change and will fight for it, if conditions permit, while the other glosses over the egregious and extensive privations of rights and economic opportunities of the people.

Prognostication and Prognosis

The outlook for Burma is bleak. In spite of an abundant natural resource base, it has mismanaged its economy and denigrated the integrity of its diverse peoples. The outlook for the medium term is for a strong, controlling, military presence in any regime that follows the present SLORC, and an important military role even if a true civilian government were to come to power. The dirigiste tendencies exhibited by the state in the past are likely to continue, with the military playing an important economic role in the society. The state will continue to try centrally to control all elements of the society, and probably would ruthlessly suppress popular protests. Only very limited authority will be given to the periphery or to indigenous nationalities. The state will be unitary in fact, even if pockets of local autonomy exist. The minority issues are unlikely to be resolved by the military, and some of the cease-fires may well collapse. The basic issues facing the state are the redistribution of power, minority relations, a more authoritative voice for the people, and further economic liberalization, all of which are interrelated. All are also unlikely to be encouraged by the SLORC.

Continued opprobrium from foreign sources and Burmese expatriates likely will hinder the regime from undertaking the most extreme excesses, but such activities in themselves will not change the government—a change that will come, when it does, internally. This opprobrium, many have suggested, should be demonstrated by applying sanctions to Burma on the South African model. Sanctions, even if universally and officially applied, often do not work, and unilateral or partial sanctions may appease a foreign nation's conscience, but are ineffective. China would veto any UN proposed sanctions on Burma. The King of Thailand expressed his strong opposition to them as unenforceable and hurting his nation.[6]

Although the moral issues in South Africa and Burma may appear similar, and Nobel laureates Nelson Mandela and Aung San Suu Kyi may invite comparisons, the effects are unlikely to be analogous. South Africa's economy was highly integrated into the West's, its neighbors, indeed most of Africa, were opposed to its policies, and its leadership trained in Western milieux which put greater pressure on them. Burma, on the other hand, is composed of some 40,000 essentially traditional and self-sufficient villages with leadership generally internally educated. Burma's neighbors oppose sanctions. Sanctions would force out major, responsible international businesses, and leave much of the remainder to laundered funds from the narcotics trade. Unilateral sanctions imposed by the United States would occupy the moral high ground, but be ineffectual economically and not induce the changes that are desired.

The external actors have various interests in Burma, including limiting the flow of refugees and the spread of disease, suppressing illegal narcotics trade, and ensuring human rights. The path the SLORC is on will not resolve any of these problems before some reach crisis proportions. But Burma's neighbors, except China, have limited capacity to influence the SLORC, and China is not now prepared to do so. The other major powers will not use their sparse good-will with China over the issue of Burma.

Of all foreign influences, that most important in addition to China is Japan. It was Japan that prompted Burmese official rethinking and liberalization of its socialist economic policies in a virtual ultimatum. The threat to withdraw for-eign economic assistance was given to the Burmese deputy prime minister in Tokyo in March 1988. The Japanese had special access to Ne Win. Japanese assistance is needed for Burma's economic growth, and although Japan would likely settle for fewer political changes than the United States might desire before reintroducing aid, it does not want to appear too far out of step with the rest of the industrialized world. The potential Japanese role is thus of importance and should be coordinated with other potential donors, multilateral and bilateral.

The foreign role in Burma is legitimate, and it is to analyze, advise, criticize, and assist those internal and external actors who see the possibilities of a more beneficial regime, one concerned with the well-being of its population and the equitable distribution of rights and the fruits of growth.

Notes

1. The views presented here are those of the author and do not necessarily represent those of any institution.

2. One eminent Burman in 1988, commenting to the author on the dire conditions in Burma, said, "The play is over, the audience is forced to remain in their seats, and the actors refuse to leave the stage."

3. Personal communication, one of the members of the Central Committee of the BSPP, 1988. The issue, he said, was not socialism, but feedback.

4. Personal communication, a Chinese military attache in Asia, 1996.

5. See Muthiah Alagappa (ed.), *Political Legitimacy in Southeast Asia. The Quest for Moral Authority* (Stanford, 1995), 11–65.

6. Personal communication, 1993.

About the Authors

John J. Brandon is an international relations associate in The Asia Foundation's Washington, D.C., office. He co-authored the International Human Rights Law Group's report on the 1990 election in Burma. He has also edited *Burma/Myanmar in the Twenty-First Century: Dynamics of Continuity and Change* (Chulalongkorn University, 1997).

Mary P. Callahan is an assistant professor in the National Security Affairs Department at the Naval Postgraduate School, Monterey, Calif. She teaches about Southeast Asia, civil-military relations, and transitions to democracy. She also serves as regional director for Asia and Africa at the Postgraduate School's Center for Civil-Military Relations. Callahan has published articles on Burmese politics, and is working on a manuscript tentatively entitled "The Origins of Military Rule in Burma."

David A. Chandler is the Burma representative for World Vision International, a non-governmental organization focusing on health, relief, and services for disadvantaged children. He has written articles on the role of NGOs in Burma.

David Dapice is a professor of economics at Tufts University, and a faculty associate at the Harvard Institute for International Development. He has conducted research on Southeast Asia since the early 1970s, focusing on Indonesia, Thailand, Vietnam, and Burma. He has written a number of papers on Burma for the United Nations Development Program, and has visited Burma several times.

Robert S. Gelbard is President Clinton's special representative for implementation of the Dayton Peace Accords. A career Foreign Service officer, he served as assistant secretary for international narcotics and law enforcement affairs at the U.S. State Department from 1993-1997. He also has served as principal deputy assistant secretary of state for inter-American affairs, ambassador to Bolivia, and deputy assistant secretary of state for South America. He was a Peace Corps volunteer in Bolivia from 1964-1966.

Frank S. Jannuzi is the East Asia specialist for the minority staff of the U.S. Senate Foreign Relations Committee. Prior to that, he worked as the East Asia political and military analyst for the U.S. State Department's Bureau of Intelligence and Research, and as a visiting lecturer at Yale University.

Bertil Lintner is the Burma correspondent for the *Far Eastern Economic Review*. He also writes for the Swedish daily *Svenska Dagbladet* and *Politiken* of Denmark. Lintner is the author of *Outrage: Burma's Struggle for Democracy* (London, 1989), *The Rise and Fall of the Communist Party of Burma* (Ithaca, N.Y., 1990), *Land of Jade: A Journey through Insurgent Burma* (Kiscadale, U.K., 1990), and *Burma in Revolt: Opium and Insurgency Since 1948* (Boulder, 1994).

J. Mohan Malik is senior lecturer and director of the Defense Studies Program at Deakin University, Victoria, Australia. He has contributed several chapters to books and published more than fifty articles on security issues in the Asia-Pacific area in international relations journals. Malik is the author of *China and Nuclear Arms Control* (Oxford, forthcoming), *The Gulf War: Australia's Role and Asian-Pacific Responses* (Victoria, Australia, 1992), and editor of the three volumes on *Asian Defense Policies* (Victoria, Australia, 1994).

Mark Mason is associate professor at the School of Management, Yale University, where he specializes in the regulation of foreign direct investment and the multinational corporation, particularly in East Asia. In addition to two books and a co-edited volume, Mason has published numerous articles in academic journals. He is the author of *American Multinationals and Japan* (Cambridge, Mass., 1992), and is currently writing a book on multinationals in the Mekong.

Marvin C. Ott is professor of national security policy at the National War College, and director of the Southeast Asia Colloquium at the Institute of National Strategic Studies, National Defense University. Previous positions include deputy staff director of the Senate Intelligence Committee, senior associate at the Carnegie Endowment, senior analyst with the CIA, and associate professor at Mount Holyoke College.

Ananda Rajah is senior lecturer in anthropology at the National University of Singapore. He was previously senior fellow and coordinator of the Social Issues in Southeast Asia Program at the Institute of Southeast Asian Studies, Singapore. His recent research interests concern ethnicity, ethnic relations and the state, and the anthropology of state-building, development, and modernity in Southeast Asia. He has published several papers on the Karen in northern Thailand, the Karen insurgency, and ethnic conflict in Burma. Rajah is joint compiler of *The ASEAN Reader* (Singapore, 1992).

Robert I. Rotberg is president of the World Peace Foundation, coordinator of the Southern Africa Program at Harvard Institute for International Development, and a teacher at the Kennedy School of Government at Harvard University. Rotberg was professor of political science and history at Massachusetts Institute of Technology from 1968 to 1987, and then became academic vice president of Tufts University and president of Lafayette College. He is the author of many books and articles and editor of *Haiti Renewed* (Washington, D.C., 1997); *Vigilance and Vengeance: NGOs Preventing Ethnic Conflict in Divided Societies* (Washington, D.C., 1996); and *From Massacres to Genocide: The Media, Public Policy, and Humanitarian Crises* (Washington, D.C., 1996).

Andrew Selth is a visiting fellow at Australian National University's Strategic and Defense Studies Center. Between 1973 and 1986 he was a member of the Australian Department of Foreign Affairs, and served as a diplomatic officer in Rangoon, Seoul, and Wellington. In 1986 he transferred to the Department of Defense and until 1994 was a senior strategic analyst with the Defense Intelligence Organization. He has published widely on strategic issues and Asian affairs, including *Death of a Hero: The U Thant Disturbances in Burma, December 1974* (Brisbane, 1989), and *Transforming the Tatmadaw: The Burmese Armed Forces Since 1988* (Canberra, 1996).

Joseph Silverstein is professor emeritus at Rutgers University. He taught at Wesleyan University from 1958-1964 and at Rutgers University from 1964-1992, retiring as distinguished professor. He was director of the Institute of Southeast Asian Studies, Singapore, from 1970-1972. Silverstein's books include *Burma: Military Rule and the Politics of Stagnation* (1977); *The Political Legacy of Aung San (1972, 1993); Independent Burma at Forty: Six Assessments* (1989).

David I. Steinberg is the director of Asian Studies, Georgetown University, and representative of The Asia Foundation for Korea. He was a member of the senior foreign service of the Department of State and a representative of The Asia Foundation in Burma. He has written extensively on Burma, Korea, and development in Asia; his books include *The Future of Burma: Crisis and Choice in Myanmar* (New York 1990).

Robert H. Taylor is vice-chancellor of the University of Buckingham, England. He was previously Pro-Director of the School of Oriental and African Studies and Professor of Politics in the University of London. His publications include *The State in Burma* (London, 1987), and *Marxism and Resistance in Burma: Thein Pe Myint's "Wartime Traveler"* (Athens, Ohio, 1985).

About the Sponsoring Institutions

The World Peace Foundation

The World Peace Foundation was created in 1910 by the imagination and fortune of Edwin Ginn, the Boston publisher, to encourage international peace and co-operation. The Foundation seeks to advance the cause of world peace through study, analysis, and the advocacy of wise action. As an operating, not a grant-giving foundation, it provides financial support only for projects which it has initiated itself.

Edwin Ginn shared the hope of many of his contemporaries that permanent peace could be achieved. That dream was denied by the outbreak of World War I, but the Foundation has continued to attempt to overcome obstacles to international peace and co-operation, drawing for its funding on the endowment bequeathed by the founder. In its early years, the Foundation focused its attention on building the peace-keeping capacity of the League of Nations, and then on the development of world order through the United Nations. The Foundation established and nurtured the premier scholarly journal in its field, *International Organization*, now in its fiftieth year.

From the 1950s to the early 1990s, mostly a period of bipolar conflict when universal collective security remained unattainable, the Foundation concentrated its activities on improving the working of world order mechanisms, regional security, transnational relations, and the impact of public opinion on American foreign policy. From 1980 to 1993, the Foundation published nineteen books and

291

seven reports on Third World security; on South Africa and other states of southern Africa; on Latin America, the Caribbean, and Puerto Rico; on migration; and on the international aspects of traffic in narcotics. In 1994 and 1995, the Foundation published books on Europe after the Cold War; on the United States, southern Europe, and the countries of the Mediterranean basin; and on reducing the world traffic in conventional arms.

The Foundation is now focusing most of its energies and resources on the Prevention of Intercommunal Conflict and Humanitarian Crises. This focus proceeds from the assumption that large-scale human suffering, wherever it occurs, is a serious and continuing threat to the peace of the world, both engendering and resulting from ethnic, religious, and other intrastate and cross-border conflicts. The Foundation is examining how the forces of world order may most effectively engage in preventive diplomacy, create early warning systems leading to early preventive action, achieve regional conflict avoidance, and eradicate the underlying causes of intergroup enmity and warfare. It is also concerned with assisting the growth of democracy in selected states like Haiti and Burma.

Harvard Institute for International Development

Founded in 1974, the Harvard Institute for International Development (HIID) has assisted developing countries to become part of, and to benefit from, the emerging global economy. As Harvard's principal center for research, teaching, and assistance related to developing and transitional economies, HIID is engaged in the analysis, design, and promotion of worldwide economic reforms.

Drawing on its own staff and the faculty and students of Harvard University, HIID analyzes developments in the world economy and proposes new approaches to pressing problems of economic development and global economic integration.

Index

GUIDE TO PHILOSOPHY

by

C. E. M. JOAD

DOVER PUBLICATIONS
NEW YORK

Published in Canada by General Publishing Company, Ltd., 30 Lesmill Road, Don Mills, Toronto, Ontario.

Published in the United Kingdom by Constable and Company, Ltd., 10 Orange Street, London WC 2.

This Dover edition, first published in 1957, is an unabridged and unaltered republication of the work originally published by Victor Gollancz, Ltd. in 1936.

Standard Book Number: 486-20297-6
Library of Congress Catalog Card Number: 57-2470

Manufactured in the United States of America
Dover Publications, Inc.
180 Varick Street
New York, N. Y. 10014

CONTENTS

* It is suggested that the chapters marked with an asterisk
should be omitted in a first reading.

PART III : CONSTRUCTIVE
METAPHYSICS

* It is suggested that the chapters marked with an asterisk
should be omitted in a first reading.

* It is suggested that the chapters marked with an asterisk should be omitted in a first reading.

INTRODUCTION

It is usual to introduce a book on philosophy intended for the general reader with some account of the subject matter of philosophy, the nature of its results and the methods which it pursues. The reader is told that he will not be made free of any definite and agreed body of knowledge ; he is warned that philosophers frequently do not even discuss the same questions and that, when they do, it is only to give diametrically opposite answers ; and he is informed that he will be asked to take part not in a steady and ordered advance from speculation to knowledge but in a series of marches and counter-marches, in the course of which he will traverse and retraverse the same territory in the company of travellers whose concern seems less to arrive at a goal than to obliterate the footsteps of their predecessors. It is conceivable that, if the book is of the lighter sort, he may be regaled at this point with a gibe about blind men searching in dark rooms for non-existent black cats. Nevertheless, and in spite of these drawbacks, it will be clearly intimated to him that the value of philosophy is, indeed, very great, although it happens to be rather difficult to say what it is.

I propose to forgo this kind of Introduction, partly because I have already written elsewhere[1] of the value and methods of philosophy, but also because I propose to pay my readers the compliment of assuming that those who have decided to embark upon the reading of a book of these dimensions have already made up their own minds as to the value, at any rate for them, of the task they have taken in hand.

Nevertheless, although I have judged a general disquisition upon the nature, scope and methods of philosophy to be superfluous, I owe my readers a few pages of introduction in explanation of the nature, scope and methods

[1] See my *Return to Philosophy*, Chapters VII and IX.

of this book. I want, in a word, to say what I have tried to do and how I have tried to do it.

I have not sought to cover the whole field of philosophy; I have not tried to bring in all the philosophers—not even all the great philosophers—and I have not dealt fully with the work of any single philosopher. My object has been to provide a general survey of the main field of philosophy; to introduce in the course of the survey the chief problems that philosophers discuss, to show why they discuss them and to give some illustrations of the methods by which their discussions are pursued. In carrying out this undertaking, I have sought to observe two conditions; the first, that no philosophical theory should be included which was not intrinsically important and interesting on its own account; the second, that no philosophical theory should be included which was not capable of being made intelligible to the educated layman who, possessing no previous acquaintance with philosophy, was yet prepared to accord his best attention to the subject and his best patience to its expositor.

The first condition needs no defence; the second requires a few words of explanation. Philosophy is an exceedingly difficult subject and cannot with the best will in the world be made into an easy one. For one thing, the understanding of philosophy is frequently found to entail some knowledge of a number of other subjects. Physics and theology, history and biology, aesthetics and literature—all these are intermittent grist to the philosopher's mill, and he who would follow its grindings must have at least a nodding acquaintance with them. For another, it is exceedingly abstract. There are many, and they are not by any means the most stupid of our species, who will always find philosophy largely unintelligible. The twists and turns of the speculative reason, the hair-splitting distinctions, the abstractness of the thinking, the remoteness of the conclusions reached from the interests of ordinary life, the absence of agreed results—all these cannot but seem to many at best a monument of energy misplaced, at worst an irritating perversion of the powers and faculties of the human mind.

But there are others who, by nature addicted to philosophising, are nevertheless, kept at arm's length by the habits of philosophers. A natural taste for speculation has too often been repelled by the difficulty and obscurity of professional speculators. In my view some part of this difficulty and obscurity is unnecessary. In Chapter XX I have ventured to make a distinction between two kinds of obscurity—obscurity of expression and the expression of obscurity. The latter, I point out, is pardonable and, perhaps, inevitable. There is no necessary reason—at least I know of none—why the universe should be readily comprehensible by a twentieth-century mind, or why persons of average capacity should be enabled easily to grasp the thoughts of the profoundest intelligences that life has yet succeeded in evolving. The human mind, after all, has only just got under way. It is very little that we know about the universe, and, as we are beginning to realise, the more we enlarge the area of the known, the more also we enlarge its area of contact with the unknown. And the unknown is also the obscure. . . . But obscurity of expression is simply bad craftsmanship. A philosopher should, like anybody else, study to make himself understood, and, if his failure is due to slovenly writing or to inadequate mastery of the arts of exposition, no profundity or originality of thought will excuse him from censure.

Writing primarily for the intelligent layman, I have taken special pains to be intelligible. I have, for example, endeavoured never to introduce a technical term without first explaining the precise sense in which it is being used. I have reduced footnotes to a minimum. In particular, I have omitted all footnotes containing chapter and page references to the quotations from the works of philosophers which appear in the text, and have limited such references to the pages of this book. To make up for this, I have appended at the end of each chapter what will, I hope, prove a useful bibliography, containing a short list of the books which can be most fruitfully consulted by those who wish to follow up the various subjects raised in the chapter.

It is, however, in determining the general plan and arrangement of the book that the insistence upon clarity of exposition has exercised the most decisive influence. Rejecting the chronological method, I have tried to follow what appeared to me to be the logical divisions of the subject, basing my arrangement of chapters upon relevances of thought rather than upon the personalities of thinkers, and allocating different groups of related topics to different chapters. The general arrangement is broadly as follows. I have begun with the problems which constitute part of what is known as epistemology or theory of knowledge. What sort of knowledge do we have of the external world ? How far can the claims of sense experience to reveal a world like that which we normally suppose ourselves to inhabit be substantiated ? If the knowledge yielded by sense experience seems dubious, what other kinds of knowledge have we ? Can reasoning give us knowledge ? If so, what are the conditions which reasoning must satisfy, if it is to do so ?

I then pass to Part II, which I have entitled Critical Metaphysics. In this part commonsense conceptions such as those of substance, change, mechanism, purpose, cause and the Self are subjected to critical examination. They are found to give a poor account of themselves—so poor, as to render it unlikely that the world to which they are normally supposed to belong and in which common sense supposes them to be valid, is the real world.

This brings us to the distinction between the world as it really is and the world as it appears, the celebrated distinction between Appearance and Reality. If the world as it appears to common sense is not the world as it really is, how is the real world to be conceived ? In the last and longest part of the book, entitled Constructive Metaphysics, I have outlined some of the answers supplied by the great philosophers to this question. Apart altogether from the question of their truth, the philosophical systems of Plato, Kant and Hegel are among the most notable productions of the human mind, and those who wish to know what great men have thought and said memorably about the universe and man's place in it may find the reading of these chapters a not unhelpful introduction to the works of these philosophers. At the end of this part, I have endeavoured, in chapters dealing with Materialism, Dialectical and Scientific, and the philosophies of Bergson and Whitehead, to give some account of the problems that bulk largely in contemporary discussion, notably those set for philosophy by the developments of modern science.

In the course of carrying out this plan I have endeavoured to say something about most of the questions which are commonly raised in philosophical discussion. There are, however, some absentees, which I have been compelled to omit owing to my inability to deal with them in a manner which would satisfy the condition of clarity of exposition I have set myself to observe. In the first two parts of the book the issues raised are treated on merits, and the views of particular philosophers are introduced only when they happen to be peculiarly relevant to the problem under discussion. Thus Hume's criticism of the notion of cause is given in the chapter on *Causation*, and Aristotle's doctrine of Form and Matter is presented in the chapter on *Substance and its Qualities*. In these two parts I have proceeded on the assumption that the themes of philosophy are more important than the philosophers who propounded them and the dates at which they were propounded, and the thought of particular philosophers is introduced, therefore, only in order to illustrate the themes. On coming to the systems of the great philosophers in Part III, I have not as a general rule criticised the views expounded. In some instances, however, for example in the case of Aristotle's criticism of Plato's theory of Ideas and the criticism which modern Realism has brought against the idealist account of perception, the criticism is not less historically important than the theory criticised. In others, for example in the case of the pragmatists' criticism of the Hegelian Absolute and the theory of truth which it entails, the criticism forms the starting-point of a new school. In special cases of this kind I have included the criticisms along with the views criticised. I have, however, usually abstained from criticisms of my own; usually, but not always—a point which brings me to the question of bias.

My concern being to expound the views of others, I have sought, so far as possible, to suppress my own. The attempt has, I think, been in the main successful. But it is not humanly possible always to maintain a complete impartiality where one's own views are concerned, and I am conscious that there are one or two places where it has broken down. In the treatment of the theory of Subsistent Objects in Chapter XI and in the development of Plato's theory of Ideas in relation to the philosophy of aesthetics, my own philosophical opinions have insisted on intruding themselves and views have been expressed which, I fear, own little better authority than that of the author. Bias, if inevitable in philosophy, is less harmful when avowed, and I have done my best to make amends for these lapses by giving the reader due warning when the passages in question are about to occur.

In pursuance of the same policy, I had better make avowal here and now of such philosophical beliefs as I hold. My general predilections are in favour of some form of Realism and Pluralism. I am not, that is to say, an idealist who believes that mind or thought is the only reality, and I do not think that the arguments which philosophers have advanced in favour of supposing that the universe is in some important sense a whole or unity are convincing. I am not, however, a materialist, since I hold that mind is a real and unique factor in the universe. Mind and matter are, I am inclined to hold, both distinct and irreducible reals, and I should be disposed to extend the bounds of reality to include elements of value such as are envisaged by Plato's theory of Ideas. My general philosophical views have, in fact, been more influenced by Plato than by any other philosopher. Among the moderns, the earlier philosophical writings of Bertrand Russell have chiefly influenced me.

Every philosophy is open to the charge of giving more

information about the philosopher than about the universe. I do not myself believe this charge to be a true one, but no philosopher would wish to deny that an element of the personal, of personal hopes and wishes, personal temperament and training, personal disposition and desire, is inevitably embedded in every philosophy. Nor can it be entirely excluded from an exposition which seeks to confine itself to giving an account of the philosophies of others. Some bias, then, there is bound to be ; I am sorry for it, but I cannot help it.

I said at the outset that I did not propose to defend the pursuit of philosophising or to give reasons why philosophy should be studied. One expression of opinion, however, I propose to permit myself. The attraction of philosophy consists, I think, very largely in its catholicity. The philosopher seeks to comprehend the universe as a whole, not, like the physicist or the biologist, a special department of it, but the whole mass of data to which the moral intuitions of the ordinary man, the religious consciousness of the saint, the aesthetic enjoyment of the artist, and the history of the human race, no less than the discoveries of the physicist and the biologist, contribute. The disadvantage of such a form of enquiry is the lack of established results. Philosophy has no agreed body of knowledge to offer, and many will be inclined to be impatient with its inconclusiveness.

Many, but not all ; for some, the very inconclusiveness of philosophy is its attraction. It is not knowledge but the quest for it which they find exciting, and there would seem to them to be something trite and obvious about a universe which permitted itself to be wholly known. It is pleasant to keep alive the sense of wonder by contemplating the richness and the strangeness of the world ; it is no less pleasant to contemplate the varieties of men's minds. Just as it takes all sorts of men to make a world, so does it take all sorts of minds to make the truth about the world. In the present age, when applied science has done much to rob the visible world of mystery and wonder, and forms of government have ironed out the variety of men's minds and frowned upon the exercise of the free intelligence, philosophy has a special value. In the pursuit of philosophy the human mind swings free. Untramelled by limitations of subject matter, unaffected by the temporal and the particular, it recognises no laws save those which govern its own reasoning. This disinterested activity of the freely functioning mind is a good, among the greatest that human beings can enjoy. It is natural to feel curious about the universe in which we find ourselves, and the effort to satisfy our curiosity, even if it can never be wholly successful, is never wholly void of satisfaction. As the English philosopher F. H. Bradley has said, metaphysics may be " the finding of bad reasons for what we believe upon instinct ; but to find these reasons is no less an instinct." In the last resort, then, the reason for the study of philosophy is the satisfaction which it brings. If this book succeeds in communicating to its readers some part of the satisfaction which philosophy has given to its writer, it will not have been written in vain.

In spite of my determination to be at all costs simple and clear, I fear that some of the ensuing pages will provide rather stiff reading for those who are approaching philosophy for the first time. I have accordingly placed an asterisk against the more difficult chapters, and would suggest that they should be omitted on a first reading.

My thanks are due to the following for kindly reading through various chapters in manuscript, and for making valuable suggestions which I have adopted : Professor L. S. Stebbing (Chapter V), Mr. H. B. Acton (Chapters XIV and XV), Mr. H. W. Durant (Chapter XVII) and Miss Dorothy Emmet (Chapter XX). Dr. A. C. Ewing has also helped me with some of the earlier part of the book. The above are, however, in no sense responsible for any of the views expressed.

I have also to thank the Oxford University Press for permission to reprint in Chapters XVI and XIX certain passages which have already appeared in my *Introduction to Modern Philosophy*.

C. E. M. JOAD.

Hampstead, *August 1935*.

GUIDE TO PHILOSOPHY

Part I

THEORY OF KNOWLEDGE

Chapter I : WHAT DO WE KNOW OF THE OUTSIDE WORLD?

1. The Problem Stated

Introductory. It is not easy to decide how to begin a book on philosophy. Philosophical problems are closely bound up with one another ; so closely, that some philosophers think that a completely satisfactory solution of any one of them would entail the solution of them all. Whether this is so we cannot tell, since it is extremely unlikely that a completely satisfactory solution of any one of them will be reached by the human mind in the present state of its development. It is, however, true that most philosophical questions are found sooner or later to raise the same problems. In philosophy all roads lead if not to the same Rome, at least into the same maze, so that it is a matter of not very great moment which you choose at the outset of your journey.

But the fact that there is no very good reason for choosing one rather than another makes it very difficult to choose any, as the logical ass of the philosopher Buridan[1] (1300-1350), placed between two equally large and equally succulent bundles of hay, is said to have starved because of an inability to discover any reason why he should proceed in the direction of one rather than of the other.

On reflection I have decided to begin with the problem of sense perception ; not because it is any easier or any nearer to solution than any other philosophical problem, but because it entails a consideration of issues which people

[1] Actually the illustration of the ass does not appear anywhere in Buridan's writings. It is, however, always associated with him. A similar image appears in Dante's *Paradiso*, and the conceit seems to have been a popular one in the Middle Ages.

can explore for themselves : can, and to some extent do, since, of all philosophical conclusions, the conclusion that the outside world is not really " there " or is not really " real " is most familiar to, and most frequently derided by, the non-philosophical. But whether people deride it, dismiss it, or embrace it for the controversial discomfiture of their friends, they are at least familiar with it.

Commonsense View of External World.   The problem may be stated fairly simply in the form of a number of questions. What kind of information do our sense organs give us about the external world? Is it reliable information? If it is, what is the nature of the objects about which we receive it ? Of what sort of things, in other words, is the external world composed ? Common sense answers these questions without much hesitation on the following lines. (1) The external world, it declares, consists of substances which possess qualities ; for example, of wood which is hard or soft, of metal which is yellow or silver. (2) These substances we perceive in the form of physical objects such as chairs and tables, gold rings and silver shillings—unless we happen to be scientists, when we perceive what are, presumably, more fundamental substances such as chemical compounds and molecules of which the ordinary substances are composed, and should perceive, if our instruments were delicate enough, which they are not, substances more fundamental still such as atoms and electrons. (3) Physical objects are " out there " in the world and are revealed to us by our senses exactly as they are. In particular, they are not dependent for their existence upon our perception of them. When our sense organs, eyes, ears or noses, are brought into suitable spatial relations with them, then we are said to know them. But common sense would hold that that which actually *knows* is not itself a sense organ, but is the mind or consciousness. The sense organs, it would be said, are the channels by which knowledge of physical objects is conveyed to the mind.

Now each one of the above propositions is denied by many

philosophers, and, although it is by no means clear what propositions ought to be substituted for them, it is reasonably certain that, in the form in which I have just stated them, none of them is true. The first proposition, that the world consists of substances possessing qualities, will be considered in Chapter VI. The consideration of the second and the third which are largely interdependent brings us to the problem of sense perception. In the present chapter we shall be mainly concerned with the third proposition, which asserts that the physical objects which we perceive are " out there " in the world, and are in no sense dependent upon our perception of them for their existence. Most philosophers have held that they are not " out there " in the world in any ordinary sense, and many have come to the conclusion that they are in some sense dependent for their existence upon the mind or minds which perceive them. Other philosophers, while maintaining that *something* exists in the world outside ourselves which is not dependent upon our minds for its existence, have, nevertheless, adduced good reasons for denying that this " something " is in the least like the physical objects with which, if the common-sense account of the matter is to be believed, we are in contact. They have, that it to say, denied the second of the three propositions asserted above. With the reasons for this latter denial we shall be concerned in the second chapter.

What do our Senses Reveal ?　　Let us call the objects of which, common sense would say, our senses make us aware sensible objects. What do our senses tell us about them ? At first sight it seems that they tell us a great deal ; but on reflection we find that much of the information which our senses seem to give us relates not to what is going on outside ourselves, but to what is going on inside ourselves, not to sensible objects, but to our own experiences.

Let us suppose that I press my tongue against my teeth and ask the question : " What is it that I experience or am aware of ? " At first sight the answer would appear to be :

" I am aware of my teeth." But is this answer really correct? Is not what I *really* experience a feeling in my tongue—a feeling caused perhaps by the contact between tongue and teeth, but a feeling nevertheless, and since it *is* a feeling, something that is mental ? Suppose now, that I press my fingers against the table, is what I experience the table ? Again, the obvious answer proves on examination to be doubtful. The *immediate* object of my experience, that of which I am directly aware, is, many would say, a sensation in my fingers, a sensation of smoothness, hardness, and coolness.

Let us take a further example. If I stand two feet away from the fire, I experience heat, and common sense tells me that this heat is a property of the fire. If, however, I move nearer to the fire, the heat increases in intensity, until it becomes pain. Now, the pain is clearly in me and not in the fire ; since, then, the pain is only a more intense degree of the heat, the inference is that the heat also was a sensation of mine, and not a property of the fire. The leg of a cheese mite is so small that, except with the aid of a microscope, we cannot see it. Are we, then, to suppose that the cheese mite cannot see its own leg ? This seems unlikely. We must infer, then, that the apparent size of the cheese mite's leg varies according to the nature of the mind perceiving it— that the leg, in fact, has one apparent size for the cheese mite and another for ourselves. But the leg cannot have two different sizes at the same time. Has it, then, any *real* size at all ? May it not rather be the case that size is not an intrinsic[1] quality of the object seen, a quality possessed by it in its own right, but is relative to and dependent upon the nature of the perceiver's mind.

The Case of the Steeple.   Let us consider the case of size in a little more detail. I am, we will suppose, looking at a church steeple. Its height appears to vary according to the distance from which I view it. It appears, for example, to have one height from a distance of half a mile, another

―――――――――
[1] For a definition of " intrinsic " see below, p. 52.

from a distance of a hundred yards, and another from a distance of five yards, while, if I stand right underneath it, I am unable to estimate its height at all. There are thus a number of different heights which the steeple *appears* to have. How am I to tell which one of them is or represents its *real* height? The commonsense answer would probably be, by applying a measuring rod or tape-measure or whatever apparatus is normally used for measuring steeples, and noting the reading on the apparatus in question. Let us suppose that the reading on the piece of apparatus—we will call it a tape-measure—is 150 feet. Then we shall say that 150 feet is the *real* height of the steeple. But will this answer bear investigation? For practical purposes no doubt it will ; but for philosophical ones it will not.

In the first place, we have admitted that the steeple *appears* to have different heights to different observers situated at different distances. What we want to know is, which one of these different appearances really *is* its height. Now, 150 feet is one of these heights, the height, namely, which it appears to have to a tape-measure extended to the whole of its very considerable length along the outside of the steeple. But why should the tape-measure be accorded the title of a privileged observer, and why should the position immediately contiguous to the outside wall be regarded as a privileged position, so that we are entitled to say that *to an observer occupying that position alone* is the *real* height revealed?

Secondly, what sort of information does a reading of 150 feet really give us? We want to know what is the real height of the steeple and we are informed that it is 150 feet. But what is 150 feet? It is a mathematical expression, a name that we give to certain sorts of height, for example to the height possessed by the steeple. Thus, when we want to know what is the real height of the steeple we are told that it is 150 feet, and when we want to know what 150 feet is, we find that it is the sort of height which the steeple, and whatever other things happen to be exactly as tall as the steeple are said to possess. Our information, in fact, is purely circular.

Thirdly, what account are we to give of the tape-measure itself? We have cited a number of illustrations above to suggest that the qualities apparently possessed by sensible objects do not belong to them in actual fact, but are either qualities of our own experience or, since our experience of them varies, are at any rate dependent upon and determined by our experience. But if this is so, we have no right to assume that a tape-measure is exempt from the conclusions suggested by the previous analysis, that it *really* owns in its own right the qualities that it appears to own, and that in particular it has a length which *really* is its length. If we may assume without question these facts about the tape-measure, there would be no need to raise questions about the height of the steeple. But whatever reasons there are for doubting whether the steeple *really* has a height are equally good reasons for doubting whether the tape-measure *really* has a length. We cannot in short establish the *real* height of the steeple by reference to the *real* length of the tape-measure, for it is precisely the meaning of the words " real height " and " real length " that is in doubt.

The Shape of the Penny.   As with height so with shape. Let us consider as an example the shape of a penny. Common sense supposes the shape to be circular, but from almost any point of view from which the penny is looked at, the penny appears, as we quickly find out when we try to draw it, to be elliptical, the ellipses which we perceive varying in degrees of fatness and thinness according to the angle of vision from which we view the penny. From two positions only does the penny appear to be circular, and these, namely, the position vertically above and the position vertically below the penny, are rather peculiar positions which are comparatively rarely occupied by the human eye.

If the shape of the penny normally appears to be elliptical, why do we call it circular? It is not easy to say.

In the first instance, perhaps, because of the prevalence of a general belief to the effect that it *is* circular, a belief so widespread and deep-seated that anyone who questioned it outside a philosophical discussion would be regarded as imperfectly sane. But how did this general belief arise? On what is it based? Probably it rests at bottom upon the fact that the penny conforms in respect of many of its attributes to the definition of a circle. There is, for example, a point on its surface such that all lines drawn from that point to the circumference are of equal length : its circumference again is equal to $2\pi r$, its area to πr^2. But, if we take our stand on this definition, similar difficulties arise to those which we considered in the case of the steeple. What we want to know is the nature of the shape to which these mathematical properties belong? If we answer that it is a *circular* shape the question arises, does a penny have it? Unfortunately the penny as usually seen does not. Nor does the penny as touched ; to feel a penny is not to feel a circular shape but either a flat surface or, if a finger is crooked round its edge, a curving line of metal. Hence, to touch and to sight the penny does not normally *appear* to be circular. But to what, then, does it *appear* to be circular? Presumably to a pair of compasses. But why should its appearance to a pair of compasses, or if the expression be preferred, the reaction of a pair of compasses to it, be presumed to acquaint us with its *real* shape, in some sense in which its appearance to eyes and fingers does not acquaint us with its real shape? Why in fact are the compasses privileged " observers " ? Moreover, what are we to say of the properties of the pair of compasses? Can we, when the existence of physical objects possessing properties in their own right is in question, steal the answer to the question in the case of the compasses in order not to beg it in the case of the penny?

As it is with texture and temperature, as with size and shape, so is it with most, if not all, of the qualities which apparently belong to objects in the external world. In regard to most, if not to all, of these apparent qualities we can truly say that in the last resort they turn out to be relative to ourselves. We have only, for example, to raise the temperatures of our bodies a few degrees, and the world will look different. Still more obviously will it feel different. Yet there is no reason why that world alone should be privileged to be considered real which is perceived by a normal, Nordic adult possessing a body which is heated to a temperature of 98·4 degrees.

Implications of Modern Science.   The force of these considerations, in so far as they purport to show the relativity to the perceiver of the qualities apparently existing in the external world, is considerably strengthened by the information which science in general and the sciences of physics and physiology in particular have obtained in regard to the machinery of perception. Before, however, we indicate the bearing of the conclusions of modern science upon the problems under consideration, it is necessary to guard ourselves against misinterpretation by the introduction of a word of warning.

In the first place, the whole question of the relation between science and philosophy is controversial, and many philosophers would maintain that no results reached by science do have or can have any bearing upon philosophical problems.

In the second place, the philosophers whose line of thought I have during the course of the foregoing illustrations been mainly following and with whose general conclusion, namely, that the objects revealed to us in perception are in some sense dependent upon the mind of the perceiver, we are in this chapter mainly concerned, did not introduce scientific considerations into their arguments, or did so only to a very small extent. The philosophers in question (who are sometimes known as subjective idealists) are Locke (1632-1704), Berkeley (1685-1753) and Hume (1711-1776)[1] who lived in the seventeenth and eighteenth

[1] The conclusions of their philosophies are indicated in greater detail below (see Chapter II, pp. 39–55).

that the physiologist is really looking at a brain outside his own becomes very great.

Touch and Smell.

Perception by touch makes the matter even plainer. Let us consider in a little more detail the case of a person who presses his fingers against the table. I am doing it now, as I write. Ordinarily I should say that there was contact between two material substances, my fingers and the table. Modern physics, however, lends no countenance to this view. What happens according to the physicist is that electrical repulsion is developed between the atoms composing the finger and those composing the table. The harder I press the table, the stronger are the electrical forces which repel my finger. These electrical forces set up in the nerve cells at the end of my finger a current which reaches my brain, as the result of which I experience the sensation of touching the table. In fact, however, I am not in contact with any object outside my body and, if appropriate parts of my nervous system are suitably stimulated, I shall experience the same sensation of touching the table, although there is no table to touch. What is more, I can experience what appears to be a sensation of a pin prick in the non-existent finger of a hand which has been amputated, provided that the nerve terminals in my arm are suitably manipulated.

As with sight and touch, so with smell. I doubt very much whether even common sense assumes that the smell of a body is something which really belongs to it. Most people would probably agree that a thing's smell is at least not *in the same place* as that which is occupied by the thing. It is, they would say, something which the thing gives off —most people, I imagine, think of smell as a sort of gas composed of molecules—and it is only when the gas reaches the place where one's nostrils are and the molecules of which it is composed stimulate the sensitive tissues inside the nostrils, that certain nervous impulses are despatched to the brain, as a result of which we have the sensation of smelling.[1] But the connection of this "some-thing," the smell which is smelt, with the object which is thought to have originated it remains vague. Similarly with sound ! Waves travel through the atmosphere and impinge on the ear drums. Complex events take place in the outer, middle and inner ears. In the inner ear, for example, there is a shell-like bony receptacle, the cochlea, filled with fluid. When the vibrations of the bones and membranes in the middle ear reach the cochlea, the fluid is agitated. The agitation of the fluid imparts a swaying motion to certain long, hair-like threads, the cilia ranged along the inside of the cochlea. The swaying cilia send neural impulses to the brain, as a result of which we hear a sound. But if we were to ask where or what is the sound that is heard, it is extremely difficult to answer.

Eddington's Idealist Conclusion.

The teaching of physics and physiology with regard to the machinery of perception seems to point to the conclusion that what we actually know, when we have sensory experience, are not the movements of matter, but certain events in ourselves connected with or produced by these movements · not objects external to ourselves, but the effects of the impact of light rays, gases, atmospheric waves and other forms of energy proceeding from these objects upon our bodies.

The following quotation from Sir Arthur Eddington's book *Science and the Unseen World* clearly indicates how large a part of what we know of the external world is conceded by a modern physicist—and in this respect, at least, Eddington's views are in no sense unrepresentative—to be inferred by our minds, instead of being directly perceived by our senses.

"Consider," says Sir Arthur Eddington, "how our supposed acquaintance with a lump of matter is attained. Some influence emanating from it plays on the extremity

---

[1] In fact, odorous substances must be dissolved in the moisture which covers the nasal mucous membrane, before they can evoke the sensation of smell.

of a nerve starting a series of physical and chemical changes which are propagated along the nerve to a brain cell ; there a mystery happens, and an image or sensation arises in the mind which cannot purport to resemble the stimulus which excites it. Everything known about the material world must in one way or another have been inferred from these stimuli transmitted along the nerves. . . . The mind as a central receiving station reads the dots and dashes of the incoming nerve-signals. By frequent repetition of their call-signals the various transmitting stations of the outside world become familiar. We begin to feel quite a homely acquaintance with 2LO and 5XX. But a broadcasting station is not *like* its call-signal ; there is no commensurability in their natures. So, too, the chairs and tables around us which broadcast to us incessantly those signals which affect our sight and touch cannot in their nature be like unto the signals or to the sensations which the signals awake at the end of their journey. . . . It is an astonishing feat of deciphering that we should have been able to infer an orderly scheme of natural knowledge from such indirect communication."

From these considerations Sir Arthur Eddington proceeds to derive conclusions which, as the reader will see in the next chapter, are almost indistinguishable from those of idealist philosophers. Having stressed the roundabout and inferential character of our knowledge of the external world, he proceeds to contrast it with the directness and immediacy of our knowledge of ourselves.

" Clearly," he continues, " there is one kind of knowledge which cannot pass through such channels, namely, knowledge of the intrinsic nature of that which lies at the far end of the lines of communication."

This is not an inferred knowledge of outside things from the messages which they send us over the telephone lines of nervous communication ; it is knowledge of something as it is in itself. And this something as it is in itself, the one thing we know directly as it really is, turns out to be mental ; it is a mind. " Mind," Sir Arthur Eddington concludes,

" is the first and most direct thing in our experience ; all else is remote inference." We have, he adds, an acquaintance with the " mental and spiritual nature of ourselves, known in our minds by an intimate contact transcending the methods of physics."

Significance of Conclusions derived from Science.

I do not wish to suggest that the above conclusion is necessarily true. As we shall see below,[1] any philosophy which asserts, as the subjective idealists did, that the objects which we know in perception are existent in or even dependent upon the mind of the perceiver is precluded from making use of any of the considerations upon which the scientist's conclusions are based. I have introduced the scientific account of perception at this stage because my present purpose is to accumulate considerations, from whatever source they may be derived, which militate against the commonsense view that the external world is composed of physical objects possessing qualities in their own right, which by a sort of divine revelation are presented to the mind exactly as they are. Whether we emphasise the part played by the mind in the process of perception or by the body and the sense organs, it seems almost impossible to resist the view that the qualities of the world we perceive depend very largely upon ourselves. For how otherwise, it may be asked, are we to explain the fact of differing perceptions of the same thing. If X sees a carnation blue, and Y, who is colour-blind, sees it green, it is very difficult to suppose that the carnation is both green and blue at the same time. On the other hand there seems no good ground for affirming that it *really* is blue because it is blue to normal vision, and that its appearance to the colour-blind man is not, therefore, its *real* appearance, merely because the colour-blind man is in a minority. The plain implication seems to be that the difference between the apparent colours is due to a difference in the physiological machineries of the two perceivers. Moreover, if we place santonin in

[1] See Chapter II, p. 58.

our eyes, we see everything yellow. Since we cannot suppose that the alteration in our visual apparatus has produced a corresponding alteration in the world outside us, we can only conclude that the appearance of yellowness is the result of a peculiar condition of our visual organs. But, if this is true in regard to yellowness, there is no reason why it should not be true in regard to all the colours which we normally believe ourselves to perceive in the outside world.

RUSSELL, BERTRAND   The Problems of Philosophy   *Home University Library*.
  Chapters I–IV contain a clear elementary account of the problem of perception.
WISDOM, JOHN   Problems of Mind and Matter, Part II.
  Short and clear, but more difficult.
MOORE, G. E.   Philosophical Studies.
  May be consulted in connection with all the problems raised in this and the next two chapters. It is likely to become a classic, but is considerably more difficult than the books mentioned above.

A summary of the relevant information with regard to the machinery of perception obtained by the sciences will be found in Bertrand Russell's *An Outline of Philosophy*, Part II, and in my *Guide to Modern Thought*, Chapter IV.

Chapter II: WHAT DO WE KNOW OF THE OUTSIDE WORLD?

2. The Answer of Subjective Idealism

General Conclusion of Subjective Idealism. The philosophers who maintain that the qualities of the world which we perceive by means of our senses are dependent on the *mind* of the perceiver are known as subjective idealists. The form in which this conclusion is usually stated is that what we know, and in the long run all that we know, is our own mental states which the subjective idealists called " ideas." Thus the quality of warmth that I perceive in the fire, the quality of squareness I perceive in the chess-board would both be described by these philosophers as ideas in my mind. Their reasons for this conclusion were based very largely upon the considerations which we advanced in the first chapter to show the dependence of the qualities which we perceive in things upon states of the perceiver's consciousness. But they do not to any substantial extent make use of the *additional* arguments derived from the scientific account of the machinery of perception which seek to show the dependence of what we perceive upon states of our *bodies*, and it never occurred to them to say that *what* we perceive is analysable into events happening inside our bodies. Nor could it ; for the general conclusion of their line of thought was, as I have just said, that everything that we perceive reveals itself on analysis to be combinations of ideas in our own minds. Now, if this conclusion is true, our bodies and sense organs will also be our ideas in our own minds. I shall return to this point later.

Locke's Theory of Perception. Let us first briefly consider the historical development of the thought of the three philosophers, Locke, Berkeley, and Hume, which culminated in this conclusion. Locke (1632-1704) set out with the avowed intention of analysing human experience —what, he wanted to know, are the contents of our minds when we think—and of determining the limits of human knowledge—how much, he asked, can we know of the world outside us ? Broadly speaking his conclusion was that the mind thinks about its own ideas. By " idea " Locke meant " whatever is the object of the understanding, when a man thinks " or " whatever it is which the mind can be employed about in thinking." The ideas are of various kinds. For example, there are ideas of sensation which are supplied to us by our sense organs, and ideas of reflection, that is to say, ideas of the operations which the mind performs when it manipulates the ideas of sensation, for example, in remembering, comparing, imagining and so forth. The ideas of sensation are the raw materials of all experience. The ideas of reflection constitute our consciousness of the operations which the mind performs upon the raw materials supplied by sensation.

The ideas of sensation are those chiefly relevant to our present enquiry. These, as has just been said, are the objects of the mind when it thinks. How they come to be in the mind Locke does not explain, but his general view is that they are the appearances or representations of outside things. Thus when a hot thing is brought into contact with the skin, and the resulting stimulus is transmitted to the brain, the occurrence in the brain produces in the mind the idea of heat—not, be it noted, of the hot thing, but of its heat. If the hot thing happened also to be red, and we saw it, there would be also produced in the mind the idea of redness. The idea of heat thus represents the temperature of a hot body, the idea of redness its colour, and these ideas are what the mind knows.

Thus the world of ideas constitutes a body of representations of the qualities of real things. It is this world of ideas which the mind knows, and not the world of real things.

Primary and Secondary Qualities.   Primary qualities
are those with which mathematicians and geometers are
chiefly concerned, for example, extension in space, number,
motion and solidity. These, Locke thought, do in fact
belong to things in the external world, his reason for this
view being that, whatever you do to things, they will still
insist on exhibiting these qualities. Melt butter, for example,
or burn wood ; their colours will change, but some shape,
some degree of solidity, some weight and mass they will
still possess. Secondary qualities, on the other hand, not
only change with varying circumstances, but in certain
circumstances vanish altogether. In other words, colour,
taste and smell, which are examples of secondary qualities,
may be possessed by things or they may not. For example,
if there is no light, things will no longer possess the quality
of being coloured. Secondary qualities, moreover, change
as conditions in the perceiver change. If, for example, I
have a cold, I shall not be able to smell.

Secondary qualities do not, then, really belong to bodies,
and they are not, therefore, " out there " in the world.
They are, said Locke, simply the " powers " which bodies
possess of producing effects in us ; whether the effects will
or will not be produced depends upon conditions prevailing
in us.

Locke's Substance.   In addition to the primary qualities
which bodies possess in their own right, Locke held that
they also possess a substance. We do not, however, experience substance. Substance is one of the ideas of the
mind, belonging to the class of what Locke called complex
ideas. We find a number of ideas of simple qualities continuously going together. Accordingly, says Locke, we combine these ideas, give them a single name, and then proceed to invoke the notion of some support or substratum
for the qualities in the thing which produced the simple
ideas in us. This notion of " some support " is what Locke
calls " Substance." An Indian philosopher declared that
the world was supported by an elephant, the elephant by a

tortoise, and the tortoise by he knew not what. Locke makes no difficulty about admitting that his substance is like the support of the Indian philosopher's tortoise. It is an obscure idea of some support, " we know not what " and " it is the same everywhere." Substance, then, in Locke's philosophy, is a something not itself experienced which lies at the base of, and supports the simple ideas of, heat, taste, colour, shape, extension and so forth, which are experienced, and which, because they are continuously found to go together, we regard as constituting a single thing.

Statement of Representationalism.

We are now in a position to sum up Locke's theory of perception. The theory is known as " Representationalism " because it asserts that we know not external things, but the representations, or copies, of external things in our own minds. These representations, or copies, are Locke's simple ideas. The external world consists of things which possess only primary qualities such as size, motion, number and extension, that is, occupancy of space. These things impinge upon our sense organs and cause representations or images of themselves to appear in consciousness. It is these representations or images, and not the external objects that produce them that the mind knows. But the representations, unlike the objects, are enriched by the mind with secondary qualities such as temperature and colour. The mind then proceeds to project the secondary qualities with which it has enriched the representations into the external world, supposing the objects to possess those characteristics which it has itself engendered. The mind is thus conceived after the model of a dark cabinet containing a brightly lit screen which is illuminated by the light of consciousness. Upon this screen our senses throw the images, or representations, of external things, and it is these that the mind knows, at the same time investing them with secondary qualities. The following quotation, a celebrated passage from Professor Whitehead's *Science and the Modern World*, admirably sums up Locke's view : " Thus the bodies are perceived as with qualities which in reality do not belong to them, qualities which in fact are purely the offspring of the mind. Thus nature gets credit which should in truth be reserved for ourselves : the rose for its scent : the nightingale for his song : and the sun for his radiance. The poets are entirely mistaken. They should address their lyrics to themselves, and should turn them into odes of self-congratulation on the excellency of the human mind. Nature is a dull affair, soundless, scentless, colourless ; merely the hurrying of material, endlessly, meaninglessly." Thus what, according to Locke, is really out there in the world is a kind of featureless stuff called " substance " which, though it is without qualities, serves as a substratum, or foundation, for the primary qualities which inhere in it.

Berkeley's Criticism and Development.   Locke's is a very confused account of perception and in the light of the considerations advanced in the last chapter, the reader will have no difficulty in picking holes in it. It represents, it is obvious, a half-way house rather than a completed journey. Either it goes too far, or it does not go far enough. Berkeley (1685-1753), Locke's successor, had little difficulty in showing that it did not go far enough. Locke had posited an external world which exists independently of perception, and which contains substance and the primary qualities inhering in substance. Berkeley departs from Locke in two particulars ; he abolishes the distinction between primary and secondary qualities, and he eliminates substance.

Let us take each point separately. So far as the qualities are concerned, the distinction between primary and secondary qualities is clearly arbitrary. Any arguments which show that a secondary quality, heat, for example, is an idea in the mind of the perceiver apply also to size, or solidity, or motion. When we were engaged in showing that the qualities of the alleged external object were not really properties owned by the object, but were dependent